HARM TO THE ENVIRONMENT:
THE RIGHT TO COMPENSATION
AND THE ASSESSMENT OF DAMAGES

Harm to the Environment: The Right to Compensation and the Assessment of Damages

edited by
PETER WETTERSTEIN

CLARENDON PRESS • OXFORD
1997

Oxford University Press, Great Clarendon Street, Oxford OX2 6DP
Oxford New York
Athens Auckland Bangkok Bogota Bombay
Buenos Aires Calcutta Cape Town Dar es Salaam
Delhi Florence Hong Kong Istanbul Karachi
Kuala Lumpur Madras Madrid Melbourne
Mexico City Nairobi Paris Singapore
Taipei Tokyo Toronto
and associated companies in
Berlin Ibadan

Oxford is a trade mark of Oxford University Press

Published in the United States by
Oxford University Press Inc., New York

British Library Cataloguing in Publication Data
Data available

Library of Congress Cataloging in Publication Data
Data available

ISBN 0–19–826274–4

1 3 5 7 9 10 8 6 4 2

Typeset by Graphicraft Typesetters Ltd., Hong Kong
Printed in Great Britain by
Biddles Ltd., Guildford and King's Lynn

Acknowledgments

This book emanates from the seminar *Harm to the Environment—The Right to Compensation and the Assessment of Damages*, held in Turku/Åbo in June 1995. The aim of the seminar was to examine legal questions related to damage caused to the environment. Special emphasis was placed on damage to the environment *per se*, such as damage to wildlife and biota.

The seminar was organized within the research project *Legal Responses to Environmental Harm* which has been carried out at the Department of Law, Åbo Akademi University, Finland, since 1990, and which is mainly sponsored by the Academy of Finland.

Many individuals lent their helping hands in the task of editing and finalizing the book. In particular, I wish to thank Raija Hanski and Kristiina Vainio for their role in the editing process.

Last but not least, I am very grateful to the authors for devoting their precious time to this enterprise and to Oxford University Press for producing the final volume.

PETER WETTERSTEIN
Turku/Åbo, April 1996

Contents

Acknowledgments   v

Contributors   ix

Abbreviations   xi

Treaties   xiii

Introduction   1

PETER WETTERSTEIN

Part I: The Tort Law Approach and Framework   9

1. Deterring, Compensating, and Remedying Environmental
   Damage: The Contribution of Tort Liability   11

   BRIAN JONES

2. A Proprietary or Possessory Interest: A *Conditio Sine Qua Non*
   for Claiming Damages for Environmental Impairment?   29

   PETER WETTERSTEIN

Part II: The International Framework and Concepts   55

3. Harm and Reparation in International Treaty Regimes:
   An Overview   57

   BJÖRN SANDVIK AND SATU SUIKKARI

4. The ILC and Environmental Damage   73

   JULIO BARBOZA

5. Remedying Harm to International Common Spaces and
   Resources: Compensation and Other Approaches   83

   ALAN E. BOYLE

**Part III: National Approaches and Practices:
Selected Examples**   101

6. Harm to the Environment in Italian Practice: The Interaction of
   International Law and Domestic Law   103

   ANDREA BIANCHI

7. How to Deal with Damage to Natural Resources: Solutions in the German Environmental Liability Act of 1990   131
   WERNER PFENNIGSTORF

8. The Compensation of Ecological Damage in Belgium   143
   HUBERT BOCKEN

9. Environmental Damages: The Emerging Law in the United States   159
   THOMAS J. SCHOENBAUM

   Part IV: Problems involved in the practical Application of New Approaches—the US example   175

10. The Role of Government Trustees in Recovering Compensation for Injury to Natural Resources   177
    WILLIAM D. BRIGHTON AND DAVID F. ASKMAN

11. Litigating and Settling a Natural Resource Damage Claim in the United States: The Defence Lawyer's Perspective   207
    CHARLES B. ANDERSON

    Part V: On Complementary Compensation   221

12. COSCA: A Complementary System for Compensation of Accidental Pollution Damage   223
    HENRI SMETS

Bibliography   249
Index   261

Contributors

Charles B. Anderson, Attorney, Haight, Gardner, Poor & Havens.

David F. Askman, Trial Attorney, Environmental Enforcement Section, Environment and Natural Resources Division, US Department of Justice.

Julio Barboza, Ambassador; Member of the International Law Commission of the United Nations.

Andrea Bianchi, Assistant Professor, Istituto di Diritto Pubblico e Internazionale, Università di Siena.

Hubert Bocken, Professor of Law, Rijksuniversiteit Gent.

Alan E. Boyle, Professor of Law, Department of Public International Law, University of Edinburgh.

William D. Brighton, Assistant Chief, Environmental Enforcement Section, Environment and Natural Resources Division, US Department of Justice.

Brian Jones, Professor of Law, Institute of Environmental Law, de Montfort University.

Werner Pfennigstorf, Dr iur. habil., M.C.L., Attorney at Law.

Björn Sandvik, Acting Assistant Professor of Private Law, Department of Law, Åbo Akademi University.

Thomas Schoenbaum, Dean and Virginia Rusk Professor of International Law, University of Georgia; Executive Director, Dean Rusk Center for International and Comparative Law.

Henri Smets, Professor; Director, Directorate of the Environment, OECD.

Satu Suikkari, Researcher, Department of Law, Åbo Akademi University.

Peter Wetterstein, Professor of Private Law, Department of Law, Åbo Akademi University.

Abbreviations

BLM	Bureau of Land Management (USA)
CCAMLR	Convention for the Conservation of Antarctic Marine Living Resources
CDA	Comprehensive Damage Assessment (USA)
CERCLA	Comprehensive Environmental Response, Compensation, and Liability Act (USA)
CLC	Convention on Civil Liability for Oil Pollution
CMI	Comité Maritime International
COSCA	Complementary System for Compensation of Accidental pollution damage
CRAMRA	Convention on the Regulation of Antarctic Mineral Resources Activities
CRISTAL	Contract Regarding an Interim Supplement to Tanker Liability for Oil Pollution
CRTD	Convention on Civil Liability for Damage Caused during Carriage of Dangerous Goods by Road, Rail and Inland Navigation Vessels
CV	Contingent Valuation (USA)
CWA	Clean Water Act (Federal Water Pollution Control Act) (USA)
CVM	Contingent Valuation Methodology (USA)
DARP	Draft Restoration Assessment Plan (USA)
DOI	Department of the Interior (USA)
EC	European Community
ECE	United Nations Economic Commission for Europe
EEC	European Economic Community
ECOSOC	United Nations Economic and Social Council
EDA	Expedited Damage Assessment (USA)
EDCA	Finnish Environmental Damage Compensation Act
EPA	Environmental Protection Agency (USA)
ESA	Endangered Species Act (USA)
FAO	Food and Agriculture Organization
FWPCA	Federal Water Pollution Act (Clean Water Act) (USA)
GDP	gross domestic product
GESAMP	UN Joint Group of Experts on the Scientific Aspects of Marine Pollution
GCHS	Geneva Convention on the High Seas
HV	Hedonic Valuation (USA)
IAEA	International Atomic Energy Agency

ICJ	International Court of Justice
ILC	International Law Commission
ILM	International Legal Materials
IMF	International Monetary Fund
IMO	International Maritime Organization
IOPC Fund	International Oil Pollution Compensation Fund
IUCN	International Union for the Conservation of Nature
MARPOL	Convention for the Prevention of Pollution from Ships
NCP	National Oil and Hazardous Substances Contingency Plan (USA)
NEPA	National Environmental Policy Act (USA)
NOAA	National Oceanic and Atmospheric Administration (USA)
NRDA	Natural Resource Damage Assessment (USA)
NRDAM/CME	Natural Resource Damage Assessment Model for Coastal and Marine Environments (USA)
OECD	Organization for Economic Co-operation and Development
OPA	Oil Pollution Act (USA)
P&I	Protection and Indemnity
SARA	Superfund Amendments and Reauthorization Act (USA)
SCLND	Standing Committee on Liability for Nuclear Damage (IAEA)
SDR	Special Drawing Right (IMF)
TAPAA	Trans-Alaska Pipeline Authorization Act (USA)
TCV	Travel Cost Valuation (USA)
TOVALOP	Tanker Owners Voluntary Agreement Concerning Liability for Oil Pollution
UN	United Nations
UN Doc.	United Nations Document
UN/ECE	United Nations Economic Commission for Europe
UNCLOS	United Nations Convention on the Law of the Sea
UNEP	United Nations Environment Programme
UNJYB	United Nations Juridical Yearbook
UNTS	United Nations Treaty Series
WHO	World Health Organization

Treaties

1958	Geneva Convention on the High Seas (GCHS). Adopted: 29 April 1958; entered into force: 30 September 1962: 450 UNTS 82.
1959	Antarctic Treaty. Adopted: 1 December 1959; entered into force: 23 June 1961: 402 UNTS 71. Protocol on Environmental Protection of 4 October 1991, not in force: 30 ILM 1461.
1960	Convention on Third Party Liability in the Field of Nuclear Energy (1960 Paris Convention). Adopted: 29 July 1960; entered into force: 1 April 1968: [1968] UKTS 69. Amended 1964. Amended 1982; entered into force: 7 October 1988: [1989] UKTS 6.
1962	Convention on the Liability of Operators of Nuclear Ships. Adopted: 25 May 1962; Not in force: 57 AJIL 268.
1963	Convention Supplementary to the Paris Convention on Third Party Liability in the Field of Nuclear Energy. Adopted: 31 January 1963; entered into force: 4 December 1974: 2 ILM 685. Amended 1964: [1975] UKTS 44. Amended 1982; entered into force: 1 August 1991: [1983] UKTS 23.
1963	Convention on Civil Liability for Nuclear Damage (1963 Vienna Convention). Adopted: 21 May 1963; entered into force: 12 November 1977: 2 ILM 727.
1967	Treaty of Principles Governing the Activities of States in Exploration and Use of Outer Space, Including the Moon and Other Celestial Bodies (Outer Space Treaty). Adopted: 27 January 1967; entered into force: 10 October 1967: 610 UNTS 205.
1969	Vienna Convention on the Law of Treaties. Adopted: 23 May 1969; entered into force: 27 January 1980: 8 ILM 679.
1969	International Convention on Civil Liability for Oil Pollution Damage (CLC). Adopted: 29 November 1969; entered into force: 19 June 1975: 9 ILM 45. 1976 Protocol: entered into force: 8 April 1981: 16 ILM 617. 1984 Protocol: never entered into force: 23 ILM 177. Protocol of 1992 to Amend the 1969 International Convention on Civil Liability for Oil Pollution Damage (1992 Protocol to the CLC): adopted: 27 November 1992; entered into force: 30 May 1996: IMO Dec. LEG/CONF.9/15.
1969	International Convention Relating to Intervention on the High Seas in Cases of Oil Pollution Casualties (the Intervention Convention). Adopted: 29 November 1969; entered into force: 6 May 1975: 9 ILM 25. 1973 Protocol: entered into force: 30 March 1983: 13 ILM 605.

1971   Convention Relating to Civil Liability in the Field of Maritime Car-
              riage of Nuclear Material. Adopted: 17 December 1971; entered
              into force: 15 July 1975: 1971 UNJYB 100.

1971   International Convention on the Establishment of an International
              Fund for Compensation for Oil Pollution Damage (Fund Conven-
              tion). Adopted: 18 December 1971; entered into force: 16 October
              1978: 11 ILM 284. Amended 1976; entered into force: 22 Novem-
              ber 1994: 16 ILM 621. 1984 Protocol: never entered into force: 23
              ILM 195. 1992 Protocol to Amend the International Convention
              on the Establishment of an International Fund for Compensation
              for Oil Pollution Damage (1992 Protocol to the Fund Convention):
              adopted: 27 November 1992; entered into force: 30 May 1996:
              IMO Dec. LEG/CONF.9/16.

1972   Convention on International Liability for Damage Caused by Space
              Objects. Adopted: 29 March 1972; entered into force: 1 September
              1972: 961 UNTS 187.

1972   Convention Concerning the Protection of the World Cultural and
              Natural Heritage (the World Heritage Convention). Adopted: 23
              November 1972; entered into force: 17 December 1975: 11 ILM
              1358.

1972   Convention on the Prevention of Marine Pollution By Dumping of
              Wastes and Other Matter (London Dumping Convention). Adopted:
              29 December 1972; entered into force: 30 August 1975: 11 ILM
              1294. Amended 1978; entered into force: 11 March 1979. Amended
              1980: entered into force: 11 March 1981. Amended 1989: entered
              into force: 19 May 1990. Amended 1993: entered into force: 20
              February 1994.

1973   International Convention on International Trade in Endangered
              Species of Wild Flora and Fauna. Adopted: 3 March 1973; entered
              into force: 1 July 1975: 12 ILM 1085.

1973/78   International Convention for the Prevention of Pollution from Ships
              (MARPOL). Adopted: 2 November 1973: 12 ILM 1319. Amended
              (before entry into force) by Protocol of 17 February 1978; entered
              into force: 2 October 1983: 17 ILM 546.

1974   Convention for the Protection of the Marine Environment of the
              Baltic Sea Area. Adopted: 22 March 1974; entered into force: 3
              May 1980: 13 ILM 546.

1976(77)   Convention on Civil Liability for Oil Pollution Damage Resulting
              from Exploration for and Exploitation of Seabed Mineral Resources.
              Adopted: 17 December 1976 (opened for signature: 1 May 1977);
              not in force: 16 ILM 1450.

1979   Geneva Convention on Long-Range Transboundary Air Pollution.
              Adopted: 13 November 1979; entered into force: 16 March 1983: 18

ILM 1442. 1984 Protocol: entered into force: 28 January 1988: 24 ILM 484. 1985 Protocol: entered into force: 2 September 1987: 27 ILM 707. 1988 Protocol: entered into force: 14 February 1991: 27 ILM 698. 1991 Protocol: not in force: 31 ILM 568. 1994 Protocol: not in force: 33 ILM 1540.

1979 Agreement Concerning the Activities of States on the Moon and Other Celestial Bodies (the Moon Treaty). Adopted: 5 December 1979; entered into force: 11 July 1984: 18 ILM 1434.

1980 Convention for the Conservation of Antarctic Marine Living Resources (CCAMLR). Adopted: 20 May 1980; entered into force: 7 April 1981: 19 ILM 841.

1982 UN Convention on the Law of the Sea (UNCLOS). Adopted: 10 December 1982; entered into force: 16 November 1994: 21 ILM 1261.

1985 Vienna Convention for the Protection of the Ozone Layer. Adopted: 22 March 1985, entered into force: 22 September 1988: 26 ILM 1529. Amended by Montreal Protocol of 16 September 1987; entered into force: 1 January 1989: 26 ILM 1550. Amended 1990; entered into force: 10 August 1992: 30 ILM 539.

1986 Single European Act. Adopted: 17 February 1986; entered into force: 1 July 1987: 25 ILM 506.

1986 Protocol for the Prevention of Pollution of the South Pacific Region by Dumping. Adopted: 25 November 1986, entered into force: 18 August 1990: 26 ILM 38.

1988 Convention on the Regulation of Antarctic Mineral Resource Activities (CRAMRA). Adopted: 2 June 1988; not in force: 27 ILM 868.

1988 Joint Protocol Relating to the Application of the 1963 Vienna Convention and the 1960 Paris Convention. Adopted: 21 September 1988; entered into force: 27 April 1992: International Transport Treaties, VI–193.

1989 Basel Convention on the Control of Transboundary Movements of Hazardous Wastes and their Disposal. Adopted: 22 March 1989; entered into force: 5 May 1992: 28 ILM 657.

1989 International Convention on Salvage. Adopted: 28 April 1989; entered into force: 14 July 1996: IMO/LEG/CONF.7/27 (1989).

1989 Convention on Civil Liability for Damage Caused During Carriage of Dangerous Goods by Road, Rail and Inland Navigation Vessels (CRTD). Adopted: 10 October 1989; not in force: International Transport Treaties IV–81.

1990 International Convention on Oil Pollution Preparedness, Response and Co-operation. Adopted: 30 November 1990; entered into force: 13 May 1995: 30 ILM 735.

1991 Bamako Convention on the Ban of the Import into Africa and the

Control of Transboundary Movement and Management of Hazardous Wastes within Africa. Adopted: 30 January 1991; not in force: 30 ILM 775.

1991   Agreement between the United States and Canada on Air Quality. Signed and entered into force: 13 March 1991: 30 ILM 678.

1992   Treaty on European Union. Adopted: 7 February 1992; entered into force: 1 November 1993: 31 ILM 247.

1992   Convention on the Protection and Use of Transboundary Watercourses and International Lakes. Adopted: 17 March 1992; not in force: 31 ILM 1312.

1992   Convention on the Transboundary Effects of Industrial Accidents. Adopted: 17 March 1992; not in force: 31 ILM 1330.

1992   Convention on the Protection of the Marine Environment of the Baltic Sea Area. Adopted: 9 April 1992; not in force: Diplomatic Conference on the Protection of the Marine Environment of the Baltic Sea Area. Conference Document No. 4, Agenda Item 4.

1992   Framework Convention on Climate Change. Adopted: 9 May 1992; entered into force: 21 March 1994: 31 ILM 848.

1992   Convention on Biological Diversity. Adopted: 5 June 1992; entered into force: 29 December 1993: 31 ILM 818.

1992   Niuë Treaty on Co-operation in Fisheries Surveillance and Law Enforcement in the South Pacific Region (South Pacific Forum Fisheries Agency). Adopted: 9 July 1992; entered into force: 20 May 1993: 32 ILM 136.

1992   Convention for the Protection of the Marine Environment of the North-East Atlantic. Adopted: 22 September 1992; not in force: 32 ILM 1069.

1993   Convention on Civil Liability for Damage Resulting From Activities Dangerous to the Environment (Council of Europe). Adopted: 21 June 1993; not in force: 32 ILM 1228.

1993   North American Agreement on Environmental Co-operation. Adopted: 14 September 1993; entered into force: 1 January 1994: 32 ILM 1480.

1993   Agreement to Promote Compliance with International Conservation and Management Measures by Fishing Vessels on the High Seas (FAO). Adopted: 24 November 1993; not in force: 33 ILM 968.

1994   Convention on the Conservation and Management of Pollock Resources in the Central Bering Sea. Adopted: 16 June 1994; entered into force: 8 December 1995: 34 ILM 67.

1994   Agreement Relating to the Implementation of Part XI of the 1982

UNCLOS. Adopted: 28 July 1994; provisionally in force since 16 November 1994: 33 ILM 1309.

1995   Agreement for the Implementation of the Provisions of the UN Convention on the Law of the Sea Relating to the Conservation and Management of Straddling Fish Stocks and Highly Migratory Fish Stocks. Adopted: 4 August 1995; not in force: 34 ILM 1542.

Introduction

PETER WETTERSTEIN

In international and comparative environmental law the notion of *environmental damage* is gaining increasing interest. Rules on liability and compensation enter into the picture when administrative etc. regulations have proved ineffective in preventing damage. When damage has occurred, interest is focused on the question of compensation, *inter alia*, in the form of reinstatement of the environment (for instance, restocking the waters with young fish, replanting new flora, and cleaning the banks after a pollution incident) or, if this is not possible or if it is not economically feasible, by making financial compensation.

Environmental impairment (for instance, an explosion of an industrial plant) may cause extensive personal injuries and property damage, and economic losses (both consequential and pure economic losses), and the damage to the environment *per se*, that is, the common goods of nature (*res communis omnium*: soil, groundwater, habitats, species of flora and fauna, æsthetic and natural values, etc.) can be difficult to evaluate and to 'repair'. Particularly in US law methods have been developed to put a monetary value on natural resources. But some of these valuation methods are highly controversial—not least from an international point of view.

The question of compensating environmental damage challenges traditional rules and concepts of tort law. Such damage does not fit neatly into the categories in existing rules, which tend to classify damage according to who can claim redress. A progressive approach presupposes a critical and analytical review of the conceptual framework. For instance, the notion of *property damage* has to be adapted to the needs of modern environmental law. Furthermore, the need for a new approach concerning compensation for non-economic dimensions of environmental damage should be discussed.

However, such efforts are impeded by the fact that the legal problems pursuant to environmental impairment are solved in diverse ways in different countries. An environmental impairment may have transboundary consequences, and thus affect several legal systems (for instance, *Amoco Cadiz*, 1978, Chernobyl, 1986, and Sandoz, 1986). There are different systems of liability, for instance, regarding the designation of the person liable, notions like damage and injury to the environment, the causal relationship, limitations of liability, etc.

Consequently, in view of the growing risks of transboundary environmental impairment, national legislation and systems of liability and compensation should be as uniform and coherent as possible. This works to the advantage of the persons involved (in this way, for instance, 'forum shopping' and other jurisdictional problems are mitigated). Furthermore, uniform liability systems are an advantage for liability insurers and enhance their potential for providing better protection. Aspects of competition may also be mentioned in this context: differences among national laws lead to unequal conditions for competition between states.

This underlines the need for international co-operation in the form of conventions, bilateral agreements, and other international co-operation. The international legal framework should be improved and adapted to existing and future needs. Despite the fact that the legislation on environmental protection and liability has developed since the 1972 Stockholm Conference on the Human Environment, international environmental treaties are, in general, weak in providing for explicit responsibility and liability regimes. Most of the treaties focus on prevention. On the other hand, a number of conventions on civil liability with respect to some specific risk-creating activities, especially in the areas of international maritime and nuclear law, have already been concluded. Furthermore, it will continue to be important and desirable to discuss state liability on the basis of international law. There is already a certain interspersion of civil and state liability regimes. This tendency should be encouraged, including the introduction of features of state liability into regimes hitherto considered as belonging to the sphere of civil liability. For instance, the International Law Commission (ILC) is doing work on bridging the gaps between state-liability and civil-liability regimes. Since 1980, the ILC has been engaged in drafting a comprehensive convention on liability for damage arising out of acts not prohibited by international law. In this context the ILC has increasingly focused on transboundary environmental damage.

Since 1990 a research project entitled *Legal Responses to Environmental Harm* has been carried out at the Department of Law, Åbo Akademi University, in Finland. The project addresses the problems related to the international law on environmental protection mainly from the reparative point of view, while recognizing that prevention and reparation are often inseparably linked. The research aims at describing what legal tools are available for dealing with the consequences of transboundary harm. This is done by focusing on the interrelations between public international law, private international law, and domestic law.

Within this research project a seminar on *Harm to the Environment—The Right to Compensation and the Assessment of Damages* was arranged in Turku/Åbo in June 1995. The purpose of the seminar was to examine legal questions related to damage caused to the environment. Special emphasis was placed on damage to the environment *per se*, such as damage to flora and fauna. The seminar in the main addressed two aspects: (1) the right to and extent of damages for environmental impairment. Who is entitled to claim for damages? What types of damages may be claimed? Which value characteristics of natural resources are compensable? etc.; and (2) the methods for conducting natural resource damage assessments. These include the determination, quantification, and measurement of damage to the environment. The questions raised were studied both from a national/ international (civil law and international law) and a *de lege lata/ferenda* perspective. The seminar papers are published in this book.

The papers are organized in a series of Parts. Part I proceeds from the traditional approach and framework in tort law. *Brian Jones* discusses the role which tortious civil liability rules should play within the general body of laws which collectively may be said to encompass liability for environmental damage. He examines how the rules which a legal system develops on the matter of tortious civil liability for environmental damage can be integrated in a way which can be rationally justified into that legal system's general body of civil liability rules. In particular Jones critically analyses the trend, in this context, towards regimes of strict liability.

In his paper *Peter Wetterstein* focuses on the right to claim damages for environmental impairment. He examines the question who can assert a claim for compensation. Special emphasis is placed on the question of compensating pure economic losses and on the distinction between private (individual) and public (collective) rights in this context. Furthermore, the question of the right to assert a claim for damage to the environment *per se* is examined: should such a claim be filed only by the authorities or could it also be laid by private citizens, for instance, by environmental associations?

Part II of the book deals with the international framework and concepts. In their paper *Björn Sandvik* and *Satu Suikkari* provide an overview of the ways in which the concept of damage has been formulated in international civil liability regimes and other environmental treaties which address the question of liability for damage. In addition to treaty law, they also cover some relevant soft law material. Sandvik and Suikkari examine the broadening of the traditional pattern in tort law regarding the concept of damage towards explicit formulations of impairment of the environment in modern civil liability conventions.

The Special Rapporteur, *Julio Barboza*, presents a summarized version of the Eleventh Report to the ILC entitled *Liability for the Injurious Consequences Arising Out of Acts Not Prohibited by International Law*. He analyses the concept of environmental damage in search for a suitable and adequate description. Furthermore, he makes suggestions about the consequences in the case of environmental damage arising out of the breach of an obligation of prevention established in the draft articles of the topic.

In his paper *Alan E. Boyle* extensively analyses the problem of remedying harm to international common spaces and their resources. He reviews the possible options, with a view to assessing their comparative utility, and poses the crucial question whether the issue should at all be looked upon from the viewpoint of a right to compensation and assessment of damages. In trying to formulate an answer to the problem posed, Boyle resorts both to state responsibility for environmental harm and to private law approaches. As preliminary issues he discusses the notion of common spaces and resources and the protection afforded to the them by international law.

Part III of the book focuses on national approaches and practices. As long as it proves difficult internationally to achieve uniform solutions to liability systems and compensation arrangements that can be widely accepted by means of conventions and other agreements, interest will be focused on national rules and their appropriateness. National legal developments must not be unnecessarily delayed by the wait for international measures (on the other hand, neither should international developments be too dependent on national steps). However, the rules covering compensation for environmental damage are in many countries heterogeneous, inconsistent, and also to some extent unclear. Such legislation is often to be found in the different countries' laws on adjoining property and general liability laws. But there is a growing awareness of the need for comprehensive rules on environmental impairment liability. Some national solutions in this field are presented in Part III.

New legislation on compensating environmental damage in Europe is exemplified by the developments in Belgian, German, and Italian law. *Hubert Bocken* gives an overview of the prevailing law in Belgium and thereafter presents and discusses the solutions proposed in a Draft Decree on Environmental Policy which has been elaborated by the Inter-university Commission for the Revision of Environmental Law in the Flemish Region. *Werner Pfennigstorf* presents the German Environmental Liability Act of 1990 as an example of the general tendency of tort law to expand the basis of liability and the range of compensatable damages. Italian law is most interesting since monetary compensation for damage to the environment can be awarded when restoration of the environment is not possible or if it is disproportionately expensive. *Andrea Bianchi* reviews Italian case law and legislation, especially Act No. 349 of 1986, whereby the Ministry of the Environment was established and the rules concerning environmental damage were set up. Furthermore, he examines whether the Italian practice of compensating purely ecological damage is consistent with contemporary international law and practice in the light of two oil pollution incidents (the *Patmos*, 1985, and the *Haven*, 1991).

Damage to natural resources is well covered under US compensation law (essentially the Clean Water Act, the Comprehensive Environmental Response, Compensation, and Liability Act of 1980 (CERCLA), and the Oil Pollution Act of 1990 (OPA)). The broad approach of approving restoration costs as a basic measure for damages and identifying both 'use values' and 'non-use values' may result in extensive amounts of natural-resource damages. According to definitions in US law 'use values' are derived from the reduction in the level of services the harmed resources provided to another resource or to humans as a result of the release or discharge (61 Fed.Reg. 448, 1996), while 'non-use values' are derived from the value of the resources to humans 'independent of direct use of a resource by the individual' (59 Fed.Reg. 1073, 1994).

In his paper *Thomas J. Schoenbaum* discusses the salient features of the emerging oil pollution compensation regime under the OPA 1990. Special emphasis is placed on the regulations on Natural Resource Damage Assessment (NRDA) promulgated by the US Department of Commerce, acting through the National Oceanic and Atmospheric Administration (NOAA). He also offers some remarks on how OPA might best be harmonized with the international system.

In Part IV of the book some problems involved in the practical application of new approaches are discussed. Since there has been considerable development in the actual field in the United States, the two papers presented here will focus on the US perspective. *Charles B. Anderson* discusses the NRDA process from the perspective of lawyers representing responsible parties in actions brought under both the OPA 1990 and the CERCLA 1980. He evaluates some of the problems likely to be encountered in trying and settling a natural resource damage action in the United States.

In their paper *William D. Brighton* and *David F. Askman* examine the powers and duties of federal and state governments as natural resource trustees under US law. The natural resource damage cause of action in CERCLA, OPA, and similar US laws is a significant expansion from common-law public trust and *parens patriae* doctrines. The paper discusses the legal character of the trusteeship and tries to clarify what duties the government trustees owe the public and what rights the public has against arbitrary or inadequate action by its trustees. The authors address the legal avenues that may be available for citizens to influence the government's exercise of its statutory trustee responsibility.

Finally, Part V of the book contains a paper on complementary compensation arrangements. It seems to be generally accepted that the person causing the environmental damage—and who also derives economic benefit from the activity—should pay for the damage caused; cf. the 'polluter pays' principle, which presupposes that the cost of pollution shall be channelled to the polluter so that the market prices of goods will better reflect the true social costs of their production and that he be persuaded to evolve and choose production methods less harmful to the environment. But a system of compensation which is based on liability rules contains weaknesses and restrictions. Apart from the fact that liability litigation may be lengthy and costly, a system of liability does not, in the absence of effective liability insurance, provide compensation when the person liable is insolvent. Nor can compensation be obtained in cases where the person liable is not identified. Furthermore, such a system does not provide compensation when the right to compensation is time-barred or when the activity causing the damage has been discontinued.

In his paper *Henri Smets* discusses the possibility for potential polluters collectively to undertake to indemnify all accidental pollution victims in all circumstances. In order to guarantee indemnity, he recommends the creation of a fund to substitute for defaulting or unknown polluters. The paper also contains some interesting figures on the cost of accidental pollution in OECD countries.

Summing up some of the findings of the seminar, one can as a start note that there seemed to be general agreement that prevention should be the focus of efforts to protect the environment. Such an approach is needed, *inter alia*, because of the limited possibilities offered by the law for adequate and effective compensation in the case of environmental damage.

Regarding the reparation issue, it was agreed that the conceptual framework related to compensation for environmental damage needs to be clarified and developed. The judicial analysis has to be renewed. The general opinion was that traditional tort law approaches restrict the development of a progressive and comprehensive system for compensating environmental damage. In this context the need for internationally uniform solutions was stressed. For instance, of concern was the fact that the emerging American regime for liability and recovery of damages for an oil spill incident differs largely from international standards. Efforts should be made to harmonize American and international practice.

Opinions were also expressed in favour of enhanced state participation in the compensation arrangements, especially as a 'guarantor' of compensation to pollution victims. However, it was acknowledged that the integration of civil and state liability elements in a comprehensive regime poses difficulties. States seem to accept inter-governmental liability only in areas where issues of global and military importance prevail over economic and civil aspects. In areas where economic aspects prevail they favour private solutions of the liability question.

On the other hand it was stated that one of the major roles of public international law when dealing with environmental problems is to facilitate resort, where appropriate, to private law solutions. These are most likely to provide the best means of remedying harm to, for instance, international common spaces. It is also interesting to note that the concept of environmental damage in the ILC's draft articles on liability for the injurious consequences arising out of acts not prohibited by international law largely follows the definition of 'damage' in many civil liability conventions.

The question of compensation for damage to the environment *per se* was much discussed during the seminar. There still seems to be a cautious approach to such compensation in European countries—with the clearest exception of Italy. However, many countries, and also civil liability conventions, have approved *reasonable* restoration costs as a basic measure for recoverable damages. This seems also to be the position taken by the European Commission in relation to a Resolution adopted by the European Parliament in April 1994, calling on the Commission, pursuant to Article 138b(2) of the EC Treaty, to submit a proposal for a directive on civil liability in respect of environmental damage. But many questions still remain largely unspecified and consequently need some clarification; for instance, the determination of the baseline to which resources are to be restored, the elaboration of standards or levels for restoration of environmental damage, and the measurement of the reasonability of the costs involved.

It was also stressed that rules and principles should be developed for situations where restoration of the environment is not possible or is not reasonable. Possible solutions could be to lay an obligation upon the polluter to introduce the equivalent of the damaged or destroyed components into the environment, or even to make monetary compensation for the diminution in values of natural resources. However, it was also acknowledged that such an extension of the liability principles would cause severe evaluation problems.

The measurement of damages for the purpose of liability for loss or destruction of natural resources touches one of the major problems of the whole environmental impairment liability question. Considerable difficulties—philosophical, legal, and practical—are involved in evaluating damage to natural resources and in defining compensatable value characteristics, for instance, when it comes to the cost of restoration not yet undertaken or compensation for irreparable natural resources. This is particularly true as regards so-called 'lost use values', not to mention 'non-use' values.

The methods for evaluating environmental damage which have been developed so far seem to be too artificial and arbitrary. They are also very costly. Further, they have methodological shortcomings and they do not take sufficiently into account differences in environmental damage situations (the migrations of sea animals, impacts on reproductive cycles, the long-term effect of, for instance, sunken oil on the ecosystem itself, etc.). Nonetheless, it is possible that lawyers, economists, scientists, etc. will be able to develop more rational and accurate methods for evaluating environmental damage in the future. To some extent the advance made in this field in the United States may serve as an example for development elsewhere. Finally, it was stressed during the seminar that the methods of quantifying environmental damage ought to be internationally as uniform as possible.

As regards the question of *locus standi*, it was recognized that the public authorities usually have the right to claim costs for restoration of the environment—in addition to a private person whose individual rights have been infringed. However, it was generally felt that there is a need to enhance private participation in the process of assessing and claiming natural resource damages. Internationally there is a growing preparedness to extend to environmental interest groups/organizations the right to recover natural resource damages—at least regarding restoration costs.

PART I

The Tort Law Approach and Framework

1

Deterring, Compensating, and Remedying Environmental Damage: The Contribution of Tort Liability

BRIAN JONES

1. INTRODUCTION

The purpose of this Chapter is to discuss the role which tortious civil liability rules should play within the general body of laws which collectively may be said to encompass liability for environmental damage.

The discussion will reflect a certain unease as regards developments which may be seen to be occurring (or are being proposed) within a number of legal jurisdictions as regards the scope and nature of tortious civil liability for environmental harm: in particular the trend, in this context, towards regimes of strict liability.

2. GUIDING PRINCIPLES

It may be helpful at the outset to offer, more by way of assertion than demonstration, two statements of general principle which it is suggested should guide our thinking on this important matter; and which are at the root of the several concerns to be expressed. In a more positive vein, these principles assist the formulation of certain policy suggestions which will be ventured at the conclusion of the discussion.

The first of these two preliminary contentions may be stated, quite simply, in the following way: the rules which a legal system develops on the matter of tortious civil liability for environmental damage should integrate in a way which can be rationally justified into that legal system's general body of civil liability rules. It will be suggested that such rational integration presents some considerable difficulty in the context of liability for environmental damage.

The second of the suggested principles which should inform discussion of this matter requires a little fuller statement and explanation. The suggestion is that, in considering the appropriate scope and nature of tortious civil liability for environmental damage, it is important to keep in mind the fact that such rules of civil liability are but one aspect of a rather broader collection of legal rules which, when taken together, may be considered to embody the more general composite notion: 'environmental liability law'.

Some explanation of this broader concept is, perhaps, necessary. As a legal concept 'environmental liability' is by no means a term of art: it is not an expression which lawyers use always according to a single and commonly understood meaning. Nevertheless it may be suggested that, at the very least, the expression can be regarded as embracing the following four broad categories of legal rules:

(i)   liability in tort under the civil law to compensate for harm done to another person (or to that person's assets, or to that person's enjoyment of those assets);

(ii) liability under the criminal law in respect of actions or omissions which may have harmed, or at least endangered, the environment;

(iii) liability to indemnify governmental agencies for the expenses incurred by such agencies in preventive or remedial work in relation to anticipated or actual environmental harm. Also, we may include in this category liability to administrative direction as regards action which may be required to be undertaken to prevent or remedy environmental damage;

(iv) liability to contribute to joint contributory solutions to the problem of securing financial resources to compensate, or to fund the repair of, environmental damage.

Something will be said about some of these various matters later in this discussion. The point to note here, however, is a simple one. It is to remind ourselves that ultimately what matters is that the combined and collective operation of these several aspects of environmental liability should deliver desired environmental benefits: benefits determined and assessed, no doubt, by reference to:

(i)   the deterrence which collectively they may afford in respect of environmentally dangerous activity; and

(ii) the repair of environmental damage, or compensation for harm done, which collectively they may secure.

To anticipate at this early stage a suggestion to be developed later, there would seem to be an ever-present danger that, in our very commendable and understandable general environmental zeal, we may all too easily lose sight of the fact that the rules of tortious civil liability are but one component of this more general picture of environmental liability: and, in so doing, we may seek to make such civil liability rules perform functions for which they are not very well suited.

3. TORTIOUS LIABILITY FOR ENVIRONMENTAL HARM

3.1. Meaning of Tortious Civil Liability

At this point it may be well to spend a moment defining, or explaining, terms. To begin with, for example, we should ask: what ordinarily do we mean when we refer to 'tortious civil liability'? Once a basic idea of the notion of such civil liability has been suggested we may be in a position to consider the way that such rules might operate in the special context of environmental damage: a concept which itself will require some discussion in order to elucidate its meaning.

It may be suggested that when ordinarily we think of tortious civil liability we have in mind the body of rules which defines the circumstances when one person may be obliged to compensate another for harm which has been done by the former (or, via an employee, by the former's business) to the latter: and, ordinarily, we will be thinking about compensation for harm in the form of bodily injury or illness, harm to the plaintiff's property (land or movable), or harm to the plaintiff's enjoyment of that property. In certain instances conduct merely affecting a plaintiff's financial well-being may be countenanced as warranting tort liability: liability for 'pure economic loss'.

3.2. Meaning(s) of 'Liability for Environmental Damage'

If this be accepted as correctly describing the conventional understanding of the ambit of rules of tortious civil liability, the question may immediately be posed: how readily does the notion of 'civil liability for environmental damage' fit into this basic scheme of ideas?

Before, however, it is possible to begin to answer that question it is necessary to consider what we mean by the expression 'civil liability for environmental damage'. In particular, what is meant by the expression 'environmental damage'? As will appear, more than one answer can be offered to this critical definitional question.

At first sight it may seem that when reference is made to liability for environmental damage what is envisaged is civil liability for having caused harm to the natural and, in most instances, the unowned environment: that is, liability to pay compensation for having polluted the air, for having polluted water resources, or for having harmed wildlife.

This notion of liability for environmental damage presents some difficulties in terms of the ready applicability of civil liability rules. It raises, for example, in the typical or standard situation of harm having been done to unowned environmental assets, the fundamental question: who should qualify to be a plaintiff in such an action?

Civil liability rules do not, ordinarily, confer upon individuals a right to sue for compensation except as regards harm done to themselves, or to their own assets, or to their enjoyment of those assets. Of course, in so far as some incident which has given rise to harm to the unowned environment may at the same time have interfered with a plaintiff's enjoyment of his own property, a 'nuisance' or 'neighbour law' action may quite readily be envisaged. Rather more conceptual difficulty arises, however, in determining or discovering the appropriate plaintiff to seek compensation in relation to harm to the (unowned) environment *per se* (i.e. unrelated to and independent of any consequences personal to the plaintiff or any asset owned or possessed by the plaintiff).

There are, as is well known, certain ways of avoiding this difficulty; and circumstances where an appropriate plaintiff may, in fact, be readily apparent. In relation to the unowned environment it is quite possible for legislation to afford a civil claim, in effect, to the community as a whole: perhaps on the rationale that what is owned by nobody may equally be considered to be owned by everyone. In this way it may be thought appropriate for a legal system to confer rights upon governmental (or similar) representative agencies to recover, on behalf of the community generally, compensation for harm done to natural resources. The natural resource damage recovery actions conferred in the United States under, for example, the Comprehensive Environmental Response, Compensation, and Liability Act (CERCLA), and the Oil Pollution Act (OPA), discussed elsewhere in this volume, are well-known examples.

Equally, an appropriate plaintiff may emerge in other ways. Imagine, for example, the situation where in response to some action of the defendant causing or threatening harm to the environment a plaintiff (let us suppose an environmental group) incurs expense in volunteering its assistance towards preventive or clean-up operations. Here we have an incidence of harm to, or threat to, the environment; and there is a potential plaintiff claiming individual financial loss consequent upon the conduct of the defendant. A case like this arose not so long ago for decision before the Dutch courts. A court in Rotterdam, in 1991 in the *Borcea* case,[1] was prepared on such facts to award compensation to a Dutch bird protection society to reimburse expenses which had been incurred in its sea-bird rescue activities following pollution of the sea caused by the defendant.

Another situation where a plaintiff may seek to identify, and sue in respect of, individual loss arising out of harm done by a defendant to the unowned environment involves claims presented in respect of pure economic loss. The stock example used to illustrate this kind of claim is the claim by a hotelier in respect of an alleged down-turn in custom following reduced tourist activity resulting from damage done by the defendant to the local amenity. Assuming that such financial loss can be demonstrated and quantified this will be a case not inapposite to a regime of civil liability as earlier depicted. The plaintiff is seeking recovery in respect of harm done which is personal and is distinct from, and different from, the more general damage done to the unowned environment.

The purpose of the discussion in the paragraphs immediately above has not been to argue in favour or against the success of such claims as there described. As is well known, claims for negligently induced financial loss, unassociated with harm to any proprietary or possessory interest of the plaintiff, tend to be

---

[1] Discussed by J. M. van Dunné *et al.*, 'Liability Developments in the Netherlands' (1993) 1 *Environmental Liability* Issue 3, 72–6, at 74.

viewed with some caution by the courts.[2] Moreover, any right of action afforded to those who may quite voluntarily have engaged in environmental repair may need to be closely circumscribed.

The three illustrative situations described should, in any case, be regarded with some caution. The first raises important questions of what is sought to be achieved by means of such a 'community' action for natural resource damages; and whether those aims might not equally, or better, be achieved by some other legal technique. If we turn our attention beyond the sphere of damage to the environment we may note that, in the main, those whose actions harm or threaten the interests of the community generally, rather than the interests of particular identifiable individuals, are usually considered more appropriate targets for the attention of the criminal law than for modified rules of civil liability. Applying this logic to the matter of harm or threatened harm to the unowned environment the true challenge would seem to be to devise criminal penalties which may serve to secure valuable environmental benefits (involving, for example, obligations to remove the threat to, or to remedy, environmental damage). Handling this matter by way of the criminal rather than the civil law may be seen to have several advantages. Criminal proceedings may be regarded as having the twin benefits of at one and the same time involving more by way of stigma and deterrence than a civil action, yet also involving what may be considered a more acceptable result in terms of the order which may be imposed upon a losing defendant. It is a significant problem of civil liability in this context that a loser in a tort claim will usually be ordered to pay full compensation to the plaintiff. A convicted defendant, on the other hand, will have a penalty assessed which is thought appropriate in all the circumstances of the case. One of those circumstances will, no doubt, be the quantum or magnitude of the damage that has been done; but this will likely be one factor amongst several others in the equation. The 'all or nothing', 'full compensation or no compensation', approach of many, albeit not all (for example the Finnish), systems of tort compensation will be returned to later in this discussion as pointing towards a relatively limited role for tortious civil liability in the context of environmental damage.

The second and third of the examples given above must also be considered with some care. They depict what may be regarded as the exceptional rather than the stock situation under review. They relate to circumstances where harm to the unowned environment may also have given rise to individual losses, and where a legal system has merely to come to a view as regards whether (and, if so, on

---

[2] See, e.g. the discussion of US case law in N. Peck and K. Page, 'USA—Natural Resource Damage: A Defence of the Economic Loss Doctrine or Bright-Line Rule Limiting Recovery' (1993) 1 *Environmental Liability* Issue 3, 53–61: contrast developments in Canada, discussed by A. Lucas in 'Canada—Economic Loss from Natural Resource Damage: The *Norsk Pacific* Case' (1994) 2 *Environmental Liability* Issue 2, 38–41.

what basis) such claims in respect of individual losses should or should not succeed).

Perhaps the more typical situation, the standard case which should be kept in mind, is where the harm done by the defendant to the unowned environment gives rise to no such appropriate plaintiff: and in this stock situation it seems inapposite to think in terms of the applicability of civil liability rules. This is not, of course, to say that there should be no legal liability for having caused such environmental harm. It is merely to suggest that the branch of environmental liability law which may be appropriate may be one other than the rules of tortious civil liability.

3.3. 'Liability for Environmental Damage': Alternative Meaning

Should this argument, suggesting the inappositeness of tortious civil liability in relation to damage to the unowned environment *per se*, be accepted, the question may legitimately be asked: what then is being considered when discussion centres, or proposals are made, as is now commonly the case, on the matter of civil liability for environmental damage?

The answer, it seems, may be stated as follows. In such discussions what is being considered is usually not—as one might have expected—the idea of bringing within the ambit of civil liability a new or different kind of damage (i.e. damage to the environment). Rather, what is being discussed is whether special (strict) liability rules should be made applicable in situations where quite standard kinds of damage (for example personal injury/illness, property damage) may have been caused by means of environmental pollution. In other words, in discussions of civil liability for environmental damage what is distinctive is, usually, not the *kind* of damage in issue, but rather the *manner in which* some quite conventional kind of harm may have been done.

It is well known that there is a clear trend towards civil liability regimes which single out this manner of having caused harm as warranting special legal treatment as regards the applicable civil liability rules. For example, one may refer to the environmental liability legislation of recent years enacted in Sweden, Norway, Germany, Luxembourg, Denmark, and Finland.[3] Equally, reference should be made to the terms of the Council of Europe Convention on Civil Liability for Damage Resulting From Activities Dangerous to the Environment, opened for signature at Lugano in 1993;[4] and the discussion and the tentative

---

[3] See G. Hager, 'Umwelthaftungsgesetz: The New German Environmental Liability Law' (1993) 1 *Environmental Liability* Issue 2, 41–5; R.-M. Lundstrom, 'Environmental Liability in Sweden: Context and Main Features' (1993) 1 *Environmental Liability*, Issue 5, 117–23; P. Pagh, 'The New Danish Act on Strict Liability for Environmental Damage' (1995) 3 *Environmental Liability* Issue 1, 15–19; P. Wetterstein, 'The Finnish Environmental Compensation Act—and Some Comparisons with Norwegian and Swedish Law' (1995) 3 *Environmental Liability* Issue 3, 41–8.

[4] See M. Bowman, 'The Convention on Civil Liability for Damage Resulting from Activities Dangerous to the Environment' (1994) 2 *Environmental Liability* Issue 1, 11–13.

proposals contained in the European Commission's Green Paper on Remedying Damage to the Environment, also of 1993.[5]

In this context (i.e. damage caused by pollution) there seems to be developing a seldom questioned assumption that civil liability should not be dependant upon proof of fault but, rather, should be strict. What is less apparent are the reasons which might be said to justify the imposition of such strict liability. The question needs, therefore, to be asked: why should such special civil liability rules apply to benefit plaintiffs who have suffered quite ordinary kinds of harm simply because they have suffered that harm by means of pollution, or some other environmental damage, caused by the defendant?

4. BASIC PRINCIPLES OF TORTIOUS CIVIL LIABILITY

To seek to address this question immediately may, however, be premature. Before we can consider and assess the reasons offered for departing from ordinary principles of tortious civil liability it is necessary to review those ordinary principles. In this part of the discussion an attempt will, therefore, be made to suggest in broadest outline the most basic principles which underlie tortious liability. The suggestions derive, in the main, from a familiarity with English tort law. However, it is believed that what follows may be true also, in general terms, of other jurisdictions.

It may be well to begin by making a point which, although fundamental, seems all too readily and all too often forgotten. The idea should be dispelled that there is any first principle of tort liability that all those who can be shown to have caused harm to others should be required to compensate such persons for the damage or loss which they have caused. It is a dangerous trap for the unwary to assume that once causality is demonstrated, liability will inevitably follow. In truth there are very many contexts in which courts have been, and remain, quite content to hold that no duty to pay compensation arises even though it may be indisputable, even undisputed, that a plaintiff's damage has been a direct consequence of the defendant's actions.

This first, negative, point, it should be noted in the environmental damage context, is one which is incompatible with any simple application of the polluter pays principle of environmental policy; and this may provide one reason why environmental lawyers and tort lawyers may not always find themselves in easy agreement.

So much by way of negative warning. What can be suggested more positively as regards the nature of ordinary tort liability principles? Perhaps the following suggestions may be ventured:

[5] See, e.g. O. McIntyre, 'European Community Proposals on Civil Liability for Environmental Damage—Issues and Implications' (1995) 3 *Environmental Liability* Issue 2, 29–38; and B. Jones, 'Remedying Environmental Damage: The European Commission's Green Paper' (1994) 8 *TMA* (*Tidschrift voor Milieu-Aansprakelijkheid*) Issue 1, 1–7.

(i) Where one person can be shown to have deliberately caused harm to
     another there will quite commonly be a liability to pay compensation.
     This will not, however, invariably be the case. There are plenty of situ-
     ations in which the courts have held that one may deliberately, and yet
     with impunity, act so as to cause damage (particularly financial disadvant-
     age) to another person. For the mischievously inclined such situations may,
     perhaps, constitute one of the fascinations of the study of the law of tort.
(ii) Where harm has not been caused deliberately the tendency has been for
     the courts to restrict liability to instances of proven negligence or of want
     of due care: to situations where the defendant has failed to act in accord-
     ance with a standard of care prescribed by the law.

Generally this will involve a comparison of the conduct of the defendant with
that which may be ascribed to a hypothetical reasonable citizen. It is for having
failed to live up to the standard deemed to be complied with by such a reasonably exemplary individual that liability is thought appropriate. Again, though, a
word of warning is necessary. Not all negligently caused harm is likely to be
actionable: not all instances of carelessly caused loss will sound in damages.
Even quite moderate students of the English law of tort can compile a not
insubstantial list of court decisions holding that in the circumstances of the
particular case, and regardless of demonstrable carelessness and causality, no
duty to pay damages should be countenanced.

This is not an appropriate occasion to examine this matter in any detail.
Nevertheless, it may be worth referring to the reticence of the English courts as
regards allowing actions in three particular situations: (i) where a defendant's
carelessness may have caused very widespread damage and to a large number
of potential plaintiffs; (ii) where recovery is sought in respect of negligently
induced purely economic loss; and (iii) where recovery is sought in respect of
(mere) pained emotions as distinct from compensation for physical injury or
illness. Any reader seeking to explore the concerns of the judges as regards
imposing liability in these contexts should review the hesitant development of
liability under English law in respect of the negligent infliction of nervous trauma.

(iii) Where a defendant neither intended the harm which has resulted, nor has
      failed to take reasonable care to prevent such harm from occurring, the
      tendency is for the courts to have held that no obligation to pay compen-
      sation arises. Once again, of course, exceptions may be found. The English
      Rule in *Rylands* v. *Fletcher* is quite well known. More will be said later
      about this particular principle of strict liability. For the moment, and
      notwithstanding its recent judicial rejuvenation in the *Cambridge Water
      Company* case,[6] it may simply be noted that to an English tort lawyer

---

[6] *Cambridge Water Company* v. *Eastern Counties Leather plc* [1994] 1 All ER 53. See also M.
Bowman, 'Nuisance, Strict Liability and Environmental Hazards' (1994) 2 *Environmental Liability*
Issue 5, 105–10.

strict liability remains something exceptional rather than something which is of widespread applicability.

What lesson may be drawn from this very general, and it is hoped not too contentious, discussion of the scope of ordinary tort liability? Perhaps it should be this. Given the fact that the judges have tended to be quite cautious as regards the contexts and circumstances in which those who have caused harm should be required to pay compensation, it may be legitimate to ask that cogent justifications be given by those who advocate, in any particular kind of case, an extension of such liability: be it to introduce liability where none previously existed, or to make liability strict where liability has hitherto been conditional upon the demonstration of fault.

Ultimately, we should acknowledge and remember the plain fact that the spectre of the uncompensated victim of another's actions is one with which tort lawyers seem less uncomfortable than do others. It is all too easy to wish to compensate all who have been caused harm; and, conversely, to feel that all those who have caused harm must, in some way and to some body, be 'made to pay'. But before decisions are taken to extend tort liability it is well to acknowledge the existence of reasons which may have underpinned the denial of compensation hitherto.

The onus, therefore, would seem to be upon those who favour strict liability for environmental damage (in either of the earlier discussed senses of that expression) to explain convincingly why this matter should be governed by such special rules. Moreover, as indicated at the start of this discussion, such proponents should also be called upon to demonstrate that the changes which they may suggest will integrate rationally into the more general body of civil liability rules. It is a principal contention of this discussion that neither of these burdens is easily discharged.

5. STRICT LIABILITY: SUGGESTED RATIONALES

What reasons are typically offered by way of advocacy of the introduction of special strict liability regimes for harm caused either to the environment, or, more narrowly, in respect of harm caused by pollution of the environment? A number of rationales for such proposals may be listed and considered.

First, it is often stated that the imposition of strict liability is justified on the basis of its being an application of the polluter pays principle of environmental policy. That it is such an application would certainly appear to be the case. However, it is a justification which merely requires that our attention be transferred to the reasons which may justify such wholesale application of the polluter pays principle to civil liability. This is not an occasion for any full discussion of the polluter pays principle. For environmentalists and also, it may be said, for environmental lawyers, this somewhat ill-defined principle constitutes an important aspect of their most fundamental thinking: something ingrained within their 'mind-sets'.

As a guiding principle of general environmental policy it has, to be sure, much to recommend it. Its essence, the internalization of environmental costs into the costs of environmentally burdensome activity is salutary. But this does not mean that all the implications, and all the ramifications, of implementation of the policy should be accepted without question. In particular it should be emphasized that when its requirements are applied to matters of civil liability it produces results which are fundamentally at odds with traditional tort liability notions. It seeks to make demonstration of causality (by evidence, or perhaps by legal presumption) sufficient for liability. It fails to address the more sophisticated issues which tort lawyers will tend to want to review and to assess before deciding whether or not one who has caused harm should be required to pay compensation.

A second reason sometimes offered for the imposition of strict liability is based upon the deterrent effect which is asserted to result from such a liability regime. Whether or not, and if so to what degree, the imposition of strict liability may influence the conduct of potential defendants is very much a matter of speculation. It seems to be something of an 'article of faith' to some who advocate strict liability: it is regarded as at best unproven and at worst implausible by those who are sceptical about strict liability.

No pretence is made here to any empirical knowledge of the impact that strict civil liability in this context has had, or would have, amongst potential defendants. Research into this matter would be difficult indeed. To relate the motivation for any change of attitude or conduct to any particular legal change amongst the very many influences on modern business operations would very likely be impossible.

Nevertheless, some suggestions may be offered. To begin with a distinction may, perhaps, be drawn between two principal kinds of activity which might be made subject to strict liability. The first category comprises activities which for some reason the law may choose to seek to discourage. In essence the approach of tort liability may here be said to be that the activity is regarded as having no substantial social or communal merit, so that if an individual wishes to engage in that activity he or she should do so on the clear understanding of strict liability for any harm demonstrably resulting from the activity. It may be suggested that the judge-made strict liability rules of the English law of tort seem to have been developed very much upon this rationale. Those who, for their own gratification, keep animals dangerous by nature should face such liability consequences; and at least until its recent revisionist interpretation, in the House of Lords in the *Cambridge Water Company* case, the Rule in *Rylands* v. *Fletcher* could be regarded as a doctrine applicable essentially only to those persisting in engaging in certain forms of purely self-serving and potentially dangerous activities upon their land.

In situations such as these one may offer the following comments. First, it is plausible here that a strict liability regime may indeed, at least if it is well known, discourage individuals from embarking upon, or continuing in, the activities in question. However, by way of further comment it may be suggested that it is argu- able that such liability, in such instances, may as appropriately be regarded as being 'fault based' as being 'strict': certainly liability is not dependant upon proof of carelessness; it is, however, dependant upon a characterization by the court of what may be described as the 'unworthiness', or the 'un-neighbourliness', of the defendant's activities.

A second category of activity, in contrast, is rather different. Here we need to consider activities which it is not in any way the aim of the law of tort to seek to discourage. Indeed, the activities are likely to be ones in respect of which there is a general consensus that enterprises so engaged in should flourish. The purpose of strict liability is here not to discourage such activity; its rationale, it is argued, involves a belief that the activity will be conducted all the more carefully because of the enhanced likelihood of a successful compensation claim in the event of damage being caused. But this justification rests more on asser- tion than on demonstration: proof of the impact on conduct of strict liability seems to be lacking. If the justificatory onus be on proponents of strict liability the absence of such evidence would seem to rebound against such advocates.

One further point may be worth making here. In the last paragraph it was suggested that it is no function of the law of tort to provide discouragement to persons or enterprises from engaging in what, as a community, we regard as legitimate and valuable activity. Perhaps one caveat to this assertion should be considered. It may be that in the context of the kinds of activity with which we are principally concerned (i.e. those with a potential for 'environmental dam- age') the law of tort, by the imposition of stringent liability rules, may play a role in limiting the enterprises which choose to engage in such activities to those with the financial resources to bear such more prominent liabilities and also pos- sess the technical expertise to minimize the risk of such liability being incurred. It is, certainly, possible that awareness that an activity carries with it strict liability for any harm which may be caused may have a beneficial effect in discouraging less 'suitable' enterprises from becoming involved, or from con- tinuing their involvement. The purpose of this comment is simply to acknow- ledge that this may be a consequence of the imposition of such strict tort liability. It is debatable, however, whether this should be a function of tort liability. It might be thought to be more appropriate for regulatory licensing and inspection arrangements to be utilized for this purpose. Further, the influence of stringent civil liability rules on small and medium-sized enterprises, as compared with large corporations, may be undesirable in more general economic terms.

A third statement sometimes made in the purported justification of strict liab- ility is that it is necessary in order to ease the difficulties confronting plaintiffs in succeeding in the actions which they may seek to bring. This, however, only begs further questions.

If strict liability is considered necessary in order to allow plaintiffs to succeed against defendants who have not been at fault it remains necessary to revert to our basic question of why we should seek to achieve this result.

If strict liability is considered necessary because of the difficulties faced by plaintiffs in proving fault even in instances where in fact there has been fault the response should be that the remedy is not the appropriate one. If there is something about environmental damage cases, or certain categories of such cases, which makes it particularly problematic for plaintiffs to demonstrate fault there may well be a good argument for altering ordinary civil liability rules so as to reverse the onus of proof. It may be arguable that in certain contexts, maybe because the facts are peculiarly within the realm of the defendant or because of the highly technical or scientific nature of the evidence, it is appropriate to require that the defendant disprove fault rather than to require fault to be demonstrated by the plaintiff. This is a not unfamiliar device within the field of tort liability. It retains the principle that liability is fault-based, but responds with some sensitivity to the practicalities of proof of this matter, and seeks to preserve a proper strategic balance between the two parties to a claim. It is not peculiar to statutory reform, nor is it peculiar to continental legal systems: witness the *res ipsa loquitur* doctrine developed over the years by the English judges.

Before moving on a further point may be noted. If the aim of strict liability is indeed to ease the lot of plaintiffs in environmental damage claims there is a danger that too much may be expected to be achieved by a move from fault-based to strict liability. Although this change may be critically important to some plaintiffs who may, following such a change, be put in a position to succeed, it is important not to lose sight of two important matters.

The first is that ultimately the difference between fault-based liability and strict liability may not be as great as may sometimes be suggested or imagined. A regime even of strict liability may contain within its particulars a number of defences enabling a defendant to avoid liability in certain situations. Moreover, even where liability remains fault-based experience suggests that there may be opportunities for judges to rule that the fault threshold has been satisfied on relatively little, or none too grave, evidence.[7] Further, in some of the jurisdictions where strict liability regimes for environmental damage have been enacted lawyers have been heard to acknowledge that, even prior to such legislation, the hurdle to be surmounted in persuading a judge that a defendant's conduct should be characterized by fault was not a very substantial one.

The second point to note is that the imposition of strict liability does nothing, in itself, to assist in the situation where the most significant problem for the plaintiff relates not to proof of fault but to proof of causality. Recent litigation in the United Kingdom has produced valuable reminders that in the kinds of cases

---

[7] See, e.g. on this trend in Dutch law van Dunné *et al.*, n. 1 above, referring to the judicial development of so-called 'pseudo-strict' liability.

under consideration it is this which is likely often to be the greatest difficulty for plaintiffs.[8] Causality problems may in some situations be eased by reversing evidential burdens (as in the German legislation). However, the difficulty ultimately remains that the various branches of environmental science are at a quite early stage of development, and ultimately there may be real doubt or uncertainty as regards any link between the actions or activities of the defendant and the plaintiff's damage. In such circumstances even a system of civil liability which only demands proof on a 'more likely than not' basis should be uneasy about affording redress.

6. PROBLEMS OF INTEGRATION

There is a risk that the tenor of the discussion above may suggest a lack of concern for, or sympathy towards, the damaged environment and for those who may have suffered damage by environmental means. As will appear as the discussion progresses, this is by no means the case. The present aim, however, is simply to question why plaintiffs in such cases as the ones under consideration should be afforded advantages denied to other plaintiffs perhaps equally, maybe even more, deserving of our general sympathy and goodwill.

A simple example may be useful to explain the doubts felt on this matter. Suppose an explosion has occurred at a chemical factory. Two people passing by suffer harm. One has been made ill by chemical vapours which leaked into the atmosphere following the explosion. The other was injured by flying glass and masonry: by the force of the explosion itself. Each of the injured persons seeks advice about a compensation claim. What advice should they receive?

Take, first, the person made ill. It seems that many would like to be able to say that this person should benefit from a strict liability regime; the victim being a person who has suffered illness as a result of breathing air polluted by the incident at the defendant's factory.

So far, so good. The matter which gives rise to concern, though, is the advice we should give to the other person injured. This person cannot be regarded as having suffered 'environmental damage' in either of the senses outlined earlier. The injured person is not, let us assume, 'the environment'; nor have his or her injuries been sustained by means of the damaged environmental medium. It is a standard personal injury, accident, claim. As such it is a typical instance of a case where liability ordinarily depends upon the court being satisfied that the injuries flowed from the fault of the defendant.

If this be the advice to be given it is suggested that the resulting contrast between the two cases is somewhat grotesque. But an even starker illustration might have been offered. Compare the claim of the physically injured person

---

[8] See, e.g. *Hope and Reay* v. *British Nuclear Fuels* [1994] *Environmental Law Reports* 320; and *Graham and Graham* v. *ReChem International*, ENDS Report 245, June 1995, 17–19.

with that of a neighbouring landowner whose trees may have been tarnished and rendered marginally less æsthetically attractive. Environmental lawyers (and others) are very properly lovers of trees: but they should also have due regard for people, and should be concerned if such stark contrasts in liability principles are produced by legislative reforms.

Is there not, however, some easy solution to this problem? A solution some-times suggested is that an environmental liability regime is likely to apply in relation to particular categories of plant or installation only. These may be listed in detailed categories (as in Germany) or may be more broadly defined. In either case certain installations will be subject to this liability regime and others will not. All that is then necessary, it may be argued, is for the strict liability regime to extend its remit to include personal injuries suffered as a result of any event or occurrence emanating from the plant. In this way our hypothetical victims will both have an equal opportunity to succeed in a damages claim.

It might be nice if this simple arrangement produced the solution desired. Unfortunately it does not. Whilst it may produce some rationality as between the situations of the two victims we have been considering it is only necessary to alter the facts a little to produce a further and unresolved anomaly.

Imagine, now, that two separate and unrelated factory explosions occur in the same city and on the same day. A passer-by at one is made ill; a passer-by at the other is physically injured. The former factory is one in which chemical processes potentially hazardous to the environment are undertaken and is listed in the Annex to our imaginary liability statute. The latter factory makes inert products from inert material and has, therefore, been considered to present no significant environmental risk. Both victims seek legal advice. Assuming neither is able to demonstrate fault, should one succeed and the other fail? If so, why should this be so? As will be apparent, the present writer does not have answers to these questions.

Such contrasts should be avoided in any rationally defensible system of civil liability. And, indeed, such avoidance is by no means difficult. It may be achieved either by extending the ambit of strict liability enormously; or by deciding against such piecemeal extension of strict liability. The latter seems the more acceptable and practical approach.

7. FAULT-BASED LIABILITY: PROBLEMS IN THE CONTEXT OF ENVIRONMENTAL DAMAGE

The discussion above indicates substantial misgivings about the introduction of strict liability in relation to environmental damage. The tenor of the discussion might be thought to suggest that such misgivings are confined to the introduction of strict liability, and are not also possessed as regards the operation of fault-based tort liability. In truth there would appear to be good reasons to have sub-stantial reservations on this matter also.

Such reservations have been prompted by an instance of tort litigation which was heard by the various tiers of the English civil courts between 1991–3, *Cambridge Water Company* v. *Eastern Counties Leather plc*. The case reveals certain characteristics of environmental damage claims which seem in a general way to render the operation of civil liability rules problematic.

It is not necessary to discuss the decision in the case itself in any detail. It involved the question of the liability of a relatively small industrial company to compensate a water supply company for substantial expenses that the latter had incurred when solvent chemicals, spilled over the course of several years during its manufacturing process, proceeded to contaminate an aquifer, and in so doing rendered one of the water company's water-supply bore-holes unusable.

The point about the case which is of relevance here is this: 'environmental damage' is rather unusual in at least one important potential characteristic. The magnitude of damage which may be caused seems to bear no necessary relation to the likely financial resources of the defendant polluter. Very substantial environmental damage is in no way the preserve of the giant industrial corporations. Quite small enterprises may quite easily cause very substantial harm. The defendant in the *Cambridge Water Company* case was itself quite a small business. The claim against it was for compensation exceeding £1 million. Moreover, it may be noted that this represented only the expense incurred by Cambridge Water Company in locating a fresh bore-hole supply and linking it to the distribution system. Had clean-up of the polluted bore-hole supply water been technically feasible, this, no doubt, might have been an environmentally sound yet more expensive solution. Further, the figure contained no element in respect of natural resource damage or remediation costs as regards the contaminated aquifer itself.

Environmental damage cases may be regarded as somewhat unusual in this particular respect. In other contexts where special liability rules have been developed the position seems somewhat different. It is, for example, only the largest of corporations which can build aeroplanes or motor vehicles (which may crash), develop and market pharmaceutical drugs (which may have harmful side-effects). In the field of product liability there would seem to be at least some, albeit very approximate, degree of proportionality between the likely financial resources of a potential defendant manufacturer and the magnitude of damage which may be done by its product. Even such very approximate proportionality seems to be no necessary element in environmental damage claims. As the facts of the *Cambridge Water Company* case make us very much aware, it is quite feasible for tiny enterprises, even for individuals not acting in the way of business, to do very substantial environmental damage.

In such cases, even assuming that fault of some kind is demonstrable, is there not something deeply unsatisfactory, and ultimately rather pointless, about civil liability rules which may render defendants liable to sums out of all proportion to their capacity to pay. Moreover, it is very much the possibility of such a result that may be considered to be one of the principal reasons behind the difficulties being experienced in securing reasonably affordable insurance of environmental risks.

In other contexts, where a diverse liability insurance market operates, there is relatively little need for discussion about the scope and ambit of liability rules. So long as the rules about, and the magnitude of, liabilities are reasonably clear the impact of those rules on individuals and enterprises may be softened by insurance. In the context of environmental damage liability such comfort from insurance is not readily attainable. The liability 'buck' may genuinely rest where the tort rules have placed it.

8. CONCLUSIONS

The discussion above may, if its argument be accepted, seem to make somewhat gloomy reading because of the suggested absence of justification for the intrusion of strict liability rules in this context; and the 'structural' problems associated with the operation even of fault-based liability.

In truth there is only any cause for despondency if one is for some reason wedded to the achievement of environmental goals by means, in a substantial way, of the operation of tort liability rules. If only one casts one's eyes beyond this particular body of rules it may be seen that there remains much scope for the attainment of desired and shared environmental objectives by the appropriate utilization of various other aspects of environmental liability law.

This is not the place to seek to explain, even quite briefly, the considerable potential of such mechanisms. Nevertheless, given the essentially negative tenor of the discussion so far, it may be appropriate to mention two facets of environmental liability law upon which it is believed greater attention should focus and reliance be placed.

To begin with, the potentiality of the criminal law should be noted. In many jurisdictions there appears to be increasing resort to the penal law to seek to secure compliance with environmental laws, to deter environmentally damaging activity, and to impose penalties which may themselves have environmentally beneficial effects (for example remediation orders, disqualifications from involvement in certain activities).

Equally, further attention should focus on techniques for spreading the risks and burdens associated with environmental damage by means of joint or collectively funded arrangements. Indeed, it is this approach which would appear to offer the most fruitful way forward in terms of securing the funding of environmental repair.

This represents, of course, very much the second limb of the 'dual', 'integrated', approach suggested by the European Commission in its Green Paper of 1993. This part of the Commission's proposal should be afforded the strongest support. Indeed support for, and more detailed (and costed) proposals in relation to, this second of the two limbs may be of considerable assistance in the securing of an acceptable and satisfactory overall package of measures.

The aim should be to produce detailed and costed proposals for joint contributory arrangements whereby the various sectors of the economy largely responsible for the environmental damage requiring remediation may fuel, by means of regular contributions, a fund (or funds) from which assistance towards environmental improvement projects may be sought.

This is, of course, work essentially for the skills of economists rather than for lawyers. The magnitude and burden (big or small) of the figures to be worked out will, of course, be of critical importance and cannot be estimated even in the most general way here. However, there must be reason for some optimism that levels of contribution may be set which may at one and the same time: (i) produce reasonable sums for remediation purposes; (ii) not impose undue burdens upon industrial concerns; and (iii) produce some security for contributing concerns as regards the measure of their environmental liabilities, thereby assisting their forward-planning and decision-making in numerous ways. Awareness of the kind of aggregate sums which may reasonably be generated by these means may have a valuable effect in terms both of prioritizing remediation projects, and determining remedial standards.

If some such package can be devised (broadly acceptable to industry, to governments, and to the environmental lobby) it may be that the former of the two limbs of the European Commission's proposed 'dual' approach (strict tort liability) may come to be seen to be of much-reduced significance. Indeed what may perhaps be expected is that a compromise package may be devised under which, in return for strict liability being imposed upon certain sectors of industry, an upper limit to tortious environmental liability would be set. Such a package might meet certain at least of the concerns voiced earlier in this Chapter. Depending on the detail of such a package it might be appropriate to entitle any resulting legislation either an 'environmental liability' measure or, alternatively, an 'environmental damage (defendant protection: limitation of liability)' measure. Provided any such limits to liability be not set too low; provided they are set in a way which relates, even in some approximate way only, to the financial capacity of the particular defendant (or category of defendant); and provided the limits apply equally to instances where fault (at least in the sense of 'mere' negligence) may be apparent as well as where strict liability is being relied upon, it may be that a compromise reasonably acceptable to all may be devised.

2

A Proprietary or Possessory Interest: A Conditio Sine Qua Non *for Claiming Damages for Environmental Impairment?*

1. INTRODUCTION

Environmental impairment can cause a great variety of harm and damage. The negative effects may result both from *accidents* occurring in the course of production, transport, storage, waste-handling, etc., of hazardous and noxious substances and from *gradual pollution* from environmentally harmful activity, for instance, emissions, spills, or waste generation on a continuing or repetitive basis.[1]

Loss of lives and personal injuries have been sustained in connection with accidents such as Chernobyl (1986),[2] Bhopal (1984),[3] and Texas City (1947).[4] These accidents also caused extensive material damage, that is, damage to property and consequential economic losses. Such damage is further continuously caused by gradual pollution. However, mainly because of the difficulties in proving a causal link between a polluting activity and inflicted harm, claims for personal injury have so far not been common in the latter context. Many incidents involving

---

[1] The distinction between accidental damage and gradual and long-term effects is important from the viewpoint of damage reduction and risk management. Accidental damage usually arises from active operations (production plants, etc.), whereas the risk of gradual pollution is more typical of passive operations, exemplified by stores and refuse tips. See P. Linkola, 'Försäkringsprincipen som miljöekonomiskt styrmedel' (1989) 69 *Nordisk Försäkringstidskrift*, No. 2, 90–100, at 92.

[2] According to official information provided by the Soviet Union, 32 persons died and more than 200 were injured in the Chernobyl accident in the Soviet Union. No effects on human life seem to have been registered outside the (former) Soviet Union. However, it is difficult to prove the long-term effects of radiation. For instance, the World Health Organization (WHO) reported on 24 Mar. 1995, that the number of children suffering from thyroid cancer has increased a hundredfold in the Chernobyl area.

[3] In the Bhopal accident in Dec. 1984 a leak of methyl isocyanate gas killed more than 2,800 people and injured 200,000.

[4] A total of 468 people were killed when the freighter *Grandcamp* caught fire and exploded in Apr. 1947 while being loaded with ammonium nitrate in the port of Texas City.

personal injury may also be of the kind where the consequences become apparent only after a long time, for instance, injuries caused by radiation.[5]

The number of claims for pure economic loss, that is, economic loss unconnected with personal injury or property damage, has recently increased. For instance, three recent oil pollution cases in Europe, the *Haven* (1991), the *Aegean Sea* (1992), and the *Braer* (1993), have resulted in a wide variety of claims for pure economic loss. As a consequence of sea pollution, fishermen have lost the preconditions for fishing and have suffered reduced catches. Hoteliers, restaurateurs, shopkeepers, etc., whose establishments are located in adjacent tourist resorts, have suffered economic loss when tourists have avoided the area because the beach has become polluted.[6]

In addition to personal injury, property damage, and pure economic losses, environmental impairment may cause damage to the environment as such, for instance, to species of flora and fauna, to food chains in the environment, to æsthetic and cultural values, etc. Damage to the environment *per se*[7] can be very extensive. For instance, when the *Amoco Cadiz* sank off the French coast in 1978 more than 220,000 tons of crude oil were released into the sea and approximately 180 miles of coastline in one of the most important tourist and fishing regions in France were badly polluted. The clean-up took more than six months and involved equipment and resources from all over the country. The disaster had severe effects on the environment, the economy, and the people of Brittany.[8] Damage to the environment can also be difficult to evaluate and above all to 'repair'.[9]

The aim of this Chapter is to discuss the right to claim damages for environmental impairment. Who can assert a claim for compensation? Traditional liability rules are normally concerned with proprietary or other *private* (individual) rights, as opposed to *public* (collective) rights, for instance, fishing rights in the sea and the right to use recreational areas.[10] Consequently, in cases of loss of life or personal injury claimants are able to recover damages. Also persons having a proprietary or possessory interest in damaged property generally have the right to assert a claim for compensation.

---

[5] See, e.g. P. Ståhlberg, 'Causation and the Problem of Evidence in Cases of Nuclear Damage', (1994) 53 *Nuclear Law Bulletin* 22–9.

[6] See IOPC FUND/WGR.7/2, 4 Jan. 1994, 8. See also overview in: *International Oil Pollution Compensation Fund: Annual Report 1994*, 46 ff.

[7] For a discussion of damage caused to the environment *per se*, see, e.g. B. Sandvik and S. Suikkari, 'Harm and Reparation in International Treaty Regimes: An Overview', Ch. 3 in this book, with references.

[8] Cf. also the *Exxon Valdez* grounding in Mar. 1989, spilling over 11 million gallons of crude oil into the sea and polluting the pristine area surrounding Alaska's Prince William Sound.

[9] On the very complex issues of evaluating harmed natural resources and calculating compensation, see, e.g. P. Wetterstein, 'Trends in Maritime Environmental Impairment Liability', [1994] 2 *Lloyd's Maritime and Commercial Law Quarterly* 230–47, at 237 ff. with references. Cf. also, the text between nn. 102–12 below.

[10] It is admitted, however, that the distinction between private and public rights in tort law is not entirely clear. See, e.g. H. Saxén, *Skadeståndsrätt* (1975), 71.

Traditionally the concept of proprietary rights has referred above all to individual rights over things which normally can be transferred from one person to another and entail a more or less absolute power to use the thing to the exclusion of others. However, there has been a certain tendency during the last decades to redefine it so as to include certain claim-rights and possessory rights which are not 'owned' in the traditional sense.[11]

In the United States the Fifth Circuit has stated that the requirements for *proprietary interest* are actual possession or control, responsibility for repair, and responsibility for maintenance.[12] In *State of La. Ex Rel. Guste* v. *M/V Testbank*,[13] the Fifth Circuit defined the term 'proprietary interest' to mean that a party must have control over the property tantamount to full ownership. Further, it may be mentioned that under the Oil Pollution Act of 1990 (OPA),[14] damages for injury to, or economic losses resulting from destruction of, real or personal property shall be recoverable by a claimant who owns or leases that property.[15]

Also outside US, law claims for property damage generally presuppose that an individual and concrete right to property has been infringed. In Nordic tort law—and also under many other legal systems—such individual and concrete rights are those held by the owner, mortgagee, or lessee, etc. of a property. The looser and less concrete the link with the property which has been damaged, the less certain that the right to compensation exists.[16]

However, regarding the right to compensation for pure economic losses the distinction between individual defined rights and public rights becomes topical. A successful claim for pure economic losses presupposes in many countries that an individual defined right has been infringed.[17] In the case of environmental impairment, however, interest is often directed towards cases where public rights

[11] Sandvik and Suikkari, n. 7 above. In his interesting article, 'Private and Non-Private Property: What Is the Difference?' (1995) 111 *Law Quarterly Review* 421–44, J. W. Harris analyses the notion of property. As an institution, property has a dual function, since it governs both the use of things and the allocation of items of social wealth. This duality of function comprises many elements, from relatively determinate prescriptive or permissive rules to open-ended principles of exclusive use and allocation. These elements vary in time and place. Notwithstanding these complexities, Harris makes the submission that the essentials of a property institution are trespassory rules and the ownership spectrum (425 ff.).

[12] See *Louisville & Nashville R. Co.* v. *M/V Bayou Lacombe*, 597 F.2d 469 (1979) (railroad did not have a proprietary interest in a damaged bridge which it used under contract), *Texas Eastern Trans.* v. *McMoRan Offshore Explor.*, 877 F.2d 1214 (1989) (natural gas producer could not recover for loss of production based upon damage to 20-inch pipeline owned by another company which was ruptured by drilling rig's anchor during attempt to relocate drilling rig, as gas producer did not have proprietary interest in pipeline; gas producer neither owned nor contributed to construction of pipeline and was able to transport its gas through its own modified 12-line pipeline during repair of 20-inch pipeline), and *Imtt-Gretna* v. *Robert E. Lee SS*, 993 F.2d 1193 (1993) (a tortfeasor is liable only to the owner of the dock and he has no responsibility to a third party lessee). See also *Plaza Marine, Inc.* v. *Exxon Corp.*, 814 F.Supp. 334 (1993) ('exclusive bunkering rights' granted plaintiffs neither a property interest in the damaged docks nor the exclusive right to use the docks).

[13] 752 F.2d 1019 (1985).   [14] 33 USC § 2702(b)(2)(B).

[15] See also *Sekco Energy, Inc.* v. *M/V Margaret Chouest*, 820 F.Supp. 1008 (1993).

[16] For instance, see the discussion in Finnish Supreme Court decision 1994:94.

[17] See 2.2.1 below.

have been infringed. I have especially in mind claimants exercising their public rights (using roads, waters, and lands for travelling, fishing, hunting, picking berries, and mushrooms, etc.) and suffering economic losses. Does a pure economic loss, when the right is exercised on a public basis, qualify for compensation?

The question of the right to assert a claim for damage to the environment *per se* is complex but most interesting. The award of natural resource damages can provide an effective tool for the protection of the environment. The right to recover such damages can force the internalization of many pollution costs and thus create a deterrent to future environmental harm.

The general opinion seems to have been that the goods of nature are common property (*res communis omnium*) and that nobody has individual rights to them. Thus the private citizen cannot normally act as a plaintiff to recover environmental damages. Instead, public authorities have been authorized to act as plaintiffs.[18] Consequently, the question whether a claim for natural resource damages should be filed only by the authorities (state agencies, municipalities, etc.) or whether a claim could be laid also by private citizens, for example, by environmental associations, is worth discussion.

Also the question of the right to claim costs for measures aimed at preventing and mitigating damage is relevant in this context. However, that question will not be dealt with in this Chapter. Generally it can be said that there are special rules in many countries providing for such compensation—often based on international treaties, for instance, in cases of oil spill (or threat of spill) from ships. Such a right to compensation may also be based on general tort principles.[19]

This Chapter deals mainly with civil liability under domestic law, but in a comparative context and also taking into account international treaties on liability.

2. PRIVATE (INDIVIDUAL) RIGHTS

2.1. Personal Injury and Damage to Property

Cases of loss of life or personal injury do not, as such, raise unusual problems under liability law in the pollution context. As was mentioned above, claimants can usually recover damages—provided that they are able to show the causal links between the harm suffered and the alleged polluting activity. But, of course, there may be difficult questions regarding both the issue of compensatable losses (economic losses, pain and suffering, permanent disability, loss of amenities or

---

[18] See, e.g. P. Wetterstein, *Damage from International Disasters in the Light of Tort and Insurance Law* (general report submitted to Association Internationale du Droit des Assurances [AIDA], 8th World Congress on Insurance Law in Copenhagen, 18–22 June 1990) (1990), 2–187, at 76 ff.
[19] *Ibid.* 83 ff. See also H. Bocken, 'Achievements and Proposals with Respect to the Unification of the Law on Environmental Liability for Damages Caused by Particular Types of Operation', in Dr. C. von Bar (ed.), *Internationales Umwelthaftungsrecht I: Auf dem Weg zu einer Konvention über Fragen des Internationalen Umwelthaftungsrechts* (1995), 31–67, at 47 ff.

of consortium, etc.) and the evaluation of the injury. On these matters national legal systems differ considerably.[20]

In the case of property damage with an ecological dimension the question of compensation is easier if it is possible to repair/replace the object. In such a case the cost of repair/replacement determines the amount of compensation. However, there may be situations where, for instance, objects with historical or cultural values are destroyed. In such cases the normal market value of the damaged property does not catch the ecological dimension. Therefore, more or less arbitrary evaluations on a case-by-case basis may be necessary.[21]

Furthermore, according to the tort law of many countries the right to claim compensation for property damage is restricted to economic losses only. Non-economic losses, for instance, discomfort because of smell or noise or æsthetic unpleasantness following upon deterioration of the environment, are compensated only exceptionally and on the basis of special rules (often rules of neighbouring law[22]). However, when environmental disturbance makes difficult or limits the exercise of a right to property, it seems reasonable and justified to award compensation. This is the solution under many new laws on environmental impairment liability.[23] But compensation for non-economic loss is a difficult area because of the difficulty of evaluating the damage.[24]

2.2. Pure Economic Losses

2.2.1. The Right to Compensation

On the question of compensating pure economic losses, legal practice varies considerably from country to country. In many legal systems there has traditionally been a reluctance to award compensation for pure economic losses. In general,

---

[20] See, e.g. Wetterstein, n. 18 above, at 72 ff. See also W. Pfennigstorf (ed.), *Personal Injury Compensation* (1993); C. Oldertz and E. Tidefelt (eds.), *Compensation for Personal Injury in Sweden and Other Countries* (1988); P. Szöllösy, 'Compensation for Personal Injury in Western Europe' (1994) 74 *Nordisk Försäkringstidskrift* 221–42.

[21] See H. Bocken, 'Developments with Respect to Compensation for Damage Caused by Pollution', in B. S. Markesinis (ed.), *The Gradual Convergence: Foreign Ideas, Foreign Influences, and English Law on the Eve of the 21st Century* (1994), 226–51, at 241 ff.

[22] See also about 'nuisance', Wetterstein, n. 18 above, at 56 ff.

[23] For instance, the Finnish Environmental Damage Compensation Act (EDCA), which entered into force on 1 June 1995, provides (s. 5, para. 2) that environmental damage other than losses connected with personal injury or property damage or pure economic losses shall be compensated to a reasonable amount (in view of the time the disturbance or damage lasts and the possibilities of the injured party avoiding or preventing the damage). In the explanatory notes to the EDCA compensation for non-economic loss (e.g. inconvenience in exercising a right) is mentioned.

[24] Therefore it is provided in the EDCA, *ibid.*, that such compensation shall be awarded to a *reasonable* amount. It is to be noted, however, that this kind of damage often has consequences of an economic nature, e.g. in the form of reduced market value for real estate, and the claimant can then, in certain circumstances, be entitled to compensation for such economic loss. On these questions, see, e.g. S. Michelson, 'Skadeberäkning vid miljöskada' (1989) 74 *Svensk Juristtidning* 721–4. Further, the *authorities* can lay claims against the person liable for reasonable costs for restoration of the environment, see 3.2 below.

such compensation is awarded only to a limited extent.[25] The reason for this reluctance has been fear for the far-reaching consequences of the acceptance of such claims, and the acknowledgment of the difficulty in drawing a line in a consistent manner between those claims which are compensatable and those which are not. Further, one argument for a cautious approach to compensation for pure economic losses might be that it is difficult to insure against liability for such losses.[26]

Under common law systems the 'bright line' rule has restricted the right to compensation for pure economic losses.[27] Under the prevailing rule in the United States, a plaintiff may not recover in negligence for economic loss resulting from bodily harm to another or from physical damage to property in which the plaintiff has no proprietary interest.[28] The restrictive holding is also valid for cases regarding infringement of public rights (see section 3 below). The explanation for this reluctance is mainly pragmatic: it rests upon the proposition that a contrary rule, which would allow compensation for all losses of economic advantages caused by a defendant's negligence, would subject the defendant to claims based upon remote and speculative injuries which he could not foresee in any practical sense of the term.[29] Indeed, in some cases the courts have invoked the doctrine of proximate cause to reach the same result.[30]

The leading maritime case is *Robins Dry Dock & Repair Co.* v. *Flint*:[31] the operators of a dry dock were not liable in admiralty to timecharterers of a ship, placed by its owners in the dry dock, for negligent injury to the ship's propeller where the injury deprived the charterer of the use of the ship.[32] This case has been followed by many later cases.[33] But there are also some exceptions to the general

---

[25] See Wetterstein, n. 18 above, at 74 ff.

[26] *Ibid.* 75 with references. See also F. James, Jr., 'Limitations on Liability for Economic Loss Caused by Negligence: A Pragmatic Appraisal' (1972) 25 *Vanderbilt Law Review* 43–58, at 52 ff.

[27] The distinction between consequential loss, i.e. economic loss sustained as a result of damage to the plaintiff's property, and pure economic loss, i.e. loss sustained without accompanying physical damage, was observed as a hard-and-fast rule, setting a boundary between recoverable and irrecoverable loss. While this approach could lead to arbitrary results, it nevertheless offered a clear line of demarcation, and for this reason became known in the US, as the 'bright line' rule. 'Admissibility and Assessment of Claims for Pollution Damage: Report of the Chairman of the International Sub-Committee', in *Comité Maritime International, Yearbook 1993 (Sydney I, Documents for the Conference)*, 88–135, at 95.   [28] See, e.g. F. V. Harper *et al.*, *The Law of Torts* (1986), 619.

[29] *Union Oil Company* v. *Oppen*, 501 F.2d 558 (1974), 563. See also Harper *et al.*, n. 28 above, at 623.

[30] See, e.g. *Petition of Kinsman Transit Company*, 388 F.2d 821 (1968) and *Union Oil Company* v. *Oppen*, n. 29 above.   [31] 275 US 303 (1927).

[32] Holmes J., who delivered the opinion of the court, made the much quoted statement: 'no authority need be cited to show that, as a general rule, at least, a tort to the person or property of one man does not make the tortfeasor liable to another merely because the injured person was under a contract with that other, unknown to the doer of the wrong'.

[33] See, e.g. *Louisville & Nashville R. Co.* v. *M/V Bayou Lacombe*, n. 12 above; *State of La. Ex Rel. Guste* v. *M/V Testbank*, n. 13 above; *Barber Lines A/S* v. *M/V Donau Maru*, 764 F.2d 50 (1985); *Naviera Maersk Espana, S.A.* v. *Cho-Me Towing, Inc.*, 782 F.Supp. 317 (1992); *Plaza Marine, Inc.* v. *Exxon Corp.*, 814 F.Supp. 334 (1993); *In re Oriental Republic of Uruguay*, 821 F.Supp. 950 (1993); *Golnoy Barge* v. *Shinoussa*, 1994 AMC 1378; and *In re the Exxon Valdez*, 1994 US Dist, LEXIS 6009.

rule expressed in *Robins Dry Dock*.[34] Commercial fishermen who suffer economic loss absent physical damage to a proprietary interest as a result of a pollution incident have been permitted to recover.[35] The courts have often stated that fishermen are traditionally the favourites of admiralty and entitled to full protection under the law. However, some courts have also rejected the view that commercial fishermen are entitled to an exception to the *Robins Dry Dock* doctrine.[36]

The *Robins Dry Dock* doctrine has been criticized for being inequitable and too formal.[37] Much of this criticism seems justified. The new federal environmental impairment legislation, especially the Comprehensive Environmental Response, Compensation, and Liability Act of 1980 (CERCLA) and the Oil Pollution Act of 1990 (OPA), has provided broader damage provisions and thus indicated a legislative intent to modify the doctrine. The broad language of the 'damages' provision in the OPA suggests that the OPA contemplates recovery for persons with more extended connections with a discharge than fishermen.[38] In *Sekco Energy, Inc.* v. *M/V Margaret Chouest*,[39] the court noted that the plaintiff can maintain a cause of action under OPA § 2702(b)(2) subs. (E) for loss of profits. The plaintiff (platform owner) alleged that it lost profits when it was required to cease operations during a pollution investigation which was required after a seismic cable being towed by a vessel chartered and owned by the defendants struck the leg of the platform, causing the cable to rupture and mineral oil in the cable to spill into the ocean.[40]

---

[34] In general, recovery for pure economic losses in negligence has been permitted in instances in which there is some special relation between the parties. There are numerous cases indicating that economic losses may be recovered for the negligence of pension consultants, accountants, architects, attorneys, notaries public, test hole drillers, title abstractors, termite inspectors, soil engineers, surveyors, real estate brokers, drawers of cheques, directors of corporations, trustees, bailees, and public weighers. *Union Oil Company* v. *Oppen*, n. 29 above, 566. It may also be mentioned that *Robins Dry Dock* will not always be a bar to a state law action, and businesses such as marinas, boat retailers, and bait and tackle shops may be able to recover their lost profits. See T. J. Schoenbaum, 'Liability for Spills and Discharges of Oil and Hazardous Substances from Vessels' (1984) 20 *The Forum* 152–63, at 161 ff., and, e.g. *The Glacier Bay*, 746 F.Supp. 1379 (1990).

[35] See, e.g. *Union Oil Company* v. *Oppen*, n. 29 above; *State of La. Ex Rel. Guste* v. *M/V Testbank*, n. 13 above; *Golnoy Barge* v. *Shinoussa*, n. 33 above; and *In re the Exxon Valdez*, n. 33 above.

[36] See M. P. Sullivan, 'Annotation, Robins Dry Dock Doctrine Limiting Recovery for Economic Losses Due to Unintentional Maritime Torts' (1988) 88 *American Law Reports Federal* 295–334, at 311 ff., and, e.g. *Casado* v. *Schooner Pilgrim, Inc.*, 171 F.Supp. 78 (1959).

[37] See, e.g. J. Gallagher, 'In the Wake of the *Exxon Valdez*: Murky Legal Waters of Liability and Compensation' (1990) 25 *New England Law Review* 571–616, at 588. See also dissenting opinion of Circuit Judge Wisdom in *State of La. Ex Rel. Guste* v. *M/V Testbank*, n. 13 above, 1035 ff.

[38] See P. Wetterstein, *Environmental Impairment Liability in Admiralty: A Note on Compensable Damage under US Law* (1992), 75 ff. and 102 ff.   [39] 820 F.Supp. 1008.

[40] See also comment by C. H. Totten, 'Recovery for Economic Loss under Robins Dry Dock and the Oil Pollution Act of 1990: *Sekco Energy, Inc.* v. *M/V Margaret Chouest*' (1993) 18 *Tulane Maritime Law Journal* 167–78. It may be mentioned that the court in *In the Matter of the Petition of Cleveland Tankers, Inc.*, 1992 US Dist. LEXIS 6242, rejected the claimants' claims for pure economic losses since they did not fall under either the 'subsistence use' rule (§ 2702(b)(2)(C), ('such term relates to use of a natural resource, such as water, to obtain the minimum necessities for life'), or § 2702(b)(2)(E) ('loss of profits or impairment of earning capacity due to the injury, destruction, or loss of real property, personal property, or natural resources')).

Obviously there are instances where compensation for pure economic losses should be made to operators of commercial enterprises who, through no fault of their own, have suffered great losses without sustaining physical damage to their property. While this damage may be difficult to prove and measure, compensation should be made to the extent that the damage may reasonably be ascertained.[41]

The United Kingdom seems also to have upheld the rule that loss suffered consequent upon damage to the property of another is not recoverable.[42] However, in other common law systems one can find a somewhat more flexible attitude towards the 'bright line' rule. In Australia proximity seems to have emerged as the decisive factor in delimiting the class of persons to whom a duty of care is owed, whether for physical damage or pure economic loss.[43] Further, according to one commentator in Canada, '[t]he Supreme Court of Canada's 1993 decision in *Canadian National Railway Co.* v. *Norsk Pacific Steamship Co.* has now made it clear that there is no "bright line rule" in Canada for economic loss and has reaffirmed the incremental policy-based approach.'[44]

In many civil law countries, too, the negative attitude towards compensating pure economic losses seems to be changing. This trend can in particular be seen concerning environmental impairment. Many countries have new legislation on environmental impairment liability approving pure economic losses as recoverable.[45]

Turning now to international treaties, the conventions on nuclear liability (1960 Paris Convention on Third Party Liability in the Field of Nuclear Energy, 1963 Supplementary Convention to the Paris Convention, and 1963 Vienna Convention on Civil Liability for Nuclear Damage[46]) are silent on this point. The texts

---

[41] See also Gallagher, n. 37 above, at 588. It would seem important to achieve a uniform interpretation of the right to compensation for pure economic losses under both statutory and non-statutory maritime law.

[42] See, e.g. *Murphy* v. *Brentwood District Council* [1991] 1 AC 398. See also the survey by the Hon. Mr Justice C. S. C. Sheller, 'Frank Stewart Dethridge Memorial Address 1994, Pride and Precedent: Economic Loss—The Search for a New Bright Line' (1994) 10 *MLAANZ Journal*, Part 2, 7–34.

[43] See Sheller J., n. 42 above, at 24, and the discussion in *Caltex Oil (Australia) Pty. Ltd.* v. *The Dredge Willemstad* (1976) 136 CLR, 529. But cf. *Christopher* v. *M.V. Fiji Gas* [1993] LMLN 350, and the comment by S. Hetherington in [1993] 4 *Lloyd's Maritime and Commercial Law Quarterly* 462–5.

[44] A. R. Lucas, 'Canada—Economic Loss from Natural Resource Damage: The *Norsk Pacific* Case', (1994) 2 *Environmental Liability* Issue 2, 38–41, at 38. See also J. B. Wooder and R. F. Southcott, 'Canadian Maritime Law Update: 1992–1993' (1994) 25 *Journal of Maritime Law and Commerce* No. 3, 421–50, at 448 ff., where the proximity considerations of the *Norsk Pacific* case are reported. But cf. *Valleyfield Bridge*, 1994 AMC 1592: although in some cases Canada allows pure economic damages caused by tort without requiring a proprietary interest in damaged property, shipowners, charterers, etc., who suffered delays on account of failure of lift bridge over St Lawrence Seaway could not recover in tort against the Seaway Authority. Although users pay to use the Seaway, the users have no contract with the Authority to support such damages in contract.

[45] Such laws have been adopted in, e.g. Denmark, Finland, Norway, and Sweden. See P. Wetterstein, 'The Finnish Environmental Damage Compensation Act—and Some Comparisons with Norwegian and Swedish Law' (1995) 3 *Environmental Liability* Issue 3, 41–8.

[46] See also the 1971 Convention Relating to Civil Liability in the Field of Maritime Carriage of Nuclear Material and the 1988 Joint Protocol Relating to the Application of the Vienna Convention and the Paris Convention.

of the conventions mention only personal injury and damage to or loss of property.[47] Thus the question of compensating pure economic losses—and also other damage resulting from a nuclear accident—is largely left to national legislators and court practice, which in turn may lead to nationally differing solutions.[48]

In the 1969 International Convention on Civil Liability for Oil Pollution Damage (CLC), 'pollution damage' is defined as 'loss or damage caused outside the ship carrying oil by contamination resulting from the escape or discharge of oil from the ship, wherever such escape or discharge may occur, and includes the costs of preventive measures and further loss or damage caused by preventive measures' (Article I.6). However, it is unclear to what extent pure economic losses would fall within this definition. Consequently, if out-of-court settlements (by the claimant, the shipowner, the P&I club, and the International Oil Pollution Compensation Fund) are not reached, national courts have the task of deciding whether, and to what extent, such losses should be compensated.

Questions of compensating pure economic losses have, however, often arisen in cases involving the International Oil Pollution Compensation Fund (IOPC Fund) established under the 1971 International Convention on the Establishment of an International Fund for Compensation for Oil Pollution Damage (Fund Convention). The IOPC Fund has over the years gained considerable experience as regards the interpretation and application of the CLC and the Fund Convention. In the context of some seventy incidents the Fund has also had to deal with the admissibility of claims for pure economic loss.[49]

The IOPC Fund has considered as recoverable economic losses those suffered by persons who depend directly on earnings from coastal or sea-related activities, for instance, loss of earnings suffered by fishermen and by hoteliers, restaurateurs, operators of beach facilities, etc.[50] However, there may be problems in establishing the loss sustained.[51]

The CLC and the Fund Convention were revised by Protocols in 1992 which

---

[47] Paris Convention, Art. 3, and Vienna Convention, Art. I.1.(k).

[48] It may be mentioned that negotiations on all aspects of nuclear liability commenced under the auspices of the International Atomic Energy Agency (IAEA) in 1989 and are continuing within its Standing Committee on Liability for Nuclear Damage (SCLND). On the work, see, e.g. L. de la Fayette, 'Nuclear Liability Revisited' (1992) 1 *Reciel* No. 4, 443–52, and *Report of the Standing Committee on Liability for Nuclear Damage*, Eleventh Session, 20–24 Mar. 1995, SCNL/11/INF.5, 24 Apr. 1995.

[49] Statement by M. Jacobsson, in *Comité Maritime International, Yearbook 1994 Annuaire (Sydney II, Documents of the Conference)* (1995), 128–9.

[50] See M. Jacobsson and N. Trotz, 'The Definition of Pollution Damage in the 1984 Protocols to the 1969 Civil Liability Convention and the 1971 Fund Convention' (1986) 17 *Journal of Maritime Law and Commerce* No. 4, 467–91, at 478. See also IOPC FUND/WGR.7/3, 12 Jan. 1994, 5 ff. It has been emphasized that there must be reasonable proximity between the contamination and the pure economic loss for the claim to be admissible: IOPC Fund, *Record of Decisions of the Thirty-fifth Session of the Executive Committee*, FUND/EXC.35/10, 8 June 1993, 3.

[51] It may be noted that the IOPC Fund has in previous cases based its assessment of the quantum of the losses on the actual economic results of the individual claimant for comparable periods in the years prior to the relevant incident, normally the two preceding years. See IOPC Fund, n. 50 above, at 15.

entered into force on 30 May 1996.[52] An interesting amendment was the introduction of a definition of oil pollution damage taking into account aspects of
environmental damage into the CLC. The new wording seems to make it clear
that loss of profit from impairment of the environment is recoverable—also when
the loss is unrelated to damage to the claimant's property.[53] Consequently, in the
case of a pollution incident affecting a coastline, both fishermen losing income
and hoteliers, restaurateurs, and shopkeepers who obtain their income from tourists at seaside resorts will in principle be able to recover—provided that they are
able to prove that they have suffered loss of profit as a result of such contamination.[54] Thus, the 1992 Protocol seems to accept the IOPC Fund's practice as
a basis for the interpretation of the concept of 'pollution damage'.

The definition of 'pollution damage' in the 1992 Protocol has had a consid-
erable impact on the development of international environmental law.[55] Similar
definitions have been adopted in, for instance, the 1993 Convention on Damage
Resulting from Activities Dangerous to the Environment, drawn up within the
Council of Europe (Article 2.7), the 1989 Convention on Civil Liability for Dam-
age Caused during the Carriage of Dangerous Goods by Road, Rail and Inland
Navigation Vessels (CRTD) (Article 1.10), and the 1995 draft of an International
Convention on Liability and Compensation for Damage in Connection with the
Carriage of Hazardous and Noxious Substances by Sea, produced within the
International Maritime Organization (IMO) (Article 1.6).[56]

2.2.2. The Need for Delimitation of the Right to Compensation

Accepting the right to compensation for pure economic losses poses the question
of how far that right extends in cases of environmental impairment. The impact of
such impairment can reach interests beyond those directly suffering losses. I have
specifically in mind claimants with a *contractual relationship* to those primarily
suffering loss or damage as result of the impairment. An environmentally harmful

---

[52] Protocol of 1992 to Amend the International Convention on Civil Liability for Oil Pollution
Damage, 1969, and Protocol of 1992 to Amend the International Convention on the Establishment
of an International Fund for Compensation for Oil Pollution Damage, 1971.

[53] The new definition of pollution damage is: ' "[p]ollution damage" means: (a) loss or damage
caused outside the ship by contamination resulting from the escape or discharge of oil from the ship,
wherever such escape or discharge may occur, provided that compensation for impairment of the
environment other than loss of profit from such impairment shall be limited to costs of reasonable
measures of reinstatement actually undertaken or to be undertaken.'

[54] The problems of causation, quantification, and burden of proof are not solved in the 1992
Protocols, i.e. these issues will still be subject to national law.

[55] It is to be noted that the definition of 'pollution damage' mentioned above (n. 53 above)
was already adopted in the 1984 Protocols amending the CLC and the Fund Convention respectively.
By 1990, however, it had become clear that the 1984 Protocols would not enter into force, since the
required number of ratifications would not be obtained. These Protocols were replaced by the 1992
Protocols.

[56] See IMO LEG/CONF.10/6(a), 21 July 1995, *Consideration of a Draft International Convention
on Liability and Compensation for Damage in Connection with the Carriage of Hazardous and
Noxious Substances by Sea* (HNS).

incident may have so far-reaching consequences that it is doubtful whether those indirectly suffering economic losses should be compensated—even if one accepts the polluter pays principle as a starting point. A non-restrictive attitude could cause large and complicated compensation issues. Widespread natural resource damage raises the spectre of enormous and virtually indeterminate liability. Further, considering the harmonization aim of international conventions, it would be important to develop general criteria for the admissibility of claims for pure economic loss.

The question of how the line is to be drawn between those claims for economic loss which should be paid and those which should be dismissed as too remote poses, however, many problems: what is the relevance—if any—of the 'traditional' test for tort liability, involving factors such as proximate cause, foreseeability, and remoteness of the damage? What significance should be attached to elements such as the geographic proximity between the claimant's activity and the contamination of the environment (for instance, in cases of hoteliers/restaurateurs who are not in the nearest vicinity, but who nevertheless suffer loss of income because tourists shy away from the region as a whole) or the degree to which a claimant is economically dependent upon an affected resource? What is the relevance of the extent to which a claimant's business forms an integral part of the economic activity affected?[57] Further, what is the relevance of contractual clauses and insurance aspects (for instance, first party insurance) for the compensation issue in contractual relations? What impact has a cost/benefit analysis when discussing the reasonable delimitation of the right to compensation for loss of profit?

It is not possible within the confines of this short presentation to analyse in depth the complicated matter of developing criteria concerning the admissibility of claims for pure economic losses. However, some short comments can be made.

Such criteria (or parameters) should meet various requirements. They should enable claimants—and also polluters/insurers—to foresee with some degree of certainty whether a particular claim will be admissible. At the same time, the criteria should retain sufficient flexibility to change and consider each case on its merits. Where to set the bounds for what damage shall be compensated in this respect is also largely a question of policy, that is, how restrictive shall liability be in the case of environmental impairment. The problem is how to achieve a reasonable balance between all the relevant, and also conflicting (claimant/polluter), interests.

The principles and notions of proximate cause, adequate causation, foreseeability, and remoteness of the damage have been applied by courts in different countries.[58] The right to compensation may be denied because the loss or damage

---

[57] Cf. for oil pollution IOPC FUND/WGR.7/WP.1, 8 Feb. 1994.

[58] See, e.g. Wetterstein, n. 18 above, at 93 ff. with references. For a comprehensive overview see also A. M. Honoré, 'Causation and Remoteness of Damage', in A. Tunc (ed.), *International Encyclopedia of Comparative Law, Vol. XI, Torts* (1983), 7–45.

is of such an unforeseeable, untypical, or remote nature that compensation shall not be payable. For instance, an incidence of environmental impairment may have such extensive consequences that doubt may arise whether some of those consequences are so remote that they fall outside the limits of what should be compensated. With the aid of these principles it is possible to vary the effects of a compensation system.[59]

But legal theories and principles of causation and remoteness of damage vary between different courts. The substance of these principles is imprecise and differs from country to country. This is a highly discretionary and unpredictable branch of the law. It would seem difficult to include the aforementioned tests in a more general analytical or philosophical theory. Judgment must be *in casu* and take into account the differing circumstances.[60]

Consequently, such general principles and notions afford only limited guidance on the problem of delimiting compensation for losses resulting from environmental impairment.[61] For instance, the test of foreseeability is of minor use since the limits of foreseeability may be extended from one case to another.[62] The ability to foresee loss or damage is advanced by the progress made in the fields of medicine, biology, biochemistry, statistics, etc., so the area of damage which falls within the bounds of foreseeability will be extended.

When trying to develop criteria concerning the admissibility of claims, a starting-point could be to consider not giving the right to recover pure economic losses to claimants with only a *contractual relationship* to those primarily suffering loss or damage as a result of environmental impairment. Loss and damage in consequence of contractual ties can be very unpredictable and differ with the time and place.[63] Such a diversion of claimants may be justified, especially when con-

---

[59] It may be mentioned that the test for proximity seems to have been gradually eased in modern tort law. Developments have moved from the strict *conditio sine qua non* theory over the foreseeability ('adequacy') test to a less stringent causation test requiring only the 'reasonable imputation' of damage. See J. M. van Dunné, 'Environmental Liability—Continental Style' (1992) 1 *Reciel* 394–401, at 396 ff.

[60] These factors are described in an illuminating way by Judge Andrews in the famous case of *Palsgraf* v. *Long Island Railroad Co.*, 248 N.Y. 339, 162 N.E. 99 (1928).

[61] Cf. Honoré, n. 58 above, at 7–105: '[b]ut though forensically the vaguest formula may often be the best, from the standpoint of legal science it is important to recognize that just as there are several different grounds for imposing a duty to compensate, so there are several different grounds for limiting compensation.' It may also be mentioned that, e.g. the Scandinavian writer H. Andersson has, in *Skyddsändamål och adekvans: Om skadeståndsansvarets gränser* (1993), critically analysed the doctrine of adequate causation. See also A. Agell, 'Adekvans eller skyddsändamål: Om rättsvetenskaplig metod och skadeståndsrättslig regelbildning' (1994–5) 13 *Juridisk Tidskrift* 799–810, at 805 ff.

[62] For instance, in US law the courts have often stated that foreseeability is an inadequate control mechanism. See the discussion in, e.g. *State of La. Ex Rel. Guste* v. *M/V Testbank*, n. 13 above; *Barber Lines A/S* v. *M/V Donau Maru*, n. 33 above; *Imtt-Gretna* v. *Robert E. Lee SS*, n. 12 above; and *In re the Exxon Valdez*, n. 33 above. But as was mentioned above, in Australia proximity seems to have emerged as the delimiting factor, see the discussion by Sheller, n. 42 above, at 24 ff.

[63] Such indirect claims are, e.g. claims by fish processors for loss of income due to lack of deliveries from fishermen prevented from fishing in a polluted sea area, and by wholesalers to which processed fish is usually delivered by a fish processor which has had to close down its

sidering the restrictive attitude of many national tort laws and the interpretational difficulties concerning concepts such as *direct* loss. Furthermore, contractual clauses and insurance aspects are relevant for the compensation issue in contractual relations. It must be kept in mind that tort action is a very expensive administrative device for compensating victims of accidents. Those having indirectly suffered financial harm may find it easier to arrange for cheaper, alternative compensation, for instance first party insurance.[64]

However, strict adherence to such a rule cannot take into account all the differing cases and circumstances. Some exceptions may be needed, for instance, regarding employees of those directly suffering damage, such as employees of fishermen, hoteliers, restaurateurs, etc.[65] Legal policy and social reasons may support giving the right to claim for pure economic losses to such employees made redundant as a consequence of the environmental impairment.[66]

As regards the position of those claimants who suffer pure economic losses more directly, that is, without the aforementioned contractual ties, it seems clear that those in the 'front line' of the pollution/contamination should be able to recover. In particular this concerns claimants whose businesses form an integral part of the economic activity within the area affected by the impairment.[67] But what about claimants who are not in the nearest vicinity, but who nevertheless suffer loss of income because tourists shy away from the region as a whole? Or

processing activity due to the lack of deliveries of fish from fishermen. Further examples are claims by wholesalers of victuals to hotels and restaurants in an area affected by oil pollution, and by enterprises depending on supply of electricity from a power plant station which has to close down because polluted sea water is unsuitable for its cooling system.

[64] Cf. also the discussion by James, Jr., n. 26 above, at 53 ff. However, it may be noted that claims relating to pure economic loss as presented by fish processors, who were deprived of their supply of fish due to the destruction of salmon and the imposition of an exclusion zone, were compensated in the *Braer* case. Even though their economic losses were only indirectly caused by the contamination, they were compensated because it was felt that the harm to the fish processors was a foreseeable consequence of the oil spill and should be considered as damage caused by contamination. See E. H. P. Brans, 'The *Braer* and the Admissibility of Claims for Pollution Damage under the 1992 Protocols to the Civil Liability Convention and the Fund Convention' (1995) 3 *Environmental Liability* 61–9, at 64 ff.

[65] It may be mentioned that following the *Aegean Sea* and *Braer* incidents, claims for loss of income were submitted by employees at fish processing plants, mussel farms, or shellfish purification plants who had either been placed on part-time work or who had been made redundant. See IOPC FUND/WGR.7/3, 12 Jan. 1994, 11. However, according to Brans, n. 64 above, at 65, claims for compensation by employees of fish-processing plants who suffered reduced working hours were rejected. These losses were not considered as damage caused by contamination.

[66] It may be noted that, e.g. the Norwegian comprehensive rules on compensation for pollution damage (Pollution Act of 1981 with amendments concerning compensation for pollution damage of 1989) give employees the right to claim compensation from the polluter in cases where environmental damage leads to partial or total stoppages. See [1988–9] Ot prp. nr 33, 57 ff.

[67] The IOPC Fund has considered as recoverable economic losses those suffered by persons who depend directly on earnings from coastal or sea-related activities. Here one can find fishery-related, port-related, and tourism-related businesses. Examples of claimants belonging to the first category are fishermen, fish farmers (damage suffered by fish farmers has sometimes been considered as damage to property, i.e. to the fish), and cultivators of mussels, oysters, and scallops. See IOPC

claimants who are economically dependent on an affected resource only to a minor degree? Should there be a differentiation according to geographic or economic proximity?

It may be mentioned that an Intersessional Working Group, set up by the IOPC Fund Assembly, has developed some criteria for the admissibility of claims for pure economic loss in the field of oil pollution from ships.[68] When considering whether the requirement of the link of causation between the contamination and the loss was fulfilled, the Working Group took the position that, *inter alia*, the geographic proximity between the claimant's activity and the contamination and the degree to which a claimant is economically dependent on an affected resource were relevant factors.[69] The Fund Assembly has endorsed the report of the Working Group.[70]

I believe, however, that the criterion of geographic proximity gives only limited guidance in this context. All hotels, restaurants, shops, etc., in the same town or village should be treated equally in principle, regardless of their precise location, because if there has been contamination of sea and beaches which has resulted in a reduction in tourist activity in the town or village, it has probably affected all establishments of the same kind in the locality. Neither does the criterion of the percentage of the activity affected within the claimant's overall activity seem very manageable. What would be the relevant percentage? Consequently, principles of proximity—albeit not irrelevant—will provide only a limited contribution to the certainty and consistency of results in this field.

However, in this context it is also important to note the claimant's burden of proof. First, he must establish a link of causation between the loss/damage and the environmental impairment, a task that is often difficult to fulfil. Further, the claimant must prove that he has suffered actual economic loss. The amounts claimed must be substantiated by sufficient proof.[71] It is to be observed, however,

FUND/WGR.7/3, 12 Jan. 1994, at 6 ff. For ferry operators, shipowners, and time charterers loss of income could arise as a consequence of a ship being prevented from entering or leaving a port due to the fact that the oil pollution incident has made the authorities close the harbour area to traffic. Tourism-related claimants are hoteliers, restaurateurs, operators of beach facilities, shopkeepers, etc. Claims for loss of income as a result of alleged reduction in tourism were presented in the *Tanio*, *Haven*, *Aegean Sea*, and *Braer* cases: *ibid.*, at 12 ff.

[68] The Working Group should, *inter alia*, 'study in particular problems relating to claims in respect of so-called "pure economic loss" and "preventive measures" taken to prevent or minimise pure economic loss'. See IOPC FUND/WGR.7/10, 11 Mar. 1994, 2.

[69] See IOPC FUND/WGR.7/10, 11 Mar. 1994, 6. See also *International Oil Pollution Compensation Fund: Annual Report 1994*, n. 6 above, at 25.

[70] See IOPC FUND/A.17/35, 21 Oct. 1994, 12 ff. It may be mentioned that in the *Comité Maritime International (CMI) Guidelines on Oil Pollution Damage* (Part II.6) geographic proximity and degree of economic dependence are mentioned among the general criteria in ascertaining whether a reasonable degree of proximity exists between the contamination and the loss. These Guidelines were adopted at the 35th International Conference of the CMI, held in Sydney on 2–8 Oct. 1994. The guidelines are concerned with the admissibility and assessment of claims for oil pollution damage.

[71] It may be noted that the Executive Committee of the IOPC Fund has endorsed the policy that the assessment of the quantum of claims for pure economic loss should be based on the actual financial results of the individual claimant for appropriate periods during years preceding the incident;

that the further away (both geographically and in terms of economic dependence) the claimant is from the pollution/contamination, the more difficult it may be for him to prove the link of causation, the alleged economic loss, etc. Consequently, the rules of the claimant's burden of proof reduce the need for *criteria* concerning the admissibility of claims for pure economic loss.

3. PUBLIC (COLLECTIVE) RIGHTS

3.1. The Right to Claim for Pure Economic Losses

Let us return to the question put forward in the introductory part, that is, does a right to compensation for pure economic loss exist in cases where public rights have been infringed? On this question, too, legal practice varies from country to country.

Of particular interest in US law is *Burgess* v. *M/V Tamano*,[72] which dealt with infringement of public rights. In this case commercial fishermen and clam diggers were entitled to recover lost profits due to oil spill. The court stated, *inter alia*:

It is also uncontroverted that the right to fish or to harvest clams in Maine's coastal waters is not the private right of any individual, but is a public right held by the State 'in trust for the common benefit of the people'.... Since the fishermen and clam diggers have no individual property rights with respect to the waters and marine life allegedly harmed by the oil spill, their right to recover in the present action depends upon whether they may maintain private actions for damages based upon the alleged tortious invasion of public rights which are held by the State of Maine in trust for the common benefit of all the people. As to this issue, the long standing rule of law is that a private individual can recover in tort for invasion of a public right only if he has suffered damage particular to him—that is, damage different in kind, rather than simply in degree, from that sustained by the public generally.... The commercial fishermen and clam diggers in the present case clearly have a special interest, quite apart from that of the public generally, to take fish and harvest clams from the coastal waters of the State of Maine. The injury of which they complain has resulted from defendant's alleged interference with *their* direct exercise of the public right to fish and to dig clams.[73]

There seems to be a holding in US law that economic loss will be regarded as different in kind—and recoverable—where the claimant is making commercial

---

the assessment should thus not be based on budgeted figures. However, the Committee also stated that the IOPC Fund should be prepared to take into account the particular circumstances of the claimant and consider any evidence presented by him in respect of the quantum of his loss. See IOPC FUND/WGR.7/3, at p. 5.

[72] 370 F.Supp. 247 (1973).   [73] *Ibid*. 249 ff. (emphasis in the original).

use of the infringed public right. This also means that hotel owners, restaurateurs, etc., not directly exercising a public right would not be entitled to recover their pure economic losses.[74] Reference is also made to other cases.[75]

There are also some relevant provisions in federal legislation. The provisions under the OPA (1990) regarding recovery for pure economic losses are particularly broad. Both those considered 'subsistence' users of natural resources and others who suffer economic losses (loss of profits or impairment of earning capacity) due to damage to natural resources are entitled to recover. In addition, the federal government, a state, etc., are allowed to recover lost revenues and costs of providing additional public services.[76] However, under CERCLA (1980) the right to recovery for private claimants seems to be restricted. Although there is a right to recovery of necessary response costs,[77] the CERCLA does not authorize lost-profit damage actions by private claimants[78]—with the possible exception for such claims in the maritime tort law context.[79]

It may also be noted that the Canadian 'incremental policy-based approach' referred to above[80] suggests that persons or classes of persons who rely economically on public resources, for instance, fishermen, should be entitled to recover losses when these resources are damaged. Similarly, operators of recreational and tourism activities that are based on the existence and quality of certain natural resources or amenities should be able to recover economic loss.[81]

---

[74] The court in *Burgess* v. *M/V Tamano* also stated: '[u]nlike the commercial fishermen and clam diggers, the Old Orchard Beach businessmen do not assert any interference with *their* direct exercise of a public right. They complain only of loss of customers indirectly resulting from alleged pollution of the coastal waters and beaches in which they do not have a property interest. Although in some instances their damage may be greater in degree, the injury of which they complain, which is derivative from that of the public at large, is common to all businesses and residents of the Old Orchard Beach area. In such circumstances, the line is drawn and the courts have consistently denied recovery' (emphasis in the original). See also *Pruitt* v. *Allied Chemical Corp.*, 523 F.Supp. 975 (1981) and T. W. Kinnane, 'Recovery for Economic Losses by the Commercial Fishing Industry: Rules, Exceptions, and Rationales' (1994) 4 *Journal of Environmental Law* 86–112, at 98 ff.

[75] See *Oppen* v. *Aetna Insurance Co.*, 485 F.2d 252 (1973): under California law, where private pleasure boat owners' claim was not for loss of use of their boats, which were perfectly usable, but rather for loss of navigation rights in channel and harbour due to oil spill disaster, and where damage suffered on account of their loss of navigation rights with respect to their pleasure boats was no different in kind from that suffered by the public generally, plaintiffs' claim was one for damages arising out of a public nuisance and was not compensable, and *State of La. Ex Rel. Guste* v. *M/V Testbank*, n. 13 above: various plaintiffs, including shipping interests, marina and boat operators, seafood enterprises, tackle and bait shops, and recreational fishermen were denied recovery for pure economic losses. See also the discussion in *Adams* v. *Star Enterprise*, 1995 US App., LEXIS 7648 and in *In re the Exxon Valdez* No. 146, 1995 AMC 1409.

[76] 33 USC § 2702(b)(2)(C–F). See Wetterstein, n. 38 above, at 88 ff. See also Totten, n. 40 above, at 171 ff.   [77] See Wetterstein, n. 38 above, at 121 with references.

[78] See also J. T. Smith II, 'Natural Resource Damages under CERCLA and OPA: Some Basics for Maritime Operators' (1993) 18 *Tulane Maritime Law Journal* 1–32, at 28.

[79] See 42 USC § 9607(h): '[t]he owner or operator of a vessel shall be liable in accordance with this section, under maritime tort law, and as provided under section 9614 of this title notwithstanding any provision of the Act of March 3, 1851 (46 USC 183 et seq.) or the absence of any physical damage to the proprietary interest of the claimant'. See also Wetterstein, n. 38 above, at 120 ff.

[80] See n. 44 above.   [81] See Lucas, n. 44 above, at 40.

Many civil law countries, too, seem to be more open to such claims for pure economic losses. Such countries are, for instance, Belgium, France, and the Netherlands.[82] A difference between many civil law systems and the common law seems to be that the common law courts have more inclined towards a clear but arbitrary rule, while in civil law jurisdictions the general nature of the relevant criteria leaves a great deal to the discretion of the judge in the particular case.[83]

For the Nordic countries, both the Swedish Environmental Damage Act (1986) and the Finnish Environmental Damage Compensation Act (EDCA, 1994) are silent on the point whether pure economic losses are compensated when public rights have been infringed. These Acts contain only a general provision that pure economic losses (provided they are not insignificant) shall be compensated.[84] The Norwegian Pollution Act (1981), on the other hand, has arrived at the solution of awarding compensation only to those who suffer economic loss in their *business*—also ancillary business—as the result of an infringement of public rights.[85]

As was mentioned above, the 1992 Protocols to the 1969 CLC and the 1971 Fund Convention, as well as some other environmental impairment liability treaties,[86] have explicitly adopted the wording *loss of profit* into their definitions of 'pollution damage'. It seems that the draftsmen of these definitions did not intend in cases of lost profit to make a distinction between the infringement of private and public rights.[87]

Since environmental impairment may often result in economic losses, there seem to be good reasons for extending the right to compensation to encompass infringement of public rights. Risk-spreading and preventive considerations (cf. the polluter pays principle) favour such a right. But compensation should be restricted, as in Norway, to those who suffer economic losses in the exercise of their *commercial activity* because they are unable to enjoy their public rights. Such losses may, for instance, hit commercial fishermen and people who are

---

[82] See, e.g. National Reports to *Damage from International Disasters in the Light of Tort and Insurance Law* (general report submitted to Association Internationale du Droit des Assurances [AIDA] 8th World Congress on Insurance Law in Copenhagen, 18–22 June 1990) (1990), at 65, 172, and 340.

[83] See CMI Conference 1994, Admissibility and Assessment of Claims for Pollution Damage, n. 27 above, at 18.

[84] The Swedish Environmental Damage Act, s. 1, and the Finnish EDCA, s. 5.1. It may be noted that during the preparation of the EDCA it was not considered feasible to include in the Act a general rule on compensation for infringed public rights. However, the Legal Committee of Parliament expressed the view that so-called *general users* should have the right to compensation for pure economic losses. See Opinion of the Legal Committee of the Parliament concerning Governmental Bill 165/1992, 1994 vp–LaVM10–HE 165/1992 vp, 6. The concept of *general user*, however, remains somewhat unclear.   [85] The Norwegian Pollution Act, 1981, s. 57.

[86] See the text between nn. 52–56 above.

[87] It may be noted, however, that the right to compensation for *loss of profit* under the 1992 Protocols seems to be narrower than the right of those considered 'subsistence' users of natural resources under, e.g. the OPA (1990).

dependent upon unrestricted travel in their business. People who are dependent upon the ecosystem for their subsistence should also be able to recover.[88]

There are, in law, for instance, technical arguments for not awarding compensation in all cases where public rights have been infringed. To give everybody the right to compensation would not be a satisfactory solution from the viewpoint of the legal system. In cases when pollution restricts the exercise of public rights it is often a large and vague group of people which suffers. Moreover, the individual losses caused by such incidents may vary greatly from person to person. If the right to claim compensation is afforded to all these people, it may result in a large number of claimants and consequently many problems of a practical, procedural, and technical nature. The assessment of damage on the basis of the different claims would also pose great difficulty. The situation is different when, for example, an organization or an authority is allowed to claim on behalf of society. Then, naturally, the number of claimants and claims is restricted.[89] Finally, insurance considerations should also be taken into account. Liability insurance, which plays a key role in a functional compensation system,[90] presupposes that the risks involved can be fairly accurately calculated. A multiplicity of possible individual claims from the public would therefore not be a successful solution from the insurance point of view.

However, allowing recovery for those involved in *commercial activity* makes the question of a reasonable delimitation of this right even more topical.[91] For instance, interruption of traffic as a result of environmental impairment may give rise to a large variety of claims for economic losses: claims from ships using waterways, from firms and other businesses whose employees regularly use roads to commute, etc. Should all these costs be laid upon the polluter? Would this be suitable in view of principles and aspects such as cost-efficiency, insurability (third party/first party insurance), and procedural rationality?

Even if principles of proximity may provide some guidance in this context, the burden of proof rules *de facto* function as a limitation of the right to compensation for economic losses even when public rights have been infringed. In such cases it may be difficult for the claimant to prove both the link of causation and the amount of his loss. Apart from this, it seems very difficult to develop general criteria for the admissibility of claims for pure economic loss. Here, too, it is ultimately a question of achieving a reasonable balance between all the relevant interests.

3.2. Natural Resource Damages

As was mentioned in the introductory part, the common goods of nature are not the object of individual property rights. A country's natural spaces, resources,

---

[88] Cf. the situation under the American OPA (1990): see Wetterstein, n. 38 above, at 87 ff.

[89] Cf. the current discussion in US law, Wetterstein, n. 38 above, at 145 ff.

[90] See, e.g. Wetterstein, n. 18 above, at 109 ff.   [91] Cf. 2.2.2 above.

and environments, its animal and vegetable species, and the biological diversity and balance of which they form part are part of a common, national heritage. Their protection, restoration, management, etc. are of general interest, and thus the individual citizen is not normally entitled to act as a plaintiff to recover natural resource damages.[92] However, it must be clarified in this context that in cases of property damage with an ecological dimension individual interests are naturally involved.[93]

Even though it is not appropriate or practical to give everyone the right to claim individual compensation when, for instance, public rights have been infringed, there are solutions that indirectly look after their interests. More recently the environment has in many countries been included among objects that enjoy protection in tort law, that is, damage to the environment is being recognized as a separate category of actionable harm. A usual solution is to give the public authorities the right to claim costs for *reasonable*[94] measures undertaken to restore the environment from the person(s) liable.[95] Such legislation

---

[92] See also Bocken, n. 21 above, at 244.   [93] See 2.1 above.

[94] Even the most vigorous advocates of restoration-cost recovery recognize that restoration cost should not be used when it yields a result that is grossly disproportionate to the actual damages. See F. B. Cross, 'Natural Resource Damage Valuation' (1989) 42 *Vanderbilt Law Review* 269–315. The reasonableness criterion has also been included in many international treaties: see, e.g. the 1992 Protocol to the 1969 CLC (Art. 2.3); the 1993 Convention on Damage Resulting from Activities Dangerous to the Environment (Art. 2.8); the 1989 Convention on Civil Liability for Damage Caused during the Carriage of Dangerous Goods by Road, Rail and Inland Navigation Vessels (CRTD) (Art. 1.10); and the 1995 draft of an International Convention on Liability and Compensation for Damage in Connection with the Carriage of Hazardous and Noxious Substances by Sea (Art. 1.6). Cf. also Art. 4.2 of the amended EC proposal for a Council Directive on Civil Liability for Damage Caused by Waste (Doc. COM(91) 219 final–SYN 217): one cannot claim the cost of restoration measures if their 'costs substantially exceed the benefit arising for the environment from such *reinstatement* and other alternative measures to the *reinstatement* of the environment may be undertaken at a substantially lower cost'. However, the value of cost/benefit assessment seems questionable in such cases, since the 'benefits' of æsthetic, scenic, wildlife, and comparable resources are not easily reduced to economic quantification. Consequently, the cost/benefit considerations will be based as much on political and economic imperatives as on environmental functional concerns. See P.-A. Trepte, 'Civil Liability for Environmental Damage: The Green Shoots of a Community Policy' (1992) 1 *Reciel* 402–10 at 404, 407. Furthermore, it is to be noted that in order to conclude that restoration costs are grossly disproportionate to the resource value, one needs a yardstick against which these costs are tested. The choice of yardstick methodology is central to the ultimate measure of damages. If the reasonableness of restoration costs is tested against a valuation methodology that tends to produce low natural resource values, restoration may often seem excessively costly. On valuation methodologies see the references in n. 112 below. Finally, it may be mentioned that the US Court of Appeals in *Commonwealth of Puerto Rico* v. *The SS Zoe Colocotroni*, 628 F.2d 652 (1980), stated that the determination of whether costs of reinstatement were reasonable depended on factors such as technical feasibility of the restoration, the ability of the ecosystem to recover naturally, and the expenditures necessary to rehabilitate the affected environment.

[95] Conceptually restoration of the environment is larger than just cleaning up spilled oil and other substances; cf. the terms 'removal' and 'remedial actions' under the American CERCLA: see Wetterstein, n. 38 above, at 118 ff. In the Convention on Civil Liability for Damage Resulting from Activities Dangerous to the Environment (Council of Europe, 1993), 'measures of reinstatement' are defined as 'any reasonable measures aiming to reinstate or restore damaged or destroyed components of the environment, or to introduce, where reasonable, the equivalent of these components into the environment' (Art. 2.8).

has been adopted in, for instance, the United States,[96] Canada,[97] Italy,[98] the United Kingdom,[99] Denmark, Finland, and Norway,[100] and to a limited extent in Germany.[101] The international treaties mentioned above also cover restoration costs.[102]

I can agree with Hubert Bocken when he declares that 'from an ecological point of view, restoration of the environment is preferable to monetary compensation'.[103] Restoration of the environment mitigates pollution damage of a non-economic nature suffered by the public. The environment is restored as far as possible so that fishing, berry-picking, swimming, etc.—the exercise of public rights—are possible again.

However, there are also problems involved in restoring and replacing natural resources,[104] and, furthermore, one can ask whether reinstatement is enough, in view of the need to protect the environment and compensate damage caused to natural resources? To be more effective, recovery should capture the full value of the harm done to the environment.[105] Should, for instance, the diminution in value of natural resources pending restoration be made compensatable? If we

---

[96] See, e.g. the OPA (1990), 33 USC § 2706(d)(1)(A); the CERCLA (1980), 42 USC § 9607(a)(4)(A–D); the Federal Water Pollution Control Act (FWPCA), 33 USC § 1321(f); and the Trans-Alaska Pipeline Authorization Act (TAPAA) 1973, 43 USC § 1653(c)(1).

[97] See, e.g. D. Saxe, 'Canadian Reflections on Environmental Restoration: The Legal Questions', (1994) 2 *Environmental Liability*, Issue 2, 51–6, at 53.

[98] See A. Bianchi, 'Harm to the Environment in Italian Practice: The Interaction of International Law and Domestic Law', Ch. 6 in this book. See also M. C. Maffei, 'The Compensation for Ecological Damage in the "Patmos" Case', in F. Francioni and T. Scovazzi (eds.), *International Responsibility for Environmental Harm* (1991), 381–94, and Brans, n. 64 above, at 63 ff.

[99] In England and Wales there are numerous statutory provisions giving extensive powers to government or public agencies either to order action to be taken or to take action itself and recoup costs. The provisions on contaminated land contained in the recently enacted Environment Act 1995 (it is expected that the Act will be brought into operation during 1996) will enhance the powers of public authorities to require the restoration of contaminated land. See further B. Jones, 'Liability for Environmental Damage—The Tightening Screw—A Plea for Rationality', paper presented at the seminar 'Harm to the Environment: The Right to Compensation and the Assessment of Damages', held in Turku/Åbo, Finland, 15–18 June 1995, at 11 ff. See also A. Layard, 'Contaminated Land: Law and Policy in the United Kingdom, The Environment Bill, Clause 54' (1995) 3 *Environmental Liability* Issue 1, 52–60.

[100] See Wetterstein, n. 45 above, at 46 ff. See also P. Pagh, 'The New Danish Act on Strict Liability for Environmental Damage' (1995) 3 *Environmental Liability* Issue 1, 15–19.

[101] The powers of the authorities will increase in Germany if the draft of an Environmental Code (*Umweltgesetzbuch*) is adopted. See further W. Pfennigstorf, 'How to Deal with Damage to Natural Resources: Solutions in the German Environmental Liability Act of 1990', Ch. 7 in this book.

[102] See the text between nn. 52–56 above. It is to be noted that the definition of 'pollution damage' in these treaties also covers *future* measures ('costs of reasonable measures of reinstatement actually undertaken or to be undertaken'). A right to claim compensation also for measures *to be undertaken* enhances the possibilities of safeguarding the interests of the public/society. Compensation can be claimed 'in advance' from the polluter.   [103] Bocken, n. 21 above, at 242.

[104] Such as the determination of the baseline to which resources are to be restored, the often huge expenses involved, the time it takes for the ecosystem superficially to resemble its original condition (if at all possible), the determination of when restoration has succeeded, etc. See further, Cross, n. 94 above, at 298 ff. See also Saxe, n. 97 above, at 58.

[105] The award of natural resource damages can provide an effective tool for the protection of the environment. The right to recover such damages can force the internalization of many pollution costs and thus create a deterrent to future environmental harm: Cross, n. 94 above.

strive for full protection of natural resources, compensation should also be paid for such lost use values.[106] Furthermore, if restoration of the environment is not possible[107] or, if it is disproportionately expensive,[108] the obligation should be laid upon the polluter to make financial compensation.[109] In this case, diminution in use values would include compensation to the public for non-reparable damage such as the permanent loss of wildlife and fisheries.[110] Alternatively, the obligation might be laid upon the polluter to provide an equivalent area elsewhere in the same general vicinity.[111] Finally, before any award on damages is

[106] Diminution of use values is based upon the reduction in the level of services the injured resources provided to another resource or to the public (e.g. fishing) as a result of the discharge or release. It does not address any private economic damages related to the indirect economic effects on individuals, businesses, etc. See further Wetterstein, n. 38 above, at 168 ff. with references. It may be mentioned that focusing on the use value of natural resources is consistent with a tradition in US law. According to 43 CFR, Part 11, para. 11.83, use value is 'the value of the resources to the public attributable to the direct use of the services provided by the natural resources', and further, compensatable value is 'the amount of money required to compensate the public for the loss in services provided by the injured resources between the time of the discharge or release and the time the resources and the services those resources provided are fully returned to their baseline conditions. . . . Compensable value is measured by changes in consumer surplus, economic rent, and any fees or other payments collectable by a Federal or State agency or an Indian tribe for a private party's use of the natural resources; and any economic rent accruing to a private party because the Federal or State agency or Indian tribe does not charge a fee or price for the use of the resources'. Use value is more precise and less speculative than other types of resource value because it measures actual behaviour, rather than attitudes. See Cross, n. 94 above, at 282 ff. It may also be noted that according to the OPA (1990) 'the diminution in value of those natural resources pending restoration' is recoverable (33 USC § 2706(d)(1)(A–C)).

[107] Such irreparable damage could e.g. be damage caused by a nuclear accident, damage to archaeological and historical values, and the destruction of an animal species or of a biotope.

[108] See n. 94 above.

[109] Monetary compensation for damage to the environment is possible under US law: see Wetterstein, n. 38 above, at 141 ff., and under Italian law. According to Bianchi, n. 98 above, restoration in kind should be ordered by Italian courts whenever possible. Otherwise, damages can be awarded. Should the assessment of such damages prove to be difficult, 'courts may resort to an equitable appraisal that takes into account, respectively, the degree of fault, the costs of restoration and the profit unduly gained by the tortfeasor as a consequence of the wrong'. On the question of monetary compensation for damage to the environment, see also International Law Commission, Special Rapporteur Julio Barboza, *Eleventh Report on International Liability for Injurious Consequences Arising out of Acts Not Prohibited by International Law*, UN Doc. A/CN.4/468, 26 Apr. 1995, 11 ff. Further, see Art. 2.2(b)(iv) of the Draft Arts. of a Protocol on Liability and Compensation for Damage Resulting from the Transboundary Movements of Hazardous Wastes and their Disposal (n. 135 below), and the definition of 'damage' in the 1990 ECE Guidelines on Responsibility and Liability Regarding Transboundary Water Pollution (I.1(m)).

[110] On the interesting question of compensating so-called existence and bequest values (non-use values), see Wetterstein, n. 38 above, at 149 ff. with references. See also the interesting discussion by B. Sandvik in 'Broadening the Scope of Compensation for Damage to Natural Resources—What Can We Learn from US Law?', *Marius*, No. 218 (1995). A measurement of natural resource damages that takes into account also non-use values may result in extensive amounts of damages.

[111] According to the American OPA (1990) compensation to the ecosystem covers not only the costs of removal (i.e. the costs of cleaning up spilled oil) but also 'the cost of restoring, rehabilitating, replacing, or acquiring the equivalent of, the damaged natural resources' (33 USC § 2706(d)(1)(A–C)). See also 43 CFR, Part 11, para. 11.82. It should also be noted that the acquisition of equivalent resources is mentioned in the definition of 'measures of reinstatement' in the 1993 Convention on Civil Liability for Damage Resulting from Activities Dangerous to the Environment (Art. 2.8). The Explanatory Report to the Convention (Council of Europe, Draft Convention on Civil Liability for Damage Resulting from Activities Dangerous to the Environment and Explanatory

given, it will be necessary to arrive at a methodology for evaluation of the harmed resources.[112]

Returning now to the question of *locus standi*, it was mentioned above that the public authorities usually have the right to claim the costs of restoration of the environment—in addition to a private person whose individual rights have been infringed. In US law the right to bring claims for natural resource damages (the right to compensation is greater than merely the recovery of restoration costs[113]) has been gradually extended. From federal and state officials (the Federal Water Pollution Control Act[114] and non-statutory maritime law[115]) the group of plaintiffs that can bring actions has been expanded to Indian tribes and, in some cases, to foreign governments.

The OPA (1990) gives the right to claim natural resource damages to the US Government, a state, an Indian tribe, and a foreign government.[116] Under the CERCLA (1980) (amended in 1986 by the Superfund Amendments and Reauthorization Act (SARA)) natural resource damage claims may be brought exclusively by the federal government and authorized representatives of states as 'trustees' of natural resources, acting on behalf of the public, or by designated trustees of Indian tribes.[117] Consequently, private entities may not bring CERCLA natural resource damage claims.[118] Further, it is to be noted that 'double recovery'

Report, Strasbourg, 15 Jan. 1993) contains the following explanation: '[w]hen it is impossible to restore or re-establish the environment, the measures of reinstatement may be in the form of the reintroduction of equivalent components into the environment. This applies for example in the case of the disappearance of an animal species or the irreparable destruction of a biotope. Such damage cannot be evaluated financially and any reinstatement of the environment is in theory impossible. Since such difficulties must not lead to a complete absence of compensation, a specific method of compensation has been introduced. This method of compensation is based on achieving an equivalent instead of an identical environment' (28). See also C. de la Rue, 'Environmental Damage Assessment', in R. R. Kroner (ed.), *Transnational Environmental Liability and Insurance* (1993), 67–78, at 71 ff., for the discussion concerning the possibility of creating an equivalent site as an alternative to restoration.

[112] On these complex issues, see, e.g. Wetterstein, n. 38 above, at 148 ff., 160 ff.; Sandvik, n. 110 above, and also E. Louderbough, 'The Role of Science in Valuing Natural Resources after *State of Ohio* v. *Department of Interior*, 880 F.2d 432 (D.C. Cir. 1989)' (1992) 32 *Natural Resources Journal* 137–48.   [113] See Wetterstein, n. 38 above, 141 ff.

[114] See the FWPCA 33 USC § 1321(f). See also Wetterstein, n. 38 above, at 158 ff.

[115] See Wetterstein, n. 38 above, at 181 ff.   [116] 33 USC § 2706(a), cf. § 2702(b)(2)(A).

[117] 42 USC § 9607(f). Only officials or agencies specifically designated by the President or by the governor of a state are entitled to act as public trustees under the CERCLA, see § 9607(f)(2)(A–B). Those agencies that the President has designated as federal trustees include the Department of the Interior (DOI), the Department of Commerce, the Department of Agriculture, the Department of Defense, and the Department of Energy. Further, 'Environmental Protection Agency regulations indicate that tribal chairmen or heads of tribes are to act as trustees for Indian tribes': C. W. Breeding and L. R. Cress, Jr., 'Natural Resource Damages under CERCLA: A New Beginning?' (1992) 20 *Northern Kentucky Law Review* 23–45, at 26.

[118] It may be noted that cases prior to the 1986 CERCLA amendments allowed municipalities to bring actions for natural resource damages—even if they were not designated as trustees by the State Governor. See paper by W. D. Brighton, 'Natural Resource Damages under the Comprehensive Environmental Response, Compensation, and Liability Act' (Sept. 1994), 3 ff. See also Breeding and Cress, Jr., n. 117 above, at 26.

for natural resource damages, including the costs of damage assessment or restoration, rehabilitation, or acquisition for the same release and natural resource, is not possible.[119]

In many European countries the public authorities have been given the right to claim restoration costs. Such countries are, for instance, Finland,[120] Italy,[121] Spain,[122] and the United Kingdom. The Norwegian Pollution Act of 1981 has adopted a progressive approach by offering a solution by which public authorities (primarily the municipal pollution control authority) and *private organizations/societies* with legal interest in the matter have the right to claim reasonable costs from the defendant(s) for restoration of the environment.[123] In France, some environmental associations have the right to claim compensation in criminal cases involving the violation of certain environmental statutes.[124] Other countries grant environmental associations the right to seek an injunction against activities violating certain environmental statutes.[125]

The environmental treaties do not usually give any answers to the question of who can claim the cost of restoration of the environment.[126] However, some explicit provisions exist granting rights to environmental associations.[127]

---

[119] 42 USC § 9607(f)(1).

[120] According to s. 6 of the Finnish EDCA 1994 the authorities have the right to claim reasonable (in view of the disturbance or the risk of disturbance and the benefit of the restoration measures) costs from the person(s) liable for measures undertaken to restore the environment. As a comparison, the Swedish Environmental Damage Act 1986 does not explicitly mention restoration costs.

[121] The Italian state and its subdivisions, i.e. municipalities, provinces, and regions, are the only entities that are entitled to ask for redress as trustees, respectively, for the national and local community: see Bianchi, n. 98 above.

[122] See 'Repairing Damage to the Environment—A Community System of Civil Liability' (European Environmental Law Association, Report of Working Party: Submission to the Commission of the European Communities) (1994) 2 *Environmental Liability* 1–10, at 10.

[123] The Norwegian Pollution Act, s. 58. See also the decision of the Norwegian Supreme Court in [1992] Rt (Norsk Retstidende) 1618. As a comparison, it may be mentioned that the new (1994) Danish Act on Compensation for Damage to the Environment does not grant environmental organizations or private citizens any right to compensation for measures to prevent environmental harm or to restore the environment: Pagh, n. 100 above, at 19.

[124] Bocken, n. 21 above, at 244. However, a new environmental protection law in France, enacted on 2 Feb. 1995, has introduced a number of new provisions, including important rights for environmental groups. *Associations agrées de protection de l'environnement* will have rights to participate in various ways in environmental regulation, including legal standing in cases which concern breaches of statutory regulations giving rise to direct or indirect harm to the collective interests which it is their object to defend. See (1995) *Environmental Liability Report* Issue No. 018, 3.

[125] New laws to this effect have been introduced in Belgium, see N. Van Crombrugghe, 'Belgium: Class Action for Environmental Issues' (1993) 2 *European Environmental Law Review*, No. 10, 275–6, and in the Netherlands, see P. Klik, 'Group Actions in Civil Lawsuits: The New Law in the Netherlands' (1995) 4 *European Environmental Law Review* No. 1, 14–16. In Canada, Part 6 of Ontario's new Environmental Bill of Rights authorizes judges to order the making good of environmental damage on the basis of civil law suits, see further D. Saxe, 'Canadian Reflections on Environmental Restoration: The Legal Questions (Continued)' (1994) 2 *Environmental Liability* Issue 3, 57–64, at 57.   [126] See the treaties mentioned in the text between nn. 52–56 above.

[127] See Art. 4.3 of the amended EC proposal for a Council Directive on Civil Liability for Damage Caused by Waste (1991), and Art. 18 of the Convention on Civil Liability for Damage Resulting from Activities Dangerous to the Environment (1993).

The question of giving the right to claim restoration costs also to certain environmental interest groups and organizations is interesting. Such a restricted right to claim natural resource damages is worth considering.[128] After all, there are some limitations on the ability authorities have effectively to safeguard the interests of their citizens. The authorities may lack the political will and preparedness to tackle the problems in earnest. They may be too 'tied' to the interests of industry. Short-term economic interests may prevail over long term ecological concerns. Environmental groups and organizations, on the other hand, often function as 'watchdogs' over industries and activities hazardous to the environment[129] and they could form an important part in a comprehensive system to protect the environment. This would be particularly important when the possibilities of claiming restoration costs 'in advance' (that is, for measures *to be undertaken*) from the polluter are enhanced.[130]

If environmental associations are granted *locus standi*, the question arises under what conditions such right may be exercised. The decisive issue seems to be what kind of legal interest in the relevant matter should be demanded of the association. In my opinion, some conditions should be fulfilled. The association should have obtained legal personality in accordance with applicable (national) law. Further, it must have 'a certain permanence' which can be fulfilled by the time element and/or the number of members. And, which is very important, the legal actions conducted by the association must correspond to its corporate aims and purpose (as defined in the articles of the association).[131] Finally, it is self-evident that the money raised should be used for non-profit-making purposes,

---

[128] It may be mentioned that this question was discussed within the Legal Committee of the Finnish Parliament. The Committee postponed the matter pending the implementation of the Council of Europe Convention: see Opinion of the Legal Committee of the Parliament concerning Governmental Bill 165/1992, 1994 vp-LaVM 10-He 165/1992 vp, 6 ff. The granting of legal standing to sue to environmental groups with 'a certain permanence' and fishermen's organizations has also been proposed in Sweden. See (1994) *Environmental Liability Report* Issue No. 013, 5. In the US, too, there have been recommendations that citizens' groups be allowed to sue on behalf of the public for natural resource damages when federal or state trustees fail to act: D. Woodard and M. R. Hope, 'Natural Resource Damage Litigation under the Comprehensive Environmental Response, Compensation, and Liability Act' (1990) 14 *Harvard Environmental Law Review* 189–215, at 215, state: '[w]e believe that such a provision would increase the number of recoveries on behalf of the public at no cost to the taxpayers and without the need for creating a new right of action for recovery of damages by private parties.'

[129] Cf. M. J. Uda, 'The Oil Pollution Act of 1990: Is There a Bright Future Beyond Valdez?' (1991) 10 *Virginia Environmental Law Journal* 403–33, at 432.   [130] See n. 102 above.

[131] Cf. Van Crombrugghe, n. 125 above, at 275. See also P. v. Wilmowsky and G. Roller, *Civil Liability for Waste* (1992), who, at 90 ff., generally support the approach of the proposed directive (the amended EC proposal for a Council Directive on Civil Liability for Damage Caused by Waste, 1991) to granting standing to common interest groups and associations. Further, in their view, only three general conditions appear acceptable to restrict the right of associations to litigate: 'the condition of "persistence", which means that the group has to demonstrate a permanent and not merely temporary commitment to promoting the cause of environmental protection; the condition of "openness", which means that the association should admit as a member anybody willing to support its declared aims; and finally environmental protection being the principal goal of the association' (138). Also of interest in this context is the Norwegian Supreme Court decision n. 123 above.

that is, for the restoration of the environment. These are some possible conditions and, of course, there may be others. In any case, it is important that these issues are discussed.

Another problem in this context is the issue of competition between claims. For instance, should an environmental association (or the authorities) be entitled to claim restoration costs on an equal footing to a land/water-owner or only if the latter declines to do so? It would seem appropriate that the owner be entitled to take action before environmental associations/public authorities.[132] In this way the risk of 'double recovery' from the person liable is mitigated.[133] But the competition between owner and other claimants relates only to proprietary or other individual rights, not to the *res communis* part of the environment.[134] Furthermore, it is also very important that there are provisions for sufficient and effective co-operation between the authorities and the environmental associations. The question of competition between claims should be solved also concerning these claimants.

It is interesting to note that the 1993 Convention on Civil Liability for Damage Resulting from Activities Dangerous to the Environment covers 'loss or damage by impairment of the environment in so far as this is not considered to be damage within the meaning of sub-paragraphs a or b above' (Article 2.7.c). Sub-paragraphs a and b cover loss of life or personal injury and loss of or damage to property (with some restrictions). However, the wording of Article 2.7.c seems somewhat ambiguous. There is no clarifying statement in the Explanatory Report to the Convention. Is the meaning, as it appears, that the rules relating to impairment of the environment are only to be applied in cases where the private assets involved present an ecological value which exceeds the personal interest of the owner?[135] Since, for instance, land and water are usually owned by somebody, and impairment of the environment thus often also constitutes property damage, such a view seems to restrict the possibilities of public authorities/environmental associations to take measures of reinstatement in cases where those having proprietary interests decline to do so. Further, such a solution puts special emphasis on the difficult question of defining 'property

---

[132] See also 'Repairing Damage to the Environment—A Community System of Civil Liability', n. 122 above, at 9.

[133] However, if several parties are to be given the right to take action, mechanisms have been mentioned to ensure that restoration is the end result and to prevent double recovery. Such devices could *inter alia*, be the establishment of a trust for this purpose or to give the court the discretion to settle this issue as a preliminary point. See 'Repairing Damage to the Environment—A Community System of Civil Liability', n. 122 above, at 10.   [134] Cf. pp. 30–2 above.

[135] Cf. also Art. 2.2 of the Draft Arts. of a Protocol on Liability and Compensation for Damage Resulting from the Transboundary Movements of Hazardous Wastes and their Disposal: 'For the purposes of this Protocol: . . . (b) "Damage" means: (i) loss of life of personal injury; (ii) loss or damage to property other than property held by the person liable for the damage in accordance with the present Protocol; (iii) loss of profit from impairment of the environment; (iv) impairment of the environment, in so far as this is not considered to be damage within the meaning of sub-paragraphs (i), (ii) or (iii) above': *Report of the Ad Hoc Working Group on the Work of Its Third Session*, UNEP/CHW.1/WG.1/3/2, 17 Mar. 1995, 20.

damage'.[136] With regard to this, the definition of pollution damage in the international treaties mentioned above, that is, the 1992 Protocols to the CLC and the Fund Convention, the 1989 CRTD Convention, and the 1995 draft HNS Convention, would perhaps have been preferable.

4. CONCLUSIONS

The foregoing survey has indicated that the traditional approach in tort law to tying the right to claim for environmental impairment to individual rights (proprietary, possessory, etc.) is changing. For instance, many new international treaties dealing with environmental impairment liability seem to have accepted both claims for pure economic losses regardless of the distinction individual/public rights and claims for the restoration of the environment—including the unowned environment. But this enlargement of the scope of environmental liability poses many new questions: how shall we delimit in an appropriate and fair way the right to compensation for pure economic losses? What are reasonable measures to restore the environment? Is the right to claim restoration enough, in view of the need to protect the environment and compensate damage caused to natural resources, or should there also be a possibility to claim monetary compensation? What is the right methodology for evaluation of the harmed resources? Should environmental associations also be given the right to claim costs for restoration of the environment? If so, under what conditions? How is the question of competition between claims solved?

All these complex questions are relevant, and they should be answered in order to achieve a modern and comprehensive liability regime.

[136] See the text between nn. 10–16 above.

PART II

The International Framework and Concepts

3

Harm and Reparation in International Treaty Regimes: An Overview

BJÖRN SANDVIK AND SATU SUIKKARI*

1. INTRODUCTION

At the time of the negotiation of the first international civil liability treaties it was envisaged that the type of damage to be compensated would concern individual rights in the strict sense: personal injury, and loss of or damage to property. It has long been recognized that the range of potential damage is much broader. Environmental incidents may involve high costs of preventive measures, the costs of cleaning up the contaminated environment, and the costs of reinstatement of the environment. Furthermore, economic losses or loss of profit as a result of the contamination of the environment, even when unrelated to personal or property damage, are often substantial. The experience of such incidents has required the drafters of international liability treaties to broaden the scope of compensable damage accordingly.

This Chapter aims at describing how the concept of environmental damage has been formulated in international civil liability regimes and other environmental treaties which address the question of liability for environmental damage. It should be emphasized that the purpose of this Chapter is to provide a general treaty overview only. The international civil liability treaties set up a general framework for a system of compensating damage, and the task of elaborating more detailed arrangements rests with the national authorities. Thus, a more profound treatment of the substantive liability issues would require not only a careful analysis of each treaty regime, but also a discussion on the national implementation of the treaty in question as well as on the interrelation between international treaty law and domestic law in this context. Such discussions are to be found in other chapters of this volume.

Areas regulated by existing civil liability treaties (as amended by additional protocols relevant to the concept of environmental damage) include:

* The authors would like to thank Professor P. Wetterstein and Professor A. Rosas for helpful comments on this Ch.

(1) *Peaceful use of nuclear energy*
1960 Paris Convention on Third Party Liability in the Field of Nuclear
Energy (1960 Paris Convention);
1963 Vienna Convention on Civil Liability for Nuclear Damage (1963)
Vienna Convention);

(2) *Operation of nuclear ships*
1962 Convention on the Liability of Operators of Nuclear Ships;

(3) *Maritime carriage of nuclear material*
1971 Convention relating to Civil Liability in the Field of Maritime
Carriage of Nuclear Material;

(4) *Oil pollution*
1969 International Convention on Civil Liability for Oil Pollution Damage
(1969 CLC) and Protocol of 1992 to Amend the International Convention
on Civil Liability for Oil Pollution Damage 1969 (1992 Protocol to the CLC);
1971 International Convention on the Establishment of an International
Fund for Compensation for Oil Pollution Damage (1971 Fund Convention) and Protocol of 1992 to Amend the International Convention on the
Establishment of an International Fund for Compensation for Oil Pollution Damage (1992 Protocol to the Fund Convention);
1977 Convention on Civil Liability for Oil Pollution Damage Resulting
from Exploration for and Exploitation of Seabed Mineral Resources;

(5) *Carriage of dangerous goods by road, rail, and inland navigation vessels*
1989 Convention on Civil Liability for Damage caused during Carriage
of Dangerous Goods by Road, Rail and Inland Navigation Vessels (1989
CRTD);

(6) *Activities dangerous to the environment*
1993 Convention on Civil Liability for Damage Resulting from Activities
Dangerous to the Environment (1993 European Convention).

Moreover, negotiations on civil liability for certain areas are under way, namely
damage in connection with the carriage of hazardous and noxious substances by
sea (1995 HNS Draft Convention)[1], damage resulting from the transboundary
movements of hazardous wastes and their disposal (1995 Draft Protocol to the
1989 Basel Convention)[2], and peaceful use of nuclear energy (the 1995 Proposal
for a Revision of the 1963 Vienna Convention).[3]

As regards state liability[4] reference may be made, for example, to the 1972

---

[1] 1995 Draft International Convention on Liability and Compensation for Damage in Connection
with the Carriage of Hazardous and Noxious Substances by Sea.
[2] 1995 Draft Protocol on Liability and Compensation for Damages Resulting from the Transboundary Movements of Hazardous Wastes and Their Disposal. See the *Report of the Ad Hoc Working
Group on the Work of Its Third Session*, UNEP/CHW.1/WG/1/3/2 of 17 Mar. 1995.
[3] See the *Report of the Standing Committe on Liability for Nuclear Damage*, Eleventh Session,
20–24 Mar. 1995, SCNL/11/INF.5, 24 Apr. 1995.
[4] Apart from treaty regimes providing for state liability, reference may be made to the liability
regime established by the UN Security Council adressing the liability of Iraq for any direct loss, or

Convention on International Liability for Damage Caused by Space Objects which includes a direct obligation for the state to compensate damage caused. A corresponding provision can be found in the 1988 Convention on the Regulation of Antarctic Mineral Resources Activities (1988 CRAMRA). However, the latter Convention has not entered into force. Moreover, the 1963 Convention Supplementary to the Paris Convention of 1960 on Third Party Liability in the Field of Nuclear Energy provides for residual state liability. The question of state liability is also being addressed by the International Law Commission of the United Nations within the topic 'injurious consequences arising out of acts not prohibited by international law'.[5]

Liability for damage or loss is also addressed, albeit generally, in some of the existing multilateral environmental protection treaties. Such treaties usually merely state that the parties shall deal with liability in accordance with international law.[6] For instance, the Draft Agreement for the Implementation of the provisions of the UN Convention on the Law of the Sea relating to the conservation and management of straddling fish stocks and highly migratory fish stocks provides, in Article 35, that 'States Parties are liable in accordance with international law for damage or loss attributable to them in regard to this agreement'.[7] None of these treaties, however, defines in any more detail, for instance, the nature of liability or the scope of compensatable damage, and they are therefore not of particular interest in the present context.

Under some of these treaties the parties have undertaken the task of developing specific rules on the matter of liability, but very little progress has been made in the field. However, the development of a detailed liability regime is currently under discussion, for example, in the 1995 Draft Protocol to the 1989 Basel Convention[8] and within the ILC under the topic referred to above.[9]

damage, including environmental damage and the depletion of natural resources as a result of Iraq's unlawful invasion and occupation of Kuwait. See Security Council Resolutions 687 (1991) of 3 Apr. 1991, and 692 (1991) of 20 May 1991.

[5] For the recent developments in this field see J. Barboza, 'Environmental Damage in the International Law Commission', Ch. 4 in this book. See also sect. 6 of this Ch. Further reference may also be made to ILC, *Survey of Liability Regimes Relevant to the Topic of International Liability for Injurious Consequences Arising out of Acts not Prohibited by International Law* (A/CN.4/471, 23 June 1995).

[6] See, e.g. 1972 Convention on the Prevention of Marine Pollution by Dumping of Wastes and Other Matter; 1974 Convention for the Protection of the Marine Environment of the Baltic Sea Area; 1982 UN Convention on the Law of the Sea; 1992 Convention on the Protection of the Marine Environment of the Baltic Sea Area; 1992 Convention for the Protection of the Marine Environment of the North-East Atlantic.

[7] The Agreement was adopted by the UN Conference on Straddling Fish Stocks and Highly Migratory Fish Stocks on 4 Aug. 1995.

[8] The present draft of the liability protocol is based on a three-tier liability system, where primary liability shall be through civil liability of private operators. This would be supplemented by a compensation fund, and as a last resort the state would be liable.

[9] The work on developing rules on liability has also been pursued under some other agreements, but such efforts have failed. See M. Koskenniemi, 'Transfrontier Pollution Damage Liability' (1990) 2 *International Environmental Affairs* No. 2, 309–16, at 311.

Among relevant soft law instruments reference may, for instance, be made to the UN/ECE Guidelines on Responsibility and Liability Regarding Transboundary Water Pollution of 1990 (1990 UN/ECE Guidelines).[10] The question of liability and responsibility is also touched upon in several international key documents in the field of environmental law, but again very generally and without giving any guidance as regards the scope of compensatable damage.

2. THE ELEMENTS OF THE CONCEPT OF 'ENVIRONMENTAL DAMAGE'

The concept of 'environmental damage' can, generally speaking, be referred to in at least two different ways. In a narrow sense it refers only to harm to the environment, that is, damage to the environment *per se*, pure environmental damage, or 'impairment of the environment', which is the terminology frequently used in civil liability treaties. These concepts again are somewhat blurred and have to be interpreted on the basis of the exact meaning of the term 'environment' in each treaty regime; the broader the definition of environment, the broader is the scope of compensatable damage to the environment *per se*.

Civil liability treaties, however, seldom expressly define what is meant by 'environment'. Nevertheless, reference may be made to the 1993 European Convention. According to Article 2, paragraph 10, 'environment' includes:

— natural resources both abiotic and biotic, such as air, water, soil, fauna, and flora, and the interaction between the same factors;
— property which forms part of the cultural heritage; and
— the characteristic aspects of the landscape.

The rather broad definition of environment in the 1993 European Convention, covering even the man-made environment as distinct from natural resources, can be related, for example, to the 1988 CRAMRA. Damage to the Antarctic environment or ecosystems is defined in Article 1, paragraph 15, as:

any impact on living or non-living components of that environment or those ecosystems, including harm to atmospheric, marine or terrestial life, beyond that which is negligible or which has been assessed and judged to be acceptable pursuant to the convention.

The narrower definition of 'environment' and consequently a narrower scope of compensatable damage to the environment *per se* in the latter treaty seems to restrict liability to so-called 'ecological damage' or 'natural resource damage', although it should be stressed that the meaning of these expressions is not univocal.[11]

---

[10] Reprinted in H. Hohmann (ed.), *Basic Documents of International Environmental Law* (1992), i, 310–4. See further on the Guidelines in sect. 6 of this Ch.

[11] For a discussion of the notion of ecological damage or natural resource damage, see, e.g. H.-U. Marticke, 'Liability for Ecological Damage: Report' (1992) 22 *Environmental Policy and Law* 28–31, at 28; M. C. Maffei, 'The Compensation for Ecological Damage in the "Patmos" Case', in

The term 'environmental damage *per se*' has also been used in contradistinction to those aspects of the environment which constitute private property. On the other hand, since no distinction between the owned and the unowned environment, or private and public property[12] is made, for example, in the 1969 CLC, the 1971 Fund Convention or the 1992 Protocols, it is arguable that none of these regimes would disallow claims for environmental damage simply on the ground that no owner has suffered loss.[13] And the opposite is also true of damage to the owned environment, whether private or public property, may constitute compensatable damage to the environment *per se* under these treaty regimes.

In a wider sense the term 'environmental damage' is not restricted to damage to the environment *per se*, but is understood also to cover other aspects of losses resulting from environmental impairment ('consequential environmental damage'). This includes personal injury, damage to property, and economic losses resulting, for instance, from the release or discharge of toxic substances, or noise, vibrations, or other emissions into the environment.[14]

As has been noted above, international civil liability treaty law at first followed the traditional pattern in tort law as far as the concept of damage was concerned. Thus, the first conventions on nuclear liability focused on compensation for damage to persons and property only.[15] However, the revision of these treaties is under way, and one of the major issues in the negotiations has been the formulation of a new definition of damage.[16] In other fields the concept of compensatable environmental damage has already been broadened to include economic losses (both consequential and pure economic loss), costs of preventive measures, clean-up costs, and costs of reinstatement including the acquisition of

F. Francioni and T. Scavazzi (eds.), *International Responsibility for Environmental Harm* (1991), 381–94, at 381; L. Teclaff, 'Beyond Restoration—The Case of Ecocide' (1994) 34 *Natural Resources Journal* 933–56; B. R. Binger, R. F. Copple, and E. Hoffman, 'The Use of Contingent Valuation Methodology in Natural Resource Damage Assessments: Legal Fact and Economic Fiction' (1995) 89 *Northwestern University Law Review* 1029–115, at 1107.

[12] For a discussion on the distinctions between private and public property, see, e.g. J. W. Harris, 'Private and Non-private Property. What is the Difference?' (1995) 111 *The Law Quarterly Review* 421–44.

[13] D. Wilkinson, 'Moving the Boundaries of Compensable Environmental Damage Caused by Marine Oil Spills: The Effect of Two New International Protocols' (1993) 5 *Journal of Environmental Law* 71–90, at 83, n. 71.

[14] See further on the notion of environmental damage, T. Kuokkanen, 'Defining Environmental Damage in International and Nordic Environmental Law', in T. Tervashonka (ed.), *The Legal Status of the Individual in Nordic Environmental Law* (1994), 53–62, at 53 and 61.

[15] However, there is an explicit provision in these conventions which allows parties to extend this definition, but the legislation of OECD states closely follows the provisions of the conventions: see A. Boyle, 'Nuclear Energy and International Law: An Environmental Perspective' (1989) 60 *British Year Book of International Law* 257–314, at 309, quoting OECD, *Nuclear Legislation; Third Party Liability* (1976). But see also, e.g. s. 39 of the Polish Atomic Law of 1986, according to which compensation can be awarded even for diminution of common interest arising from radioactive contamination of the environment.

[16] See the document referred to in n. 3 above. See also OECD, *Liability and Compensation for Nuclear Damage. An International Overview* (1994), especially 127–8.

equivalent resources. Further, provisions including even monetary compensation for diminished environmental values have been included, *inter alia*, in draft documents addressing liability for environmental impairment.[17]

Certain issues related to each of the different categories of damage will be briefly touched upon in the following sections, while compensation for damage to the environment *per se* is the only category described in any more detail.

3. PERSONAL INJURY

Personal injury is explicitly covered in the definitions in most of the existing civil liability treaties. However, the 1969 CLC and the 1971 Fund Convention, for example, do not explicitly mention personal injury, although it seems to be covered by the vague definition of pollution damage. Oil pollution incidents nevertheless relatively seldom cause personal injury. Thus, the International Oil Pollution Fund (IOPC Fund) has had only limited experience regarding claims for this type of damage.[18]

Yet, there are certain problems attached to claims for personal injury, concerning in particular the time limits for submitting a claim and the proof of causality. Personal injury resulting from environmental harm may sometimes not become apparent until decades after an accident, and may even affect the unborn. This is particularly the case with nuclear injury and injury caused by highly toxic substances.[19] In the light of this, for example, the ten-year time limits provided for in the nuclear liability conventions are far too low. There have been proposals to extend the claims period of the nuclear conventions to thirty years. All problems would not, however, be resolved by such an amendment. First, it is difficult to obtain insurance covering long periods. Secondly, there is the problem of distributing funds among claimants.[20] Since the funds available for compensating the injury are limited, a situation may arise where no funds are left for those who file their claims at a very late stage.

Proof of causality between an incident and personal injury can be very difficult to establish, especially in cases where the injury becomes observable only after a long period of time. For instance, in the case of personal injury caused by a nuclear accident, it may be difficult to establish whether the person in question has been exposed to radiation, and to estimate the effects of the dose.[21] In

---

[17] In this context reference may be made to the 1995 Draft Protocol to the Basel Convention and the work within the ILC under the topic 'Injurious Consequences Arising Out of Acts Not Prohibited By International Law': see further sect. 6 of this Ch.

[18] P. Wetterstein, 'A Proprietary or Possessory Interest: A *Conditio Sine Qua Non* for Claiming Damages dor Environmental Impairment?', Ch. 2 in this book.

[19] The most famous examples are the Chernobyl accident from 1986 and the Bhopal accident from 1984. For a recent report on the results of the Bhopal accident, see e.g. W. Morehouse, 'Unfinished Business: Bhopal Ten Years After' (1994) 24 *Ecologist* No. 5, 164–9.

[20] See L. de la Fayette, 'Towards a New Regime of State Responsibility for Nuclear Activities' (1992) 50 *Nuclear Law Bulletin* 7–35, at 15.

[21] On these questions see P. Ståhlberg, 'Causation and the Problem of Evidence in Cases of Nuclear Damage' (1994) 53 *Nuclear Law Bulletin* 22–9, at 23.

order to secure the victim's right to compensation in situations where there is doubt about the cause of damage, a provision was introduced to the 1989 CRTD according to which: '[w]here it is not reasonably possible to separate damage caused by the dangerous goods from that caused by other factors, all such damage shall be deemed to be caused by the dangerous goods.'

The 1995 Draft HNS Convention includes a similar provision.

4. PROPERTY DAMAGE

Property damage seems to be compensatable under all liability regimes considered in this Chapter. The concept of property arguably refers above all to individual rights over things which can normally be transferred from one person to another[22] and entail a more or less absolute power to use the thing to the exclusion of others.

On the other hand, it will be recalled that the concept of property is historically relative.[23] There has been a certain tendency during recent decades to redefine it so as to include certain claim-rights and user-rights which are not 'owned' in the traditional sense.[24] Consequently, denial by reason of environmental harm of the right to use natural resources and environments could then be considered as damage to property. If the state is the claimant, compensation could in such cases be awarded, for example, for specific user-rights of private persons.[25] However, in this context a clear conceptual distinction should rather be made between the infringement of individual proprietary or possessory interests, as opposed to granting public authorities *locus standi* when public (collective) rights or interests have been infringed, such as the right to use recreational areas.[26] The fact that the general provision for compensation for property damage has not been thought to be sufficient, but has been supplemented in more recent instruments by additional references to impairment of the environment, also points to the limits of extensive definitions of the concept of property. On the other hand, there is no escape from the fact that 'property' invites a broad spectrum of properties and rights in relation to them, and that the drawing of a line between 'property' and 'environment' is no easy task.

---

[22] This person may, of course, also be a body corporate, the state or another public body.

[23] See, e.g. K. R. Minogue, 'The Concept of Property and Its Contemporary Significance', in J. R. Pennock and J. W. Chapman (eds.), *Property* (1980), 3–27, at 12–15; E. F. Paul *et al.* (eds.), *Property Rights* (1994).

[24] One of the by now classic contributions is C. Reich, 'The New Property' (1964) 73 *Yale Law Journal* 733–87. See further, e.g. J. Nedelsky, *Private Property and the Limits of American Constitutionalism: The Madisonian Framework and Its Legacy* (1990), 240–6; A. Rosas, 'Property Rights', in A. Rosas and J. Helgesen (eds.), *The Strength of Diversity: Human Rights and Pluralist Democracy* (1992), 133–57, at 150–1, 154.

[25] See A. Rosas, 'Issues of State Liability for Transboundary Environmental Damage' (1991) 60 *Nordic Journal of International Law* 29–48, at 41. Cf. also with regard to Russian law, e.g. A. Kolodkin, V. Kiselev, and N. Koroleva, 'Some New Tendencies in Legislation of the Russian Federation and Its Attitude Towards Conventions with Regard to Marine Pollution', in Colin M. de la Rue (ed.), *Liability for Damage to the Marine Environment* (1993), 33–8.

[26] See further the discussion by P. Wetterstein, n. 18 above.

5. ECONOMIC LOSSES

When discussing economic losses, a distinction must be made between *consequential* and *pure* economic losses. The former refers to losses which are consequential on personal injury or property damage, such as loss of earnings due to disablement. The latter, in turn, is not related to personal injury or property damage. Reference can, for instance, be made to a situation where commercial fishermen lose the preconditions for fishing as a result of marine pollution.

Most jurisdictions have traditionally accepted claims for consequential economic losses, while being more or less reluctant about claims for pure economic losses. Accepting claims for pure economic losses can be problematical for several reasons: the chain of causation may be very long and the question of how the line is to be drawn between those claims for economic loss which should be compensated, and those which should be dismissed as too remote poses many problems. The admissibility conditions for claims for pure economic losses have, nevertheless, been facilitated in recent years, in the domain of both domestic and treaty law.[27]

The question of compensating pure economic losses has often arisen under the definition of pollution damage in the 1969 CLC and the 1971 Fund Convention.[28] In particular, the *Haven* (Italy, 1991), the *Aegean Sea* (Spain, 1992), and the *Braer* (United Kingdom, 1993) incidents involved a wide variety of claims for pure economic losses. The IOPC Fund has agreed to compensate economic losses suffered by persons who depend directly on earnings from coastal or sea-related activities such as commercial fishermen, hoteliers, and restaurateurs at sea-side resorts, even if the person concerned had not suffered any damage to property.[29]

To date, apart from the nuclear liability treaties,[30] most civil liability conventions have expanded their scope of compensatable damage to loss of profit as a result of environmental impairment, even when unrelated to personal or property damage.[31]

6. DAMAGE TO THE ENVIRONMENT *PER SE*

The practical experiences of various incidents involving oil pollution damage, damage caused by highly toxic chemicals, and nuclear damage from the 1980s especially have raised one of the most controversial and difficult policy questions

[27] See, e.g. the discussion by N. J. J. Gaskell, 'Economic Loss in the Maritime Context' [1985], *Lloyd's Maritime and Commercial Law Quarterly* 81–117 with references, IOPC Fund, *Report of the Seventh Intersessional Working Group*, FUND/WGR.7/21, 20 June 1994, at 6–12.

[28] See also P. Wetterstein, n. 18 above.

[29] *International Oil Pollution Compensation Fund: Annual Report 1993*, 41.

[30] However, see also n. 15 above.

[31] Cf. also M. Jacobsson and N. Trotz, 'The Definition of Pollution Damage in the 1984 Protocols to the 1969 Civil Liability Convention and the 1971 Fund Convention' (1986) 17 *Journal of Maritime Law and Commerce* No. 4, 467–91, at 490.

of environmental impairment liability: the question of compensation for damage to the environment *per se* and the assessment of such damage. The discussion on including 'impairment of the environment' in the definition of compensatable damage began with the 1984 Oil Pollution Protocols. Although the rather vague definition of pollution damage of the 1969 CLC[32] had made it possible to claim compensation for damage to the environment *per se*,[33] it was deemed necessary to introduce a specific provision in order to clarify the state of law. The 1984 Protocols never entered into force, but were replaced by 1992 Protocols containing a similar definition of pollution damage. The 1992 Protocols entered into force 30 May 1996.

Reasonable costs of measures actually undertaken or to be undertaken in reinstating the environment are widely regarded as the most appropriate measure for damage to the environment *per se*. This approach is followed up, for example, in the 1992 Protocol amending the 1969 CLC, making it clear that only 'costs of reasonable measures of reinstatement actually undertaken or to be undertaken' are compensatable (Article 2, paragraph 6(a)). The 1969 CLC and the 1992 Protocol have served as models for several other conventions, for instance, the 1989 CRTD, the 1995 HNS Draft Convention, and the 1995 proposal for the Revision of the 1963 Vienna Convention.

It is, however, argued that several unreasonable consequences may derive from restricting compensation for damage to the environment *per se* to reasonable costs of reinstatement. An example frequently cited is that while 'minor damage' is compensated as it is reparable, severe irreparable damage would not be fully compensated. The case would be similar if, for example, reinstatement would not be undertaken because it is deemed unreasonable.[34] Consequently, it has been asserted that the environmental damage cannot be measured solely in terms of reasonable reinstatement costs when the aim is to give full effect to the 'polluter pays' principle[35] and to attain a more effective liability system. Possible solutions could, for example, be to lay down an obligation upon the polluter to *introduce the equivalent of the harmed or destroyed resources* into the environment and/or even to make *monetary compensation* for the diminution in value of the environment.

---

[32] Art. 1, para. 6 defining 'pollution damage' as meaning 'loss or damage caused outside the ship carrying oil by contamination resulting from the escape or discharge of oil from the ship, wherever such escape or discharge may occur, and includes the costs of preventive measures and further loss or damage caused by preventive measures'.

[33] See further nn. 42–45 below and accompanying text.

[34] See, e.g. M. C. Maffei, n. 11 above, at 390; B. Sandvik, 'Broadening the Scope of Compensation for Damage to Natural Resources—What Can We Learn from US law' (1995) *Marius*, No. 218 at 4 with references.

[35] The polluter pays principle is strongly supported within the Organization for Economic Cooperation and Development (OECD), as well as within the European Community. The principle is also emerging at a more global level. See the Rio Declaration on Environment and Development (A/Conf. 151/5/Rev. 1, 13 June 1992), Principle 16, which recognizes that 'the polluter should, in principle, bear the costs of pollution'.

The 1993 European Convention moves in this direction by giving a broad definition of 'reinstatement of the environment' in Article 2, paragraph 8, which reads as follows: 'any reasonable measure aiming to reinstate or restore damaged or destroyed components of the environment, or *to introduce, where reasonable, the equivalent of these components into the environment*' (emphasis added). Thus, in cases where the reinstatement of the contaminated environment is not feasible, or unreasonable, the polluter still has to make reparation, not in the form of monetary compensation for diminished values, but in the form of replacing destroyed habitats etc.[36] However, it is unlikely that a broad definition of 'reinstatement' alone will solve all problems, and at worst it may even create several distortions. For example, what would be reasonable close equivalent resources and to what level or extent should equivalent resources reasonably be introduced etc.? In addition, there is a potential risk that in some cases the possibility of granting reparation in the form of acquisition of equivalent resources may in fact lower the threshold for deeming actual restoration of the harmed components of the environment to be unreasonable. One further and more obvious legal loophole is, for instance, that even the 1993 European Convention, Article 2, paragraph 8 is insufficient in dealing with compensation for diminution in value of the components pending restoration.

The liability provisions in the 1988 CRAMRA are not restricted to costs of reinstatement of the contaminated environment but also include 'payment in the event that there has been no restoration to the *status quo ante*' (Article 8, paragraph 2). It is not specified in the treaty whether the term 'payment' in such cases refers to monetary compensation for diminished values, or merely to payment for the acquisition of equivalent resources as described above.[37] The broad definition of environmental damage in Article 1(m) of the 1990 UN/ECE Guidelines,[38] on the other hand, merely mentions acquisition of equivalent resources as *one* possible solution:

'Damage' means: . . . [d]etrimental changes in ecosystems, including:
(i)   The equivalent costs of reasonable measures of reinstatement actually undertaken or to be undertaken; and
(ii) Further damages exceeding those referred to under (i) *such as* (emphasis added) the equivalent costs of measures of replacement of habitats of particular conservation concern.

The International Law Commission of the UN goes one step further within the topic of state liability for 'injurious consequences arising out of acts not pro-

---

[36] See further on this provision the Draft Convention on Civil Liability for Damage Resulting from Activities Dangerous to the Environment and Explanatory Report, Strasbourg, 15 Jan. 1993, at 28.

[37] In this context reference may also be made to Resolution 687 of 3 Apr. 1991, of the UN Security Council concerning the Iraq–Kuwait conflict, which lays down a liability under international law for any direct loss or damage, including environmental damage, and the depletion of natural resources. However, the resolution is silent as to the forms of compensation for environmental damage (that is, reinstatement, acquisition of equivalent resources, or monetary compensation for diminished values, etc.).   [38] N. 10 above and accompanying text.

hibited by international law' in explicitly providing for monetary compensation if reinstatement or acquisition of equivalent resources 'were impossible, unreasonable or insufficient to achieve a situation acceptably close to the *status quo ante*'.[39] However, neither the 1988 CRAMRA nor the UN/ECE Guidelines provide any definition of compensatable value characteristics.

In this respect the Draft Protocol to the 1989 Basel Convention of 1995 has to be considered fairly innovative. According to Draft Article 2, paragraph 2(a)(iv), 'damage' means 'impairment of the environment in so far as this is not considered to be damage within the meaning of subparagraphs (i), (ii), or (iii)'. With regard to the scope of compensation for 'impairment of the environment' and compensatable value characteristics, interest is focused on draft Article 4*ter*, especially 4*ter*(2), Alternative 2:

(a) if the environment can be reinstated, compensation shall be limited to:
    (i) the costs of measures of reinstatement actually undertaken or to be undertaken; or
    (ii) the costs of returning the environment to a comparable state, where reasonable;
(b) if the environment can not be reinstated,
    Alternative 1
    Compensation shall be limited to an amount calculated as if the environment could be reinstated.
    Alternative 2
    Compensation shall be calculated only taking into account the following: *intrinsic value* of the ecological systems involved including their *æsthetic and cultural values* and in particular the *potential loss of value entailed in the destruction of species of flora or fauna* (emphasis added).[40]

But even if there has been some movement towards including monetary compensation for diminished environmental values, and even to define compensatable value characteristics, very few efforts have been made to develop parameters for damage assessment. For example, the only guideline given by ILC within the topic referred to above is that '[t]he court should . . . have some leeway to make an equitable assessment of the damage in terms of a sum of money'.[41]

In this context it may also be recalled that the IOPC Fund has dealt with claims for monetary compensation for diminution in value of the environment in a number of cases under the 1969 CLC and the 1971 Fund Convention. The IOPC Fund Assembly in 1980 adopted a resolution in which it stated that damages should not be allowed 'on the basis of an abstract quantification of damage

---

[39] See ILC, Special Rapporteur J. Barboza, *Eleventh Report on International Liability for Injurious Consequences Arising out of Acts not Prohibited by International Law*, UN Doc. A/CN.4/468, 26 Apr. 1995.
[40] See UNEP/CHW.1/WG/1/4/2 of 3 July 1995. Cf. also UNEP/CHW.1/WG/1/2/4 of 24 Oct. 1994.   [41] See the document referred to in n. 39 above, at 15.

calculated in accordance with theoretical models'.[42] Compensation can be paid by the IOPC Fund only if a claimant, who has a legal right to claim under national law, has suffered *quantifiable economic loss*. Non-economic environmental damage is not compensated.[43] Only two exceptions of limited importance from this interpretation are to be found,[44] which was later codified in the 1992 Protocols.[45]

Nevertheless, if we strive to provide monetary compensation for damage to the environment *per se*, we will sooner or later inevitably be confronted with problems involved in damage assessment. Courts are not—as has been noted[46]— likely to be at ease with an equitable award of damages without support from valuation techniques in such a highly technical and extremely difficult matter as natural recource assessment. Further, a lack of assessment methodologies, or at least common acceptable standards for damage assessment, as well as clearly defined compensatable value characteristics, may turn out to be serious threats to a uniform interpretation and implementation of international rules recognizing monetary compensation for diminished environmental values. However, considerable legal and economical (as well as philosophical) difficulties are involved in evaluating damage to the environment *per se* and in defining compensatable value characteristics. And further, under which specific circumstances should monetary compensation be awarded?[47] For example, even if the affected environment is completely restored there may be a reduction in value of that environment during the interim period. Consequently, should this interim diminution in

---

[42] IOPC Fund, Resolution No. 3 on Pollution Damage (Oct. 1980). This Resolution was adopted as a consequence of an oil spill in 1979 involving the vessel *Antonio Gramsci* and a claim for monetary compensation by the USSR based on the 'Methodica' in response to that spill. 'Methodica' is a formula, according to which the amount of damages is calculated on the basis that each ton of oil that escapes from a ship pollutes a given quantity of water. Damages are awarded in an amount that corresponds to a given sum per cubic metre of water that is considered polluted. See Jacobsson and Trotz, n. 31 above, at 480. Cf. also A. Kolodkin, V. Kiselev, and N. Koroleva, n. 25 above.

[43] IOPC Fund, *General Information on Liability and Compensation for Oil Pollution Damage* (July 1994), 14. Cf. also Art. 11 of the *Guidelines on Oil Pollution Damage*, approved by the XXXVth Conference of the Comité Maritime International, Sydney, 8 Oct. 1994.

[44] See A. Bianchi, 'Harm to the Environment in Italian Practice: The Interaction Between International Law and Domestic Law', Ch. 8 in this book, with regard to the so-called *'Patmos* case'. In one other case the USSR successfully claimed monetary compensation for damage to the environment in response to an oil spill in 1987 involving the vessel *Antonio Gramsci*. The damages were assessed in accordance with the 'Methodica' (see n. 42 above with references). The IOPC Fund did not alter its interpretation from 1980 (n. 42 above and accompanying text). However, the Fund eventually awarded damages referring to the limited amount of damages claimed, the high cost of intervening in the proceedings, and the number of complex legal issues arising from the case. See *International Oil Pollution Compensation Fund: Annual Report 1990*, at 29.

[45] The term 'quantifiable economic loss' means damage to the environment in respect of which the value of the damage can be assessed in terms of market price. The terms 'non-economic environmental damage', or 'non-quantifiable elements' of the environment mean damage in respect of which the quantum cannot be assessed in accordance with market prices. See, e.g. IOPC Fund, *Report of the Seventh Intersessional Working Group*, FUND/WGR.7/21, 20 June 1994, at 12.

[46] See A. Bianchi, n. 44 above. Cf. also, e.g. B. Sandvik, n. 34 above, 37–8, 40.

[47] Cf., e.g. the discussion in B. Sandvik, n. 34 above, 5, 16–17, 38–9 with references.

value also be compensated, or should compensation be awarded only in cases of non-feasible or unreasonable reinstatement?

Quite clearly, the experience gained under US law in particular[48] indicates that these are—and will probably remain—the most burning problems of the entire environmental impairment liability debate. With this in view the emerging international trend recognizing monetary compensation could even be accused of being too innovative and progressive. On the other hand, considering the complex nature of problems which remain unanswered one might as well question whether the recent efforts to provide for monetary compensation are sufficient and innovative *enough* to be accepted at an international level.

7. COSTS OF PREVENTIVE MEASURES

Rules on liability and compensation enter into the picture when administrative provisions and provisions on environmental protection have proved to be ineffective or insufficient in preventing damage. However, prevention and reparation are often inseparably linked, especially in the environmental law context. The costs of preventive measures as well as further loss or damage caused by such measures are consequently covered by the definition of compensatable damage in most of the treaties relevant in the context.

Preventive measures are defined, for example, in the 1969 CLC as 'any reasonable measures taken by any person after an incident has occurred to prevent or minimize pollution damage' (Article 1, paragraph 7). The definition is qualified by the words 'after an incident has occurred', which seem to exlude recovery for costs of pre-spill preventive measures.[49] This interpretation is supported by that of the IOPC Fund which has explicitly stated that the Fund does not pay compensation for costs incurred for pre-spill preventive measures.[50] Such a limitation

---

[48] See B. Anderson, 'Litigating and Settling a Natural Resource Damage Claim in the United States: The Defence Lawyer's Perspective', Ch. 11 in this book; W. D. Brighton and D. F. Askman, 'The Role of Government Trustees in Recovering Compensation for Injury to Natural Resources', Ch. 10 in this book; T. J. Schoenbaum, 'Environmental Damages: The Emerging Law in the United States', Ch. 9 in this book. See also, e.g. the following articles: F. B. Cross, 'Restoring Restoration for Natural Resource Damages' (1993) 24 *University of Toledo Law Review* 319–44; J. Dobbins, 'The Pain and Suffering of Environmental Loss: Using Contingent Valuation to Estimate Non-use Values' (1994) 43 *Duke Law Journal* 879–946; J. Heyde, 'Is Contingent Valuation Worth the Trouble?' (1995) 62 *The University of Chicago Law Review* 331–62; D. Willimas, 'Valuing Natural Environments: Compensation, Market Norms, and the Idea of Public Goods' (1995) 27 *Connecticut Law Review* 365–491; B. R. Binger, R. F. Copple, and E. Hoffman, n. 11 above.

[49] See, e.g. J. H. Bates and C. Benson, *Marine Environmental Law* (1993), at paras. 4.14–4.19 with references. However, the application of the 1969 CLC revealed that there were divergent views on the correct interpretation of the concept of 'preventive measures'. The question was whether the definition covered pre-spill measures and what has been referred to as 'pure-threat situations', that is, measures to prevent pollution taken before a spill occurred and measures that were so successfull that no oil spill occurred at all. See M. Jacobsson and N. Trotz, n. 31 above, at 485–6.

[50] See IOPC Fund, *General Information on Liability and Compensation for Oil Pollution Damage* (July 1994), 13: '[t]he IOPC Fund does not pay compensation for costs incurred for *pre-spill preventive measures*. Losses which *do not result directly* from an incident are not compensated.'

is clearly unsatisfactory. However, unlike the original convention, expenses incurred for preventive measures will be recoverable under the 1992 Protocol even when there is no actual spill of oil as a result of an incident, provided that the incident 'creates a grave and imminent threat of causing [pollution] damage' (Article 1, paragraph 6(a), and paragraph 8).[51]

A similar solution is to be found in, for example, the 1989 CRTD Convention, the 1993 European Convention, the Draft HNS Convention, and the 1995 Draft Protocol to the Basel Convention. Thus, costs for preventive measures that have been taken before actual damage has occurred seem also to be recoverable. This allows action to be taken at an early stage—it is no longer primarily a question of preventing or mitigating damage after it has occurred.[52] Such provisions are in conformity with 'the preventive principle' which requires action to be taken at an early stage and, if possible, before any damage has occurred.[53] The provisions defining the term 'incident' broadly seem to move the liability regimes slightly towards the so-called 'liability for risk'.

8. CONCLUDING REMARKS

International civil liability law initially followed the traditional pattern in tort law as far as the concept of damage was concerned: the liability provisions focused on personal injury and damage to property, including consequential economic loss. However, environmental incidents have shown that the range of potential damage may be much broader. Costs of preventive measures (including 'pre-spill' measures), costs of clean-up, and costs of reinstatement may be high. Further, economic losses or loss of profit as a result of the contamination of the environment, even when unrelated to personal or property damage, are often substantial. The experience of such incidents has required the drafters of international liability treaties to broaden the scope of compensatable damage accordingly.

The next step towards a more effective liability system and more efficient implementation of the 'polluter pays' principle could be to impose upon the polluter an obligation to make monetary compensation for diminished environmental values. Efforts in this direction have been made, *inter alia*, in recent draft instruments, although concern may be expressed whether they will be accepted. Due to the complex nature of problems associated with such an approach existing civil liability treaties restrict compensation to costs of reinstatement or acquisition

---

[51] Cf. also, e.g. E. Brans, 'The *Braer* and the Admissibility of Claims for Pollution Damage under the 1992 Protocols to the Civil Liability Convention and the Fund Convention' [1994] *Environmental Liability* 61–9, at 66.

[52] See also L. Krämer, *EEC Treaty and Environmental Protection* (1990), 60.

[53] On the preventive principle, see, e.g. P. Sands, *Principles of International Environmental Law* (1994), i, 195.

of equivalent resources. It would not be suprising if the recent efforts to provide for monetary compensation would ultimately meet the same fate. However, as long as this is the case a paradox regarding compensation for personal damage under tort law in several countries may also be confirmed in the context of enviro-nmental impairment liability: in some cases it may be cheaper for the polluter to destroy the environment rather than, merely to harm it.

4

The ILC and Environmental Damage

JULIO BARBOZA

1. INTRODUCTION

The concept of environmental damage was introduced in the International Law Commission's (ILC) draft articles proposed by the Special Rapporteur on *Liability for the Injurious Consequences Arising Out of Acts Not Prohibited by International Law*.[1] In his Fifth Report (1989), paragraph (c) of Article 2 included, within the meaning of 'transboundary harm', the physical consequences of activities referred to in Article 1 which were 'appreciably detrimental to . . . the use or enjoyment of areas or to the environment'.[2]

In his *Eighth Report*, a new paragraph in Article 2 (meaning of terms) was proposed, which reads as follows:

'Damage' means: (a) any loss of life, impairment of health or any personal injury; (b) damage to property; (c) detrimental alteration of the environment, provided that the corresponding compensation would comprise, in addition to loss of profit, the cost of reasonable reinstatement or restorative measures actually taken or to be taken; (d) the cost of preventive measures and additional harm caused by such measures.[3]

Another paragraph was introduced: ' "[r]estorative measures" means reasonable measures to reinstate or restore damaged or destroyed components of the environment, or to reintroduce, when reasonable, the equivalent of those components into the environment.' The ensuing debate on that proposal, which is summarized in paragraphs 337 to 340 of the ILC Report to the General Assembly,[4]

---

[1] The Special Rapporteur for that topic is the author of this article.

[2] Activities referred to in Art. 1 were, in that version of the draft, those activities the physical consequences of which caused, or created an appreciable risk of causing, transboundary harm. Later on, the Commission decided to consider first only the activities which *create a significant risk* of such harm, and leave those which *cause* transboundary harm for a later stage: *Yearbook of the International Law Commission* (1989), ii, Part 1, at 135. Para. 33 of the commentary reads: '[a] reference to the environment has been added after the "persons and objects" and "the use or enjoyment of areas" to which harm may be caused. Although it could be considered covered by the earlier definition, it is felt that the environment has become such a major concern that it must be included in the definition of harm in order to leave no room for doubt that the draft seeks also to protect the environment', at 137.   [3] UN General Assembly Document A/CN.4/443, 15 Apr. 1992, at 32.

[4] *Yearbook of the International Law Commission* (1992), ii, Part 2, at 50–1 and n. 118.

shows that the Commission implicitly accepted the notion of environmental harm since there is no record in those paragraphs of any criticism of its inclusion in the Article.[5]

The question of environmental damage was revisited in the *Eleventh Report* of the Special Rapporteur,[6] of which the following is a summarized version.

2. THE CONCEPT OF ENVIRONMENT

A definition of environment may be the starting-point. There is at present no universally accepted concept of environment: elements considered to be part of the environment in some conventions dealing with environmental harm are not present in others. Existing conventions include in their definitions of environment, or within the concept of environmental harm, elements which may not properly belong to the environment. As the Green Paper of the Commission of the European Communities puts it: '[r]egarding the definition of environment, some argue that only plant and animal life and other naturally occurring objects, as well as their relationships, should be included. Others would include objects of human origin, if important to a people's cultural heritage.'[7] An effort should be made to eliminate foreign elements.

On the other hand, such definitions in conventions dealing with environmental harm are not exclusively guided by a scientific criterion. For the sake of pragmatism, that practice may be maintained.[8]

I submit that the definition of environment should be restricted to the notion of 'natural' environment, in order to avoid confusion and reduce compensation for 'environmental damage' to its correct proportions. Protection of nonenvironmental elements or values, however valid, should not pass under the guise of environmental protection.

[5] Besides all the conventions which accept that notion, (see n. 8 below) the Security Council recognized the existence of environmental damage in international law, as well as the corresponding reparation, in its Resolution 687 of 8 Apr. 1991, para. 16: 'Iraq, without prejudice to the debts and obligations of Iraq arising prior to 2 August 1990, . . . is liable under international law for any direct loss, damage, including environmental damage and the depletion of natural resources, or injury to foreign Governments, nationals and corporations, as a result of [its] unlawful invasion and occupation of Kuwait'.   [6] UN General Assembly Document A/CN.4/468, 26 Apr. 1995.

[7] COM(93)47, at 10.

[8] Harm to the environment has been included in some international conventions, drafts, and judgments, such as Art. 2(7)(d) of the 1993 Lugano Convention (Council of Europe Convention on Civil Liability for Damage Resulting from Activities Dangerous to the Environment), confirmed by Art. 1(c) of the 1992 ECE (UN Economic Commission for Europe) Convention on the Transboundary Effects of Industrial Accidents; Art. 1(2) of the 1992 ECE Convention on the Protection and Use of Transboundary Watercourses and International Lakes and the 1985 EEC Directive ([1985] OJ L175/40); Art. 8(2)(a), (b), and (d) of the 1988 Convention on the Regulation of Antarctic Mineral Resources Activities (CRAMRA); and Art. 9(c) and (d) of the 1989 Convention on Civil Liability for Damage Caused during Carriage of Dangerous Goods by Road, Rail and Inland Navigation Vessels (CRTD), to which must be added the directives proposed by the ECE task force on responsibility and liability regarding transboundary water pollution and the draft protocol on liability to the Basel Convention

3. PURIFICATION OF THE CONCEPT

Some such elements as do not belong to the notion of 'environment', like human health, or to the notion of 'natural environment' (cultural elements) should, therefore, be discarded.

3.1. Human Health

'Environment' is 'human environment', i.e. the environment in which mankind lives.

Human health belongs to human beings (mankind), and human environment surrounds or environs mankind, which occupies a central position. Neither mankind nor the health of human beings forms part of the environment. That does not mean that human health is less valuable than the environment: it simply should be covered—as it normally is—under another item within the concept of damage.

3.2. Cultural and other 'Non-natural' Elements

Damage caused to 'cultural property', such as certain monuments, should also be left to be covered by the common notion of damage, be it material or moral damage.

4. ENVIRONMENT COMPONENTS AND VALUES

A further distinction should be necessary, namely between environment proper, that is, natural resources, and 'environmental values'. The latter are not part of the environment, but rather (a) human uses of that environment: in the case of a lake, for instance, fishing, skiing, wind-surfing, and commercial uses. They all may be called 'use values' or (b) emotions that the environment provokes in human beings, such as æsthetic emotions caused by the landscape, or the satisfaction for the continued existence of familiar features of the environment, etc., which may be called 'non-use values'.

on the Control of Transboundary Movements of Hazardous Wastes and their Disposal being prepared by a working group appointed by the Conference of the Parties to that Convention (Ad Hoc Working Group of Legal and Technical Experts to Consider and Develop a Draft Protocol on Liability and Compensation of Damage Resulting from Transboundary Movements of Hazardous Wastes and Their Disposal. See Art. 2(a)(iii), (iv), and (v), document UN/CHW.2/3, 10). The issue has also been the subject of studies and has been included in some documents drafted by study groups and working groups, for instance, in Art. 47 of the draft Convention on Environment and Development of the International Union for the Conservation of Nature (IUCN) and in the research project conducted by the Universities of Sienna and Parma and sponsored by the Italian Council for Scientific Research. Furthermore, the concept of harm to the environment has been incorporated into the domestic laws of a number of countries, such as Brazil, Finland, Germany, Norway, Sweden, and the US.

5. ENVIRONMENTAL DAMAGE

Environmental values do not form part of the environment proper, but are affected by damage to it and deterioration to them, as well as the frustration caused by that deterioration or by their loss, should be considered environmental damage.

Then environmental damage will be damage done to the components of the environment, as well as the loss or diminution of environmental values caused by the deterioration or destruction of such components.

Most aspects of the damage caused to persons or property as a consequence of the deterioration of the environment are already covered in the existing notion of damage to persons or property.

Let us take an example: a small lake is polluted by chemicals. (A) The pollution diminishes the fish population of the lake, and changes the quality of the water. It can no longer be used for fishing, bathing, or windsurfing (because falls or any other contact with the water are dangerous to people). The vegetation on the coast suffers; the landscape is altered. (B) Some people inadvertently drink water from it, become very ill and must be hospitalized. The owner of the hotel by the lake suffers serious economic loss from lack of clients.

Under (A) there are cases of damage to the components of the environment. Such damage is usually called 'damage to the environment *per se*'. The deterioration of environmental components (pollution of the water, diminution of the fish stocks, change of landscape) affect values of the environment (use-values, like fishing or wind-surfing, non-use values like æsthetic or other emotional appreciation of the landscape). This should be included within an enlarged concept of 'environmental damage', in order to obtain compensation for the loss or diminution. The cases under (B) are forms which may be considered as already covered by the existing notions of damage to persons or property (including loss of profit).

6. THE INJURED PARTY

Environment belongs to everybody in general and to no one in particular. It is vital for human beings, and, for that reason, communities like the state formulate environment protection policies and enforce them.

Communities also seem to be the natural injured parties in the case of so-called 'damage to the environment *per se*'. As the natural representative of the national community, the state appears to be the entity most suited to be considered, on the international plane, as the injured party in such cases and should be entitled to take legal action. Under US law (the Comprehensive Environmental Response, Compensation, and Liability Act of 1980;[9] the Federal Water Pollution Act of 1977;[10] and the Oil Pollution Act of 1990[11]):

[9] 42 USC § 9601 ff.   [10] 33 USC § 1251 ff.   [11] 33 USC § 2701 ff.

Congress empowered government agencies with management jurisdiction over natural resources to act as trustees to assess and recover damages . . . [the] public trust is defined broadly to encompass 'natural resources' . . . belonging to, managed by, held in trust by, appertaining to or otherwise controlled by, federal, state or local governments or Indian tribes.[12]

The state is, on any score, the injured party on the international plane: even if damage to the environment *per se* would be considered to affect individuals instead of communities, the state is also the representative of such individuals in international law. The damage caused to the nationals of a state by another state is considered to be 'mediate damage' to the former, which can extend its diplomatic protection.

7. THE 'INTRINSIC' VALUE OF THE ENVIRONMENT

A closer look should be taken at the notion of 'intrinsic' value of the environment, which has been gaining some ground.[13] 'Damage' in law is always damage to somebody (a physical or a juridical person, and in the last analysis individual human beings in both cases).

The utilization of the word 'intrinsic' cannot therefore change that essential category of legal thought. Therefore, the so-called 'intrinsic' damage, or damage to the environment *per se* is, after all, damage to human beings who are affected by the deterioration or destruction of the components of the environment, mainly because some of the use or non-use values of such environment are lost or diminished for them.

If the previous analysis is correct, damage to the environment *per se* is also damage done to persons through the deterioration of the environment, and there is really no essential difference between environmental damage, i.e. damage done to persons or property through damage to the environment and the 'classical' concept of damage.

Strictly speaking, there would be no need to include this type of damage as

---

[12] See R. B. Stewart, 'Liability for Natural Resources Injury: Beyond Tort', in R. L. Revesz and R. Stewart (eds.), *Analysing Superfund, Economics, Science and Law* (1995), 219–47, at 219.

[13] Art. 3 of the 1991 Protocol on Environmental Protection to the Antarctic Treaty recognizes and attempts to protect 'the intrinsic value of Antarctica, including its wilderness and æsthetic values'. A similar mention is also made in the Convention on Biological Diversity, in the first paragraph of the preamble, which reads as follows: '*Conscious* of the intrinsic value of biological diversity'. According to the *Diccionario de la Real Academica Española*, intrinsic means 'essential', and the *Concise Oxford Dictionary* defines intrinsic as 'belonging naturally, inherent, essential, esp. *intrinsic value*'. *Roget's International Thesaurus*, under the entry for 'intrinsic' includes the word 'characteristic'. This latter definition should be the real meaning of 'intrinsic' as used in these legal instruments, and in any case the words 'essential' and 'inherent' may not be made to mean that the adverse effects on the environment *per se* constitute a form of harm which is independent of human beings. It is difficult to understand who could be harmed by the loss of the wilderness or of the æsthetic values of Antarctica if there were no human beings on the planet to appreciate them.

a new category: damage to the environmental components which affect the life, health, or property of people is a form of 'material damage'—including loss of profit—and damage which affects the feelings of people could be included in an enlarged notion of 'moral' damage.

However, conventions have described damage to the environment as a separate category within the concept of damage (together with the other 'classical' items, usually in the same Article) in order to make sure that reparation follows in such cases. I submit that such practice should be continued so as to assure that reparation is forthcoming, but purifying the notions of 'environment' and of 'environmental damage' as above, in order to avoid doubts and confusion regarding reparation.

From another viewpoint, there seem to be two categories of damage caused through the deterioration of environmental components. One is the harm which affects a community of people, as in (A) of the above example. It affects a community of people because it has *general* consequences.

The cases mentioned in (B), however, affect only determinate individuals: those who drank the water, or the hotel owner who happened to have his business in that particular place. There would be no difficulty—I believe—in making reparation to those individuals under the existing categories of damage: suffice it to find out who caused the pollution and to prove the causal relationship between the pollution of the lake and the noxious effect.

The consequences of the deterioration of the environment components are, in these cases, *peculiar* to some people. I submit, therefore, that what has been called damage to the environment *per se* is only that damage to the environment which immediately affects a collective subject. In international law, that injured party is the state.

8. REPARATION

Reparation for environmental damage caused by a wrongful act should follow the so-called 'Chorzów factory' rule, so as to wipe out all the consequences of the act and establish the situation which would, in all probability, have existed if that act had not been committed.[14]

Such consequences are established by customary law, and according to the Articles proposed by the International Law Commission to codify the field of state responsibility, they are: cessation; *restitutio naturalis*; compensation by equivalent; satisfaction; and guarantees of non-repetition.

Reparation for damage caused under *sine delicto* liability would be fixed by treaty in every particular case, since general international law is not considered

---

[14] Judgment No. 8, *Case concerning the Factory at Chorzów*, Publications of the Permanent Court of International Justice, Series A, Vol. 2, No. 9, 1–44.

to have any rule imposing such liability on states. Where damage is thus produced by an act which is not prohibited by international law, the compensation is ascribed to the operation of the primary rule: it is not reparation imposed by the secondary rule as a consequence of the violation of a primary obligation, but rather conduct imposed by the primary rule itself. As a result, it does not necessarily have to meet all the criteria of *restitutio in integrum* imposed by customary law for responsibility for a wrongful act. There does not appear to be a clear international custom with respect to the *content, form, and degree* of reparation corresponding to the damage under *sine delicto* liability, but there are some indications that international practice is not necessarily following the same lines as the Chorzów factory rule. *Restitutio in integrum* is not being as rigorously respected in this field as in that of wrongful acts, as illustrated by the existence of thresholds below which the harmful effects do not meet the criteria of reparable damage, as well as the imposition, in legislative and international practice, of ceilings on compensation. Both the upper and lower limitations, which were imposed for practical reasons, create categories of non-recoverable harmful effects. However, the Chorzów factory rule obviously serves as a guideline, although not a strict benchmark, in the field of *sine delicto* liability, too, because of the reasonableness and justice it embodies.

8.1. The Consequences

In the case of environmental damage arising out of the breach of an obligation of prevention established in the draft Articles under discussion, the consequences would be the following:

— Cessation, in cases where the breach of the obligation is performed through a continuous act.

— Restitution in kind, that is, return to the *status quo ante* whenever possible is normally the best solution. It is preferable to restore the environment than to pay compensation and, on the other hand, the best measure of the value of the loss or injury is the cost of replacement of the damaged components.

— However, if restoration is impossible, or its cost unreasonably high, other forms of reparation may be considered. It seems important, however, that in such a case, the state of origin for the deterioration suffered does not save the costs that would have been its responsibility had the restoration been possible.

— If reasonable, elements equivalent to those destroyed may be accepted as reparation.

— As regards the reparation for the loss of environmental values, I suggest that monetary compensation should be awarded if restoration of former conditions—which would bring about restoration of its values—is impossible. Whenever there is a market price for the damaged components, that price would give a good measure of the damage.

Where there is no market value, the Commission should have some leeway to make an equitable assessment of the damage in terms of a sum of money, which could perhaps be used for ecological purposes in the damaged region, something for instance like a 'nature swap', namely, the improvement of the environment in other parts of the same zone (the creation of a natural park, or some other form of enhancing the existing environment, or of repairing other damage to the environment already existing before the commission of the wrongful act).

Abstract methods, such as the 'travel costing method' or 'hedonic pricing method',[15] could, in my opinion, provide only a very general guide to the sense of justice and equity of the court in assessing the monetary compensation to be fixed, but I submit that they would not necessarily be resorted to.

— On the list of consequences are the guarantees of non-repetition. The idea behind such measures—which may have far-reaching effects—may have inspired some of the sanctions applied by the Security Council to Iraq in regard to its aggression against Kuwait (for instance, a no-fly zone to avoid the commission of certain acts).

— Where it would be reasonable to wait for natural recovery of damaged elements of the environment, compensation for the diminished use of the resource until its full restoration should be in order.

The conclusions on breach of obligation, with the exception of cessation and guarantees of non-repetition seem also applicable to damage by way of *sine delicto* liability.

9. TEXTS SUGGESTED IN THE *ELEVENTH REPORT*

The following were the texts of paragraphs proposed by the Special Rapporteur to be included in Article 2 of the draft (meaning of terms):[16]

'Harm' means:
(a) Loss of life, personal injury or impairment of the health or physical integrity of persons;
(b) Damage to property or loss of profit;
(c) Harm to the environment, including:

---

[15] 'Travel costing methods' use the amounts spent by individuals in visiting and enjoying resources as a basis for the calculation. 'Hedonic pricing methods' look at the added market value commanded by private property with designated environmental amenities and seek to transpose such values into public resources with comparable amenities.

[16] Texts suggested by Special Rapporteurs should be considered tentative, as they are usually subject to considerable modifications after being examined in plenary debates, and particularly in the Drafting Committee.

(i)   the cost of reasonable measures taken or to be taken to restore or replace destroyed or damaged natural resources or, where reasonable, to introduce the equivalent of these resources into the environment;

(ii) the cost of preventive measures and of any further damage caused by such measures;

(iii) the compensation that may be granted by a judge in accordance with the principles of equity and justice if the measures indicated in subparagraph (i) were impossible, unreasonable or insufficient to achieve a situation acceptably close to the *status quo ante*. Such compensation should be used to improve the environment of the affected region.

In a different (new) paragraph of the same Article 2, the following definition of environment was proposed: '[t]he environment includes ecosystems and natural, biotic and abiotic resources, such as air, water, soil, fauna and flora and the interaction among these factors.' Yet another new paragraph, the position of which has yet to be decided, was suggested as following: '[t]he affected State or the bodies which it designates under its domestic law shall have the right of action for reparation of environmental damage.' This, however, should only apply in cases of civil liability, i.e. where a domestic court is competent.

5

Remedying Harm to International Common Spaces and Resources: Compensation and Other Approaches

ALAN E. BOYLE

1. INTRODUCTION

There is no single approach to the problem of remedying harm to international common spaces and their resources which presents itself as self-evidently correct. The purpose of this Chapter will be primarily to review the possible options, with a view to assessing their comparative utility, and to raise perhaps the most important question, which is whether we want to look at the issue in terms of a right to compensation and assessment of damages at all. A second major question is whether, if we do, an approach which emphasizes the responsibility of states or the liability of individuals should be preferred. Lastly, and remembering that it is the global commons we are addressing and not harm to the territory of other states, a third question of some importance is who will assume responsibility for seeking whatever form of redress is potentially available.

Preliminary to all these questions, however, are two further issues: what are 'common spaces and resources', and does international law protect them *per se*, or only in so far as the right of individual states to make use of them is affected.

1.1. What are Common Spaces and Resources?

In contemporary international law there are now three different, and in some ways competing, senses of the term 'common spaces' or 'global commons': (i) the classical or Grotian doctrine of *common property* exemplified by the high seas and their resources, but also applicable to outer space and, arguably, Antarctica;[1] (ii) *common heritage*, a revisionist version of the Grotian doctrine applied

---

[1] See 1982 UN Convention on the Law of the Sea (hereafter UNCLOS 1982), Art. 87; 1958 Geneva Convention on the High Seas (hereafter GCHS 1958), Art. 2; 1967 Treaty of Principles Governing the Activities of States in the Exploration and Use of Outer Space, Including the Moon and Other Celestial Bodies (hereafter Outer Space Treaty), Arts. 1, 2; 1959 Antarctic Treaty, Arts. 2–4; 1980 Convention for the Conservation of Antarctic Marine Living Resources (hereafter CCAMLR 1980).

to deep seabed resources by the 1982 United Nations Convention on the Law of the Sea (UNCLOS)[2] and to the mineral resources of the moon and other planets by the 1979 Agreement Concerning the Activities of States on the Moon and Other Celestial Bodies (the Moon Treaty); (iii) *common interest* or *common concern*, an emerging and rather different status applied in recent international environmental law to the global atmosphere and biological diversity resources,[3] and arguably also in the 1972 Convention Concerning the Protection of the World Cultural and Natural Heritage (the World Heritage Convention). Although it may be appropriate to embrace all these terms within the umbrella description 'global commons', their distinctiveness needs to be recalled if confusion and incoherence are to be avoided in any analysis of the law relating to common spaces.

1.1.1. Common Property

The salient characteristics of the classical doctrine of common property, as applied to the high seas and their resources, are that they do not fall within the sovereignty or sovereign rights of any state, and are free for use and exploitation equally by all. This doctrine continues to apply to the remaining area of high seas, and in particular to high seas fisheries, moderated by a requirement of reasonable regard for the interests of other nations in their use of high seas freedoms, and for the needs of conservation.[4]

1.1.2. Common Heritage

Like common property, common heritage has been applied to areas and resources, such as those of the deep seabed and the celestial bodies, which are not under the sovereignty or sovereign rights of any state. In the form found in UNCLOS,[5] however, it differs from common property in two important respects: (i) access to the resource is not free but is controlled and managed by an international institution—the International Seabed Authority—with quasi-sovereign powers of licensing, regulation, and taxation, and (ii) the proceeds of access are to be distributed 'for the benefit of mankind as a whole' and not simply retained by those who do the exploitation. In effect, common heritage, as used in UNCLOS, is a form of international trusteeship. This is very different from a common property status, and not surprisingly the concept in this form has found no other applications. It has also been strongly opposed by previous US Presidents.[6] Even developing states did not support attributing a common heritage status to

---

[2] UNCLOS 1982, Arts. 136–149.

[3] UN General Assembly Resolution 43/53, Protection of global climate for present and future generations of mankind, 27 Jan. 1989; 1992 Framework Convention on Climate Change, Preamble; 1992 Convention on Biological Diversity, Preamble.

[4] UNCLOS 1982, Art. 87; GCHS 1958, Art. 2; *Fisheries Jurisdiction (United Kingdom v. Iceland), Merits*, Judgment [1974] ICJ Rep. 3.

[5] Part XI and Annex III. Note that they must now be read in conjunction with modifications made by the 1994 Agreement Relating to the Implementation of UNCLOS 1982.

[6] Presidential Statement on US Oceans Policy, 10 Mar. 1983, (1983) 22 ILM 464–5.

biological resources in the 1992 Convention on Biological Diversity because of the implications this would have for their sovereignty over natural resources. It does not follow, however, that the idea of common heritage can be defined only in the form envisaged by UNCLOS. Although not used explicitly to describe the statues of Antarctic resources, the evolving legal regime for that continent may point to an alternative form of common heritage in which resources are *preserved* for the benefit of mankind as a whole, rather than exploited.[7] On the other hand Antarctic itself, although subject to claims by seven nations, is better regarded for most purposes neither as sovereign territory nor as the common heritage of mankind, but as an area of common property access to which, for scientific research, is open to all.[8] Its marine living resources are unquestionably common property under the 1980 Convention on the Conservation of Antarctic Marine Living Resources.

1.1.3. Common Concern

The phrase 'common concern of mankind' was first used in UN General Assembly Resolution 43/53 on global climate change, and subsequently in the Conventions on Climate Change and Biological Diversity. Whereas the 1972 Stockholm Declaration on the Human Environment[9] had simply distinguished between areas within and beyond national jurisdiction, the Rio Conference instruments[10] use the concept of 'common concern' to designate those issues which involve global responsibilities, such as climate change and biological diversity. Global environmental responsibility in this developed form is not confined to climate change and biological diversity, however. Although the ozone layer is nowhere referred to as the 'common concern of mankind', it is in substance treated by the 1985 Convention for the Protection of the Ozone Layer and its 1987 Montreal Protocol[11] in the same way as climate change. The 1972 World Heritage Convention also contains features comparable to these regimes of 'common concern'.

Here we confront the basic question: what are the 'global commons'? Are they confined to areas or resources which, like the high seas, outer space, the deep seabed, or Antarctica, are clearly, or arguably, beyond the limits of national jurisdiction? Or do they now include the atmosphere, tropical forests, genetic resources, world heritage areas, and so on? Unlike the oceans or outer space, these new additions include resources and impacts which are located wholly or partly within areas of national sovereignty over land or airspace. It is evident, particularly in the Convention on Biological Diversity, that few states are willing

---

[7] 1991 Protocol to the Antarctic Convention on Environmental Protection; F. Francioni (ed.), *International Environmental Law for Antarctica* (1992).   [8] Antarctic Treaty 1959, Art. 2.
[9] UN Document A/CONF. 48/14/Rev. 1.
[10] Rio Declaration on Environment and Development 1992 and Agenda 21, in *Report of the UN Conference on Environment and Development*, UN Document A/CONF.151/26/Rev. 1 (1992), i; Conventions on Climate Change and Biological Diversity 1992.
[11] Convention for the Protection of the Ozone Layer 1985 and 1987 Protocol, as amended in 1990 and 1992.

to see such national resources either turned into common property or subjected to international trusteeship.[12] But in using the criterion of common concern to designate environmental matters as 'global', the Rio Conference instruments do not seek and do not need to redefine, the legal status of biological resources, or of the global climate. What common concern does imply is that the international community has both a legitimate interest in resources of global significance and a common responsibility to assist in their protection. In legal terms, 'common concern' both gives other states standing with regard to matters which, like human rights, might otherwise fall within the protected sphere of domestic jurisdiction, and brings with it shared obligations of international solidarity.

In this limited sense we can probably treat the atmosphere, or biological diversity, as part of the global commons. But we do have to recognize that in various contexts it may not be particularly useful to do so. Compensating for harm is probably one of those contexts; in so far as we can point to 'harm' in the context of climate change or loss of biological diversity this will of necessity either be harm which affects states, or, in the case of oceans and Antarctica, it will be harm to common spaces and their ecology. It is not plausible to conceive of 'harm' to the climate or to biodiversity which has no such impacts. Thus for the purposes of this Chapter, the better view is that 'common concern' does not represent a separate category requiring further discussion, and we can confine our attention to areas or resources which are common property or common heritage.

1.2. Does International Law protect Common Spaces?

Whereas older formulations of the 'no harm' principle, in cases such as *Trail Smelter*,[13] had dealt only with transboundary harm to other states, the subsequent development of international law points to widespread international acceptance of the proposition that states are now required to protect global common areas, including Antarctica and those areas beyond the limits of national jurisdiction, such as the high seas, deep seabed, and outer space. As regards Antarctica and outer space, the 1991 Protocol to the Antarctic Treaty on Environmental Protection, the 1967 Outer Space Treaty and the 1979 Moon Treaty all provide in varying degrees for environmental protection of these areas. Among several treaties dealing with the marine environment, UNCLOS 1982 is particularly important in confirming an obligation to protect common spaces, and not merely the marine environment of other states. Thus, Article 194(1) requires states to prevent, reduce, and control pollution of the *marine environment*, while Article 194(2) emphasizes the point by requiring states to prevent pollution spreading beyond areas where they exercise sovereign rights. Similarly Article 145 requires

---

[12] See A. E. Boyle, 'The Convention on Biological Diversity', in L. Campiglio *et al.* (eds.), *The Environment after Rio: International Law and Economics* (1994), 111–27.

[13] (1939) 33 *American Journal of International Law* 182 ff. and (1941) 35 *American, Journal of International Law* 684 ff.

measures to be taken to ensure effective protection of the marine environment against pollution and harmful effects from deep seabed operations. For this purpose the 'marine environment' includes 'the ecological balance' and flora and fauna. Moreover the convention's broad definition of 'pollution' in Article 1(4), including 'harm to living resources and marine life', and its requirement in Article 194(5) that pollution control measures must protect and preserve 'rare or fragile ecosystems as well as the habitat of depleted, threatened or endangered species and other forms of marine life' also indicate that the scope of its provisions on the marine environment is not dependent on actual or intended human usage of the sea and its contents but focuses instead on the interdependence of human activity and nature. This broad formulation presents a more clearly environmental perspective than is found in some earlier definitions of marine pollution,[14] and reflects both Principle 21 of the 1972 Stockholm Declaration on the Human Environment and its subsequent reiteration in Principle 2 of the 1992 Rio Declaration on Environment and Development. Both declarations affirm the responsibility of states 'to ensure that activities within their jurisdiction and control do not cause damage to the environment of other states or of areas beyond the limits of national jurisdiction'. Moreover, the global conventions which now regulate ozone depletion, climate change, and biological diversity afford clear evidence that Stockholm Principle 21/Rio Principle 2 have been further extended in scope and now also apply to this category of global environmental concerns.[15]

There is thus no reason for doubting that international law does protect common spaces and resources. The more important question, however, is not whether, but how, it does so.

2. STATE RESPONSIBILITY FOR ENVIRONMENTAL HARM

2.1. Are States Responsible for Environmental Harm?

This is a serious question, too little reflected on in the literature.[16] The precedents, whether they relate to the territory of other states or to common spaces,

---

[14] Compare the definition of marine pollution adopted by the UN Joint Group of Experts on the Scientific Aspects of Marine Pollution (GESAMP), which refers only to 'harm to living resources, hazard to human health, hindrance to marine activities including fishing, impairment of quality for use of sea water and reduction of amenities', and see M. Tomczak, 'Defining Marine Pollution' (1984) 8 *Marine Policy* 311–22; A. Springer, 'Towards a Meaningful Concept of Pollution in International Law' (1977) 26 *International and Comparative Law Quarterly* 531–57; P. Wetterstein, 'Trends in Maritime Environmental Impairment Liability' [1994] 2 Lloyd's Maritime and Commercial Law Quarterly 230–47.

[15] See Convention for the Protection of the Ozone Layer 1985, Preamble; Framework Convention on Climate Change 1992, Preamble; Convention on Biological Diversity 1992, Art. 3.

[16] But see B. Conforti, 'Do States Really Accept Responsibility for Environmental Damage', in F. Francioni and T. Scovazzi (eds.), *International Responsibility for Environmental Harm* (1991), 179–80.

are few, particularly if what is sought is compensation for harm. Arbitral or judicial awards such as the *Trail Smelter*[17] case remain the exception. The *Nauru*[18] case before the International Court of Justice (ICJ) did result in the payment of damages by way of a friendly settlement, but the trusteeship context and the preliminary nature of the Court's judgment make the case an uncertain precedent. Decisions of international tribunals dealing with high seas resources have not been concerned with compensation for harm or ecological damage but only with allocation of the resource, and with co-operation for conservation purposes, as in the *Behring Sea*[19] and *Icelandic Fisheries*[20] cases. The *Nuclear Tests*[21] cases were too inconclusive on the issues of responsibility for harm and interference with high seas freedoms to offer useful guidance.

There are additionally a number of inter-state claims which have resulted in payments of compensation for what can be seen as environmental damage. In its claim for damage caused by the crash of a Soviet nuclear satellite, Cosmos 954,[22] Canada relied on the 1972 Convention on International Liability for Damage Caused by Space Objects (the Space Objects Liability Convention) and general principles of law favouring the absolute liability of the launching state. Out of a total clean-up cost of $14 million Canada claimed $6 million and settled for $3 million, representing only the removal of satellite debris. A Japanese claim that US atmospheric nuclear tests in the Marshall Islands had caused death and injury to fishermen and contaminated large quantities of fish also resulted in an *ex gratia* payment,[23] the implications of which as regards responsibility for harm to common property resources are not easy to determine, however.

These are exceptional examples. More noticeable are the situations where environmental harm has been caused but the matter is not dealt with through inter-state claims, either because no claim is made, or because the issue is handled in a different way. Responses to the Chernobyl nuclear disaster provide some of the most telling evidence of state practice. This accident caused widespread harm to agricultural produce and livestock in Europe and affected wildlife, in some cases severely. Clean-up costs were incurred and compensation paid by several governments to their own citizens for produce destroyed as a precaution or rendered unusable. Evidence of long-term health risks and loss of life within

---

[17] N. 13 above.

[18] *Certain Phosphate Lands in Nauru (Nauru v. Australia), Preliminary Objections*, Judgment [1992] ICJ Rep. 240. For the settlement, see (1993) 32 ILM 1471. A supplementary Joint Declaration of Principles, *ibid.*, at 1476, commits both governments to 'work together to facilitate the progressive rehabilitation of Nauru and the protection of Nauru's environment'.

[19] J. B. Moore, '*Hisber and Digest of the International Arbitration to which the United States has been a Party*' (1898), i, 755.   [20] N. 4 above.

[21] *Nuclear Tests (Australia v. France), Interim Protection*, Order of 22 June 1973 [1973] ICJ Rep. 99, and *Nuclear Tests (New Zealand v. France), Interim Protection*, Order of 22 June 1973 [1973] ICJ Rep. 135; *Nuclear Tests (Australia v. France)*, Judgment of 20 Dec. 1974 [1974] ICJ Rep. 253, and *Nuclear Tests (New Zealand v. France)*, Judgment of 20 Dec. 1974 [1974] ICJ Rep. 457.

[22] (1979) 18 ILM 899.

[23] *Settlement of Japanese Claims for Personal and Property Damage Resulting from Nuclear Tests in the Marshall Islands* (1955) 1 UST (United States Treaties) 1, TIAS 3160.

the former USSR has also begun to emerge. Despite these provable losses, no claims were made against the Soviet Union by any affected state, although the possibility was considered by some governments. The main reasons for this silence appear to be uncertainty over the basis for such a claim, reluctance to establish a precedent with possible future implications for states which themselves operate nuclear power plants, and the absence of any appropriate treaty binding on the Soviet Union. It is also unclear whether liability would extend to damage to the environment, or to the costs of precautionary measures taken by governments. The Soviet Union made no voluntary offer of compensation and questioned the need for the precautionary measures taken by its neighbours. The failure to demand, or to offer, compensation in this case shows the difficulty of reconciling doctrinal support for state responsibility for environmental damage with the realities of state practice.[24]

The same is true in other contexts. State practice in bilateral air pollution disputes involving the United States, Canada, Norway, Sweden, the United Kingdom, Germany, and France does not as such cast doubt on the principle that states are responsible for harm caused in breach of obligation by transboundary air pollution. But it does show that the solution to regional problems of air pollution and acid rain in North America and Europe has not been found in compensating for past harm. Although those states which are net importers of pollution, such as the Nordic countries or Canada, have from time to time invoked Principle 21 of the Stockholm Declaration, or *Trail Smelter*, the preferred approach of all parties has been to negotiate agreed future emission standards with polluting states, and to seek international regulation on a basis which takes account of the interests of both sides, while leaving aside the question of compensation for long-term damage previously inflicted.[25] Both the 1979 Geneva Convention on Long-Range Transboundary Air Pollution and the 1991 United States–Canadian Air Quality Agreement indicate that in practice equitable considerations have played an important part in resolving questions concerning the legality of transboundary air pollution.[26] Much the same can be said of global climate change; the Convention on Climate Change also carefully avoids confronting the issue of damage in terms of compensation, in favour of a regulatory regime based on principles of precautionary action, common but differentiated responsibility, and equitable distribution of burdens and benefits.[27]

---

[24] See generally A. E. Boyle, 'Nuclear Energy and International Law: An Environmental Perspective' (1989) 60 *British Year Book of International Law* 257–313; and G. Handl, 'Après Tchernobyl: Quelques Réflexions sur le Programme Legislatif Multilateral' (1988) 92 *Revue Générale de Droit International Public* 5–62, at 47–55.

[25] See, generally, G. Handl, 'National Uses of Transboundary Air Resources: The International Entitlement Issue Reconsidered' (1986) 26 *Natural Resources Journal* 405–67.

[26] On both agreements, see P. W. Birnie and A. E. Boyle, *International Law and the Environment* (1992), 397 ff.

[27] D. Bodansky, 'The United Nations Framework Convention on Climate Change: A Commentary' (1993) 18 *Yale Journal of International Law* 451–558 and 'Managing Climate Change' (1992) 3 *Yearbook of International Environmental Law* 60–74.

Although it remains correct to observe that 'it will be customary international legal principles and rules which will principally shape the parties' respective starting positions and guide states in their negotiations',[28] these examples show that effective solutions are often best provided by co-operative regimes of international regulation, and not by inter-state claims for compensation. This does not mean that compensation issues have been entirely disregarded, only that states have preferred to facilitate compensation for transboundary injury by encouraging resort to national legal remedies for private parties, or by negotiating more complex civil liability and compensation schemes. The former approach is observable in Western European practice regarding pollution of the Rhine,[29] in the 1993 North American Agreement on Environmental Co-operation,[30] and in the policy of the Organization for Economic Co-operation and Development (OECD).[31] The latter approach is evident in the 1992 Protocol amending the 1969 Convention on Civil Liability for Oil Pollution Damage,[32] in the nuclear liability conventions,[33] in the 1993 Council of Europe Convention on Civil Liability for Damage Resulting from Activities Dangerous to the Environment and in negotiations concerning liability for transboundary transport of hazardous wastes and the carriage of hazardous and noxious substances at sea.[34] All of these schemes de-emphasize the responsibility of states in international law by focusing liability either exclusively or mainly onto private actors.[35] In most cases states bear only a subsidiary liability, either to contribute to a compensation fund, as in the case of the 1960 Paris Convention on Third Party Liability in the Field of Nuclear Energy with its 1963 Supplementary Convention, or to guarantee the liability of private parties, as in the 1963 Vienna Convention on Civil Liability for Nuclear Damage and in proposals for a Liability Annex to the Antarctic Environmental Protocol.[36]

The only existing precedents where liability for environmental damage has

---

[28] Handl, n. 25 above, at 467. Cf remarks by L. Gündling, in *Proceedings of the American Society of International Law* (1989), 72–5.

[29] J. D'Oliveira, 'The Sandoz Blaze: The Damage and the Public and Private Liabilities', in Francioni and Scovazzi, n. 16 above, 429–45. See also Case 21/76 *Handelskwekerij G. J. Bier B. V.* v. *Mines de Potasse d'Alsace S. A.* [1976] ECR 1735.   [30] Arts. 6–7.

[31] See the text at n. 57 below.

[32] Text in P. W. Birnie and A. E. Boyle, *Basic Documents on International Law and the Environment* (1995).

[33] Convention on Third Party Liability in the Field of Nuclear Energy 1960, with 1963 Supplementary Agreement; Convention on Civil Liability for Nuclear Damage 1963; Convention Relating to Civil Liability in the Field of Maritime Carriage of Nuclear Material 1971.

[34] For work on the elaboration of a liability protocol on transboundary transport of wastes see UNEP/CHW/WG.1/5/5; UNEP/CHW/1/5, and on the draft Convention on Liability for the carriage by sea of hazardous and noxious substances, see Wetterstein, n. 14 above.

[35] See also UNCLOS 1982, Art. 139 and Annex III, Art. 22 in regard to liability for damage caused by deep seabed activities.

[36] See S. Blay and J. Green, 'The Development of a Liability Annex to the Madrid Protocol' (1995) 25 *Environmental Policy and Law* 24–37, and Antarctic Treaty Consultative Parties, Liability Annex to the Protocol on Environmental Protection (1994) doc. XVIII/ATCM/WP2. See generally A. Rosas, 'State Responsibility and Liability under Civil Liability Regimes', in O. Bring and S. Mahmoudi (eds.), *Current International Law Issues: Nordic Perspectives* (1994), 161–82.

been placed squarely and unequivocally on states alone are the 1972 Space Objects Liability Convention (and only as regards damage on Earth) and Security Council Resolution 687, dealing with Iraq's responsibility for environmental damage following its invasion and occupation of Kuwait. In both cases there are of course no private parties who could be made liable for the damage.

This analysis does not show unequivocally that states are not responsible in international law for environmental harm, whether to other states or to common spaces. What it does show is that there is sufficient uncertainty regarding the subject, and its utility in preference to alternative approaches, to pose serious doubts about the concept. Nor does this conclusion necessarily reflect a cynical conspiracy on the part of states to evade their liabilities. Rather it raises questions about the right legal strategy to adopt in dealing with environmental problems. The most important objection to a strategy which relies on state responsibility, in the form of an obligation for states to compensate for harm, remains the argument that it is an inadequate model for the enforcement of international standards of environmental protection. Like tort law it can complement, but does not displace, the primary need for the setting and enforcement of adequate international standards of environmental protection. It is this failing which helps explain and rationalize the emphasis states have placed on the development of treaty regimes of environmental protection, including those which apply to common spaces,[37] and their supervision by international institutions. It is also a partial reason for the failure to develop or reform the law of state responsibility for environmental harm.[38] The fact that such treaty regimes are negotiated multilaterally, while compensation claims can only be adjudicated bilaterally, is another major factor in this preference.

Moreover, as we have seen, states have in many cases found equal access and other civil liability and compensation schemes a better means of allowing the recovery of environmental costs. For most forms of transboundary or marine pollution damage such schemes now represent the primary resourse available to individual claimants. Such remedies also emphasize the liability of individual polluters for damage to the environment. In this respect state responsibility operates too indirectly and may appear to exempt those corporations or officials whose actions, policies, or decisions have led to harmful consequences.

Quite apart from these objections of principle, there remain additionally the unresolved issues of the standard of liability in international law—whether absolute, or strict, or based on a failure of due diligence—and of the role of knowledge, foreseeability, and estoppel.[39] It is too often forgotten that much environmental damage is cumulative, takes place over long periods of time, and in circumstances

---

[37] International Convention on the Prevention of Marine Pollution by Dumping of Wastes 1972 (hereafter London Dumping Convention), as amended 1993; Convention for the Prevention of Pollution from Ships 1973/8 (hereafter MARPOL); UNCLOS 1982.

[38] See Rio Declaration on Environment and Development 1992, Principle 13.

[39] On these issues see R. Pisillo-Mazzeschi, 'Forms of International Responsibility for Environmental Harm', in Francioni and Scovazzi, n. 16 above, 15–35; Birnie and Boyle, n. 26 above, at 139 ff.

where few of those involved could realistically have foreseen the consequences. Contemporary adoption of the precautionary principle[40] cannot mask the obvious legal difficulties likely to confront many potential claims for environmental damage in international law. While a few cases in the ICJ might well clarify some of these issues, it is scarcely surprising that most states have thought it wiser to invest their limited environmental energy in addressing future conduct rather than establishing historic liabilities.

If this is so in the case of damage to the environment of other states, it is even more the case with damage to common spaces. What this suggests is that attempts to fashion a regime of compensation for damage to common spaces are better formulated in terms of civil law liabilities of individual actors, rather than of states. This approach can also make use of compensation funds. In those relatively few cases, such as nuclear power, where the potential loss far exceeds the resources of private parties or compensation funds, or where, as in Antarctica, jurisdictional considerations and the preponderance of state activity may make reliance on civil liability difficult, *ad hoc* development of mixed regimes of state and civil liability may remain desirable.[41] But these are exceptional cases, not the norm. They provide no justification for a special regime for harm to common spaces.

2.2. Standing to Seek International Remedies

Quite apart from the arguments just considered there remains the additional question of standing to seek whatever remedies, including compensation, international law provides for harm to common spaces. Standing to bring inter-state claims in international law is in principle confined to 'injured states'.[42] This is a less difficult problem than it may at first sight appear. What 'injured state' means can be observed in the second phase of the *South West Africa* case.[43] Liberia and Ethiopia, although original members of the League of Nations with certain rights under the mandates agreement, were held to have no legal right or interest in South Africa's compliance with its treaty obligations towards the inhabitants of the territory. That was a matter for the League alone and individual members acquired no independent standing to bring violations of the mandate before the ICJ. Although the term 'injured state' is defined in Part Two of the International Law Commission's (ILC) draft Articles on State Responsibility[44] in broadly comparable terms and includes a state whose legal rights or

---

[40] Rio Declaration 1992, Principle 15, on which see Birnie and Boyle, n. 26 above, at 95 ff.
[41] See G. Handl, 'Towards a Global System of Compensation for Transboundary Nuclear Damage', in *Nuclear Accidents, Liabilities and Guarantees: Proceedings of the Helsinki Symposium 31 August–3 September 1992* (1993), 497–520.
[42] Draft Arts. on State Responsibility, Part 2, Art. 5, *Report of the International Law Commission on the Work of Its Forty-fifth Session*, UN General Assembly, Official Records, Forty-eighth Session, Supplement No. 10 (A/48/10) (1993), 128 ff.
[43] *South West Africa, Second Phase*, Judgment [1966] ICJ Rep. 6, especially at 20–3; I. Brownlie, *Principles of Public International Law* (1990), 466–73.   [44] N. 42 above.

interests, whether arising under customary law or under multilateral treaties, are directly or indirectly infringed by the defendant state, this will cause little difficulty in most inter-state environmental disputes, even if they relate to common spaces. Thus a denial of high seas fishing rights, as in the *Icelandic Fisheries* cases, or high seas pollution which affects coastal state interests, or interferes with fishing rights, would clearly fall within the ILC's definition.[45]

The more problematic case of interest here is the situation where harm occurs in common spaces without affecting the rights or interests of any other state.[46] A real example is the oil spill from the tanker *Bahia Paraiso* in Antarctic coastal waters,[47] where of course there are no recognized coastal states.

This problem is susceptible of several answers. First, it may be said that individual states do have standing to the extent that they may be involved in expenditure on clean-up operations or restoration costs. Why should it make any difference if these costs relate to common spaces rather than to a state's own territory, as in the Cosmos 954 claim? The fact that the 1971 International Convention on the Establishment of an International Fund for Compensation for Oil Pollution Damage would not cover such costs if they relate to damage occurring on the high seas[48] does not demonstrate that international law could not do so.

Secondly, it may be said that individual states have, or should have, standing to enforce international law for the good of the community at large—an *actio popularis*. This is difficult to reconcile both with the ILC's formulation of 'injured state' and with the case law of the ICJ. It also runs counter to arguments frequently found in other legal systems against allowing litigation to be complicated by multiple plaintiffs, which may render settlement of a dispute more difficult, or lead to measures disproportionate to the violation or injury. Another obvious problem is that even if some form of *actio popularis* is contemplated, why should the applicant state be entitled to compensation when it has incurred no expense and suffered no loss?[49]

A third, more refined, version of the previous argument limits standing for individual states to situations where the rights themselves are clearly designated as community interests. This can be put in several ways. The ILC draft Articles on State Responsibility designate massive pollution of the sea or the air as 'international crimes' in respect of which all states are injured states.[50] Another

---

[45] See further K. Leigh, 'Liability for Damage to the Global Commons' (1993) 14 *Australian Year Book of International Law* 129–56, at 143–5. [46] See *Nuclear Tests* cases, n. 21 above.
[47] See J. Charney, 'Third State Remedies for Environmental Damage to the World's Common Spaces', in Francioni and Scovazzi, n. 16 above, 149–77. [48] See the text at n. 65 below.
[49] See Charney, n. 47 above.
[50] Draft Arts. on State Responsibility, Part 1, Art. 19 [1990] II Yearbook of the International Law Commission, Part 2, at 32; Draft Arts. on State Responsibility, Part 2, Art. 5, *Report of the ILC on the Work of Its Forty-fifth Session*, n. 42 above. For the ILC's reconsideration of Art. 19, see *Fifth Report on State Responsibility by Special Rapporteur Gaetano Arangio-Ruiz*, UN Document A/CN. 4/453/Add.2 and 3 (1993), and the *Report of the ILC on the Work of Its Forty-sixth Session*, UN General Assembly, Official Records, Forty-ninth Session, Supplement No. 10 (A/49/10) (1994), 329 ff.

possibility is to rely on the concept of *erga omnes* obligations which may be enforced by third states on behalf of the international community. In the *Nuclear Tests* cases the ICJ was unsympathetic to the notion of an *actio popularis* allowing high seas freedoms to be enforced as *erga omnes* obligations.[51] Unlike the protection of human rights, the ILC has not explicitly recognized protection of the environment as an *erga omnes* obligation in its draft Article 5, but it does include rights under multilateral treaties 'expressly stipulated in that treaty for the protection of the collective interests of the states parties thereto'.[52] Multilateral treaties concerned with protection of the global environment or of global common spaces are obvious candidates for this category in cases of violation. Moreover the designation of climate change and biological diversity as the 'common concern of mankind' may have the same impact. But, even if all these cases do already represent international law, which is doubtful, once again it does not follow that the remedy obtainable will include compensation.

A fourth possibility is to accept that states are inappropriate claimants on behalf of community interests, and that standing to seek an *actio popularis* should lie elsewhere, probably in international organizations such as the UN Economic and Social Council (ECOSOC), UN Environmental Programme (UNEP), International Maritime Organization (IMO) and so on. A contemporary example of precisely this possibility is the application to the ICJ for an advisory opinion on the legality of the use of nuclear weapons,[53] requested by the UN General Assembly and the World Health Organisation (WHO). While there are good reasons for doubting whether the Court will agree to decide such a hypothetical issue, a case concerning actual harm to global commons would not encounter this objection.[54] Another obstacle is that such a request may not be within the competence of UN specialized agencies; however, the UN General Assembly and Security Council are not limited in their competence to seek the advice of the Court.[55] Of course, once again, the outcome would not be an award of damages or compensation, but merely a declaratory judgment.[56]

Thus, while it is possible to envisage actions to protect the global commons, it is less obvious that this is a suitable way to secure compensation for harm which does not as such affect any particular state. In such a case the vindication of community legal rights can almost always be satisfied by a declaratory judgment.

---

[51] N. 21 above.

[52] Part 2, Art. 5, *Report of the ILC on the Work of Its Forty-fifth Session*, n. 42 above, and see Birnie and Boyle, n. 26 above, at 154 ff. On human rights, see also *Barcelona Traction, Light and Power Company, Limited*, Judgment [1970] ICJ Rep. 3.

[53] See WHO Resolution, 8 May 1993, 46th World Health Assembly, Agenda Item 33.

[54] On this point see in particular *Western Sahara*, Advisory Opinion [1975] ICJ Rep. 12, at para. 23.   [55] UN Charter, Art. 96(1).

[56] See, e.g. *Legal Consequences for States of the Continued Presence of South Africa in Namibia (South West Africa) notwithstanding Security Council Resolution 276 (1970)*, Advisory Opinion, [1971] ICJ Rep. 16, but note that in this case the declared illegality resulted in a duty of non-recognition on the part of other states.

2.3. Conclusion

Viewed in terms of orthodox interstate claims, state responsibility can scarcely be presented as a satisfactory or suitable basis for securing compensation or damages for harm to the global commons, unless individual states are in some way themselves harmed or affected. If they are, then it is less obvious that we are really talking about harm to common spaces. It seems reasonably clear that if harm to common spaces is perceived as a *sui generis* problem then other, more appropriate, solutions must be found. These, it has already been suggested, lie more in the fields of private law than in public international law.

3. RESORT TO PRIVATE LAW APPROACHES

One of the major roles of public international law when dealing with environmental problems is to facilitate resort, where appropriate, to private law solutions. These are most likely to provide the best means of remedying harm to common spaces.

3.1. Compensation Schemes and the Polluter Pays Principle

The polluter pays principle is essentially an economic policy for allocating the costs of pollution or environmental damage to the private party responsible for the harm in question. It has significant implications for the development of international and national law as regards liability for damage and more generally in regard to environmental costs borne by public authorities. As defined by OECD, its principal exponent, the principle entails that the polluter should bear the expense of carrying out measures decided by public authorities to ensure that the environment is in an 'acceptable state', or 'in other words the costs of these measures should be reflected in the cost of goods and services which cause pollution in production or in consumption'.[57] Apart from its adoption by OECD and the European Economic Community,[58] the polluter pays principle secured international support for the first time at the UN Conference on Environment and Development in 1992. Principle 16 of the Rio Declaration provides, in somewhat qualified terms, that:

National authorities should endeavour to promote the internalization of environmental costs and the use of economic instruments, taking into account the approach that the polluter should, in principle, bear the cost of pollution, with due regard to the public interest and without distorting international trade and investment.

---

[57] OECD, Recommendations C(72)128 and C(74)223, reproduced in *OECD and the Environment* (1986); C(89)88, reproduced in (1989) 28 ILM 1320; and C(90)177.
[58] Art. 130R, Treaty on European Union 1992 (TEU).

The principle is also reflected in a number of treaties dealing with marine pollution, including the 1990 Convention on Oil Pollution Preparedness, Response and Co-operation.[59]

OECD practice has generally taken a relatively conservative view of the categories of costs to be internalized, and it has also permitted a relatively liberal range of exceptions. Thus its recommendations are mainly concerned with the cost of preventive measures, the cost of control measures, such as monitoring, and the costs of clean-up and restoration following accidents.[60] OECD has allowed governmental assistance to be treated as an exception to the principle in cases where transitional arrangements leading to a more stringent control regime are needed, or where steps to protect the environment would 'jeopardize the sound and economic policy objectives of a country or region'.[61] The broad and somewhat subjective character of these exceptions is reflected in Principle 16 of the Rio Declaration, which, as we have seen, allows national authorities to apply the polluter pays principle 'with due regard to the public interest and without distorting international trade and investment'. Principle 16 differs significantly from earlier OECD definitions, however, in referring to the 'internalization of environmental costs' and the polluter 'bearing the cost of pollution'. This wording shifts the focus to the environmental *impact* of pollution, in terms of the damage which it causes and not simply the cost of preventing it. OECD has itself begun to move in this direction, in its Recommendation C(90)177 on the Use of Economic Instruments in Environmental Policy, which for the first time includes the cost of compensating for damage to the environment.[62] These developments in the application of the principle favour a much fuller internalization of environmental costs than hitherto, although, as we have seen, qualified by reference to the public interest and by a deliberately 'soft' wording which leaves much to the discretion of each state.[63]

The inclusion of compensation for the costs of environmental damage is a sensible and inevitable development if the economic logic of the polluter pays principle is to be followed through. But it remains a principle which cannot safely be used by lawyers without further clarification of its precise content in the context in which it is employed. As one distinguished commentator observes: '[t]he main difficulty with the full internalization policy is that it cannot be implemented in practice unless some agreement is reached on the respective rights of the polluters and the victims.'[64]

What are the implications of this principle for damage to the global commons

---

[59] See also Convention for the Protection of the Marine Environment of the North-East Atlantic 1992, Art. 2(2)(b); Convention for the Protection of the Marine Environment of the Baltic Sea Area 1992, Art. (3)4.   [60] See, e.g. OECD Council Recommendation C(89)88.
[61] See *The Polluter Pays Principle* (1992), 5, 26–7, 37.   [62] *Ibid.*, at 6–7.
[63] For a survey of practice in OECD countries see J. B. Opschoor, *Economic Instruments for Environmental Protection* (1989).
[64] H. Smets, 'The Polluter Pays Principle in the Early 1990s', in Campiglio *et al.* (eds.), n. 12 above, 131–47, at 141, and see also *The Polluter Pays Principle*, n. 61 above, at 39–44.

or their resources? As implemented in the present series of treaties which deal with the costs of pollution at sea the main conclusion to be drawn is that the polluter pays principle has not been applied in full, and that it does not yet cover harm not related to the territory, territorial waters, or exclusive economic zones of states or resources located therein. Harm confined exclusively to the high seas is not within the scope of any of these conventions. The point is exemplified by Article 3 of the 1992 Convention on the Establishment of an International Fund for Compensation for Oil Pollution Damage, which is expressly confined to pollution damage in the territory, territorial sea, exclusive economic zone, or within 200 miles of the state concerned, and to 'preventive measures, wherever taken, to prevent or minimize *such* damage'.[65] The 1989 International Convention on Salvage is similarly limited; although it provides a salvor 'special compensation' for salvage which prevents or minimizes 'damage to the environment', this phrase is defined to mean 'substantial physical damage to human health or to marine life or resources in coastal or inland waters or areas adjacent thereto'.[66] This clearly does not include salvage on the high seas where no state is likely to benefit from the actions taken.

The question posed by this conclusion is whether the exclusion of damage to common spaces is justifiable. The same issue arises in the context of negotiations for an Antarctic liability regime and the possible establishment of a fund to cover damage there. Should it apply only to damage to national interests, which would largely defeat the point of having a liability scheme in Antarctica, or should it apply more broadly and simply to the Antarctic environment and its resources?[67]

There is no inherent reason why liability and compensation schemes of this kind could not apply to damage to common spaces and resources. The point, however, is the one posed at the outset: does it make sense to deal with the problem in this way? There is a strong case for doing so in regard to clean-up and restoration costs. Modern science, and the philosophy of the precautionary approach with its emphasis on uncertainty,[68] suggest that it is unwise to assume that pollution or damage to common areas is ever wholly free of potential impacts on states and their use of those areas.[69] From this perspective a distinction between harm to states and harm to common spaces may well be illusory. Clean-up and restoration should therefore always be encouraged.[70]

---

[65] Art. 3 (emphasis added). See also Convention on Civil Liability for Oil Pollution Damage 1992, Art. 2, and Leigh, n. 45 above, at 129.   [66] See Arts. 1(d), 8, and 14.

[67] N. 36 above. See also Leigh, n. 45 above, at 152–5, and compared Convention for the Regulation of Antarctic Mineral Resource Activities 1988, Art. 1(15) (hereafter CRAMRA).

[68] See Rio Declaration 1992, Principle 15; D. Freestone, 'The Precautionary Principle', in R. Churchill and D. Freestone (eds.), *International Law and Global Climate Change* (1991), 21–39; J. Cameron and T. O'Riordan (eds.), *Interpreting the Precautionary Principle* (1994).

[69] For an assessment of the impact of the marine pollution see GESAMP, *The State of the Marine Environment* (1990).

[70] Such costs were included in the 1988 CRAMRA, Art. 8. See further Blay and Green, n. 36 above, at 27–8.

But suppose the harm cannot be restored, or cleaned up, and no tangible harm to other states can be demonstrated? The role, if any, of damages in this context cannot be compensatory, since there is no measurable loss to anyone. Rather, it must necessarily be punitive. The question which then arises is whether it is not simpler and more honest to acknowledge that this is a case for criminal law, not for civil liability.

3.2. Criminal Jurisdiction and Harm to Common Spaces

National law is the medium through which states will usually implement their international obligations and regulate the conduct of their nationals and companies inside their borders and beyond. In this sense it enables the notion of individual responsibility to become part of the system of enforcement. How a state effects the performance of its obligations will depend on what is required by the particular treaty or rule of international law, but in many cases the choice of means is left to the state's discretion. Whether it relies on criminal law will then depend on the legal system in question.

However, there are some situations for which states have agreed that conduct is sufficiently objectionable that criminal penalties must be employed. This is typically the case in treaties covering trade in wastes, conservation of living resources, and marine pollution.[71] Thus it will generally be criminal law which regulates illegal pollution under the MARPOL or London Dumping Conventions. In these cases it will be irrelevant where the offence took place; while questions of evidence may be problematic, the mere fact that offence took place on the high seas does not preclude the flag state from prosecuting.[72]

Flag states may, of course, have limited interest, or limited means, to pursue this remedy vigorously. International law in certain situations also affords other states an extraterritorial protective jurisdiction to act against non-nationals, as in the case of coastal state regulation of the exclusive economic zone,[73] or to treat certain offences as crimes over which all states have jurisdiction. The application of the universality principle to environmental offences has been a feature of the ILC's continuing work on a draft Code of Crimes Against the Peace and Security of Mankind.[74]

---

[71] Basel Convention on the Control of Transboundary Movements of Hazardous Wastes and Their Disposal 1989, Art. 4(3), (4); Bamako Convention on the Ban of the Import into Africa and the Control of Transboundary Movement and Management of Hazardous Wastes within Africa 1991, Art. 9(2); MARPOL Convention 1973/8, Art. 4(2), (4); London Dumping Convention 1972, Art. 6(2); Protocol for the Prevention of Pollution of the South Pacific Region by Dumping 1986, Art. 12(2); UNCLOS 1982, Arts. 217(8), 230; Convention on International Trade in Endangered Species of Wild Flora and Fauna 1973, Art. 8(1).   [72] UNCLOS 1982, Art. 217.

[73] UNCLOS 1982, Arts. 211, 220.

[74] See Draft Code of Crimes Against the Peace and Security of Mankind, *Report of the International Law Commission on the Work of Its Forty-third Session*, UN General Assembly, Official Records, Forty-sixth Session, Supplement No. 10 (A/46/10) (1991). Art. 26 applies to: '[a]n individual who wilfully causes or orders the causing of widespread, long-term and severe damage to the natural environment': *Ibid.*, at 250. For commentary see T. McCormack and G. Simpson, 'The

The inclusion of environmental offences in this category may prove a significant development, if adopted in practice, precisely because of its potential utility in protecting the global commons. Here there is a case for treating very serious and deliberate pollution as equivalent to piracy, since the public interest of all states is affected and effective enforcement may otherwise be lacking. In this respect the argument for universal jurisdiction over individuals mirrors the argument for an *actio popularis* covering 'international crimes' under Article 19 of the ILC's Articles on State Responsibility, with the added advantage, however, that it is very much easier to implement.

Significantly, it is precisely the approach of universalizing jurisdiction which Article 218 of UNCLOS 1982 applies to high seas pollution in violation of international standards. The crucial feature of this Article is that it gives the state in whose port the vessel is present the right to prosecute for pollution offences committed on the high seas or in the maritime zones of other states, subject only to a right of pre-emption by the flag state. This, it is suggested, represents a very much more realistic approach to the problem of protecting common spaces than attempting to extend the polluter pays principle or to employ compensation schemes, at least as regards the high seas. The peculiarities of Antarctica's legal and jurisdictional status may dictate a different solution there, but for the oceans, the world's major common space, the better policy appears clear, and, as regards pollution is already encapsulated in international law. Moreover, in the context of fisheries conservation, there is similar pressure for extended powers of high seas enforcement using criminal law and some evolving precedents for this in fisheries agreements.[75]

4. CONCLUSIONS

(1) Securing compensation for harm to common spaces through the law of state responsibility, in situations where there is no tangible harm to other states and no clean-up or restoration costs, is unrealistic, unprecedented, and largely unworkable.

International Commission's Draft Code of Crimes against the Peace and Security of Mankind: An Appraisal of the Substantive Provisions' (1994) 5 *Criminal Law Forum* 1–55. However, environmental offences have not been included in the draft statute of the proposed International Criminal Court, on which see *Report of the International Law Commission on the Work of Its Forty-sixth Session*, UN General Assembly, Official Records, Forty-ninth Session, Supplement No. 10 (A/49/10) (1994).

[75] See, *inter alia*, Canada, Coastal Fisheries Protection Act, as amended 1994 (1994) 33 ILM 1383; US, High Seas Driftnet Fisheries Enforcement Act, 1992 (1993) 32 ILM 530; Agreement for the Implementation of the Provisions of UNCLOS 1982 Relating to the Conservation and Management of Straddling Fish Stocks and Highly Migratory Fish Stocks, Arts. 20–3; Convention on the Conservation and Management of Pollock Resources in the Central Bering Sea 1994, Art. XI; Agreement to Promote Compliance with International Conservation and Management Measures by Fishing Vessels on the High Seas 1993; Niuë Treaty on Co-operation in Fisheries Surveillance and Law Enforcement in the South Pacific Region 1992.

(2) Extending the polluter pays principle to provide compensation for harm to common spaces in national law or through compensation funds is possible but of doubtful utility and limited practical effect, except as regards clean-up and restoration costs, where incurred.

(3) The most realistic way of protecting common spaces and resources against illegal pollution or damage by private parties is through criminal law, relying where appropriate on universal jurisdiction to ensure maximum effectiveness. This is consistent with existing law of the sea, and is the easiest solution to implement.

PART III

National Approaches and Practices:
Selected Examples

6

Harm to the Environment in Italian Practice: The Interaction of International Law and Domestic Law

ANDREA BIANCHI

1. INTRODUCTION

The award of damages for environmental harm in the *Patmos* litigation,[1] as well as the claim set forth by the Italian Government in relation to the *Haven* incident,[2] causes one to wonder whether Italian practice is consistent with contemporary international law and practice. The stance taken by the Italian Government as regards purely ecological damage caused by oil spills, which was upheld by the Court of Appeal of the Messina district in the *Patmos* case,[3] *prima facie* marks a notable departure from the practice of the states that are parties to both the 1969 Convention on Civil Liability for Oil Pollution Damage (CLC) and the 1971 Convention on the Establishment of an International Fund for Compensation for Oil Pollution Damage (Fund Convention).[4] The evaluation of Italian practice entails an investigation of complex issues of treaty interpretation and an in-depth analysis of the relationship between international and domestic law in the Italian legal system.

The vast echo that the *Patmos* case has had in the international community partly accounts for the special emphasis put on it in this Chapter. However, the

---

[1] The Court of Appeal of Messina issued the final damage award on 24 Dec. 1993: see *Ministero della marina mercantile e Ministero dell'interno* v. *Patmos Shipping Co., The United Kingdom Steamship Co., International Oil Pollution Fund* (henceforward *Patmos III*), reproduced in (1994): 9 Rivista giuridica dell'ambiente 683–94.

[2] See *International Oil Pollution Compensation Fund: Annual Report 1994*, 46 ff.

[3] The principle that ecological damage must be compensated had been asserted by the Court of Appeal of Messina in its judgment of 22 May 1989: *Ministero della marina mercantile e Ministero dell'interno* v. *Patmos Shipping Co., The United Kingdom Mutual Steamship Assurance Ass., International Oil Pollution Fund* (henceforward *Patmos II*), reproduced in 1049–58.

[4] Both Conventions entered into force for Italy on 28 May 1979. For a comment, see M. Jacobsson, 'The International Convention on Liability and Compensation for Oil Pollution Damage and the Activities of the International Oil Pollution Compensation Fund', in C. M. De La Rue (ed.), *Liability for Damage to the Marine Environment* (1993), 39–55.

distinctive features of Italian practice concerning claims for environmental damage could hardly be grasped, were one to look only at this case. In fact, the fairly recent development of a liability regime for environmental damage is the necessary background to frame the *Patmos* case correctly and to evaluate how Italian legislation and case law deal with the much debated questions of whether purely ecological damage should be compensated and, if so, according to what criteria.[5]

In order to provide the above queries with an adequate answer, a cursory review of Italian legislation and case law will be made against the background of some recently adopted international instruments regulating liability for environmental damage. Presumably, the latter will have a major impact on the Italian legal system once they enter into force. With particular regard to the *Patmos* litigation, due heed will be paid to the techniques of legal argumentation used by domestic courts to justify their rulings. This should pave the way for a better understanding of the conduct of the Italian Government in the *Haven* litigation, which we will evaluate tentatively at the end of the Chapter, in the light of the applicable rules of international law.

2. THE EMERGENCE OF A REGIME OF LIABILITY FOR ENVIRONMENTAL DAMAGE: FROM JUDICIAL ACTIVISM TO CODIFICATION

The emergence of a distinct liability regime for environmental damage was prompted by the judicial activism of Italian administrative courts. In particular, the State Auditors' Court asserted jurisdiction over cases concerning environmental damage on the assumption that harm to the environment should be equated to financial damage to the state's accounts.[6] Damage to the environment was qualified as damage to public goods and the state as a trustee for the whole national community was entitled to compensation.[7] For this purpose, the General Public Prosecutor at the State Auditors' Court could bring an action for damages.[8] Interestingly enough, punitive damages were occasionally awarded in addition to purely economic damages.[9]

Some of the principles that the case law of the Auditors' Court had already

---

[5] For an overview of the Italian regime of liability for environmental damage, see F. Giampietro, *La responsabilità per il danno all'ambiente* (1988); P. Maddalena, *Il danno pubblico ambientale* (1990); L. Francario, *Danni ambientali e tutela civile* (1990).

[6] The leading cases in the case law of the Corte dei Conti (State Auditors' Court) are the following: judgment No. 39 of 15 May 1973 (Sezione I), in (1973) 49 *Foro Amministrativo* I, 247; judgment No. 108 of 20 Dec. 1975 (Sezione I), in (1977) 102 *Foro Italiano* II, 349; judgment No. 61 of 8 Oct. 1979 (Sezione I), in (1979) 104 *Foro Italiano* III, 593; judgment No. 378/A of 16 June 1984 (Sezioni Unite), in (1985) 110 *Foro Italiano* III, 38.

[7] See judgment No. 86 of 18 Sept. 1980 (Sezione I), in (1981) 106 Foro Italiano III, 167.

[8] For an accurate retrospective analysis of the Corte dei Conti case law, see C. Malinconico, *I beni ambientali* (1991), 265 ff.

[9] See M. R. Maugeri, 'Liability for Environmental Damage in Italy', in I. Koppen *et al.*, *Environmental Liability in a European Perspective*, European University Institute Working Paper EPU No. 91/12 (1991), 59–86, at 61, n. 4, where reference to relevant case law is made.

highlighted were later codified in Act No. 349 of 1986, whereby the Ministry of the Environment was established and rules for environmental damage were set up.[10] In particular, Article 18 laid down specific provisions concerning environmental damage. Even if tortious liability claims are still available whenever individual rights are infringed,[11] Article 18 is now the sole basis upon which ecological damage can be claimed. Jurisdiction in such cases is vested in ordinary courts. As to the type of liability, the legislator opted for a regime based on fault. Anyone who wilfully or negligently violates a statute or administrative rules concerning environmental protection, thus causing ecological damage, is held liable. The state and its subdivisions (municipalities, provinces, and regions) are the only entities that are entitled to ask for means of redress as trustees for, respectively, the national and local community. As far as remedies are concerned restoration in kind should be ordered by courts whenever possible. Otherwise, damages can be awarded. Should the assessment of such damages prove to be difficult, courts may resort to an equitable appraisal,[12] that takes into account, respectively, the degree of fault, the costs of restoration, and the profit unduly gained by the tortfeasor as a consequence of the wrong.[13]

Mention should also be made of Act No. 979 of 1982 on the protection of the sea.[14] Although environmental damage is not expressly referred to as such, Article 21 provides that where damage is caused by the discharge into the sea of prohibited substances by merchant ships, the master and the owner or the builder of the ship will be held jointly and severally liable and will have to compensate the state for both clean-up operations of the waters and shores and damage caused to marine resources. Contrary to Article 18 of the 1986 Act, the 1982 Act provides for a strict standard of liability.

---

[10] Act No. 349 of 8 July 1986, 'Istituzione del Ministero dell'ambiente e norme in materia di danno ambientale', in [1986] 162 *Gazzetta Ufficiale*, Suppl. Ord. No. 59, 5 ff.

[11] See the judgment of the Tribunale Vallo della Lucania of 13 Nov. 1986, in (1987) 139 *Giurisprudenza Italiana* II, 184 and the judgment of the Tribunale di Verona of 19 Oct. 1988, in (1989) 21 *Giurisprudenza di merito* 552.

[12] Recourse to equity to assess environmental damage had already been envisaged by the Corte dei Conti: see judgment No. 1423 of 31 Oct. 1985 (Sezione Sicilia), in (1986) 62 *Foro amministrativo* 258. It may be worth recalling that the term *equity* in Italian law corresponds to the Roman law concept of *aequitas*. In a comparative perspective it is rather similar to such concepts as *reasonableness* and *fairness* as they emerged in the common law tradition. Nowadays, the concept of equity is relevant in the Italian legal order especially as regards the evaluation of damage in tortious liability cases (Art. 1226 of the Civil Code) and the interpretation of contracts (Art. 1371 of the Civil Code).

[13] Other criteria that are relevant to the assessment of the economic value of environmental damage were later indicated by the Constitutional Court (Corte Costituzionale) in its judgment No. 641 of 30 Dec. 1987, in (1988) 113 *Foro Italiano* I, 694. Such criteria include costs of patrolling and monitoring compliance with law requirements, economic management of the environment so as to maximize its enjoyment either by individuals or by the community at large and developing environmental resources. Further elements for assessing the economic value of damage to the environment may be derived from the costs necessary to preserve the environment or to restore it once damage has occurred.

[14] Act No. 979 of 31 Dec. 1982, in [1983] 16 *Gazzetta Ufficiale*.

3. THE SHORTCOMINGS OF THE CURRENT LEGISLATIVE FRAMEWORK

Article 18 of Act No. 349 of 1986 was hailed as a breakthrough in environmental protection. The enactment of a statute providing for liability for purely ecological damage was seen as a powerful tool to deter would-be polluters and to ensure that in case of damage the environment would be restored to the state prior to its occurrence. At worst, compensation would be available to remedy detrimental effects on the environment caused by intentional misconduct or negligence. As practice has shown, the expectations raised by such a new legal regime largely overlooked the many shortcomings of the provisions laid down in Article 18.

The first weakness of the above regime is the requirement that some laws or regulations be violated in order to establish fault and make Article 18 operative. The obvious consequence is that entire environmental sectors not yet regulated by laws or administrative regulations are deprived of legal protection.[15] In fact, the structure of Act No. 349 and its substantive provisions are shaped by the typical command and control scheme of criminal legislation which is not well suited to cope with some of the liability issues involved in environmental damage cases. Further, as recent case law indicates, only violations of environmental laws and regulations may entail the liability of the wrongdoer.[16] For instance, if environmental damage is caused by such a hazardous activity as the transport of toxic chemicals by road, the carrier would be strictly liable, under Article 2050 of the Italian Civil Code, for any damage caused to property or to the life or health of persons but would not be liable for ecological damage if it can be proved that he or she had complied with relevant environmental laws or regulations. As I have shown elsewhere, the requirement of fault laid down in Article 18 may lead to the paradoxical result that different activities that jointly cause environmental damage may be subjected to different liability regimes.[17]

As regards legal standing, only the state or the municipality or region in which the damage has occurred may bring an action for environmental damage. If they fail to do so no one else can substitute for them as plaintiffs in an action to recover ecological damage. Citizen suits are not allowed and environmental associations may simply bring it to the attention of public authorities that damage to the environment has occurred. They may also intervene in legal proceedings and provide, for example, expert testimony, but they cannot start an action

---

[15] See B. Caravita, *Diritto pubblico del'ambiente* (1990), 365.

[16] In a recent judgment the Court of Cassation (Corte di Cassazione) specified that 'purely formal breaches of environmental laws and regulations do not give rise to an obligation to compensate'. See judgment of 19 Mar. 1992 (Sezione III), reproduced in (1993) 33 *Cassazione penale*, 1534 ff. The ruling of the Court is important, for it holds that Art. 18 of Law no. 349 does not have a sanctioning character.

[17] See A. Bianchi, 'The Harmonization of Laws on Liability for Environmental Damage in Europe: An Italian Perspective' (1994) 6 *Journal of Environmental Law* 21–42, at 24 ff.

for environmental damage on their own initiative.[18] Still unsettled is the issue whether interim measures may be requested by environmental associations in order to suspend an activity which poses a major threat to the environment.[19] The many restraints imposed on environmental associations are all the more significant when one realizes that the state has hardly ever acted to seek compensation for environmental damage. Regions, provinces, and municipalities have shown no greater initiative in this respect. One possible explanation of their attitude is the unfortunate circumstance that most of the time damage awards are channelled directly to the state, giving no incentive to local governments to act promptly in cases of environmental damage.[20]

Environmental associations may play a somewhat more active role by lodging a claim with administrative tribunals that have the power of judicial review over administrative acts. Upon the ascertainment of an infringement of individual or collective interests, administrative tribunals may suspend the operation of and eventually annul administrative acts which are proved to cause detrimental effects to the environment. The settled case law of administrative tribunals already recognizes such a power to environmental associations of a national character.[21] This power can also be exercised when damage to the environment has not yet occurred.[22] Given the wide range of public control over activities that may be detrimental to the environment, this power is not at all negligible.

The provisions of Article 18 which are concerned with means of redress also lend themselves to criticism. Restoration in kind should be imposed by courts whenever possible. The approach inherent in this proviso falls short of efficiency in all those cases in which reinstatement of the environment to the state prior to the occurrence of damage involves excessive costs. For instance, when the reclamation of a polluted site requires an enormous amount of money if undertaken independently of a general scheme of reclamation of similarly polluted areas, should the court disregard this fact and impose restoration in any case? The

[18] The power to intervene in judicial proceedings has been limited by two ministerial decrees, of 20 Feb. 1987 and 26 May 1987 respectively, to associations of a national character having environmental protection as a primary objective in their statutes.

[19] The issue is still controversial. See A. Postiglione, 'Danno ambientale e Corte di Cassazione', (1989) 4 *Rivista giuridica dell'ambiente*, 106–9.

[20] See Caravita, n. 15 above, 374 ff.; and Malinconico, n. 8 above, at 311. In one case, however, the Court decided to channel compensation directly to the region of Lombardy that had brought a claim for environmental damage. See the judgment of the Pretura di Vigevano of 13 May 1987, in (1987) 2 *Rivista giuridica dell'ambiente* 80 ff.

[21] See the following judgments: Consiglio di Stato (State Council), Sezione VI, No. 756 of 14 Oct. 1992, in (1992) 68 *Foro amministrativo*, fasc. 10; TAR (Regional Administrative Tribunal) Veneto, Sezione II, No. 475 of 9 June 1992, in (1992) 18 T.a.r. I, 3342; TAR Lazio, Sezione I, 23 Nov. 1990, No. 1124, in (1991) 67 *Foro amministrativo* 1223; Consiglio di Stato, Sezione IV, No. 181 of 13 Mar. 1991, in (1991) 42 *Consiglio di Stato* I, 347; TAR Marche, No. 58 of 8 Mar. 1990, in (1991) 6 *Rivista giuridica dell'ambiente* 531: TAR Abruzzo, Sezione I, No. 100 of 14 Feb. 1990, in (1991) 116 *Foro italiano* III, 461; TAR Lazio, Sezione II, No. 2235 of 19 Dec. 1990, in (1991) 116 *Foro italiano* III, 179.

[22] See the judgment of the Consiglio di Stato, Sezione VI, No. 728 of 16 July 1990, in (1991) 116 Foro italiano III, 485.

wording of Article 18 seems to suggest that courts should do so regardless of whether or not the costs involved in the operation are reasonable. Thus, the natural practicability of restoration seems to be the only relevant criterion. If restoration in kind is not practicable, compensation should be awarded. When damage cannot easily be quantified, courts should decide on the basis of an equitable appraisal. This paves the way for pointing to a further difficulty in applying Article 18. Quite apart from the factors listed in the same Article 18 as relevant to make an equitable appraisal of damage, what is deemed to be equitable depends on several other elements, including the possibility of relying on qualified expert testimony, on the technical preparation of judges ruling on the case, and on their sensitivity to environmental matters.

As the enforcement practice of Article 18 clearly shows, there have been only a few instances in which courts have relied directly on Article 18 of Act No. 349 to issue an award for environmental damage.[23] Many factors account for such an unsatisfactory balance sheet of enforcement. First of all, since the coming into force of the new regime, the state has seldom initiated legal proceedings for environmental damage. In particular, only a few civil awards, in which a final quantification of damage on the basis of equity has been reached, can be traced in the case law of Italian courts.[24] There are further judgments in which courts, in the course of criminal proceedings against violators of environmental statutes and regulations that provide for criminal penalties, have on a provisional basis issued awards of damages to be settled in separate proceedings by civil courts. If the state subsequently fails to initiate such civil proceedings to recover damages for the harm caused to the environment, the money award usually set in the course of the criminal proceedings as a lump-sum on account of the final award on damages takes on a somewhat different character as if it concerned punitive damages.[25]

Specific provisions on environmental damage, which are in some respects complementary to the general regime of Article 18, appear in three decrees enacted in 1992 to implement a series of EC environmental directives on water management.[26] Where damage is done to the waters, soil, subsoil, or other envir-

---

[23] See, for instance, the judgment of the Pretura di Milano (Sezione di Rho) of 29 June 1989 (in (1990) 115 *Foro italiano* II, 526), concerning the unlawful discharge into the river Laura of toxic waste. For a comment, see F. Giampietro, 'La valutazione del danno all'ambiente. I primi passi dell'Art. 18 della legge n. 349 del 1986' (1989) 65 *Foro amministrativo* 2957–61; and P. Bossi, 'Sulla quantificazione del danno all'ambiente ex art. 18 legge n. 349/1986; la prima pronuncia del giudice penale' [1989] Diritto e pratica nell'assicurazione 867–76. For an overall assessment of the case law of Italian courts on the application of Art. 18, see D. Feola, 'L'Art. 18 L.349/1986 sulla responsabilità civile per il danno all'ambiente: dalle ricostruzioni della dottrina alle applicazioni giurisprudenziali' (1992) 9 *Quadrimestre* 541–68.

[24] See F. Giampietro, 'Access to Environmental Justice in Italy: The Innovative Role of the Judge', Paper delivered at the Conference 'Access to Environmental Justice in Europe', organized by the Robert Schumann Centre (Working Group on Environmental Studies) at the European University Institute in Florence, 18–19 Mar. 1994, 6–7.   [25] *Ibid.* 6.

[26] See in particular Decree No. 130 of 25 Jan. 1992, implementing EEC Directive 78/659 on the quality of freshwaters needing protection or improvement in order to support fish life; Decree No. 132 of 27 Jan. 1992, implementing EEC Directive 80/68 on the protection of groundwater against

onmental resources the competent administrative authority has the duty to impose an obligation to reinstate the damaged resource(s) on whoever has caused such damage. Should the latter fail to comply with the order, public authorities may themselves take measures of reinstatement and later recover the costs incurred. This proviso greatly enhances the efficacy of the legal regime of liability for environmental damage. Public authorities must act in cases of damage. No proof of fault on the part of the alleged wrongdoer is required. To establish liability it suffices that a causal nexus be proved between the damage and the relevant conduct. Finally, particular measures may be ordered to eliminate the damage or to prevent its recurrence. Obviously, this remedy is of a different nature from Article 18, to which the above provisions are without prejudice. The state may also decide to act under Article 18, either at the same time or later. However, given the scant number of cases in which legal proceedings have been initiated by the state to recover environmental damage,[27] the legal remedy provided in the above decrees is, in principle, a very useful instrument in terms both of expediency and efficacy.

4. THE FORESEEABLE IMPACT OF THE 1993 LUGANO CONVENTION ON THE ITALIAN LEGAL SYSTEM

In 1993, the Council of Europe Convention on Damage Resulting from Activities Dangerous to the Environment (the Lugano Convention) was adopted.[28] Italy signed the convention, which will enter into force after the third ratification.[29] Undoubtedly, the convention will have a major impact on the Italian liability regime for environmental damage and create some interpretive issues, which the courts will have to address. In principle, once the convention is ratified by Italy and incorporated into the Italian legal system, domestic courts should give priority to its provisions over conflicting provisions of domestic law. This result is usually achieved by interpretive techniques which justify such priority either on the basis of a presumption of consistency of domestic law with international law or on the *lex specialis* character of international legal rules with respect to domestic ones. In this particular case, the primacy of the convention, at least with respect to Act No. 349, would also be ensured by applying the

pollution caused by certain dangerous substances; and Decree No. 133 of 27 Jan. 1992, implementing several EC directives on limit values and quality objectives for discharges into the water of certain dangerous substances. For a comment, see F. Giampietro, 'Responsabilità per danno all' ambiente: la Convenzione di Lugano, il Libro verde della Commissione CEE e le novità italiane', (1994) 9 *Rivista giuridica dell'ambiente* 19–33, at 32–3.

[27] See sect. 3 above.

[28] Council of Europe, Convention on Civil Liability for Damage Resulting from Activities Dangerous to the Environment and Explanatory Report, Lugano, 21 June 1993, ETS No. 150.

[29] The Convention was opened for signature on 21 June 1993. On the same day, a group of seven countries signed it (Cyprus, Finland, Greece, Iceland, Italy, Liechtenstein, the Netherlands). Luxembourg signed the following day. As at July 1995, no country is reported to have ratified the Convention.

lex posterior principle which, between rules that enjoy the same formal rank in the hierarchy of sources, gives priority to the rule enacted later.[30]

Ratione materiae the convention applies only to damage caused by hazardous activities. In this respect Italian Act No. 349 of 1986 has a broader scope of application, since it is meant to apply generally to environmental damage provided that such damage originates as a consequence of a breach of the law. However, the convention will force a change in the Italian legal system by bringing all kinds of damage, including ecological damage deriving from dangerous activities, under a strict liability regime.[31] This will have the effect of making Italian legislation consistent with current trends in both national[32] and international practice,[33] where strict liability is the prevailing legislative choice for the regulation of hazardous activities.

[30] For an extensive survey of the techniques used by domestic courts to give priority to international law over domestic law, see B. Conforti, *International Law and the Role of Domestic Legal Systems* (1993), 41 ff.

[31] A strict liability regime for damage, apart from the case of dangerous activities regulated by Article 2050 of the Italian Civil Code, is provided by Italian law for marine pollution (see Art. 21 of Act No. 979 of 1982 which also includes the notion of environmental damage) and for nuclear activities (see Art. 15 of Act No. 1860 of 1962, implementing the 1960 Paris Convention on Third Party Liability in the Field of Nuclear Energy). As was mentioned above (n. 4), Italy is also a party to the 1969 CLC, as amended, and to the 1971 Fund Convention, as subsequently amended.

[32] Several European states have recently enacted environmental liability statutes which provide for strict liability for dangerous activities or installations. See, for instance, Art. 29 of the Greek Act for the Protection of the Environment (No. 1650/1986, in Official Gazette, 160/a of 16 Oct. 1986); Art. 41 of the Portuguese Basic Act on the Environment (*Lei de Bases do Ambiente*) of 7 Apr. 1987, in 81 Diario da República, 1386; and the German Environmental Liability Act (*Umwelthaftungsgesetz*) of 10 Dec. 1990, in [1990] I S BGBl 2634. Also other states have laws which provide for strict liability in particular areas. For example, this is the case for Belgium as far as toxic waste and the control of organisms harmful to plants and plant products are concerned (see Act of 22 Feb. 1974, and Royal Decree of 16 Oct. 1991, respectively); France (Act of 15 July 1975 on waste); Spain (Art. 3(5) of Act No. 42 of 19 Nov. 1975 on waste); the UK (Control of Pollution Act of 1974, s. 88); Germany (Water Resources Act of 1960). For an up-to-date survey of environmental liability laws, see K. Kreuzer, 'Environmental Disturbance and Damage in the Context of Private International Law' (1992) 44 *Revista española de derecho internacional* 57–78. See also House of Lords Select Committee on the European Communities, Session 1989–90, 25th Report, *Paying for Pollution: Civil Liability for Damage Caused by Waste* (1990). For common law jurisdictions, see the proceedings of the seventh Residential Seminar on Environmental Law of the IBA Section on Business Law, Committee F (International Environmental Law), held at Montreux (Switzerland) on 9–13 June 1990, and chaired by Patricia Thomas, subsequently published as *Environmental Liability* (1991).
In order to establish strict liability for damage to the environment, recourse is frequently had to general rules on torts. See, for instance, the expansion of the rule of strict liability in *Rylands* v. *Fletcher* ([1868] 1 Exch. 265, (1868) 3 App. Cas. 330 (H.L.)) by English courts. See S. Tromans, 'Environmental Liability' (1992) 22 *Environmental Policy and Law* 43–8. For other examples see Kreuzer, *ibid.* 63.

[33] See the Paris Convention on Third Party Liability in the Field of Nuclear Energy 1960 (Art. 3 and 9); the Brussels Convention on the Liability of Operators of Nuclear Ships 1962 (Arts. II and VIII); the Vienna Convention on Civil Liability for Nuclear Damage 1963 (Art. IV); the CLC 1969 (Art. 3); the Brussels Convention Relating to Civil Liability in the Field of Maritime Carriage of Nuclear Material 1971 (Arts. 1–3); the Convention on International Liability for Damage Caused by Space Objects 1972 (Art. II); the Convention on Civil Liability for Oil Pollution Damage Resulting from Exploration and Exploitation of Seabed Mineral Resources 1977 (Art. 3); the Geneva Convention on Civil Liability for Damage Caused During Carriage of Dangerous Goods by Road, Rail and

As far as remedies are concerned the Convention provides that in case of damage or impairment of the environment compensation shall be limited to measures of reinstatement. According to Article 1(9) measures of reinstatement are defined as 'any reasonable measure aiming to reinstate or restore damaged or destroyed natural resources or, where reasonable, to introduce the equivalent of these resources into the environment'. In line with Italian legislation measures of reinstatement are given priority over other means of redress.[34] A notable difference is that such measures should be reasonable. What a reasonable measure is or should be is specified neither in the text of the convention nor in its Explanatory Report. In the absence of objective parameters of interpretation in relevant legal instruments it will be left to the case law of domestic courts to determine on a case-by-case basis what amounts to a reasonable measure.[35] The notion of natural equivalent is equally unclear and will require a similar approach.[36]

Inland Navigation Vessels 1989; and the Council of Europe Convention on Civil Liability for Damage Resulting from Activities Dangerous to the Environment 1993 (Arts. 6 and 7). For a recent contribution, see T. Treves, 'Aspetti internazionali sulla responsabilità civile per danni all'ambiente' (1994) 9 *Rivista giuridica dell'ambiente* 105–16.

[34] Art. 18, para. 8, of Act No. 349 of 1986 prescribes the principle of *restitutio in integrum*, wherever possible. The Corte di Cassazione, in its judgment No. 440 of 25 Jan. 1989 ((1989) 4 Rivista giuridica dell'ambiente 103) stated that such a remedy has to be given priority over the others. The assessment of the feasibility of restoration in kind is left to the discretionary powers of the court. The issue of whether such evaluation has to be made simply on scientific grounds or whether the social costs of restoration as well as other interests have to be taken into account is still unsettled in the case law. Some scholars have argued that a balance of interests analysis should always be carried out by the courts, also in the light of governmental interests as presented to the court by competent public authorities (see Caravita, n. 15 above, 381–2).

[35] A much clearer and more realistic approach to the definition of reasonable measures characterized the 1991 EC Draft Directive on damage caused by waste. See Commission, Amended Proposal for a Council Directive on Civil Liability for Damage Caused by Waste, COM(91)219 final, in [1991] OJ C192/6 ff. In the Draft Directive an exception to the obligation to restore the environment was conceived when the costs substantially exceed the benefits arising for the environment from such reinstatement and when other alternative measures to the reinstatement of the environment may be undertaken at a substantially lower cost (*ibid.* 13). The Commission is currently considering action generally in the field of civil liability for environmental damage. See Communication from the Commission to the Council and Parliament and the Economic and Social Committee: Green Paper on Remedying Environmental Damage, COM(92)47 final of 14 May 1993. For a short summary and tentative evaluation of the Green Paper, see D. Wilkinson, 'EC Green Paper on Remedying Damage to the Environment COM (93)47' (1993) 2 *European Environmental Law Review* 159–61; and Bianchi, n. 17 above, at 32 ff.

[36] The Explanatory Report (n. 28 above) commenting on the definition of measures of reinstatement explicitly refers to the disappearance of an animal species or irreparable destruction of a biotope as typical cases for impossibility of reinstatement: '[s]uch damage cannot be evaluated financially and any reinstatement of the environment is in theory impossible. Since such difficulties must not lead to a complete absence of compensation, a specific method of compensation has been introduced. This method of compensation is based on achieving an equivalent instead of an identical environment. This notion relies on the given circumstances of each individual case of damage and is not defined in the Convention itself' (at 10). On the issue of remedying techniques other than reinstatement, see F. Giampietro, 'Damage to the Environment: Meaning and Function of the Assessment of Damage', in F. Giampietro and S. Miccoli, *Assessment of Damage to the Environment* (1992), 9–28, at 25 ff.

The issue of legal standing is worth an additional remark. In particular, environmental associations or foundations which, according to their statutes, take care of the environment and comply with any further conditions imposed by national law, are given the power to bring an action in court or before an administrative authority to seek an injunction against the operator of a plant to reinstate or clean up the environment. They can also seek an injunction either to discontinue an activity which is unlawful and poses a grave threat to the environment or to order the operator to take measures to prevent an incident or damage. Such a power is somewhat constrained by the clause in the Lugano Convention that states may stipulate cases where the action is inadmissible.[37] This paves the way for broaching another issue.

In fact, the Convention leaves states with too wide a measure of discretion as regards the implementation of many of its provisions.[38] While favouring some degree of harmonization of national laws on liability, the Convention does not aim at providing a set of detailed and uniform rules.[39] The interpretation of the Lugano Convention as a treaty providing for a minimum standard is indirectly confirmed by Article 25, which states that the Convention is applicable only in so far as its provisions are more favourable to the victim(s) and/or to the environment than domestic law or other international treaties.[40] This will inevitably entail on the part of domestic courts a complex process of balancing in order to determine case by case whether the provisions of the Convention are more favourable to the victim or to the environment than domestic law. Such an exercise may prove to be difficult for the courts to handle. For instance, should Italian courts deem that the strict liability regime provided in the Convention is more favourable to the environment than the regime provided in Article 18 of Act No. 349, on the basis of the difficulty of establishing fault? Or should they rather hold that the remedies laid down in Italian law are more favourable in terms of efficacy than the corresponding norms of the convention? Furthermore, should such an evaluation be made only with regard to legal provisions or should it also include the practice of enforcement? The way these questions will be answered by domestic courts is crucial to harmonization. Hopefully, the

---

[37] See Art. 18(2) of the Lugano Convention.

[38] National law may determine, *inter alia*, who is to take measures of reinstatement (Art. 2(8)); when operators are required to have and maintain insurance or other financial security up to a certain limit and what type and terms of insurance or other financial guarantee have to be taken to cover the liability under the convention (Art. 12). It may also set up the practical arrangements under which the information held by public authorities is effectively made available and restrict access to such information in certain instances (Art. 14(1)(2)). Further, national law may stipulate cases where action brought by organizations is inadmissible (Art. 18(2)).

[39] See Bianchi, n. 17 above, 26 ff.

[40] It is unfortunate that Art. 4 of the Convention provides an exception to the application of the Convention for agreements on liability for nuclear damage and for 'damage arising from carriage' (see Bianchi, n. 17 above, at n. 24). The interpretation of the latter expression will be particularly important. Were it to include carriage of oil by sea, the CLC 1969 as amended and, in particular, its narrow definition of damage would not be affected by the Council of Europe Convention.

Committee established under Chapter VII of the Convention with the specific task of considering questions of a general nature concerning the interpretation and the application of the convention will help to solve such complex interpretative issues.[41]

5. THE *PATMOS* LITIGATION: COMMENTS ON THE INTERPRETATION OF RELEVANT INTERNATIONAL LAW BY ITALIAN COURTS

5.1. Patmos I

The *Patmos* litigation originated from the collision in the Strait of Messina on 21 March 1985, between the Greek oil tanker *Patmos* and the Spanish tanker *Castillo de Monte Aragón*. As a consequence of the collision more than 1,000 tonnes of oil were spilt into the sea.[42] Shortly afterwards limitation proceedings, in conformity with the CLC 1969, were initiated before the court of Messina. Focusing only on the matter of ecological damage, it is worth recalling that the Government of Italy lodged with the court a claim for ecological damage amounting to 5,000 million lire.[43] According to the Italian Government, Articles I(6), II, and IX(1) of the CLC and Article 3 of the Fund Convention provided for compensation of pollution damage caused on the territory of the state, including its territorial waters. The Court dismissed the claim and held that Article II of the CLC was to be interpreted as referring to damage done *on* the territory and not *to* the territory or territorial waters of the contracting states.[44] The right of territorial sovereignty enjoyed by each and every state over its territory and territorial waters cannot be violated by wrongful acts of a private nature. Nor can such acts give rise to any obligation to compensate the state. Only when a state has rights in property can domestic courts provide a remedy and protect such rights. Had Italy suffered damage to its shores—over which it has proprietary rights—it could have laid a claim for damage.[45] On a similar line of reasoning the court ruled out compensation for damage to marine flora and fauna. By qualifying territorial waters as *res communis omnium*, over which the territorial state has sovereignty, the court said that no private act could impair a right of such a nature.

Further, the court held that Italy had not suffered any direct or indirect economic

---

[41] See Art. 27 of the Lugano Convention.

[42] For a detailed account of the facts of the case see M. Medugno, 'Il caso della Patmos' (1989) 4 *Rivista giuridica dell'ambiente* 35–52.

[43] See M. C. Maffei, 'The Compensation for Ecological Damage in the "Patmos" Case', in F. Francioni and T. Scovazzi (eds.), *International Responsibility for Environmental Harm* (1991), 381–94.

[44] See the judgment of the court of Messina, issued on 30 July 1986: *ESSO Italiana S.P.A., SMEB S.P.A., Ministero dell'interno and Ministero della marina mercantile* v. *Patmos Shipping Co., The United Kingdom Mutual Steamship Assurance Association (Bermuda) Ltd, International Oil Pollution Compensation Fund et al.* (henceforward *Patmos I*), in [1986] *Il diritto marittimo* 996 ff.

[45] *Ibid.* 1008–9.

damage or loss of income. Nor had it incurred expenses in the clean up of its shores.[46] Therefore, it had no entitlement to be compensated for pollution damage. Finally, the court held that Resolution No. 3 of 1980, adopted by the Assembly of the International Oil Pollution Compensation Fund (IOPC Fund), to which Italy is a party, did not allow it to assess compensation to be paid by the Fund on the basis of an abstract quantification of damage calculated in accordance with theoretical models.[47] On these grounds the court refused to admit the expert evidence provided by the defence. Nor did the court order an independent expert's report, since the latter may not be used as evidence. It may only be used indirectly to support to evaluate evidence that has been already established.[48]

Quite apart from the conclusion reached by the court, its reasoning is not persuasive. Rather than for interpretive purposes linking the relevant treaty provisions with Resolution No. 3 of 1980, which would have been a much more convincing argument, the court distinguished the prepositions used by the drafters of the CLC to qualify the word 'damage'. As rightly pointed out,[49] an overall scrutiny of the CLC and its *travaux préparatoires* shows that such prepositions used after the word damage as 'on', 'in', or 'to' are used almost interchangeably. Therefore, the argument based on the wording of the relevant provisions loses much of its force if one frames it in a broader interpretive context. Equally unconvincing is the distinction made by the court between the proprietary rights enjoyed by the state over parts of its territory such as its shores and internal waters, which would entitle it to be compensated for damage caused by private parties, and the sovereign rights that the state has over its territorial waters, which can never be infringed by private acts and can only be protected by measures of self-help at the international level. The argument, which is shaped by an old-fashioned notion of international law, unduly complicates an already difficult matter. It would have been much better if the court had addressed the issue of legal standing in the light of the relevant provisions of the CLC.[50]

---

[46] *Ibid.* 1008.

[47] The IOPC Fund Resolution No. 3 on Pollution Damage (October 1980) provides: 'The Assembly of the International Oil Pollution Compensation Fund:

Conscious of the dangers of pollution posed by the world-wide maritime carriage of oil in bulk,
   Aware of the detrimental effect of the escape or discharge of persistent oil into the sea may have
   on the environment and, in particular, on the ecology of the sea,

Conscious of the problem of assessing the extent of such damage in monetary terms,

Noting that under the Civil Liability Convention a claim for ecological pollution damage has been
   raised against the shipowner which was based on a theoretical model for assessment,

Confirms its intention that the assessment of compensation to be paid by the International Oil
   Pollution Compensation Fund is not to be made on the basis of an abstract quantification of
   damage calculated in accordance with theoretical models'.

[48] *Patmos I*, n. 44 above, 1009.   [49] Maffei, n. 43 above, at 388.

[50] For the purpose of the Convention, the legal standing of states is not in question, as Art. I(2) defines as a person 'any individual or partnership or any public or private body, whether corporate or not, including a State or any of its constituent subdivisions'.

5.2. Patmos II

The Ministry of the Merchant Navy, which appeared throughout the proceedings on behalf of the Italian Government, appealed the decision on the basis of the following arguments. First, the Ministry reasserted its claim on the basis that damage had been caused to the marine environment, to marine resources, including fauna and flora, and to the shores of Calabria and Sicily, the two regions affected by the oil spill. As damage could not be quantified in exact terms, its relevance could only be assessed by means of expert testimony that could provide the court with some useful parameters in order to make an equitable appraisal of damage in conformity with Article 1226 and Article 2056 of the Italian Civil Code. Secondly, the Ministry argued that the expression pollution damage as appears in the CLC and Fund Convention provides for the compensation of the damage caused both to the territory and territorial waters of the contracting parties and the measures taken or to be undertaken to eliminate or limit the damage. Further, the Ministry argued that only the state is entitled to lay a claim for damage to the marine environment since it has a proprietary right over its territory and territorial waters under international law. Such a principle is also acknowledged in the 1982 Act on the protection of the sea that clearly entitles the state to compensation for damage caused to marine resources. Also the argument based on the private nature of the relations regulated by the CLC and Fund Convention should be rejected, according to the Ministry, since the provisions are without prejudice to the right of sovereignty of the state affected. The sovereignty of the coastal state over its territorial waters accounts for its direct interest in preserving the integrity of its resources. Finally, the Ministry makes reference not only to the CLC and Fund Convention but also to the 1969 Convention Relating to Intervention on the High Seas in Cases of Oil Pollution Casualties (the Intervention Convention) to assume that the purpose of all the above treaties is to prevent or limit the detrimental effects that oil spills may cause to the territorial waters of the contracting states.[51]

The Court partly upheld the arguments set forth by the Ministry of the Merchant Navy and reversed the judgment of the court of first instance. In particular, the court, faced with the question whether environmental damage can be compensated, examined the wording of the relevant provisions of both the CLC and the Intervention Convention, which the court regarded as clearly related to each other. Also in the light of Articles 1 and 2(4) of the Intervention Convention that protect such interests related to the coastal state as the conservation of marine biological resources as well as the marine flora and fauna, the court interpreted Article I(6) of the CLC broadly so as to include environmental damage in the

---

[51] The arguments put forth by the Ministry of the Merchant Navy can be read in *Patmos II*, n. 3 above, 1051–4.

notion of compensable damages. On the nature of environmental damage the court referred to judgment No. 641 of 1987 by the Italian Constitutional Court. The latter qualified such damage as economic damage, which, although having no market value, can be assessed by reference to non-use value or loss of enjoyment. According to the court, although the notion of environmental damage cannot be grasped by resorting to any mathematical or accounting method, it can be evaluated in the light of the economic relevance that the destruction, deterioration, or alteration of the environment has *per se* and for the community, which benefits from environmental resources and, in particular, from marine resources in a variety of ways (food, health, tourism, research, biological studies). Such benefits are deemed worthy of special legal protection by the state. The loss of enjoyment of all these benefits inevitably diminishes the economic value of the environment. As environmental damage cannot be the object of any pecuniary appraisal, since it has no market value, it can only be compensated on the basis of an equitable appraisal.

On the issue of legal standing, the court recognized that the state as a trustee for the national community was entitled to compensation for the damage caused to the environment. On the objection raised by the defence and upheld by the court of first instance that the relevant treaty law provisions were meant to regulate only legal relations among private parties, the court disposed of it by referring to the CLC, which does not distinguish between the rights of private parties and those of public bodies. Finally, the Court of Appeal, contrary to what the court of first instance had stated, authorized the preparation of an expert's report in order to appraise environmental damage in more concrete terms. Since the relevant evidence, due to its peculiar nature, could not be evaluated by a reasonable man in the instant case, the expert testimony, contrary to generally admitted practice, would have the function of both producing and evaluating evidence.[52]

The judgment of the Court of Appeal was hailed at the time of the decision as an important step taken by domestic courts to ensure environmental protection and to deter oil tanker owners. Rather than having the community bear the costs of environmental damage, the polluters would pay for the damage they had caused. The problem is that in the instant case the CLC and Fund Convention applied. Therefore, the matter had to be settled in the light of the treaty law provisions which were applicable to the case. The court stressed the broad language of Article I(6) of the CLC, but failed to articulate persuasive reasoning to justify its decision. In particular, the interpretation of the CLC in the light of the Intervention Convention is hardly justifiable under any international rule of treaty interpretation. The parties to the two treaties are not the same and the objects and purposes of the treaties are substantially different. While the Intervention Convention aims 'to prevent, mitigate or eliminate grave and imminent

---

[52] *Ibid.* 1054–8. See also n. 48 above and accompanying text.

danger . . . to [the coastal states'] coastline or related interests, following upon a maritime casualty',[53] the CLC and Fund Convention were meant to lay down uniform international rules and procedures for determining questions of liability and provide 'adequate compensation to persons who suffer damage caused by pollution resulting from the escape or discharge of oil from ships'.[54] Only vaguely are the two conventions related. Even less convincing is the fact that the court ignored Resolution No. 3 of the IOPC Fund Assembly, which had played a significant role in providing the *ratio decidendi* in the judgment of the court of first instance. The court should have addressed the issue, regardless of its conclusion. Had the court wanted to dismiss the argument, it could have rejected the contention that the Resolution was relevant for interpretive purposes as subsequent practice of the parties to a treaty under Article 31(3) of the 1969 Vienna Convention on the Law of Treaties, on the grounds that Article 31(3) does not reflect a rule of customary international law and is not applicable *qua* treaty law.[55] On similar grounds the court could dispose of the argument that the subsequent specification of the expression 'pollution damage' in the 1984 Protocol to the CLC could not be assumed to have relevance for interpretive purposes, since Italy had not ratified the Protocol.[56] In any event, failure to mention such an important interpretive issue did not strengthen the persuasive force of the ruling.

In conclusion, the court did not succeed in grounding its definition of environmental damage in a persuasive interpretative framework. Basically, it adopted the definition of the Italian Constitutional Court. It did not explain, however, why it did so. It could have argued that, in order to enforce a claim based on a broadly and somewhat unclearly drafted provision on pollution damage, it was forced to refer to domestic law to make such a provision self-executing.[57] Alternatively, it could have insisted on the primary value of the environment in the Italian

---

[53] See the Preamble to the CLC.   [54] See Art. I of the Intervention Convention.

[55] According to Art. 4, the Convention *qua* treaty law only applies to treaties concluded by states after its entry into force.

[56] Art. 2(3) of the London Protocol to Amend the International Convention on Civil Liability for Oil Pollution Damage 1984 provides that the expression 'pollution damage' means: '(a) loss or damage caused outside the ship by contamination resulting from the escape or discharge of oil from the ship, wherever such escape or discharge may occur, provided that compensation or impairment of the environment other than loss of profit from such impairment shall be limited to costs of reasonable measures of reinstatement actually undertaken or to be undertaken; (b) the costs of preventive measures and further loss or damage caused by preventive measures'. The 1992 Protocol contains an identical provision (Art. 2). Neither Protocol has entered into force. For a comment on the two Protocols, see M. Göransson, 'The 1984 and 1992 Protocols to the Civil Liability Convention, 1969 and the Fund Convention', in De La Rue, n. 4 above, 71–82. See also *International Oil Pollution Compensation Fund: Annual Report 1994*, 30 ff.

[57] Generally on the notion of self-executing international law see Conforti, n. 30 above, 25 ff. On the concept of self-executing treaties see Y. Iwasawa, 'The Doctrine of Self-Executing Treaties in the United States' (1986) 26 *Virginia Journal of International Law* 627–92. On the approach of Italian courts to the problem, see L. Condorelli, *Il giudice italiano e i trattati internazionali (gli accordi self-executing e non self-executing nell'ottica della giurisprudenza)* (1974).

legal system and on its constitutional underpinnings.[58] Such an argument could eventually account for giving priority to claims related to environmental protection over any inconsistent provision of international or domestic law. Article 21 of the 1982 Act on the protection of the sea and Article 18 of the 1986 Act on environmental damage could give further strength to the argument and provide the rule of decision. In fact, one gets the impression that, when the Court ruled that the evaluation of environmental damage had to be made on the basis of an equitable appraisal, it meant to enforce Article 18.[59] No mention was made, however, of this proviso.[60] Be that as it may, the Court of Appeal set an important precedent in so far as it acknowledged that ecological damage can be compensated under the CLC.

5.3. Patmos III

Upon the submission of evidence in the form of a written report by the group of experts appointed by the same court, the Court of Appeal issued the final award of damages on 24 December 1994.[61] After a cursory summary of its findings on the merits of the case, the Court of Appeal held that, in the light of the expert evidence and of all the other relevant acts submitted to it, environmental damage had been established even though it had not been quantified in precise terms. This finding will be instrumental in triggering the applicability of Article 1226 of the Italian Civil Code, which allows courts to make an equitable appraisal of damages, when the latter have been clearly established but cannot be quantified. Meanwhile, the court went on to address in detail the report that the experts had filed.

The expert evidence was premised on the following grounds. Once oil is spilt into the sea it affects the whole spectrum of marine life ranging from bacteria to phytoplankton, zooplankton, algae, benthos organisms, fish, birds, and marine mammals. Depending on the characteristics of the affected site and on the nature of the oil, the chemical and physical alterations of the marine environment may to a varying extent, affect the superficial layer of the sea, the mass of water,

---

[58] On the constitutional foundation of environmental protection, see Malinconico, n. 8 above, 128 ff.

[59] Some authors have argued that since Art. 18 requires a breach of environmental laws or regulations there would be no overlapping with the scope of application of the CLC. Cf F. Berlingieri, 'Il sistema internazionale di risarcimento dei danni causati da inquinamento da idrocarburi' (1992) 94 *Il diritto marittimo* 3–29, at 27.

[60] In some instances, courts have omitted any reference to Art. 18 in cases directly concerned with environmental damage. See Court of Cassation judgment No. 8318 of 21 July 1988 (Cassazione penale), in (1989) 115 Riv.pen. I, 515; and the Order of the Pretura di Vasto of 5 Apr. 1990, in (1991) 56 Resp. civ. e prev. 294. The uncertainty relating to the application of Art. 18 caused some authors to refer to it as 'the dreadful Art. 18' (Feola, n. 23 above, 544), who also speaks of 'the embarrassing presence of Art. 18 in the Italian legal order'.

[61] *Patmos III*, n. 1 above. For a comment see A. Merialdi, 'La sentenza sulla quantificazione del danno all'ambiente nel caso *Patmos*' (1995) 10 *Rivista giuridica dell'ambiente* 145–52.

and the seabed. Such alterations may cause disturbances, which can potentially affect pelagic organisms living in the different layers of the sea as well as those living on the seabed like shellfish. The overall intensity of such detrimental effects largely depends on such varying factors as the width of the affected area, the dimension of the oil spill, and the evolution of clean-up operations. Oil pollution can be very dangerous to the marine environment either when the concentration of oil reaches such a level as to be lethal to certain organisms or when a long time is required for the reclamation of the site. In the instant case it was doubtful whether the ecosystem could be reinstated even in a long term perspective. The group of experts then concluded that in the area of the Strait of Messina, including the shores and related interests of the coastal community, the marine environment had suffered from serious, albeit reversible, damage. More particularly, the experts calculated that 2,000 tonnes of oil had escaped from the tanker and that still 1,000 tonnes were spilt into the sea after 24 hours from the incident. The affected area was thought to be 500 square kilometres to a depth of ten metres. Comparing the volume of the affected waters with the quantity of oil they reached the conclusion that the concentration of oil could be estimated as 0.1 square metres per litre, which amounts to the threshold toxic value for causing harm to the planktonic mass, that is the biomass which is suspended in the waters. According to a complex theoretical model the experts calculated that damage to the biomass had produced a loss in terms of fish production in the range of 290 tonnes. Assuming that the proper market value would be 15,000 lire per kilogram of fish, the loss was quantified at 4,350 million lire. As only a part of the fish supply is harvested such a figure was considerably reduced (between a minimum of 375 million and a maximum of 1,275 million lire).[62]

The court basically upheld the expert evidence, although it did not fully endorse all the findings of the experts. First, it stressed that the experts had not at all ruled out, as the defence had argued, that damage to benthos had occurred. On the contrary, they held that due to the settlement of oil on the seabed for some months benthonic organisms had been affected. This damage, which in the opinion of the court could—quite obviously—not be quantified, should be taken into account in liquidating damages. The court rejected the objections raised by the defence on the alleged miscalculations of the experts with regard to the quantity of oil that had been spilt and the width of the affected area. Such a miscalculation according to the defence would have deprived of any evidentiary value the toxic rate of oil concentration in the waters. The court, while rejecting the allegation, acknowledged that Article II of the CLC only provides for compensation for pollution damage that has been caused to the territorial waters of the affected state. Therefore, damage to the marine area beyond Italian territorial waters could not be taken into account for the purpose of compensation. The

---

[62] *Patmos III*, n. 1 above, 687 ff.

court decided that, in the light of the difference between the polluted area and the extent of the Italian territorial waters, the quantification of damage made by the experts should be reduced up to a maximum of 20 per cent. Finally, the court pointed to the finding that the use of solvents and dispersants by the Navy officials, who had intervened to limit the effects of damage, had worsened the environmental alteration. Under Article III(3) of the CLC, if the owner proves that the pollution damage resulted wholly or partly from the negligence of the person who suffered the damage, the owner may be exonerated wholly or partly from his liability to such person. A somewhat similar provision exists in Italian law to exempt the wrongdoer from tortious liability.[63] In the light of both national and international law the court held that the Ministry of the Merchant Navy by its negligence contributed to causing environmental damage and that, therefore, the compensation to which it was entitled should be reduced accordingly.[64]

On the quantification of damage the court found that the experts mistakenly confined damage to the quantity of necton (fish) which the biomass could have produced had it not been polluted which could potentially have been harvested. To limit environmental damage to such a restricted notion amounts, in the opinion of the court, to giving to the environment a market value. Paradoxically, the court says, in the case of an oil spill into a fishing preserve no one would be entitled to be compensated for the damage caused to pelagic organisms living in it. As the court had already stressed, environmental damage materializes whenever there is a loss of enjoyment on the part of the community. As regards the precise quantification of damage the court decided to avail itself of the possibility of issuing a damage award on the basis of an equitable appraisal under Article 1226 of the Italian Civil Code. This provision allows courts in cases of tortious liability to resort to an equitable appraisal of damage whenever such damage cannot be quantified in precise terms. Such an equitable appraisal was made by the court: (i) on the basis of such objective criteria provided by the expert evidence as damage to benthos, the quantity of fish that had been destroyed, the market value of the fish (duly reduced to an estimated wholesale value at the time of the accident of 8,000 lire per kg); (ii) in the light of the circumstance that the damage had affected not only Italian territorial waters; and (iii) taking into account that the negligent conduct of the Navy officials had contributed to causing the damage. A damage award in the amount of 2,100 million lire was issued to the benefit of the Ministry of the Merchant Navy as compensation for environmental damage.[65] The damage award did not exceed the limit of liability of the owner and the IOPC Fund did not appeal the decision. Such a fortunate, although perhaps not fortuitous, circumstance seems to have brought to an end the lengthy proceedings related to the *Patmos* incident.[66]

The final damage award deserves a few additional comments. The court did

---

[63] See Arts. 2056 and 1227 of the Italian Civil Code.   [64] *Patmos III*, n. 1 above, 692–3.
[65] *Ibid.* 693–4.   [66] See Merialdi, n. 61 above, 150.

not seem at ease with the equitable appraisal it was to make. For instance, while rejecting the experts' contention that damage should be quantified in terms of the market value of the potential quantity of fish which could not be harvested since the oil spill had damaged the biomass, which is essential to the fish reproductive chain, it eventually referred to the market value of the fish as a parameter to be taken into account for its appraisal of damage. Overall, the indirect support that the court drew from the expert evidence was crucial to orientate the Court in a highly technical and extremely difficult matter. As compared to the *Jasenice* case,[67] in which the pollution damage arising out of an oil spill in Venice harbour had been compensated on the basis of an equitable appraisal under Article 1226 of the Civil Code, but without the support of expert evidence, the *Patmos* case marks an improvement. In the absence of any reliable guidance from settled case law, the equitable appraisal of damage of such a complex nature needs to be anchored in some sort of objective parameters provided by independent expert evidence. On the choice of tracing to Article 1226 the legal basis for making an equitable appraisal of damage, an additional remark is in order. Once it had established that ecological damage could be compensated under the CLC, the court had to determine how such damage could be compensated for. Since the CLC sheds no light on how compensation for pollution damage should be provided, the court relied on domestic law to enforce the claim. What certainly comes as a surprise is the failure by the court even to mention Article 18 of the 1986 Act for interpretive purposes. Since the ruling is based on the equitable appraisal of environmental damage mandated by Article 18, reference to the latter rule would have framed the ruling in its natural context of reference.[68]

6. THE STANCE TAKEN BY THE ITALIAN GOVERNMENT IN THE *HAVEN* LITIGATION AND ITS CONSISTENCY WITH INTERNATIONAL LAW

The outcome of the *Patmos* litigation paves the way for broaching the question of whether or not the decision of the Court of Appeal is consistent with international law and, in particular, with the CLC and related instruments. The question seems all the more interesting when one realizes that the IOPC Fund has consistently opposed the claim presented by the Italian Government.

[67] The judgment of the court of Venice of 10 July 1981, in (1981) 83 Il diritto marittimo 589 ff.
[68] With regard to the objection that the wrecking of the *Patmos* and the ensuing damage took place prior to the enactment of Act No. 349 of 1987, it should be noticed that courts have often made the application of Art. 18 retroactive (see Feola, n. 23 above, 544 ff.). This may be explained by the fact that Art. 18 is not regarded as a completely new cause of action. Many cases of tortious liability decided under the general regime provided by Art. 2043 of the Civil Code have made reference to Art. 18, which would simply provide for new modalities of compensation in specific cases. Be that as it may, a mere interpretive reference to Art. 18 would have raised no question of judicial propriety, as the rule of decision was clearly identified with Art. 1226.

The issue has come to the fore again, since the government of Italy set forth an analogous claim in connection with the *Haven* incident.[69] This time the government was joined by the Region of Liguria, two provinces, and fourteen communes that lodged separate claims for environmental damage. Originally, none of these claims contained any indication of the type of environmental damage which they had allegedly suffered. Nor when the alleged damage to the environment was finally quantified and an amount of money was specified, at least for certain types of damage, did the Italian Government state how such an amount was calculated.[70] In conformity with its settled practice the IOPC Fund has reasserted in strong terms its opposition to such claims and has repeatedly held that environmental damage cannot be recovered under the CLC unless it relates to quantifiable elements of damage to the marine environment, such as reasonable costs of reinstatement of the damaged environment and loss of profit (income, revenue) from the damage to the marine environment suffered by persons who depend directly on earnings from coastal or sea-related activities, e.g. loss of earnings suffered by fishermen or by hoteliers and restaurateurs at seaside resorts. In the latter case, however, only claims directly brought by damaged individuals can be accepted.[71]

Therefore, the IOPC Fund does not admit claims relating to unquantifiable elements of damage to the marine environment. Along the same lines of reasoning, the Assembly of the Fund in Resolution No. 3 of 1980 rejected claims for compensation to the environment calculated on the basis of abstract theoretical

---

[69] See *International Oil Pollution Compensation Fund: Annual Report 1994*, 46–55. The incident occurred in Apr. 1991, when the Cypriot tanker *Haven* caught fire and suffered a series of explosions and subsequently sank off Genoa (Italy). The incident caused serious pollution in Italy and also affected France and Monaco. For an accurate description of both the modalities of the incident and the precise location of its occurrence see Doc. FUND/EXC/21 of 31 May 1991, and Doc. FUND/EXC.28/6 of 2 Sept. 1991. For the stance taken by the Italian Government, a few months after the incident, on the matter of the admissibility of claims relating to damage to the marine environment, see the intervention made by the Italian delegation during the 30th session of the Executive Committee of the Fund (Doc. FUND/EXC.30/WP.1 of 16 Dec. 1991).

[70] See Criteria for the Admissibility of Claims for Compensation. Environmental Damage Claims, Note by the Director of the IOPC Fund, Doc. FUND/WGR.7/4, 4 Jan. 1991, 4–5.

[71] In June 1994, the Italian Government quantified the alleged damage to the environment as follows:

— restoration of 43 hectares of phanerogams; 266,042 million lire (£ 102 million);
— consequences of the beach erosion caused by damage to the phanerogams; not quantified but left to the assessment of the court on the basis of equity;
— wreck removal; 20,000 million lire (£ 7.7 million);
— damage restored by the natural biologic recovery of the resources; 591,364 million lire (£ 227 million) for the sea and 6,029 million lire (£ 2.3 million) for the atmosphere, in a total of some £ 229 million;
— irreparable damage to the sea and the atmosphere; not quantified but left to the assessment of the court on the basis of equity; and
— compensation for inflation and interest.

See Doc. FUND/EXC.43/2 of 19 May 1995, 3–4. The figures in British pounds slightly diverge from those published in *International Oil Pollution Compensation Fund: Annual Report 1994*, 50, due to the fluctuations in the exchange rate. It is worth noting also that a French public body (*Parc National de Port Cros*) has claimed compensation for damage to the marine environment (*ibid.* 4).

models.[72] The approach of the Assembly is reflected in both the 1984 and 1992 Protocols to the CLC.

The Fund further contends that the object and purpose of both the CLC and the Fund Convention is to provide compensation to the victims of oil pollution damage. According to a recent report by the Director of the Fund such domestic law provisions as the Italian 1986 Act on environmental damage, which provides for the award of damages of a punitive character, are not consistent with the Conventions. Damages awarded on that basis are not appropriate within the scope of application of the Conventions. The deterrent effect of punitive damages would be meaningless within the CLC system, since any amount in excess of the shipowner's limitation amount will have to be paid by the Fund. Paradoxically, the Fund will have to pay for the fault of the shipowner and for the profit which he or she unduly earned. Without having any deterrent effect on the conduct of shipowners, this would be to the detriment of those who have suffered actual and quantifiable economic loss, whose share in the total amount would be reduced. Italy rejected the contention that the concept of compensation embodied in the 1986 Act has a sanctioning character and further argued that compensation for damage to the marine environment would be regulated by the 1982 Act on the protection of the sea, which includes both quantifiable and unquantifiable elements.[73]

As the negotiations between Italy and the IOPC Fund seem stalled at the time of writing and the proceedings before the court of Genoa have been delayed by the controversy on how the limitation amounts should be calculated,[74] it is worth wondering whether the conduct of the Government of Italy is lawful under international law. The whole issue hinges upon the interpretation of the relevant treaty law provisions and on the legal value of Resolution No. 3 of 1980.

It should be borne in mind that Italy is a party to both the CLC and the Fund

---

[72] See n. 47 above. It may be worth recalling that the peculiar wording of the Resolution is due to the fact that in the aftermath of the *Antonio Gramsci* incident, which occurred in the USSR in 1979, the USSR had presented a claim for damage to the marine environment based on a mathematical formula, the so-called 'methodica'. According to Soviet legislation, the formula had to be used to assess the damage, which had to be linked with the quantity of oil collected in USSR territorial waters (see Doc. FUND/EXC.30.2 of 29 Nov. 1991). On the *Gramsci* incident see also Maffei, n. 43 above, 389.   [73] Criteria for Admissibility of Claims for Compensation, n. 70 above, 4–7.

[74] The major controversy was which method had to be used to convert into national currency the limitation amounts of the shipowner. On the one hand, the IOPC Fund held: (i) that the amounts must be converted into the national currency of the state in which the limitation fund is being constituted on the basis of the value of that currency by reference to the Special Drawing Right (SDR) established by the International Monetary Fund (IMF) after the demise of the 'gold exchange standard system'; and (ii) that the value of the national currency in terms of the Special Drawing Right has to be calculated in accordance with the method of valuation applied by the IMF in effect at the date of the constitution of the Fund for its operations and transactions. This solution was adopted in the two 1976 Protocols amending respectively the CLC and the Fund Convention (the 1976 Protocol to the Fund Convention is not yet in force), which, as is known, had originally adopted the gold franc as the unit of account for calculating the amounts of limitation. The claimants, on the other hand, argued that the amounts had to be calculated by reference to the market price of gold contained in the gold francs, which would lead to considerably higher amounts. The court of Genoa in two judgments, respectively of 14 Mar. 1992 ((1992) 94 *Il diritto marittimo* 164–80.

Convention, but it is not a signatory of either the 1984 or 1992 Protocol, where more precise rules on pollution damage are laid down.[75] Had Italy been a signatory to either Protocol the argument could have been made that it has an obligation, under customary international law as reflected in Article 18 of the Vienna Convention on the Law of Treaties, to refrain from any act which would defeat the object and purpose of the treaty. A similar argument was made with reference to the position of Italy with regard to the 1976 Protocol which adopts the Special Drawing Right (SDR) as the unit of account to be used for computing the limits of liability of the shipowner.[76]

Therefore, the main issue of interpretation concerns the expression 'pollution damage' as it appears in Article I(6) of the CLC. According to the Fund, even pending the entry into force of the 1984 and 1992 Protocols, Resolution No. 3 of 1980 has to be framed as an 'authentic interpretation' of the expression 'pollution damage' and as such binding on the contracting parties. Further, when the Resolution was unanimously adopted in 1980, Italy was a party to the Fund Assembly. The argument of the Fund deserves careful attention. The Assembly, according to Article 18(14) of the Fund Convention, may perform the functions that are necessary to ensure the proper operation of the Fund. Undoubtedly, Resolution No. 3 of 1980 contributes to the proper operation of the Fund since it tends to avoid practices which may undermine the object of the Fund. Looking at international practice, and in particular at the two Advisory Opinions issued by the International Court of Justice (ICJ) respectively in the *Namibia* and *Western Sahara* cases, it must be noticed that binding effects have occasionally been attached to non-binding resolutions of organs of international organizations when such resolutions provided an interpretation of treaty provisions[77] or when they made determinations or had an operative design.[78]

For an English translation of the judgment see Doc. FUND/EXC.31/2, Annex 1 of 30 Apr. 1992) and 22 July 1993 ((1993) 95 *Il diritto marittimo* 780–808. For an English translation of the judgment see Doc. FUND/EXC.36/3 Add.1 of 29 Sept. 1993), held that the conversion into Italian lire had to be made by reference to the market value of the gold contained in the gold franc. The IOPC Fund has appealed against this judgment (see Doc. FUND/EXC.36/10 of 5 Oct. 1993, 3. See also Doc. FUND/EXC.36/3 of 10 Sept. 1993, indicating the main arguments of the IOPC Fund in its deed of appeal, at 13). For an extensive survey of the international regime regulating civil liability for oil pollution damage see Berlingieri, n. 59 above.

[75] See n. 56 above.

[76] See the Opinion given by Dr T. Mensah upon the request of the IOPC Fund on 'The Question of the Unit of Account for the Limitation Amounts under the 1971 Fund Convention and the Method of Conversion into National Currency' (1992) 94 *Il diritto marittimo* 547–61, at 559–60: 'Italy has ratified the 1976 Protocol to the 1971 Fund Convention, which also adopts the SDR as the unit of account, with an identical provision regarding the value of national currencies in terms of the SDR. Although the 1976 Protocol to the 1971 Fund Convention is not yet in force, the State of Italy, as a Contracting State to that Protocol, is under an obligation to refrain from any act which would "defeat the object and purpose" of the Protocol, in accordance with the provisions of the 1969 Convention on the law of Treaties (footnote omitted).'

[77] See *Western Sahara*, Advisory Opinion [1975] ICJ Rep. 12.

[78] See *Legal Consequences for States of the Continued Presence of South Africa in Namibia (South West Africa) notwithstanding Security Council Resolution 276(1970)*, Advisory Opinion, [1971] ICJ Rep. 16, at 50.

Quite apart from the issue whether the analogy with the UN General Assembly is correct as a matter of methodology, given the major differences between the treaties involved, it is arguable that the Assembly of the Fund has the competence to interpret the CLC. However intertwined the two treaties may be, they are two distinct legal instruments.[79] The Assembly may decide that the Fund will not pay any compensation on the basis of an abstract quantification of damage calculated in accordance with theoretical models, but may not provide an authentic interpretation of the expression 'pollution damage' as it appears in the CLC. Furthermore, if the shipowner is financially capable of meeting his obligations under the CLC and his insurance is sufficient to satisfy the claims for compensation for pollution damage and the damage does not exceed the tanker owner's liability under the CLC, the Fund does not come into play. As a matter of treaty interpretation, the Fund should have been more careful in setting forth the argument that Resolution No. 3 is an authoritative interpretation of the expression 'pollution damage'.

Another way of attaching binding effects to Resolution No. 3 is to qualify the Resolution as an executive agreement between the parties to the Fund Convention. In particular, by agreeing on the Resolution the parties would have expressed their consent to be bound by an interpretation of the Convention that rules out the possibility of compensating claims for purely ecological damage. However attractive, this qualification falls short of accuracy in so far as it does not take into account that the willingness to be bound must be expressed in clear terms by the parties or unequivocally result from their conduct. In fact, it is difficult to draw from the wording of the Resolution the willingness of the parties to be bound by it. The issue of the legal value of the Fund Assembly resolutions arose, albeit in a slightly different context, in the proceedings before the court of Genoa concerning the *Haven* incident.[80] The court ruled that it is not possible for such resolutions to amend the text of the Convention, for specific provisions for the revision and amendment of the Convention exist which provide for the convening of a Conference of the Parties.[81] The argument seems correct and is supported by the subsequent practice of the parties, which negotiated and concluded in the form of a protocol amendments to the CLC and in particular to the meaning of the expression 'pollution damage'.[82] Moreover, from the standpoint of domestic law, it would be difficult to circumvent the obligation laid down in Article 80 of the Italian Constitution that requires the

---

[79] Evidence of this can be traced to the necessity of adopting two distinct amending Protocols to change the unit of account in both the CLC and the Fund Convention.

[80] The IOPC Fund had argued that the Assembly of the Fund, while awaiting the entry into force of the 1976 Protocol, had adopted Resolution No. 1 of 1978 (in which it was agreed that reference to the gold franc in the Fund Convention would be interpreted as reference to the SDR) in order to ensure the provisional application of the 1976 Protocol. For this reason the Resolution could be regarded as an executive agreement binding on the parties.

[81] See the judgment of the court of Genoa of 14 Mar. 1992, n. 74 above, 174–5. The art. of the Fund Convention that provides for the procedure of amendment and revision of the convention is Art. 4.   [82] See n. 56 above.

authorization of the Parliament for any international agreement which modifies existing legislation.[83]

Assuming the applicability of the Fund Assembly resolutions *qua* customary law, reference could be made to the rules of interpretation laid down in Article 31 of the Vienna Convention on the Law of Treaties.[84] As is known, the fundamental criterion is to interpret the treaty in good faith in accordance with the ordinary meaning to be given to its terms. Looking at the wording of the relevant provision of the CLC, the somewhat loosely drafted definition of pollution damage would theoretically render it possible to include such claims as those presented by the Italian Government. However, the proviso has also to be interpreted in the context of the treaty and in the light of its object and purpose. Indisputably, the object of both the CLC and the Fund Convention is to ensure that adequate compensation is available to persons who suffer damage caused by pollution resulting from the escape or discharge of oil from ships. The definition of person provided by the CLC is broad enough to include public bodies. Therefore, it cannot be ruled out that states or state subdivisions as trustees for the national or local communities may lodge claims for ecological damage. On the other hand, one could argue that the lodging of claims for ecological damage, based on theoretical models, may be detrimental to private parties who have suffered actual losses and whose capacity to recover might be hampered by excessive claims set forth by public bodies.

The same Article 31 of the Vienna Convention further provides that account shall be taken, together with the context, of any subsequent agreement between the parties regarding the interpretation of the treaty and the application of its provisions. Undoubtedly, the 1984 and 1992 Protocols attain that status, but Italy has not even signed them. Once again one has to revert to Resolution No. 3. Even if the Resolution has no binding effect *per se*, it might be relevant for interpretive purposes to defeat the interpretation given by the Italian Government and by the Court of Appeal of Messina to the expression 'pollution damage'. In particular, such a unanimously adopted resolution of the Fund Assembly could be regarded as *subsequent practice* of the parties to the Fund Convention in the application of the treaty which establishes the agreement of the parties regarding its interpretation. This qualification is given further support by the fact that the states parties to the Fund Convention have since generally abstained, with the only notable exception of Italy, from laying claims for purely ecological damage.[85] In any case, the interpretive relevance of the Resolution should be limited to the Fund Convention.

---

[83] Moreover, such a manifest violation of a fundamental rule of its internal law regarding competence to conclude treaties (Art. 80 of the Constitution) could be invoked by Italy as a ground for the invalidity of the treaty, according to Art. 46 of the Vienna Convention on the Law of Treaties.

[84] See n. 55 above.

[85] Apparently, even France and Monaco, which had been affected by the *Haven* incident, abode by the terms of Resolution No. 3 (see *International Oil Pollution Compensation Fund: Annual Report 1994*, 51), with the only notable exception of the French *Parc National de Port Cros* (see n. 71 above).

Theoretically, one solution to the problem could be to interpret the expression pollution damage as including claims for environmental damage, even when such claims are not based on actual losses or when they cannot be quantified in precise terms, provided that compensation does not exceed the liability of the shipowner and that the Fund need not pay any compensation. This might safeguard the interests of the Fund and be a deterrent for shipowners. As the practice of the Fund shows, however, in almost all the incidents that occurred since the establishment of the Fund the damage has exceeded the tanker owner's liability.[86] A radical alternative would be to allow claims for ecological damage to be made outside the ambit of the CLC.[87] This has been acknowledged as a theoretically viable solution,[88] especially in the light of the fact that claims other than those related to the losses caused by contamination are to be dealt with separately. However, to admit such claims may have disruptive effects on the whole system of the CLC and the Fund Convention. It would have adverse effects on the insurance market and alter the agreed apportionment of the financial burden of oil spills between the shipping industry and the oil industry.[89] Ultimately, this might defeat the object and purpose of the two treaties and undermine the international regime, which was meant to ensure that adequate compensation was paid to the victims of oil spills. Furthermore, once the persons who have suffered damage decide to act outside the CLC, they may not be able to rely on the principle of the strict liability of the shipowner. In most cases, they will be forced to bring an action in tort and establish negligence. The burden of proof will then be reversed and it may not be easy for the victims to obtain compensation.[90]

A more convincing argument—which apparently has never been raised directly by the Fund—could be that Italy is estopped from laying a claim for environmental damage, calculated on the basis of theoretical models.[91] In particular, the conduct of the Italian delegation in the Fund Assembly, which unanimously adopted Resolution No. 3, could create an estoppel in so far as the other parties to the Fund Convention relied on it in good faith. The loss that the Fund would suffer from the duty to compensate claims for ecological damage, which were not meant to be compensated according to the terms of the Resolution,

---

[86] See B. Browne, 'Compensating Marine Oil Pollution Victims: A Case Study', Paper delivered at the Conference 'Access to Environmental Justice in Europe', organized by the Robert Schumann Centre (Working Group on Environmental Studies) at the European University Institute in Florence, 18–19 Mar. 1994, 11.

[87] Art. III(4) of the CLC bars action against the owner and the owner's servants and agents otherwise than in accordance with the Convention. This limit could be circumvented either by bringing claims against persons other than the abovementioned subjects or interpreting narrowly the term pollution damage so that states may grant a wider right of recovery.

[88] See 'Admissibility and Assessment of Claims for Pollution Damage: Report of the Chairman of the International Sub-Committee', in *Comité Maritime International, Yearbook 1993 (Sydney I, Documents for the Conference)*, 88–139; reproduced in (1994) 96 *Il diritto marittimo* 298–338, at 327 ff.   [89] *Ibid.*

[90] See Browne, n. 86 above, at 6.

[91] On the doctrine of estoppel under international law see I. Brownlie, *Principles of Public International Law* (1990), 640 ff.

which Italy also adopted, could be seen as sufficient ground to invoke the doctrine of estoppel and preclude Italy from laying claims for ecological damage, which do not meet the requirements set forth by the Fund. Although the doctrine of estoppel has been the object of some controversy in international legal scholarship,[92] some decisions by the ICJ seem to have definitely acknowledged its existence and validity in international law, presumably as a general principle of law under Article 38 of the ICJ Statute.[93]

7. CONCLUDING REMARKS

As we examined above, to evaluate the consistency of Italian practice with international law is no easy task. In particular, if one is to ascertain whether the decision of the Court of Appeal of Messina in the *Patmos* case and the diplomatic stance taken by the Italian Government as regards the *Haven* incident amount to violations of the international treaty law regime regulating liability for damage resulting from oil spills, the difficulty arises of establishing the precise content of relevant treaty rules. Sound arguments exist to support both the interpretation given by Italy and the stance taken by the IOPC Fund. In fact, international law rules on treaty interpretation are hardly apt to determine with a sufficient degree of accuracy which interpretation should prevail. As is often the case, such interpretive conflicts are ultimately solved by domestic courts with reference to the values that the national legal order wants to foster.

As regards Italy, the enactment of legislation that provides for the compensation of ecological damage (Article 18 of Act No. 349 of 1986) and of damage to marine resources (Article 21 of Act No. 979 of 1982) seems to have affected the outcome of the *Patmos* litigation as well as the claim of the Italian Government. The constitutional underpinnings of environmental protection may have had, at least indirectly, some bearing on the *ratio decidendi* in the *Patmos* case. This may account also for the odd reversal of a long-applied rule of statutory construction, namely that domestic statutes ought to be construed as far as possible in conformity with international law. In fact, the Court of Appeal of Messina

---

[92] See D. Bowett, 'Estoppel before International Tribunals and Its Relations to Acquiescence' (1957) 34 *British Year Book of International Law* 176–202.

[93] Beside the classic *Case concerning the Temple of Preah Vihear (Cambodia v. Thailand), Merits,* Judgment of 15 June 1962 [1962] ICJ Rep. 6, at 32, reference to the doctrine of estoppel was also made by the ICJ in the following cases: *North Sea Continental Shelf,* Judgment [1969] ICJ Rep. 3, at 26; *Military and Paramilitary Activities in and against Nicaragua (Nicaragua v. United States of America), Merits,* Judgment, [1986] ICJ Rep. 14, at 414–5; *Elettronica Sicilia S.p.A. (ELSI),* Judgment [1969] ICJ Rep. 15, at 44; and *Land, Island and Maritime Frontier Dispute (El Salvador/ Honduras), Application to Intervene,* Judgment, [1990] ICJ Rep. 92, where essential elements of estoppel were deemed to include 'a statement or representation made by one party to another and reliance upon it by that other party to his detriment or to the advantage of the party making it' (at 118).

seems to have done just the opposite by interpreting the applicable international treaty rules consistently with domestic rules.[94]

On closer scrutiny, however, the positions taken respectively by the IOPC Fund and by the Italian Government on compensation for ecological damage are not irreconcilable. After all, there must be something between an assessment of damage based on mathematical formulae and a firm refusal to compensate ecological damage as such. Of course, the core of the problem is one of proof and to establish what damage the environment has suffered is not a matter to be tackled by jurists.

The final award of damages by the Court of Appeal of Messina in the *Patmos* case is a good illustration of how domestic courts may reconcile such conflicting approaches. Regardless of its many shortcomings in terms of legal argumentation, the court by making an equitable appraisal of damage did not jeopardize any of the different interests involved. On the one hand, the principle that environmental damage must be compensated was reasserted. On the other, since the damages award did not exceed that limit of liability of the shipowner, the apportionment of the losses arising out of oil spills as devised by the CLC and the Fund Convention was not disrupted. It must be conceded that this may not be possible in every single case and that cases differ widely from one another. However, such flexible concepts as reasonableness and equitable appraisal of damage are better suited to addressing the complexities of cases, to which the strict application of narrowly interpreted legal rules will often fail to do justice.

---

[94] The future entry into force of the 1993 Lugano Convention may bring an element of novelty into the Italian legislative framework. In particular, as far as remedial measures are concerned, the requirement that measures of restoration of the environment be reasonable may introduce a guarantee against over-generous damage awards. Even though the Convention applies only to dangerous activities and carriage is excluded from its scope of application, its provisions, once incorporated into the legal system, will be an additional hermeneutical canon for the courts to use.

7

How to Deal with Damage to Natural Resources: Solutions in the German Environmental Liability Act of 1990

WERNER PFENNIGSTORF

1. INTRODUCTION

Compensation is normally provided by the law as a second-best remedy if the consequences of an injury or damage cannot be undone by the person responsible through restoration of the exact condition existing before the damaging event. The standard measure of compensation in such cases is the economic loss caused by the injury or damage.

Losses of natural resources are often difficult to measure in economic terms. That constitutes a double challenge: to find new ways to define and measure the economic value of natural resources, or to include damage to natural resources among the types of non-economic losses for which the law, exceptionally, does provide compensation.

All efforts to determine the economic value of nature are at best hampered and at worst frustrated by the age-old ambivalence of mankind's attitude toward nature. It is easy to find agreement, in general terms, that nature must be protected, if not for its own sake, then at least for preserving the conditions and resources on which this generation and future generations of humans rely for survival and, among affluent societies like ours, for enjoyment. However, agreement on the details is difficult, indeed impossible, especially on the kinds of resources that need to be protected, in contrast to those that may be used, exploited, and consumed, and the measures to be taken for effective protection.

Apart from conflicting economic interests, value judgements tend to be influenced by temporary public anxieties and sentiments, by isolated and overrated incidents, incomplete information, or media campaigns.

The current state of German law reflects all of these difficulties. It is the result of many small adjustments on different points over a long period of time, and consequently presents neither a comprehensive nor a perfectly consistent treatment of liability in respect of natural resources.

2. SURVEY OF REMEDIES UNDER PRIVATE AND PUBLIC LAW

Environmental protection legislation has been concerned primarily with conservation and prevention by such means as restrictions on use and prohibitions against actions that might damage or disturb the protected parts of the environment. For example, persons who damage or destroy protected plants, wildlife, or inanimate parts of the environment in a nature reserve are subject to punishment, usually in the form of a fine.[1]

Private-law liability for damages can result if the damaged part of nature happens to be a subject of private-law rights or if its loss otherwise affects such rights (2.1 below). In addition, a duty to bear the cost of restoring or replacing a damaged part of nature may arise under public law in special situation (2.2 below).

2.1. Compensation under Private Law

Under the tort law rules of the Civil Code, a person who has unlawfully and negligently caused damage to privately owned property (including property owned by the state) must make good the resulting economic loss.[2] Natural resources to which these rules have been applied so far have primarily been trees and other plants, and fish (in privately owned ponds or other enclosed waters). Where causation and fault are clear and there are generally accepted standards for determining the amount of the economic loss, such losses are routinely compensated.

Pure economic loss, for example reduction of business due to adverse publicity (rather than direct physical impact) of a pollution incident is not compensatable under the general rules. Losses of a non-economic nature are compensatable only where statutory law specifically so provides.[3] So far, this has been done only for culpable bodily injury and restrictions of personal freedom.[4] Both the legislature and the courts have been extremely reluctant to expand the scope of compensatability for such losses.

Liability to pay compensation may arise under nuisance rules if a neighbour's property is affected by emissions exceeding the degree to be tolerated as consistent with prevailing local use.[5]

The general rules have been supplemented (but not replaced) for water pollution by the Water Resources Act of 1976[6] and, for damage through environmental impairments of all kinds, by the Environmental Liability Act of 1990.[7] Both laws establish strict liability regimes for owners of certain installations

---

[1] Thus, e.g. §§ 30 and 30a of the Federal Nature Protection Act (*Bundesnaturschutzgesetz*) and the corresponding laws of the individual states (*Länder*).

[2] *Bürgerliches Gesetzbuch* (hereafter BGB), §§ 823(1) and 249–55.   [3] BGB, § 253.

[4] BGB, § 847(1).   [5] BGB, § 906(2), 2nd sentence.

[6] Water Resources Act (*Wasserhaushaltsgesetz*) of 1976, § 22.

[7] *Umwelthaftungsgesetz* of 10 Dec. 1990, § 1.

or (in the case of water pollution) persons who commit certain actions.[8] General tort law remains relevant for installations or activities that do not generate strict liability under the special laws, and for claims to recover damages for pain and suffering and similar losses of a non-economic nature, which are not compensatable under such laws. The Environmental Liability Act is discussed in more detail below (at 3).

2.2. Obligations under Public Law

A public-law obligation to remedy damage to natural resources or to bear the cost may arise under general rules relating to public safety or under special provisions of nature preservation laws.

Under the general rules of the laws relating to public safety (roughly equivalent to the rules of public nuisance in common law countries[9]), if pollution of water, the air, or the ground constitutes a danger to public safety or health, the person whose actions or property have caused the danger may be ordered by the competent administrative authority to remedy it or bear the expense of remedial measures.[10]

These rules have routinely been applied not only in cases of accidental pollution but also where hazardous chemicals were present in the ground for a long time as a result of past waste disposal or industrial activities, and were recently found to threaten to contaminate the groundwater.[11] The person responsible may not be required to undertake, or pay for, any measures beyond those necessary to avert the present danger to public safety and health. Restoration of the environment to an unspoiled condition may not be required.

Several *Länder* have enacted, as part of their waste treatment and disposal laws, more detailed provisions for the 'old burdens' (*Altlasten*). Under these laws, remedial measures may be ordered not only in the event of a threat to public safety, but also if the 'public good' (*Wohl der Allgemeinheit*, defined as including the comfort of the people and the interests of nature preservation, preservation of scenery, and urban development) is injured. Remedial measures may include, in addition to containment, rehabilitation and recultivation.[12]

Besides dangers to public safety, a limited obligation to rectify damage to natural resources may arise under nature preservation laws. The current versions

---

[8] Water Resources Act, § 22(1): actions by which polluting substances are transmitted into the water.

[9] See W. Pfennigstorf, 'Environment, Damages, and Compensation' (1979) 2 *American Bar Foundation Research Journal* 347–448, at 376–7.

[10] e.g. §§ 6(1), 7(1), and 66 of the public safety law of Lower Saxony (*Niedersächsisches Gefahrenabwehrgesetz*).

[11] e.g. Verwaltungsgerichtshof München, 13 May 1986 (1986) 5 *Neue Zeitschrift für Verwaltungsrecht* No. 12, 942. For details see P. Schimikowski, *Umwelthaftungsrecht und Umwelthaftpflichtversicherung* (1994), at 145–58.

[12] For details see A. Pohl, 'Die Altlastenregelungen der Länder' (1995) 48 *Neue Juristische Wochenschrift* 1645–50.

of these laws restrict actions, notably changes of the form of the use of land, if they 'may substantially or sustainedly impair the performance capacity of the ecology or the scenic appearance'.[13] Actions of such kind may not be taken without having been approved by the appropriate authorities. The person undertaking the action must rehabilitate or restructure the land so that no substantial impairment remains.[14] If that is not possible, the person responsible must restore the affected functions or values of the ecology or scenic appearance in a similar way by substitute measures at another place in the affected area.[15]

These provisions are meant to apply primarily to large-scale activities like surface mining, canal construction, or hydro-electric power projects. The art of reclaiming and redesigning such areas has been developed to such level that the reclaimed parts are sometimes more attractive than those they replaced. Other than the substitutes mentioned, no remedy is available for unique natural resources (such as a scenic rock formation or animal species) that are lost.

3. COMPENSATION FOR THE COST OF RESTORING PRIVATELY OWNED NATURAL RESOURCES UNDER THE ENVIRONMENTAL LIABILITY ACT OF 1990

The Environmental Liability Act is concerned only with economic loss through violation of private rights. Its purpose is to supplement existing legal rules, rather than to create a comprehensive, entirely self-contained legal regime for environmental damage. It was designed to fill some gaps and to remove some inconsistencies in private-law remedies, and in particular to lighten the claimant's burden of proof. It refers to the environment not as the *object* sustaining compensatable damage (with one exception, discussed at 3.2 below) but primarily as the *medium* through which injury or damage to private property is caused. Damage to natural resources that are not privately owned is considered beyond the reach of private law, and is left to the rules and instruments of public law.[16]

3.1. The Principal Features

The principal features of the Act are as follows:

— Strict liability is attached to certain hazardous installations, specified in an Annex to the Act. The list corresponds essentially to the list of installations

---

[13] *Bundesnaturschutzgesetz*, § 8; *Niedersächsisches Naturschutzgesetz*, §§ 7–12.
[14] *Niedersächsisches Naturschutzgesetz*, § 10(1).　　　[15] *Ibid.*, § 12(1).
[16] For details see W. Pfennigstorf, 'Liability and Insurance for Pollution Damage: New Approaches in the Federal Republic of Germany' (1990) 71 *Nordisk Försäkringstidskrift* No. 2, 139–51, at 141–4; G. Hager, 'Das neue Umwelthaftungsgesetz' (1991) 44 *Neue Juristische Wochenschrift* 134–43; P. Salje, *Umwelthaftungsgesetz* (1993); Schimikowski, no. 11 above, at 85–140; J. Schmidt-Salzer, *Kommentar zum Umwelthaftungsrecht* (1992).

for which a special permit is needed under the Environmental Protection Act.[17]

— Liability covers injuries or damage caused by 'effect on the environment' emanating from such installations, whether during regular operation or due to a disruption by accident or fault.[18]

— It is presumed that damage was caused by an individual installation if that installation, considering its location, design, operating details, and all other facts of the case, was capable of causing such damage.[19]

— Compensatable damages are limited to those resulting from bodily injury or property damage. They do not include 'pure economic losses' of any kind.
    In contrast, the Water Resources Act recognizes economic losses of any kind sustained by water users (including water supply authorities, holders of fishing rights, and operators of open baths) as a result of a change in the water quality. The only limits on the range of potential claimants and compensatable losses are those inherent in the protective purposes of the law.[20]

— Also, losses of a non-economic nature (pain and suffering, loss of enjoyment of life) are not compensatable under the Environmental Liability Act.

3.2. Limitations

Consistently with its general design, the Environmental Liability Act relates to natural resources only if and to the extent that they are privately owned property. Within these limits, the Act does make a modest effort to recognize their special value beyond strictly economic standards, by providing, in § 16:

§ 16 Costs of restoration
(1) If damage to property also constitutes an impairment of nature or scenery, then, to the extent that the damaged person restores the state that would exist if the impairment had not occurred, § 251 para. 2 of the civil code shall apply, provided that expenses for restoration of the previous state shall not be considered unreasonable for the sole reason that they exceed the value of the property.
(2) The liable person must, upon the damaged person's demand, advance the necessary expenses.

To understand this provision, it is necessary to refer to § 251(2) of the Civil Code which provides: '(2) The person owing compensation may compensate the creditor by payment of money if restoration is possible only at unreasonable expense. Costs incurred by treatment of an injured animal shall not be considered unreasonable for the sole reason that they considerably exceed the animal's value.' The first sentence of this section has been interpreted as providing a double

---

[17] *Umwelthaftungsgesetz*, §§ 1 and 3.
[18] As defined in § 3(1) of the Act, 'damage results from an environmental effect if it is caused by substances, vibrations, noise, pressure, rays, gases, vapours, temperature or other phenomena that have spread in the ground, air or water'.   [19] *Umwelthaftungsgesetz*, § 6.
[20] *Wasserhaushaltsgesetz*, § 22; Schimikowski, n. 11 above, at 60–1.

limit—precluding restoration if that would be unreasonably expensive (usually interpreted to mean costs exceeding 130 per cent of market value), and, in such cases, limiting compensation to an economically reasonable amount. In the case of damage to property, that amount is usually the price of a reasonably acceptable replacement object.[21] The word 'may' indicates that the debtor (not the claimant) may still choose restoration over compensation, ignoring the limit.

The second sentence did not exist when the Environmental Liability Act was drafted and discussed. It was added in August 1990 as part of a law designed to lift animals to a legal status somewhat above mere inanimate objects.[22] The new sentence merely confirmed established case law.[23] Apart from animals, a special emotional value attached to property (such as unique creations of handicraft) has not so far been recognized.[24]

Section 251(2) would also be the appropriate place for the parallel provision freeing nature and scenery from the value limit. No reason is given, and indeed no sound reason is to be seen, why recovery for damage to nature and scenery should be privileged only within the scope of the Environmental Liability Act (i.e. the damage is caused by an environmental effect from a listed hazardous installation), and not in cases of liability under general rules.

Section 16 of the Environmental Liability Act permits owners of damaged natural resources to recover the cost of restoration without being limited to the market value. It does not, however, allow unlimited recovery of such costs.

The defence of unreasonableness is eliminated only as regards the reference to the value of the damaged property. As a general precept, the principle of reasonableness continues to govern and to limit the responsible person's obligation.

In particular, a defendant may argue, and a court may agree, that certain restoration expenses are unreasonable on other grounds, for instance because they pertain to measures that are ineffective or are unrelated to, or go beyond, the purpose of restoring the environment to its previous state, and instead serve purely cosmetic purposes. Where the limit of reasonableness is to be drawn will depend on future development of public attitudes towards the environment as well as on the facts of each individual case.[25]

As a further limit, recovery may be claimed only for expenses that are actually incurred for restoration. Recovery meets a natural limit where no restoration, at whatever expense, is possible because a part of nature has irretrievably been lost. In such a case, the parties and the courts are thrown back to the old problem of placing a market value on something that defies measurement in monetary terms.

---

[21] For details and references, see G. Schlegelmilch, in G. Schlegelmilch (ed.), *Geigel, Der Haftpflichtprozeß* (1986), 63–73.   [22] Act of 20 Aug. 1990 [1990] I BGBl. 1762.
[23] e.g. Landgericht München, 21 June 1978 (1978) 31 *Neue Juristische Wochenschrift* 1862 (three times replacement value not considered unreasonable for veterinary treatment of pet dog).
[24] Schlegelmilch, n. 21 above, at 63–4.
[25] Thus the official notes accompanying the legislative bill: *Entwurf eines Umwelthaftungsgesetzes*, Bundesrat, Drucksache 127/90, at 55.

On the occasion of several Rhine pollution incidents in 1986 and 1987, it was proposed to establish the value of uncontaminated Rhine water by way of a public opinion poll.[26] As the author of that proposal admits, that would be an extremely difficult undertaking. It would also be likely to produce highly unreliable results. Indeed, it would seem more appropriate to recognize the inherent limits of compensation as a means to protect natural resources and to concentrate instead on more effective prevention.

4. UNSOLVED TASKS

The Environmental Liability Act has not been able to overcome the problems posed by impairments that cannot be traced to one or several specific installations but are due to a combination of many and to some extent unclear circumstances. The presumption of causation (3.1 above) may be rebutted by proving that a different circumstance is (also) capable of causing the damage in question.[27]

In particular, no solution has yet been found for compensating private forest owners for the loss suffered as a result of damage caused by 'acid rain' and a variety of other causes, including, in addition to chemicals emitted by power plants and industrial establishments, exhausts from domestic heating and general motor vehicle traffic, and also such natural factors as soil exhaustion, pests, and climatic changes.[28] Efforts by forest owners to recover their losses from the federal and *Länder* governments, on the grounds that their property had been taken for a public use, that the legislature by inaction had violated its duty to protect their property, and on other grounds, were rejected by the Supreme Court on the basis of existing law.[29]

The court did recognize a need to provide an alternative basis of compensation by appropriate legislation, and the federal government expressly accepted that responsibility.[30] However, despite general agreement that compensation must be provided and that some kind of fund is the appropriate means to provide it, it has been impossible to agree on a suitable way to organize and to finance such a fund, let alone define the conditions for entitlement to compensation.[31] Unfavourable economic developments have compounded the problems. It seems at present that the issue has ceased to be a political priority.

As noted, the Environmental Liability Act deals only with damage to privately owned parts of nature. Damage to natural resources that are not subject

---

[26] K.-H. Ladeur, 'Schadenersatzansprüche des Bundes für die durch den Sandoz-Unfall entstandenen "ökologischen Schäden"?' (1987) 40 *Neue Juristische Wochenschrift* 1236–41, at 1240–41.

[27] *Umwelthaftungsgesetz*, § 7.

[28] For details see K. Kinkel, 'Möglichkeiten und Grenzen der Bewältigung von umwelttypischen Distanz- und Summationsschäden' (1989) 22 *Zeitschrift für Rechtspolitik* 293–8.

[29] Bundesgerichtshof, 10 Dec. 1987, 102 BGHZ, 350.

[30] For references see Schimikowski, n. 11 above, at 97, n. 372.

[31] Kinkel, n. 28 above, at 294–8, K.-H. Ladeur, 'Der "Umwelthaftungsfonds"—ein Irrweg der Flexibilisierung des Umweltrechts?' (1993) 44 *Versicherungsrecht* 257–65.

to private rights is considered a matter of public law, to be dealt with by separate legislation. Appropriate proposals are discussed below (at 6 below).

5. ILLUSTRATIONS

The legal rules described so far form a confusing patchwork. Depending on the facts of a given case, they may apply alternatively or cumulatively, and may lead to widely differing results. A few hypothetical or actual cases may serve to illustrate how the different regimes operate in practice.

5.1. The Hunter's Pond

In early 1995, a loud explosion was heard, and a huge fountain of mud and water seen rising from a remote swampy area in Bavaria. For want of another explanation, it was first attributed to a meteorite and thus became a front-page story in newspapers all over Germany. A day later, it was revealed that the explosion had actually been caused by a large charge of explosives, under the supervision of a certified explosives expert. Its purpose was to create a new aquatic habitat for waterfowl. More precisely, the holder of the hunting rights in the area wanted to attract ducks and other birds to shoot them.

The blasting master had obtained a permit for the operation from the public safety office of the regional government. However, the hunter had not bothered to approach the office in charge of nature preservation about a permit for what evidently amounted to a substantial interference with the ecology. The nature preservation office declared that it would not have permitted the operation if asked, and would not approve it now. Consequently the hunter faced an obligation to do, or pay for, whatever was necessary to fill in the crater and to restore the surrounding area to its previous condition.

This is one way in which German laws seek to achieve restoration if they fail in their primary goal, to *prevent* damage to natural resources.

5.2. Measuring Damage to Parts of Nature

If the hunter in the first case had blasted the crater for his pond not in a remote area but close to a neighbouring property, without the necessary precautions, and if as a consequence a wetland habitat, carefully preserved and tended by the neighbour, had been damaged by falling debris or by diversion of the natural water flow, there would be an ordinary claim for damages under tort law.

The only matter in dispute would probably be the amount of compensatable expenses. They are limited by § 251(2) of the Civil Code to an economically reasonable amount. In this case the limit would be determined by the difference in value between the property with damaged and with undamaged wetland habitat. That difference would probably be small and in any event difficult to determine, except in the case of a public park, a zoo, or a botanical garden. The special pride and affection of a private person for his own part of nature is not recognized by the law if it is not recognized by the market.

In this respect the Environmental Liability Act of 1990 would make a difference. Suppose the damage to the neighbour's wetland habitat was caused, not by falling debris or diverted water, but by toxic chemicals that had been released from a storage tank large enough to bring it within the range of the Act's Annex and which had, dissolved in surface water or groundwater, somehow found their way onto the neighbour's property.

These facts would trigger a claim for damages under the Environmental Liability Act. Under § 16 of the Act, restoration costs would not be considered unreasonable for exceeding the value of the property—in this case, the difference in market values. The neighbour could spend considerably more than that on restoring his wetland habitat, and the owner of the tank would have to pay, subject to the general limits of reasonability.

5.3. The Value of Trees

Now let it be assumed that the blasting operation had caused irreparable damage to an old tree on the neighbour's property. Damage to trees, bushes and hedges has been a rather frequent occurrence, and consequently there is now a generally accepted set of rules for measuring the compensatable damage, based on a decision of the German Supreme Court of 1975.[32]

In that case, a 40-year-old chestnut tree had been destroyed in a motor vehicle accident. It had been one in a row of trees lining a road. The government unit in charge of the road replaced it with a 5-year-old chestnut tree and claimed damages calculated on the basis of a widely used formula proposed by a private expert. The trial court adopted the same formula; the Court of Appeal disallowed one item of the formula (interest). In reversing the decision of the appeal court, the Supreme Court noted first that it would have been possible, at considerable cost, to replace the tree with one of about equal age. The court recognized that, in certain situations, it might be economically reasonable to do that, but agreed with the lower courts that in the actual case replacement with a young tree was the reasonable thing to do.

On the other hand, the court considered that an amount equal to the cost of the tree and its planting would not be adequate as compensation for the loss of the variety of functions and benefits that were provided by a mature tree and could not immediately be provided by a young replacement tree.

The court noted that the primary way to determine the remaining loss would be to compare the value that the affected property would have with the mature tree intact with its present, presumably reduced, actual value. The court admitted, however, that such comparison would be extremely difficult, even for privately

---

[32] Bundesgerichtshof, 13 May 1975 (1975) 28 *Neue Juristische Wochenschrift* 2061–3.

owned residential properties, and that it was not feasible for properties serving as public roads.

The court then accepted, as a *substitute* for the property value comparison, the formula used by the trial court. This formula (known as the *Koch* method) consists of adding the following items:

1. the cost (purchase price) of the replacement tree;
2. the cost of planting and initial care during the rooting period;
3. a charge reflecting the risk of failure to take root;
4. the cost of regular care up to the time the tree reaches the age of the replaced tree;
5. interest on the capital outlay represented by items 1–4, under business accounting rules.

The *Koch* method is based on principles and standards that are also used in official guidelines for determining the value of real property.[33] It is now well established. It may in time provide the pattern for solving similar valuation problems with other natural resources.

If the tree had been killed not by the blast but by toxic exhausts from a chemical facility of a kind listed in the Annex to the Environmental Liability Act, § 16 of that Act would apply. The reduction in value of the neighbour's property, however determined, would not be a limit, and consequently the neighbour could replace the tree with one of the same age, at greater cost—short of acting frivolously.

However, if we assume, finally, that the tree was a 500-year-old oak tree, a landmark, and a historical monument, replacement would not be feasible at any cost, and the *Koch* method, with its interest element, would produce a result so grotesque that I doubt whether any court would accept it. The only way to find a reasonable figure for compensation in such case would probably be to go back to a comparison of market values.

6. PROPOSED FURTHER EXPANSION OF LIABILITY

6.1. The Draft Environmental Code

Even while some of the most urgent problems of compensating damage to natural resources remain unresolved, new proposals to extend liability have emerged. Chief among them is the draft of an Environmental Code (*Umweltgesetzbuch*), prepared by a group of academic scholars commissioned by the Environmental Office of the Federal Government and published in 1991.[34]

This project was designed, in the German tradition of codification, to gather in one comprehensive piece of legislation the major principles and rules relating

---

[33] For details, see W. Koch, *Aktualisierte Gehölzwerttabellen* (1987).
[34] M. Kloepfer *et al.*, *Umweltgesetzbuch—Allgemeiner Teil* (1991).

to the environment, and in the process to eliminate the inconsistencies that now exist among the many scattered laws on the subject. The proposal carries no authority other than that of the authors, who are all recognized experts on environmental law. It is expected to be subject to public discussion and eventually to become a basis for formal legislative proposals. With respect to liability, the draft closely follows the Environmental Liability Act. It does, however, include modest expansions of liability with respect to damage to natural resources.[35]

6.2. Expanded Private-law Liability for Damage to Natural Resources

In its § 127, the draft refers to property damage that also constitutes a 'substantial impairment of the ecology' (*erhebliche Beeinträchtigung des Naturhaushalts*), and is caused by a violation of public-law provisions serving to protect the environment. In such case, § 127(1) clarifies that restoration of the previous state shall include measures to remedy the impairment. Apart from that, the section repeats § 16 of the Environmental Liability Act (3.2 above).

6.3. Expanded Public-law Liability for Damage to Natural Resources

The proposed § 118 of the Environmental Code would establish a public-law obligation similar in nature to the one recognized under existing nature protection laws (2.2 above) but with somewhat different conditions and standards.

The obligation would arise if a severe violation of public-law duties relating to the protection of the environment causes a substantial impairment of the ecology. In that case, the appropriate local authority may demand, primarily, restoration of the previous state (*Wiederherstellung*) or, if that is not possible, restoration of the impaired ecology in other ways (*Ausgleich*). If neither of the two is feasible, or would be feasible only at disproportionate expense, the impairment is to be remedied through compensating measures (*Ersatzmaßnahmen*) or in other ways.

What measures are to be taken in a given case would be determined by the competent public authority. The responsibility for carrying them out would be primarily that of the person liable. The authority could, in exercising its discretion, decide to carry out the remedial measures itself, at the expense of the person liable. The public-law obligation would be precluded to the extent that private-law claims are made under § 127 (6.2 above). As under existing nature protection law, there would be nothing to recover if a part of nature were irretrievably lost.[36]

---

[35] For details see R. Enders and B. Reiter, 'Die Umwelthaftung im System des Umweltgesetzbuches' (1991) 42 *Versicherungsrecht* 1329–41.

[36] Enders and Reiter (*ibid.*, 1335) suggest that in such cases payment of some kind of compensation for the 'ecological suffering' might be required. This is a minority view that is inconsistent with the generally accepted tradition in German law of providing compensation for non-economic losses only in cases of fault-based liability for personal injury.

7. CONCLUSION AND GENERAL REMARKS

The Environmental Liability Act is one example of the general tendency of tort law to expand the bases of liability and the range of compensatable damages. If despite this general trend the Act's approach to compensation for natural resources appears to be rather cautious, this may be attributed to six major countervailing factors:

— A tradition of changing laws incrementally, in small steps, combined with the recognition that deviations from general tort law must be justified in each instance by compelling reasons based on the significantly different nature of a new situation (damage to natural resources).

— The conflicts between environmental protection and economic policies, as well as among the priorities in environmental protection.

— The difficulties of agreeing on the value of natural resources.

— Recognition of the self-healing capacity of nature.

— Recognition of the primary role of preservation and prevention.

— Recognition of the primary role of public law in pursuing the goals of preservation and prevention.

8

The Compensation of Ecological Damage in Belgium

HUBERT BOCKEN

1. INTRODUCTION

In the first part of this Chapter a general overview is given of the basic rules on liability for environmental damage in Belgium. In the second part, the compensation and assessment of ecological damage are examined in more detail. With regard to both subjects, we first describe the prevailing law and thereafter present the solutions proposed in a Draft Decree on Environmental Policy which was recently elaborated by the Inter-university Commission for the Revision of Environmental Law in the Flemish Region.

Belgium having become a federal state, liability for environmental damage in Belgium remains mainly governed by federal law. The regions have to a limited extent enacted legislation in this area, more particularly with respect to liability for damage caused by the pumping of groundwater[1] and for the cost of soil sanitation.[2] The exact scope of their legislative powers with respect to liability for environmental damage remains debatable. One can, however, safely say that the regions are competent to legislate on the matter in so far as the allocation of certain losses is an inherent or necessary part of environmental policy for which the regions are fully competent.[3]

2. THE BASIS OF LIABILITY; CAUSATION

2.1. Present Law

The basic rules on environmental liability are found in the Civil Code, Articles 1382 and 1383 of which establish the fault liability which remains the cornerstone

[1] Flemish and Walloon Decrees of 5 May 1984 and 11 Oct. 1985.
[2] Flemish Decree on Soil Sanitation of 22 Feb. 1995.
[3] The Court of Arbitration, in its decision 58/94 of 14 July 1994, confirmed that the Flemish region is constitutionally competent to legislate with respect to the recovery of the costs related to soil clean-up measures taken by the Flemish Public Waste Company (1995) 4 *Tijdschrift voor Milieurecht* 310–18, at 312, with note by H. Bocken, 'Het arrest nr. 58 van 14 juli 1994 van het Arbitragehof en de bevoegdheid van de gewesten om aansprakelijkheidsregelen uit te vaardigen'.

of environmental liability law. The notion of fault refers to socially unacceptable behaviour. From the case law, a number of more specific criteria can be derived for the application of the vague and relative concept of fault.[4]

Most important is that the violation of a statutory or regulatory provision, in the absence of a justified cause, constitutes a fault which entails liability for the ensuing damage. The importance of this fault criterion for the compensation of accidental damage is increasing, together with the body of statutes and technical regulations governing a variety of industrial and other activities.

The fact that all statutory obligations are respected, however, does not guarantee freedom from liability. Next to statute and regulation, there is the general duty of care. In order to decide whether the defendant acted negligently or not, the judge will compare the behaviour of the defendant with the presumed normal conduct of a reasonable man. The standards applied in evaluating the acceptability of polluting activities, however, are seldom clearly expressed and rationalized in the case law. One broad principle which courts often refer to is that a professional must conform to the state of the art in his profession. In any event, the lack of clarity in the court cases is unsatisfactory for those who look for principles to determine when pollution is acceptable and when not. One can, however, safely conclude that the application by the courts of the concept of fault, especially in pollution cases, becomes more and more stringent. In many instances, the distinction from strict liability will be a rather theoretical one.

From the beginning of the twentieth century the courts and the legislator have developed a number of strict liability rules which can be applied to or are specifically designed for the compensation of environmental damage. The most important strict liability rule in Belgian law is based on an extensive interpretation of Article 1384, paragraph 1, of the Civil Code. It holds the custodian of a defective object strictly liable for the damage caused by the defect. To be considered defective, the object must show an abnormal characteristic. It must deviate from what can normally be expected from an object of the same type. However, the fact that an object is dangerous by its nature does not make it defective. Further, the defect should attach to the object itself, though it should not be inseparable from and inherent in it. A deviation in the structure of the object, its form, its parts, or their interrelationship qualifies as a defect. The fact that the object occupies an abnormal place or undergoes a sudden change (for example, an explosion) does not, in itself, constitute a defect.

Custody implies the factual use and control of the object for one's own account. Generally, the owner of the object will be its custodian. Custody and property, however, do not coincide. In the case of a lease, for example, it will have to be determined who actually has the control of the defective object, the owner or the lessee. The custodian does not escape liability by proving that he committed no

---

[4] For further references, see H. Bocken *et al.*, 'Herstel van schade door milieuverontreiniging', in Interuniversitaire Commissie tot Herziening van het Milieurecht in het Vlaamse Gewest, *Voorontwerp Decreet Milieubeleid* (1995), 833–994, at 847.

fault. The fact that the custodian had no knowledge of the defect and consequently could not avoid it is irrelevant, as is *force majeure* with respect to the origin of the defect.

Article 1384, paragraph 1, is quite important with respect to environmental damage, especially that which is due to a defective installation. Recent case law has considerably expanded the application of the rule to pollution damage by considering under certain circumstances a polluted river or polluted soil as a defective object, so that the public authority which exercised police authority over the river or the guardian of the land was held liable for the damages caused by the pollution.

Traditionally, Belgian courts have imposed liability whenever (even non-negligent) activities carried out on land result in an excessive nuisance for the neighbours. This liability is currently theoretically based on Article 540 of the Civil Code which states the principles of the right of ownership. Liability arises only if the nuisance exceeds what is normal in the region. To a large extent, whether a nuisance is actionable or not will thus depend on the degree of industrialization and urbanization of the neighbourhood.

Contrary to what is the case in the context of fault liability, the abnormal susceptibility of the victim and the prior occupation of the land can play a considerable role in nuisance law. Indeed, the notion of abnormal disturbance depends on a comparison between the nuisance resulting from the activities of the defendant and the normal levels of disturbance in the region. Thus, there will be no liability for disturbances which the victim feels to be excessive, merely because of his abnormal susceptibility. The general character of the region may also rule out liability: a nuisance is only excessive if it exceeds what is normal in the region. The fact that the individual defendant had established his installations before the victim came to live in the region, however, may influence the outcome of a nuisance action only in so far as the defendant's establishment determines the character of the neighbourhood; prior occupation in itself, however, does not imply that the tolerance due to the neighbours in the region increases.

Liability applies to anyone who carries out activities on land which create an excessive nuisance. The defendant should not necessarily be the owner of the property on which the nuisance originates; he may be the lessee or the holder of a limited right to use the property. Liability can be invoked by anybody who suffers injury and has a real or personal right to use the property affected by the nuisance. The claim for compensation is not restricted to the owner; all affected neighbours can claim compensation. The notion of neighbourhood is broadly interpreted. It is sufficient that activities on one property affect another property, even if there is a considerable distance between the two; contiguity is not required. Liability for nuisance has thus been applied to a variety of instances of damage suffered in the vicinity of construction works or various industrial installations.

Finally, there is a fairly large number of specific federal statutes providing for strict liability for the consequences of one or other form of pollution incidents. Apart from the acts by which the international treaties on nuclear damage and on pollution of the sea by oil are ratified and implemented, notable examples are Article 7 of the Act on Toxic Waste of 7 July 1974, which holds the producer liable for damage caused by toxic waste (but which was never applied) and Article 85 of the Act of 24 December 1976, which requires the government and local authorities to recover from the owner of the polluting substances the expenses of the intervention of the civil protection services or the fire brigades which have taken clean-up measures after pollution incidents.

There is also a number of regional decrees providing for some form of strict liability, such as the Flemish and Walloon Decrees of 5 May 1984 and 11 October 1985 with respect to damage caused by the pumping of groundwater. Of considerable importance is the Flemish Decree on Soil Sanitation of 22 February 1995. This decree contains liability rules the scope of which is limited, however, to the cost of the cleaning up of polluted soils. Other damage caused by the soil pollution remains governed by the common liability law. The decree distinguishes between historical pollution (which is the result of emissions which took place before the enactment of the decree) and new pollution. In the case of new soil pollution, the polluter is strictly liable for the clean-up costs. In the event of historical pollution, liability is determined on the basis of the legislation in existence prior to the enactment of the decree.

Liability obviously only arises if causation is established between the damage and the act to which the law attaches liability. Belgian courts interpret the notion of causation very broadly and generally apply the theory of the equivalence of conditions. For a causal link to exist between an injury and a fault, it is necessary but sufficient that the actual damage would not have occurred without the fault. The fault must be a necessary condition for the damage. This very broad concept of causation protects the victim, but also brings about liability in cases where this may be considered inequitable in view of the remoteness of the damage. The courts try to mitigate these results, often by means of decisions with a factual basis; they have, however, not succeeded in elaborating a rational and consistent set of exceptions to the basic rule. An example of one of these exceptions is the theory of the interruption of the causal link by the existence of a contractual or statutory obligation, which is discussed later in connection with the recovery of clean-up costs.

However broad the theoretical concept of causation may be, in Belgium, as in other countries, difficulties of proof will constitute the major obstacle for the victim of pollution damage. On this point, Belgian law does not provide for a presumption of causation or a reversal of the burden of proof which in principle lies with the victim.

2.2. The Draft Decree on Environmental Policy

In the framework of a policy of protecting the victims of pollution and applying the polluter pays principle, the current law on environmental liability is not entirely satisfactory. In certain cases, fault may be difficult to establish. The normative element in neighbourhood law includes a tolerance for the conditions prevailing in a certain neighbourhood. The area of application of the liability for defective things and other strict liability statutes remains limited. Although the theoretical concept of causation is very large, establishing causation is a major obstacle. There is no adequate system of financial guarantees. Ecological damage, as will be seen, is not compensatable. In any event, the law on pollution liability is characterized by a multitude of legal regimes most of which have not been designed to deal with environmental damage and which contradict each other.

In the Flemish region, the Inter-university Commission for the Revision of Environmental Law in the Flemish Region was established in 1989 in order to elaborate the codification of environmental law. The Commission finalized its draft at the end of 1994.[5] It covers general principles, rule-making, enforcement, safety measures, liability, and sectoral provisions on soil, waste, water, and noise.

Part of the Commission's proposals have already been translated into Flemish decrees on the principles of environmental management, environmental planning, waste, environmental covenants, and soil clean-up. It is uncertain, however, whether the Commission's proposals on liability (part 9 of the draft decree) will be approved by the government and introduced into Parliament. Much will depend on the developments at international level and, more particularly, the progress which is made with the elaboration of an EC directive on liability. Of great importance will also be whether or not the 1993 Convention on Civil Liability for Damages Resulting from Activities Dangerous to the Environment will be ratified by the major European countries. Whatever the draft's chances of being adopted, the chapter on environmental liability may be of some interest for foreign audiences; the main points thereof are thus briefly presented here.

The draft introduces a general rule of strict liability for damage caused by an emission of pollutants into air, soil, or water. If the emission results from an installation or activity which is subject to licence, liability is canalized to the licensee or the operator in fact. The causes of exoneration of liability are limited. However, the liability does not apply to pollution which is acceptable in view of local circumstances and which results from emissions which are consistent with the neighbourhood practice and not illegal. It applies only to emissions which have taken place after the coming into effect of the decree.[6] There is a period of limitation of three years, combined with a period of extinction of thirty years from the emission.

---

[5] The Dutch text of the Draft Decree is published in Interuniversitaire Commissie tot Herziening, n. 4 above. An English translation of the draft decree will be published at the beginning of 1996 by Graham & Trotman, London.

[6] This is also the case in the Decree of 22 Feb. 1995, with respect to the cost of cleaning up polluted soils, see sect. 2.1 above, 4.

Much attention is paid to the establishment of an adequate mechanism of financial guarantees. Operators of installations and activities presenting substantial risks are under the obligation to provide financial guarantees in proportion to the risk they create. Liability insurance can be used but is not made compulsory: bank guarantees and other financial guarantees can also be used. In order to remedy the limited availability of commercial financial guarantees, the draft provides for the establishment of the Environmental Guarantee Account. This new financial institution would manage deposits made by potentially liable parties on individual accounts in order to guarantee certain of their obligations. The deposits are tax deductible; the revenues are added to the individual accounts. A deposit with the Environmental Guarantee Account, rather than other forms of financial guarantees, is required in a limited number of cases, for example, where there is in fact no risk involved as clean-up costs or after-care expenses are clearly foreseeable. In other cases, the potentially liable party has the choice between providing a traditional guarantee or making a deposit with the Environmental Guarantee Account. The individual financial and tax situation will determine which is the most appropriate solution. Unpublished studies by a major financial institution have shown the Environmental Guarantee Account to be in many cases an attractive alternative to insurance and bank guarantees.

The liability is, in principle, unlimited. The draft, however, provides for an optional mechanism which allows operators to limit their liability to the level at which they have to be covered by financial guarantees. They can achieve this limitation by showing that their liability is covered by a compensation fund which they have established or adhered to and which ensures compensation up to a second, much higher financial ceiling. The proposed system is thus comparable to that applied in the area of oil pollution of the sea where the strict liability of the tanker owner, which is to be covered by financial guarantees, is complemented by the intervention of the International Oil Pollution Compensation Fund for damage exceeding the limit of individual liability. A major difference, however, is that the coverage by the proposed guarantee fund and the ensuing limitation of liability are optional. It is indeed not deemed possible at this moment to oblige the operators of the most diverse economic sectors and financial standing mutually to guarantee their solvency by contributing to a single fund. It is more likely, however, that risk-spreading initiatives are taken on industry basis.

The draft also addresses the problem of the compensation of a number of types of damage which fall out of the reach of any form of individual liability. If the source of pollution is unidentified, if there is no liability because the defendant can invoke a cause of exoneration, or if the party liable is insolvent and the financial guarantees insufficient, individual liability is of no avail to the victim. Here the only possible solution is recourse to a fund or other collective compensation mechanism. In this respect the draft proposes to make use of an existing fund financed by environmental taxes on waste and waste water. Part of this fund, which was created to finance government investments in pollution infrastructure and soil clean-up, is set aside for the compensation of victims who cannot obtain compensation for one of the reasons mentioned.

Major innovations—for Belgium—are introduced with respect to the definition of damages and its compensation. The liability regime would not only apply to traditional damage to individual interests ('damage') but also to damage to elements of the environment which remain unappropriated ('impairment of the environment'). Compensation for impairment of the environment, however, is limited to reasonable measures taken in order to restore the environment. The proposals in this respect will be discussed more extensively in the following section.

3. THE COMPENSATION AND ASSESSMENT OF ENVIRONMENTAL DAMAGE

3.1. In General

The concept of 'damage' is very broad in Belgian law. In principle, compensation may be awarded for personal injury, physical damage to immovable or movable goods, and nuisance in the enjoyment thereof. Economic losses can be compensated not only when they are the consequence of damage to life, health, or property, but also when they are unconnected thereto (pure economic loss). Non-economic consequences (pain, suffering, reduction in enjoyment) are compensated as moral damages.[7]

Harm to any factual (not illegal) interest qualifies for compensation; the infringement of a legal right is not required. The damage has to be personal; no claim will lie if the victim cannot prove having been individually affected. The damage must also be certain, be it the continuation or development in the future of a presently existing condition.

The objective of the action for compensation is to put the victim, as far as possible, in the condition in which it would have been had the act entailing liability not been committed. By preference the damage will be compensated by measures placing the victim effectively in such condition. Thus, the rule is compensation *in natura*[8] by replacement or restoration of the asset lost or damaged, which, in turn, is normally achieved by the reimbursement of the cost thereof. Compensation *in natura* will, of course, not take place if replacement or restoration in kind is in fact impossible. It will also be refused if it constitutes an abuse of rights, which would be the case if the cost of the restoration were out of proportion to the advantage thereof to the plaintiff. If damage to property is concerned, the courts will also refuse restoration if the cost thereof exceeds the replacement or market value of the object which has been damaged.[9]

---

[7] For further references, see Bocken *et al.*, n. 4 above, at 850 ff.
[8] Cass. 26 June 1980 [1980–1] *Rechtskundig Weekblad* 1661; [1980] *Journal des Tribunaux* 707.
[9] Cass. 23 Oct. 1986 [1987–8] *Rechtskundig Weekblad* 54.

In the event of economic damage, the courts will try to assess as much as possible (e.g. through an examination of the accounts) the gains which were lost. However, one often finds awards *ex aequo et bono*. The courts do not hesitate to translate pain and suffering as well as the reduction in the enjoyment of certain assets into (moral) damages estimated *ex aequo et bono*. In fact, in the event of pain and suffering following personal injury or the death of relatives, unofficial scales are used by the courts. The amounts awarded remain rather low.

As far as the nature of the loss is concerned and irrespective of its cause, a large part of the damage to the environment constitutes damage to health, property, or income of a classical type and does not raise unusual problems in the application of the principles on the assessment and compensation of damage. Under certain circumstances, however, quite specific problems do arise. This is more particularly the case with the four types of environmental damage discussed hereafter: damage to individual property which presents a collective ecological or æsthetic interest; 'pure' ecological damage to the ecosystem and to parts of the environment not individually appropriated by man; the cost of measures taken by the government or private parties in order to prevent or minimize damage to the environment; and economic losses and the loss of other benefits derived from the environment. No doubt other situations also merit attention, such as the threat of health damage due to exposure to pollutants. The scope of this Chapter, however, imposes its limitations.

3.2. Damage to Individual Property which also Presents a Public Interest in View of its Ecological or Æsthetic Value

Most of the living as well as non-living environment has been appropriated by man. It has been made subject to individual rights or has become part of the public domain over which the government exercises control. Damage to these parts of the environment (my house, my garden, my crop, my cattle, public buildings, and land) can be caused by a multitude of events and may be totally unrelated to environmental concerns. The problem of assessing the damage and determining the way it is to be compensated generally is not unusual nor specific for pollution.

The situation is different where valuable natural resources and cultural monuments constitute private property which thus also have an æsthetic or ecological value exceeding the personal interest of the owner. As a precautionary measure, one can impose, generally through rules of administrative law, restrictions on the use of private properties of this type. If such properties are damaged, the question arises, however, whether or not their non-economic dimension will be taken into account. There is not much of a problem if the value to the public is reflected in the normal market value of the property. Here, the assessment and the compensation of the damages will normally be achieved by restoration at the initiative of the owner.

The situation may be different if the ecological, æsthetic, or cultural value of the property is not reflected in its market value. Several difficulties may arise here. It is possible that the owner is not interested in the restoration of his property as he may prefer to use it in a more lucrative way once its ecological value has been destroyed. Under present law, the owner is indeed not obliged to sue for restoration. Further, restoration can be refused if its cost exceeds the market value of the object which has been damaged. Finally, the assessment of the monetary compensation due for the loss or reduction in value of the natural resources becomes quite difficult if the ecological values are not reflected in the market value or, more generally, if there is no market. Belgian case law on the subject is limited and does not set out any theoretical solutions to the problem. It does, however, give a few interesting examples where a judge, confronted with the illegal destruction of three oaks a century old, estimated their value at respectively 254,702, 200,538 and 11,019 bfr.[10] Here the judge apparently made use of a formula for the determination of the value of trees which was elaborated by the administration and which took into account factors such as the species of the tree, its size and age, position and condition. Some of these problems would be solved by the Flemish draft decree on environmental policy.

Where damage to real estate also constitutes damage to environmental values, two special rules apply in order to ensure as much as possible the actual restoration of the environment (Article 9.1.7, § 2). First, contrary to what is provided for by general tort law, restoration cannot be refused merely because its cost exceeds the market value of the property. This solution was inspired by § 17(1) of the German *Umwelthaftungsgesetz*.

Next, an exception is made to the exclusive right of the owner to decide whether to sue for restoration of his property or not. Here a rather delicate balance is struck between the interests of the owner and the public interest. The draft provides that the regional government may institute a claim for the restoration of the resource, but only to the extent that the owner was under the obligation to maintain elements of the property in a certain condition, pursuant, for example, to landscape protection legislation. If the regional government does not act within a certain time, the city government of the place where the pollution took place can sue. The owner and lessee of the property have to be sued as interveners.

The draft does not, however, solve the problem of assessing the damage where a reference to a market value or to restoration costs is not possible. It recognizes as compensatable losses resulting from death or physical injury, destruction or loss of property, nuisance, economic loss, as well as the cost of preventive measures and the damage caused by these measures (Article 9.1.1). The victim is entitled to such remedies as are provided under general tort law (Article 9.1.7, § 1).

---

[10] Vred. Antw., 25 June 1987, No. 80.284, unpublished.

3.3. Ecological Damages

Damage to the ecosystem as such or to parts of the environment which have not been individually appropriated by man raises fundamental problems under Belgian tort law. This normally deals with individual interests only and does not recognize the category of pure 'ecological damage'. If pure ecological damage is recognized as compensatable, the problems are to be solved of who should be entitled to claim compensation and how the damages are to be assessed.

According to general tort law, the plaintiff, in order to have standing in a compensation claim, must show that he has potentially suffered personal damage; in order to obtain compensation, he must show that he has actually suffered damage.

The requirement of personal damage implies that no compensation will be granted to an individual citizen in the event of the impairment of natural resources to which he has no individual right or of which he makes no individual use.[11] Thus damage claims currently have little or no success in the event of damage to *res communes* such as the water of the sea, the air, the ozone layer, the climate, or to *res nullius*, such as wild animals.

The requirement of the personal character of the damages is also valid for claims by the state and other public authorities. Under current Belgian law they cannot, as a rule, act as owner or trustee of the common natural resources which do not form part of their domain.[12] However, authorities which are entrusted with the task of maintaining the quality of the water and the fish population have been compensated for the expense of restocking with new fish after a pollution incident.[13]

In recent years, different avenues were explored in order to circumvent the requirement of personal damage and to allow private actions pursuant to damage to collective environmental interests. First, for a time, associations for the defence of the environment were allowed by the courts to sue in the public interest in the event of ecological damage, not only for injunctive relief but also for damages. In practice, only nominal damages were awarded. The Court of Cassation, however, reversed this trend by its landmark decision of 19 November 1982:[14] in order to have standing, environmental associations have to establish a personal and direct interest which is being harmed. The court stated that a sufficient personal interest of an association consists of its property and its reputation. The defence of a collective interest, even if it is a collective interest set out in the by-law of the association, is insufficient to justify a damages claim

---

[11] As will be indicated later, an individualized economic loss resulting from the impairment of common natural resources can, however, be compensated. In theory, the same should go for any reduction in the individual enjoyment of such resources.

[12] With respect to wild animals and fish see Pol. Chimay, 14 Aug. 1931 [1932] *Journal des Judges de Paix* 378.   [13] Corr. Turnhout, 18 Feb. 1992, No. 498, unpublished.

[14] [1982–3] *Arresten ven het Hof van Cassatie* No. 172.

in the event of damage to this collective interest. After a lengthy debate, the legislator adopted the Act of 12 January 1993, which grants a number of environmental associations, certain public servants, and the public prosecutor the right to sue in summary proceedings for injunctive relief in the event of a violation, or the threat thereof, of environmental legislation, broadly defined. This does not in any way affect the requirement of personal damage in the context of a claim for compensation ultimately. In so far as damages claims are concerned, the legislator thus in fact approved the position of the Court of Cassation.

More recently, a number of courts again took up a nineteenth century reasoning based on Article 714 of the Civil Code, which states that there are things which belong to nobody, but which can be used by everybody (*res nullius* and *res communes*). From this Article is derived the existence of a common right to the use of the common parts of the environment. If part of this common environment is damaged, individual citizens may also invoke personal damage as they can no longer fully exercise their collective right to use the environment. Associations can be entrusted with the exercise of this right in court. Here again, the courts award only nominal damages.[15]

As there is no substantial case law with respect to the compensation of pure ecological damage, one can say that the problem of their assessment has not arisen. For practical purposes, we can refer to what has been said above on the subject in connection with damage to personal property having an ecological value.

With respect to the compensation of ecological damage, the adoption of the Flemish draft decree would constitute a major innovation. The draft recognizes ecological damage as falling within the scope of tort law. It draws a distinction (inspired by the modified draft EC directive on damage caused by waste[16]) between damage to individual interests ('damage') and harm to elements of the environment which remain unappropriated ('impairment of the environment'). If damage has been caused to individual interests, the plaintiff may institute all such claims as the general tort law allows him to do. In the event of impairment of the environment, however, the only remedy is to claim that measures of restoration of the environment are taken or to recover the cost thereof. Monetary compensation based exclusively on an assessment in money of the intrinsic value of the damaged natural resources is excluded. In this respect, the draft rejects the solutions provided by US and Italian law.[17]

The concept of measures of restoration is expressly defined in Article 9.1.1. It is not limited to measures of restoration in the narrow sense, but includes the replacement of elements of the environment which have been destroyed by equivalent elements. In order to be recoverable, the cost of the measures taken should not be unreasonable in the light of the results to be achieved for the protection of man and the environment (Article 9.1.8, § 1).

---

[15] See, e.g. Corr. Eupen, 22 Nov. 1989, (1990) *Aménagement* No. 1, 41–2, at 41; Pol. Bastogne, 6 May 1991, (1991) *Aménagement* No. 3, 173–5, at 173.
[16] 28 June 1991 [1991] OJ C192/6.   [17] Bocken *et al.*, n. 4 above, at 905.

According to the draft, the action for restoration of the impaired environment can only be brought by the Flemish government, either at its own initiative or at the request of the city government of the place where the impairment took place. If the government fails to act, the city may step in and bring the action itself (Article 9.1.8, § 2). In order to provide as far as possible a scientific basis for the action, the government or the city shall, before bringing the action, request an expert's opinion from the Institute for Nature Conservation with respect to the nature and extent of the environmental impairment, the measures which could lead to its restoration, the cost involved, and the likely developments should no measures be adopted (Article 9.1.8, § 3).

3.4. Response Costs

Measures to prevent or minimize damage taken after a pollution incident[18] may be very costly. They may be required in order to prevent or limit the emission of pollutants or their dispersal, to avoid exposure of the population to pollutants, or to clean up the polluted soil or water. In the past, Belgium has not had to deal with any major catastrophic pollution incident. Nevertheless, it is faced with considerable response costs, resulting in particular from the many accidents on the road with cars loaded with chemicals as well as the clean-up costs of soil pollution. Under Belgian law, the application of liability law to these expenses raises a number of problems.

If the measures to prevent or minimize damage are taken by the (potential) victim, the latter will normally be able to recover them, whether they are taken prior to or after the pollution incident. In fact, the victim is under a duty to take reasonable measures in order to mitigate the damage. If a party other than the victim itself and, in particular, the government, takes the measures, recovery of the cost thereof may, however, not be without difficulty. Indeed, the Court of Cassation elaborated the rule that expenses incurred while carrying out a legal duty cannot be recovered from the person who, through his fault, obliged the plaintiff to carry out his legal duty.[19]

Many government agencies being under a statutory obligation to respond to pollution or the threat thereof, the recovery of the costs involved was thus made difficult. In 1988,[20] however, the court mitigated its rule to allow recovery if the plaintiff is only under a (secondary) duty to clean up the pollution, in order to

---

[18] General prevention costs paid apart from a specific pollution incident, with the goal of, e.g. providing the authorities with the necessary personnel and equipment to fight pollution, cannot normally be compensated on the basis of liability law, among other reasons, because there is no causal relationship between such expenditure and a specific source of pollution.

[19] Cass., 28 Apr. 1978 [1978–9] *Rechtskundig Weekblad* 1695; 7 Apr. 1979 [1978–9] *Rechtskundig Weekblad* 2664.

[20] Cass., 13 May 1988 [1988–9] *Rechtskundig Weekblad* 1126; Cass., 15 Nov. 1990 [1991] *Jurisprudence des cours d'appel de Liège, Mons et Bruxelles* 867.

remediate the negligence of the party who is under the (primary) legal obligation to do so. In many cases, but not in all, a primary clean-up obligation rests on the person who spills waste or other pollutants. If, however, no such obligation is imposed by statute, recovery of the response costs will, according to the rule, not be possible, contrary to the polluter pays principle.

This problem has to a large extent been solved by a number of statutory provisions which explicitly allow recovery of response costs.[21] One of the more remarkable texts is Article 85 of the Act of 24 December 1976, which imposes strict liability for the expenses incurred by the civil protection agency and the local fire brigades where they are under a legal duty to take remedial action after pollution incidents. This provision is often applied in transportation accidents which result in the dispersal of oil or other polluting products on roads or waterways. It not only entitles but obliges the authorities to recover the expenses made. Remarkably, liability is imposed on the owner of the polluting products. This way of channelling the liability is subject to criticism. It implies that, in order to determine the person who is liable, one often will have to examine contractual relationships which are conclusive with respect to the transfer of ownership. In any event, the owner is not necessarily the polluter.[22]

When preventive or remedial action is taken, not by public authorities pursuant to a duty, but by private parties not having a property interest in the polluted part of the environment, such as an association for the protection of birds after an oil spill, the situation is less clear. The main question under tort law will be whether the reaction of the private party in taking remedial action was reasonable or not.[23] In certain cases, recovery may also be possible on the basis of *negotiorum gestio*.

The draft of the Inter-university Commission allows a broad recovery of costs for preventive measures which are defined as 'measures taken by persons other than the persons liable in order to prevent an emission, or to limit its effects, provided that the cost of these measures is not unreasonable in the light of the results to be achieved for the protection of humans and the environment' (Article 9.1.1., § 1(e)). The draft thus follows recent treaty law on the subject, except in so far as payments made by the polluter himself are not considered

---

[21] e.g. the Flemish Waste Decree of 2 July 1981 (Art. 59); the Waste Decree of the Walloon Region (Arts. 28 and 39); Art. 85 of the Act of 24 Dec. 1976, and the recent Flemish Decree of 22 Mar. 1995, on soil clean-up.

[22] See, more extensively, H. Bocken, 'Milieuwetgeving en onroerende goederen: Aansprakelijkheid voor de kosten van bodemsanering' [1992] 1 *Tijdschrift voor Privaatrecht* 1–88, at 32; H. Bocken, 'La réparation des dommages causés par la pollution: La situation en 1992' [1992] *Revue de droit civil belge* No. 4–5, 284–327, at 294.

[23] In certain cases the question is formulated in terms of standing. A recent decision of the court of Rotterdam in the *Borcea* case (District Court of Rotterdam, 15 Mar. 1991 [1991] *Tijdschrift voor Milieuaansprakelijkheid* 1, note by Van Maanen) allows a society for the protection of marine birds to recover the expenses made in cleaning birds after a marine oil spill caused by the defendant on the basis that the general interest in the protection of birds must also be seen as the plaintiffs' own interest.

compensatable damage. The draft also expressly states that damage caused by the preventive measures equally qualifies for compensation.

3.5. Economic Losses. Loss of Other Benefits from the Environment

Pollution causes serious economic losses. For example, marine oil pollution has had major impacts on fishery interests and on tourism. The impact of Chernobyl, more particularly on agriculture and open air activities, has been tremendous. In Belgium, no spectacular major accident has taken place which gave rise to substantial litigation with respect to economic losses due to pollution cases. Nevertheless, a few cases relating to river pollution provide an interesting illustration of a number of the legal issues involved.

There is no doubt that economic losses which result from the impairment by pollution of property interests of the plaintiff will be compensated. Thus the reduction of revenue from of a crop or from a beehive affected by pollution will be compensated, as well as the loss of income from the licensing of fishing rights in a polluted non-navigable river; the same will apply to the loss of income from a hotel the land of which is affected by pollution.

Compensation of damage is in Belgium not hindered by the requirement that there must have been an infringement of a legal right in order to have compensatable damage. Damage to a factual, not illegal, certain, and personal interest is sufficient. 'Pure' economic losses which result from the impairment of the environment but do not qualify as physical damage to individually held property are thus not excluded from compensation. A form of such pure economic loss which no doubt can be compensated is, for example, the cost of clean-up measures undertaken by the government. The pure economic losses may also take the form of the loss of benefits resulting from the use of a common natural resource or from its presence nearby. Here the basic difficulty in Belgian case law appears to relate to the certainty of the loss: is it reasonably certain that the plaintiff would have continued deriving the same benefits from the environment had it not been polluted?

Compensation has thus been granted where it was no longer possible to continue to 'harvest' fish or other products of the natural environment. An adjacent natural resource may attract people to the plaintiff's business; owing to pollution, however, they stay away from the area. In at least one case, the operator of a café, who lost some of his clients after the pollution of the river nearby, was compensated for loss of income.[24] On the other hand, the state was not granted compensation for the loss of taxes on fishing licences which were not issued due to the pollution of a river.[25] The rationale for the decision was that the loss was considered uncertain.

The benefits derived from the common environment which can be lost due to

---

[24] Corr. Turnhout, n. 13 above.   [25] Pol. Chimay, n. 12 above.

pollution are not limited to economic ones. The pleasure of fishermen spoiled by river pollution has been deemed compensatable.[26] The reasoning is certainly susceptible of a broader interpretation. A few cases point in this direction.[27] They recognize that, for example, the killing by poacher of animals of a protected species affects the common right to use the environment which is recognized by Article 714 of the Civil Code. Wisely enough, only nominal damages were awarded.

4. CONCLUSIONS

Belgian tort law has, in recent decades, to a large extent been adapted to environmental problems, both by case law and by legislation relating to specific environmental problems. This development has certainly not yet come to an end. At the level of the application of the concept of damage, difficulties arise which relate in the main to the requirement that the damage be of a personal character. Thus, for example, the owner of a damaged property may decide to sue for restoration in kind but can also be satisfied with monetary compensation, although the property damaged is of common ecological interest. More importantly, pure ecological damage to elements of the environment which have not been individually appropriated and are not part of the public domain, and which thus constitute common environmental resources, remain out of the reach of tort law. For the remainder, the concept of damage is traditionally broadly interpreted in Belgium and does not raise too many problems in the area of environmental liability. An injury in fact is sufficient; an infringement of a pre-existing right is not required. Moral damage is recognized. Economic losses are compensatable, provided that they present a sufficient degree of certainty. In general, restoration in nature can be called for as a remedy. Restoration costs incurred by public authorities are generally compensated on the basis of specific statutory provisions, case law having imposed restrictions on the recoverability of expenses incurred in the execution of a legal duty.

A major change in the law on environmental liability is proposed in a draft decree on environmental policy prepared by a commission of law professors on behalf of the Flemish region. The draft generalizes strict liability for damages caused by the emission of pollutants. It attaches much attention to adequate mechanisms of financial guarantees. It provides recourse to a damage fund for a number of types of damage which fall out of the reach of any liability system as the source of pollution is unidentified or the party liable is insolvent and the financial guarantees insufficient.

At the level of the concept of damage, too, major innovations are introduced. The draft makes it, under certain conditions, possible for the government to

[26] *Ibid.*   [27] See n. 15 above.

enter a claim to have polluted private property, the presevation of which is of common environmental interest, restored to its prior state, even contrary to the wish of the owner. More importantly, it brings within the reach of tort law the pure ecological damage which results from the impairment of common environmental resources and which does not constitute individual damage. The remedy in this case, however, is limited to the restoration measures or the reimbursement of the cost thereof.

The draft does not pretend to solve all problems of the application of the concept of damage in the area of environmental liability. Thus the indentification of economic damage which is compensatable is left to case law which also recognizes damage to a factual interest, such as the loss of use of part of the common environment, as compensatable damage. No doubt, the question when the economic loss presents sufficient certainty may remain difficult. If claims for economic losses due to pollution were frequent, which is not the case in Belgium, it might be preferable that the legislator would make a policy judgment on which types of economic loss connected to pollution incidents are to be borne by the polluters and which not.

Nor does the draft give any indication for the assessment in money of damages to environmental values for which no normal market exists. It does not affect the way the courts solve the problem of assessing the value of a property with a particular æsthetic or ecological value. It does, however, not expand the problem as it does not allow, in the event of pure ecological damage, a monetary damages award based solely on a theoretical valuation of common environmental resources. As indicated before, the draft aims in principle at restoration of the environment, which is the main objective. The drafters were, however, of the opinion that, for cases where restoration is not possible, the methods presently advanced for the assessment of pure ecological damage are often artificial and inappropriate for general application in tort law. Other branches of law seem to be more appropriate to solve the problem. Criminal or administrative fines do not pretend to compensate damages, yet their amount may be determined taking into account the extent of the damage caused to the environment. If the proceeds of these fines are turned over to a fund established for the benefit of the environment, the end result comes close to what can be achieved by monetary valuation of environmental values for which no market exists, without placing more strain on tort law than is already done by the use of scales in which pleasure, love, or pain is translated into money as moral damages.

9

Environmental Damages: The Emerging Law in the United States

THOMAS J. SCHOENBAUM

1. INTRODUCTION

In the United States three federal laws currently provide for the recovery of natural resources damages: the Federal Water Pollution Control Act (FWPCA) or Clean Water Act (CWA), the Comprehensive Environmental Response, Compensation, and Liability Act (CERCLA or Superfund), and the Oil Pollution Act (OPA). A claim for natural resource damages may arise whenever a release of oil or a hazardous substance has injured a natural resource. Claims for natural resource damages may be brought by designated 'trustees', various federal agencies, state governments, and Indian tribes. From the international perspective, the most important regime for recovery of natural resource damages is OPA, which is the American counterpart of the international treaty system for oil pollution damages administered by the International Maritime Organization (IMO) and the International Oil Pollution Compensation Fund (IOPC Fund).

This Chapter will discuss the salient features of the emerging oil pollution compensation regime under OPA (1990), which was promulgated in final form in January 1996. I will offer some concluding remarks on how OPA might best be harmonized with the international system.

2. THE OIL POLLUTION ACT OF 1990

The centrepiece of federal ship pollution statutes is now the Oil Pollution Act of 1990.[1] This was passed after almost fifteen years of consideration of various approaches to oil-spill liability and compensation, in the wake of the *Exxon Valdez* tanker accident off Alaska in 1989. OPA increases substantially both the

[1] 33 USC §§ 2701–2761. OPA applies to oil spills in the navigable waters of the United States as well as in the exclusive economic zone: 33 USC § 2702(a). See generally, A. J. Rodriguez and P. A. C. Jaffe, 'The Oil Pollution Act of 1990' (1990) 15 *Tulane Maritime Law Journal* 1–35; T. J. Wagner, 'The Oil Pollution Act of 1990: An Analysis' (1990) 21 *Journal of Maritime Law and Commerce* No. 4, 569–95.

regulation and pollution liabilities of entities engaged in the transportation and production of oil within the jurisdiction of the United States.

2.1. Liability

OPA makes the 'party responsible' for a vessel or a facility from which oil is discharged (or threatened to be discharged) strictly liable for removal costs and damages.[2] Responsible parties include any person owning, operating, or demise-chartering a vessel; the owner or operator of an onshore facility; the lessee or permittee (or the holder of the right of use) of the area of an offshore facility; the owner or operator of a pipeline; and the licensee of a deep water port.[3] Liability is joint and several.[4]

2.2. Defences and Exclusions of Liability

There are only three defences to the strict liability provided by the Act: if the discharge of oil was caused *solely* by (1) act of God, (2) act of war, or (3) act or omission of a third party.[5]

The term 'third party' is defined very narrowly as not including (1) an employee or agent, or (2) an independent contractor of the party responsible.[6] Thus the third-party defence will not apply where the spill is caused by a tug, towboat, or even a compulsory pilot.[7] The party responsible must also prove by a preponderance of evidence that it (1) exercised due care, and (2) took precautions against

---

[2] 33 USC § 2702(e). Responsible parties are also liable for interest to claimants beginning 30 days after a claim is presented until it is paid: 33 USC § 2705(b)(1). The amount due in interest is not subject to limitation: *ibid.* § 2705(b)(5).

[3] *Ibid.*, § 2701(32). It is interesting that cargo owners entirely escaped being subject to any liability under OPA; cargo is not a 'responsible party'. This is contrary to international practice, which makes oil cargo owners liable in part. See International Convention on the Establishment of an International Fund for Compensation for Oil Pollution Damage 1971, Preamble and Art. 10. Industry-sponsored pollution schemes, TOVALOP, and CRISTAL also provide for contribution by cargo.

[4] The conference report provides that the standard of liability is to be consistent with that under the Federal Water Pollution Control Act. H. R. Conf.Rep. No. 653 101st Cong., 2d Sess. 102 (1990). The standard for liability under the Federal Water Pollution Control Act (FWPCA) is strict, joint, and several. See, e.g. *United States* v. *M/V Big Sam*, 682, F.2d 432 (5th Cir. 1982); *Burgess* v. *M/V Tamano*, 564 F.2d 964 (1st Cir. 1977).

[5] 33 USC § 2703(a). Act of God is defined as 'unanticipated grave natural disaster or other natural phenomenon of an exceptional, inevitable, and irresistible character, the effects of which could not have been prevented or avoided by the exercise of due care and foresight'; *ibid.* § 2701(1). Act of War is not defined but probably means a spill of oil because of a hostile act by a foreign power.

[6] 33 USC § 2703(a).

[7] See *Burgess* v. *M/V Tamano*, n. 4 above; *United States* v. *LeBeouf Brothers Towing Co.*, 621 F.2d 787 (5th Cir. 1980) rehearing denied 629 F.2d 1350 (5th Cir. 1980); *United States* v. *Hollywood Marine, Inc.*, 625 F.2d 524 (5th Cir. 1980). In the latter case, certiorari was denied over the robust dissent of Justice Rehnquist, who argued that the holding is contrary to the plain language of the statute; *Hollywood Marine, Inc.* v. *United States*, 451 US 994, 101 S.Ct. 2336, 68 L.Ed.2d 855 (1981). See also *In re Oriental Republic of Uruguay*, 821 F.Supp. 928, 1993 AMC 502 (D.Del. 1992).

any acts or omissions by the third party.[8] The party responsible loses even these limited defences if it does not report the discharge or fails to co-operate with or comply with a removal order.[9]

As regards any particular claimant, the party responsible is not liable to the extent that the discharge is caused by the gross negligence or wilful misconduct of the claimant.[10] Thus OPA codifies a version of the admiralty rule of comparative fault.

OPA excludes from its liability provision three kinds of discharges: (1) those allowed by permit, (2) those from a public vessel, and (3) those from an onshore facility subject to the Trans-Alaska Pipeline Authorization Act (TAPAA).[11]

2.3. Limits to Liability

There are limits to liability that apply only to the total of liability for removal costs and damages under section 2702 of OPA and any removal costs incurred by or on behalf of the party responsible. These limits are: (1) for tank vessels the greater of (a) $1,200 per gross ton or (b) $2 million for vessels of 3,000 gross tons or less, or (3) $10 million for vessels larger than 3,000 gross tons (and these limits do *not* apply to removal costs in connection with a discharge from a vessel transporting oil from an offshore facility); (2) for other vessels the limit is the greater of $600 per gross ton or $500,000; (3) any onshore facility or deepwater port is liable up to $350 million; (4) for offshore facilities (except deepwater ports) liability is limited to $75 million in damages, but liability for removal costs is unlimited; (5) for mobile offshore drilling units liability is first allocated to the owner or operator up to the limit applicable to a tank vessel. If that limit is exceeded, liability is allocated to the lessee or permittee of the area in which it is located, up to the liability limit applicable to an offshore facility, but reduced by the amount of liability allocated to the owner or operator.[12]

These liability limits do not apply if the incident in question was caused by the responsible party's gross negligence, wilful misconduct, or a violation of an applicable federal safety, construction, or operating regulation.[13] Moreover, liability cannot be limited if the party responsible fails to report the oil spill or fails to co-operate or comply with a removal order.[14]

---

[8] 33 USC §§ 2701(1), 2703(a)(3).   [9] 33 USC § 2703(c).   [10] *Ibid.*, § 2702(b).

[11] *Ibid.*, § 2703(c). These violations are subject to other laws and regulations.

[12] *Ibid.*, § 2704(a)–(d). Every three years the President can adjust the limits of liability according to the Consumer Price Index: 33 USC § 2704(d)(4). The tonnage determination of a vessel is that listed on the vessel's certificate of registry. See *Kyoei Kaiun Kaisha, Ltd.* v. *M/V Bering Trader*, 795 F.Supp. 1046 (W. D. Wash. 1991).

[13] *Ibid.*, § 2704(c). Guidance to the standard for breaking the limitations under OPA may be gained from prior case law under the FWPCA. Compare, for example, *Tug Ocean Prince, Inc.* v. *United States*, 584 F.2d 1151 (2d Cir. 1978); and *Steuart Transportation Co.* v. *Allied Towing Corp.*, 596 F.2d 609 (4th Cir. 1979). These cases show that the standard of wilful misconduct or gross negligence requires more than mere negligence but reckless disregard for the probable consequences of a voluntary act or omission.   [14] *Ibid.*, § 2704(c)(2).

Two points are of special note in this scheme. First, parties responsible may offset their own clean-up costs against the liability limits.[15] Secondly, the limits are applicable only to OPA damages; any state law liability is not limited.

2.4. Liability of Third Parties

Where a discharge is caused solely by the act or omission of one or more third parties (other than the party responsible), the third party or parties are subject to the same liability for damages as parties responsible.[16] Although the party responsible is not liable in such a case, the party responsible is subrogated to the rights of the United States and any claimants to the extent that it paid for removal costs or damages.[17] The third party's liability is subject to the liability limits of OPA.[18]

A key question not answered by OPA is whether there is any liability under OPA for third parties who are not solely at fault, and if, in the case of concurrent fault by the responsible party and a non-sole fault third party (such as an independent contractor), the responsible party may obtain contribution or even contract indemnification. Under the usual principles of maritime tort and prior applicable law, non-sole fault third parties should be liable[19] and maritime contribution and indemnification principles should apply.[20]

2.5. Limitation of Shipowners' Liability

Under prior law the Shipowners' Limitation of Liability Act of 1851 had at least limited applicability to oil spills.[21] However, OPA broadly supersedes the Limitation of Liability Act with respect to damages and removal costs under both federal and state law, including common law.[22] Thus the Act should no longer apply to limit any action for damages or removal costs in connection with any

---

[15] This is a change from the FWPCA rule that the owner or operator of a discharging vessel cannot offset the cost of its own clean-up efforts against its liability. See *United States* v. *Dixie Carriers, Inc.*, 736 F.2d 180, 1985 AMC 815 (5th Cir. 1984); *Steuart Transportation Co.* v. *Allied Towing Corp.*, n. 13 above.   [16] 33 USC § 2702(d)(1)(A).

[17] *Ibid.*, § 2702(d)(1)(B).   [18] *Ibid.*, § 2702(d)(2).

[19] See *United States* v. *Bear Marine Services*, 696 F.2d 1117 (5th Cir. 1983).

[20] 33 USC § 2709. Moreover, indemnification and hold harmless (indemnity) agreements are freely permitted under OPA, although a party responsible cannot avoid or transfer liability: *ibid.*, § 2701. Thus the party responsible will always bear first-level liability, but will be able to recover against third parties either through contribution according to principles of comparative fault or by invoking a hold harmless or indemnification agreement, if applicable.

[21] See *In re Hokkaido Fisheries Co., Ltd.*, 506 F.Supp. 631 (D.Alaska 1981); *United States* v. *CF Industries, Inc.*, 542 F.Supp. 952 (D.Minn. 1982). However, the Limitation Act did apply to limit liability at least under state law. See *Complaint of Harbor Towing Corp.*, 335 F.Supp. 1150 (D.Md. 1971); *Portland Pipe Line Corp.* v. *Environmental Improvement Commission*, 307 A.2d 1, 45, 1973 AMC 1341 (D.Me. 1973), appeal dismissed for want of a federal question 414 US 1035, 94 S.Ct. 532, 38 L.Ed.2d 326 (1973).   [22] 33 USC §§ 2702(a), 2718.

pollution incident.[23] Presumably, the Limitation Act would still apply, however, to a non-pollution claim, such as a claim for lost cargo against the carrier.[24]

2.6. Removal Costs

Each party responsible is liable for removal costs incurred by the United States, a state, or an Indian tribe, whether incurred under the Federal Water Pollution Control Act (FWPCA), the Intervention on the High Seas Act, or under state law.[25] There is also liability for removal costs incurred by *any person* undertaking clean-up consistent with the National Contingency Plan.[26] Removal costs are defined broadly as including the 'costs of removal . . . or . . . the costs to prevent, minimize, or mitigate oil pollution'.[27]

2.7. Damages

There are six categories of recoverable damages under OPA:[28]

(A) *Natural resources*: Damages for injury to, destruction of, loss of, or loss of use of, natural resources, including the reasonable costs of assessing the damage, which shall be recoverable by a United States trustee, a state trustee, an Indian tribe trustee, or a foreign trustee.

(B) *Real or personal property*: Damages for injury to, or economic losses resulting from destruction of, real or personal property, which shall be recoverable by a claimant who owns or leases that property.

(C) *Subsistence use*: Damages for loss of subsistence use of natural resources, which shall be recoverable by any claimant who so uses natural resources which have been injured, destroyed, or lost, without regard to the ownership or management of the resources.

(D) *Revenues*: Damages equal to the net loss of taxes, royalties, rents, fees, or net profit shares due to the injury, destruction, or loss of real property, personal property, or natural resources, which shall be recoverable by the Government of the United States, a state, or a political subdivision thereof.

(E) *Profits and earning capacity*: Damages equal to the loss of profits or impairment of earning capacity due to the injury, destruction, or loss of real property, personal property, or natural resources, which shall be recoverable by any claimant.

(F) *Public services*: Damages for net costs of providing increased or additional public services during or after removal activities, including protection from fire, safety, or health hazards, caused by a discharge of oil, which shall be recoverable by a state, or a political subdivision of a state.

---

[23] Although the OPA applies only to oil pollution, CERCLA also excludes limitation of liability for spills of hazardous substances: see 42 USC § 9607(h). TAPAA also excludes limitation of liability under either federal or state law. See *In re Glacier Bay*, 944 F.2d 577, 1992 AMC 448 (9th Cir. 1991).   [24] See, e.g. *Steuart Transp. Co.* v. *Allied Towing Co.*, n. 13 above.
[25] 33 USC § 2702(b)(1)(A).   [26] *Ibid.*, § 2702(b)(1)(B)   [27] *Ibid.*, § 2701(31).
[28] *Ibid.*, § 2702(b)(2). For a case calculating damages under French law, see *In the Matter of Oil Spill by the Amoco Cadiz*, 954 F.2d 1279, 1992 AMC 913 (7th Cir. 1992).

2.8. Damages to Natural Resources

Under OPA natural resources damages are recoverable by trustees of the United
States, state trustees, Indian tribe trustees, or by foreign trustees.[29]

The precise measurement of damages for purpose of liability for loss or destruction of natural resources is somewhat uncertain. The only reported case on this
matter, *Commonwealth of Puerto Rico* v. *The S. S. Zoe Colocotroni*,[30] rejected a
measure based upon diminution of the market value of the damaged area and
held that the applicable measure is: 'the cost reasonably to be incurred by the
sovereign or its designated agency to restore or rehabilitate the environment in
the affected area to its preexisting condition, or as close thereto as is feasible
without grossly disproportionate expenditures.'[31] The court rejected as grossly
disproportionate a measure of damages based on the replacement of damaged
trees and oil-contaminated sediments, approving instead a standard based upon
what it would cost to purchase the biota destroyed. The court's measure of
damages, then, appears to be based upon man-aided rehabilitation of the affected
area within a finite period of time, considering the restorative powers of the
natural environment as well as economic factors. The court limited its holding
to circumstances where the sovereign has an ownership interest in the area
where the environmental damage occurred, and remarked that in other factually
different cases other remedies might be appropriate.[32]

The natural resources damage provisions of OPA were very carefully crafted
because Congress was in large measure reacting to the devastation of Alaska's
Prince William Sound as a result of the *Exxon Valdez* oil spill. Under OPA:

'natural resources' includes land, fish, wildlife, biota, air, water, ground water, drinking
water supplies, and other such resources belonging to, managed by, held in trust by,
appertaining to, or otherwise controlled by the United States (including the resources of
the exclusive economic zone), any State or local government or Indian tribe, or any
foreign government.[33]

The measure of damages provided in section 2706[34] for natural resources damages is as follows:

Measure of damages
(1) In general
The measure of natural resource damage under Section 2702(b)(2)(A) of this title is:
   (A) the cost of restoring, rehabilitating, replacing, or acquiring the equivalent of, the
   damaged natural resources;
   (B) the diminution in value of those natural resources pending restoration; plus
   (C) the reasonable cost of assessing those damages.

---

[29] 33 USC §§ 2702(b)(2)(A). 2706(a).   [30] 628 F.2d 652 (1st Cir. 1980).
[31] *Ibid.* 675.   [32] *Ibid.* 676–8.   [33] 33 USC § 2701(20).   [34] *Ibid.*, § 2706(d).

(2) Determine costs with respect to plans
Costs shall be determined under paragraph (1) with respect to plans adopted under subsection (c) of this section.

(3) No double recovery
There shall be no double recovery under this chapter for natural resource damages, including with respect to the costs of damage assessment or restoration, rehabilitation, replacement, or acquisition for the same incident and natural resource.

To supplement this three-part test for natural resources damages, OPA provides for the promulgation of natural resource damage assessment regulations by the President through the Department of Commerce.[35] If the various natural resource trustees follow these regulations, their assessment will be given a rebuttable presumption 'in any administrative or judicial proceeding'.[36]

This is not the first time the federal government has been charged with formulating natural resources damage regulations. The Department of the Interior (DOI) issued such regulations under section 301(c) of CERCLA in 1988, but these were invalidated in part on judicial review in *State of Ohio* v. *US Department of the Interior*[37] on the ground that certain aspects of the rules favoured limiting recovery to lost use values, including market value, instead of implementing the CERCLA mandate to restore or replace natural resources.

OPA and CERCLA (as well as other statutes that provide for recovery of natural resources damages) have identical aims, and the respective implementing regulations should take a common approach.[38]

2.8.1. Restoration Costs

The restoration branch of the test for natural resource damage measurement is essentially a codification of the *Zoe Colocotroni* court's rule quoted above: 'the cost reasonably to be incurred . . . to restore or rehabilitate the environment . . . to its pre-existing condition . . . without grossly disproportionate expenditures'.[39] The court also enumerated the factors that should be considered in evaluating a reasonable restoration remedy: technical feasibility, harmful side effects,

---

[35] *Ibid.*, § 2706(e).   [36] *Ibid.*, § 2706(e)(2).

[37] 880 F.2d 432 (D.C. Cir. 1989), rehearing denied 897 F.2d 1151 (C.A.D.C. 1989). See also the companion case, *State of Colorado* v. *US Department of the Interior*, 880 F.2d 481 (D.C. Cir. 1989).

[38] There is a great body of theoretical work on natural resource damage valuation and the measure of damages for destruction of natural resources. See, e.g. F. B. Cross, 'Natural Resource Damage Valuation' (1989) 42 *Vanderbilt Law Review* 269–315; F. Halter and J. T. Thomas, 'Recovery of Damages by States for Fish and Wildlife Losses Caused by Pollution' (1982) 10 *Ecology Law Quarterly* 5–47; F. R. Anderson, 'Natural Resource Damages, Superfund, and the Courts' (1989) 16 *Environmental Affairs* 405–81; David A. McKay, 'CERCLA's Natural Resource Damage Provisions: A Comprehensive and Innovative Approach to Protecting the Environment' (1988) 45 *Washington and Lee Law Review* 1417–59: 'Damages from Oil Spills: A Comparison of the Ohio Decision and the Oil Pollution Act' (1992) 22 *Environmental Law Reporter* 10263–71; C. Cartwright, 'Natural Resource Damage Assessment: The Exxon Valdez Oil Spill and Its Implications' (1991) 17 *Rutgers Computer & Technology Law Journal* 451–92; J. L. Nicoll, Jr., 'Marine Pollution and Natural Resource Damages' (1993) 5 *University of San Francisco Maritime Law Journal* 323–58.

[39] 628 F.2d at 675.

compatibility with or duplication of such regeneration as is naturally to be expected, and the extent to which the effort could become either redundant or disproportionately expensive. If restoration of the affected area is not feasible or is disproportionately expensive, an alternative remedy might be the acquisition of comparable lands located elsewhere.

There are two important lessons in the *Zoe Colocotroni* case. First, in the choice of a restoration plan there will always be tension between, on the one hand, human intervention actively to restore the resources, and, on the other hand, leaving the affected area alone so that natural processes can restore the environment with minimal human involvement. Thus the pace as well as the extent of human intervention will always be of paramount importance. Secondly, the court's 'grossly disproportionate expenditure' test is relevant. It is not inconsistent to reject a market or commercial-value test for restoration, but nevertheless require that restoration must be feasible without grossly disproportionate expenditure.

2.8.2. Diminution of Value of Natural Resources Pending Restoration

The most difficult aspect of the measurement of natural resources damages is how to measure the diminution of value pending restoration. In the *State of Ohio* case, the court addressed this issue by suggesting that the Department of the Interior must not limit its calculation of lost-use values by market pricing. The court stated that 'DOI should consider a rule that would permit the trustees to derive use values for natural resources by summing up all reliably calculated use values, however measured, so long as the trustee does not double count'. The court also stated that the Department should not limit its consideration to consumptive use values, but should consider 'non-consumptive values' such as 'option' and 'existence' values. Economists have developed several different techniques for calculating 'use values' and 'non-consumptive values' of natural resources: (1) behavioural use valuation,[40]

---

[40] The incompleteness of market valuation techniques to measure loss of use of natural resources has given rise to several alternative methods that attempt to employ behavioural use valuation as a market surrogate for unpriced natural resources.

Perhaps the most important of these measurement methodologies is travel cost valuation (TCV). TCV is based upon the assumption that the value of a site to visitors is reflected in the expense they incur to visit the site. Thus, TCV produces a monetized worth for natural resources equal to a composite of the average visitor's expenses of travelling, entrance fees, and opportunity costs of time lost. A variant of travel cost valuation is unit day cost, the calculation of average per-day values for resource uses.

There are obvious problems with travel costs as an accurate tool of valuation. The travel cost model tests the value of a site as a whole and does not measure the impact of relatively slight or geographically small changes in the availability of natural resources. Visitors may lack information or have a misconception about a particular site, which will distort the resulting data. It is also very difficult and ultimately ambiguous to attempt to measure lost opportunity costs, which depend on each individual's wage rate as well as his/her ability and inclination to work during travel time. There is also an unsettled controversy over whether individual data on travel cost are better than zonal aggregation of travel costs.

(2) hedonic valuation,[41] and (3) contingent valuation.[42] All are highly controversial.

2.8.3. Damage Assessment Costs

The third branch of the OPA natural resources recovery measure of damages is damage assessment costs. Such costs are those associated with the work of the various trustees who have the two-fold task of (1) assessing natural resources damages and (2) fashioning a plan for resource restoration and rehabilitation.[43] OPA requires that the expenditures of the trustees in this regard must be 'reasonable'.[44]

2.8.4. Use of Recovered Sums

Funds recovered as natural resource damages must be used to pay for restoration work and to pay costs related to the damaged resources.[45]

2.8.5. Pure Economic Loss Damages

The majority rule in most federal circuits has been that there is no recovery for pure economic loss damages.[46] In the pollution damage cases, the rule has also

---

[41] Hedonic valuation (HV) is also used as a market surrogate to measure use values. HV attempts to measure environmental amenities by comparing property value in polluted areas with similar unspoiled environments. Hedonic valuation, however, is unreliable in oil-spill cases. The environmental value of a site is difficult to isolate in comparison studies because of the innumerable other variables that affect property values. HV methodology is also based upon questionable assumptions such as the idea that households continually re-evaluate their location decisions, that decisions are based upon current environmental quality, and that a family can easily move its entire household in response to nearby natural resource damage.

Of the variety of methods used to measure loss of use, all have imperfections and none is totally useful. However, TCV will usually be superior to HV in most cases. In future rulemaking, however, National Oceanic and Atmospheric Administration (NOAA) should set out relatively conservative criteria for TCV to preclude unreliable assumptions and models. Furthermore, TCV should always be checked against market value measures to determine its relationship and accuracy. Finally, the rules should emphasize that TCV, for the purpose of measuring lost use value, is only an interim technique to supplement restoration/replacement value during the period after the spill and before restoration. Moreover, since restoration efforts in most cases will gradually remedy the natural resource damage from its nadir within a short time after the spill, TCV should be adjusted for the improvement factor, and should be phased out entirely when restoration is complete.

[42] In *State of Ohio*, the court stated that the Department of the Interior had misconstrued CERCLA by arbitrarily limiting the consideration of non-use or non-consumptive values such as 'existence' and 'option' values: n. 37 above, at 464. The court upheld Interior's reliance on Contingent Valuation Methodology (CVM) to measure use value in some cases as well as resort to CVM in those rare cases where it would be necessary to determine 'option' or 'existence' values: *ibid*. 475–6.

It is important to note, however, that the court did not mandate the use of CVM to measure either use or non-use values, and the court further upheld the right of Interior 'to rank methodologies according to its views on their reliability': *ibid*. 464.

CVM employs surveys to ask a wide variety of people how much they would pay for a resource in a hypothetical market. Accordingly, CVM is entirely hypothetical, and it is based upon the assumption that people respond to a survey as they would a market-place transaction. Furthermore, the accuracy of CVM cannot be tested because natural resources have no established true value against which CVM may be measured. CVM regulations have been proposed by the National Oceanic and Atmospheric Administration, see 59 Fed.Reg. 1062 (7 Jan. 1994).   [43] 33 USC § 2706(c).

[44] *Ibid*., § 2706(d)(1)(c).   [45] *Ibid*., § 2706(f).

[46] This is the rule of *Robins Dry Dock & Repair Co.* v. *Flint*, 275 US 303, 48 S.Ct. 134, 72 L.Ed. 290 (1927). For applications of the rule in the pollution context, see *Complaint of Ballard Shipping Co.*,

been applied,[47] although an exception has been made for commercial fishermen.[48] OPA, however, is generally interpreted to allow the recovery of pure economic loss damages,[49] although neither the courts nor responsible federal agencies have adopted any guidelines on how broad this recovery should reach.

2.8.6. Penalties and Criminal Liability

OPA increases the penalties that may be assessed against a party responsible. The mandatory civil penalty is $25,000 for each day of offence or up to $1,000 per barrel of oil discharged. In the event of gross negligence, the penalty must be not less than $100,000 and up to $3,000 per barrel of oil discharged.[50] Criminal liability may be imposed under OPA even for negligent discharges of oil.[51]

3. ANALYSIS OF THE DEPARTMENT OF COMMERCE'S FINAL RULE ON NATURAL RESOURCES DAMAGES

The damage assessment procedure under the final rule promulgated by the Department of Commerce[52] consists of three phases: the pre-assessment phase, the restoration planning phase, and the restoration implementation phase. The pre-spill planning device is an additional component of the assessment procedure. Each of the three phases of the assessment process and the pre-spill planning component address unique issues of the injury determination and quantification process.

Throughout the rule, a theme of flexibility is stressed. It encourages trustees to perform those procedures that will produce more accurate results, but it does not *require* them to perform any of the procedures or follow any of the 'suggestions' offered by the rule. In order to receive a rebuttable presumption on review, however, the procedure the trustee selects or creates must be 'encompassed' by the rule. The National Oceanic and Atmospheric Administration (NOAA) fails to

---

810 F.Supp. 359, 1993 AMC 1413 (DRI 1993); *Sekco Energy, Inc.* v. *M/V Margaret Chouest*, 820 F.Supp. 1008, 1994 AMC 1515 (E.D.La. 1993); and *In re Oriental Republic of Uruguay*, n. 7 above.

[47] *State of Louisiana ex rel. Guste* v. *M/V Testbank*, 752 F.2d 1019, 1985 AMC 1521 (5th Cir. 1985) (*en banc*); *Barber Lines A/S* v. *M/V Donau Maru*, 764 F.2d 50, 1985 AMC 2600 (1st Cir. 1985). But see *Kinsman Transit Co.* v. *City of Buffalo*, 388 F.2d 821, 1968 AMC 293 (2d Cir. 1968) which holds that foreseeable damages are recoverable whether or not there was physical damage to a claimant's proprietary interest. See also *Pruitt* v. *Allied Chemical Corp.*, 523 F.Supp. 975 (E.D.Va. 1981) which allowed pure economic loss damages to certain claimant's under state law.

[48] *Union Oil Co.* v. *Oppen*, 501 F.2d 558, 1975 AMC 416 (9th Cir. 1974); *State of Louisiana ex rel. Guste* v. *M/V Testbank*, 524 F.Supp. 1170, 1982 AMC 2246 (E.D. La. 1981), affirmed on other grounds, 728 F.2d 748, 1984 AMC 2951 (5th Cir. 1984), affirmed *en banc* 752 F.2d 1019, 1985 AMC 1521 (5th Cir. 1985).

[49] *Ballard Shipping Co.* v. *Beach Shellfish*, 32 F.3d 623 (1st Cir. 1994).

[50] 33 USC § 1321(b)(7)(D).

[51] 33 USC § 1319(c). See S. Raucher, 'Racing Mistakes for Environmental Polluters: The Exxon Valdez Criminal Prosecution' (1992) 19 *Ecology Law Quarterly* 147.

[52] 61 Fed. Reg 439 (to be codified at 15 C.F.R. pt. 990) (5 Jan. 1996).

define this standard, and thus it appears that the rule gives the trustees extremely wide latitude.

3.1. Pre-spill Planning

Trustees use pre-spill planning to determine the pre-spill condition of a natural resource. Pre-spill planning may include a determination of baseline scientific information and plans for future data collection, and the determination of a particular damage assessment approach to be used in a future assessment. Through pre-spill planning, trustees, potential parties responsible, response agencies, and the public can co-ordinate plans for future damage assessments. These plans may be co-ordinated on a state, local, or regional basis.

Although NOAA encourages trustees to use pre-spill planning, it does not require it, and the absence of pre-spill planning will not detract from the rebuttable presumption of accuracy on review.

The development of regional restoration plans is one facet of pre-spill planning encouraged under the rule. Regional restoration plans evaluate a natural resource relative to its importance and significance to the regional resource base. This type of planning is intended to facilitate more ecologically accurate restoration of damaged resources. Trustees may develop new regional restoration plans or, as urged under the rule, existing restoration plans, such as Coastal Zone Management Plans or the National Estuary Program Plans, may be modified and adopted.

The use of pre-spill planning will help to fulfil the goals of the assessment procedures by co-ordinating and encouraging public and responsible party involvement, by simplifying the damage assessment process for the trustees, and by producing more accurate damage assessments. Despite the usefulness of pre-spill planning, its appropriateness as a damage assessment provision is questionable.

Pre-spill planning is wasteful in two respects. First, the results of pre-spill planning may be useless to trustees when they face an actual discharge with very incident-specific idiosyncrasies. Pre-spill planning, because of its general untargeted nature, would not in all cases be useful to trustees in assessing actual discharges. Although the rule provides that trustees can tailor the results to a specific discharge, the act of tailoring could be just as burdensome on trustees as performing the assessment without pre-spill planning. In order to tailor the results of planning to a specific spill, trustees will be forced to return to the field and collect data on every aspect of the spill, perform experiments and analysis, and countless other tasks, presumably alleviated by pre-spill planning. Because pre-spill planning does little to anticipate specific discharges, millions of dollars may be spent on studies and planning procedures targeting habitats that a discharge never affects. As comments to the proposed rule have suggested, this money might be better spent on other environmental purposes.

Secondly, pre-spill planning is wasteful because it utilizes public funds to facilitate an assessment and restoration process that should be financed by actual

responsible parties. Not only is pre-spill planning not funded by parties responsible; if effective, it works actually to lower damages owed by parties responsible. This result seems unfair and inconsistent with the polluter pays principle.

3.2. Pre-assessment Phase

Pre-assessment is the first phase of the damage assessment process. It is composed of a pre-assessment determination and a damage assessment determination. The pre-assessment determination is a decision by the trustees concerning
whether or not to initiate the pre-assessment phase. The damage assessment
determination is the trustees' choice of which damage assessment procedure, if
any, to use in their assessment.

3.2.1. Determination of Jurisdiction

In the pre-assessment determination the trustees must first decide whether or
not to continue with the pre-assessment phase, i.e. whether conducting the pre-
assessment phase is justified. The trustees base this decision on readily available
information on the nature of the discharge and the environmental setting. Using
this information the trustees should consider whether:

(1) An incident has occurred . . .
(2) The incident is not:
    (i)   Permitted under a permit issued under federal, state, or local law; or
    (ii) From a public vessel; or
    (iii) From an offshore facility subject to the Trans-Alaska Pipeline Authority Act . . . ;
          and
(3) Natural resources . . . may have been, or may be, injured as a result of the incident.[53]

If these conditions are satisfied, the trustees may then proceed with the pre-
assessment phase and commence the next determination, the damage assessment
determination.

3.2.2. Determination to Conduct Restoration

After going through this quite open-ended process, the trustees must make additional findings in order to pursue restoration: whether injuries have or are likely
to occur; whether response actions are inadequate to address them; and whether
feasible primary and compensatory restoration actions are possible.

   If these criteria are met, the trustees may issue a Notice of Intent to Conduct
Restoration Planning.

3.3. Restoration Planning

Restoration planning is the second phase of the damage assessment process. The
restoration planning phase is the heart of the natural resource damage process.

---

[53] 61 Fed. Reg. 505, § 990.41.

The purpose of this phase is twofold: the determination and quantification of the injury to natural resources; and the selection of a restoration plan.

Injury evaluation is divided into two proceedings: (1) injury determination and (2) injury quantification. 'Injury' is defined quite vaguely as an observable or measurable adverse change in a natural resource on the improvement of a service. The injury determination process consists of analysing the *exposure* of the resource to the discharged oil and whether a *pathway* exists from the discharge to the resource, establishing a causal link between the incident and the injury.

Once the existence of injury is determined, the trustees proceed to *quantify* the injury. Injury quantification consists of comparing the degree of injury to the baseline condition of the resource. Its purpose is to clarify the needed scale and design of future restoration actions. To quantify the injury the trustees are free to use a variety of conceptual bases, including the physical extent of damages or services lost. The trustees must also consider the time necessary for natural recovery of the resources.

This part of the regulations seems most inadequate. Not only are the trustees given very speculative bases for quantifying injury, the cost of restoration is not relevant in the injury quantification process. It would be better to put off quantifying the injury until the restoration selection process.

After determining and quantifying injury, the trustees must develop a plan to restore the injured natural resource. Before selecting their preferred restoration plan, the trustees must develop and consider a range of possible alternatives, including natural (no action) restoration. Each alternative must provide for two different restoration requirements: (1) a *primary restoration* action, which consists of a plan to return the damaged area to its baseline physical, chemical and biological condition; and (2) *compensatory* restoration, which is a monetary damage assessment that represents the interim resource loss between the time of damage to the time of full recovery.

In selecting between the alternatives the trustees must employ a process referred to in the regulations as *scaling*, which ensures that the restoration action appropriately addresses the injury resulting from the discharge. Scaling appears to be 'bureaucracy-speak' for determining the appropriate extent of a restoration action.

The scaling process, which is employed both for primary and compensatory restoration, is an analysis of the injury on the basis of resources and/or services lost. This appears to be another exercise in attempting to quantify the damage caused by the incident; in this respect scaling is a duplication of the injury quantification process.

If the trustees determine that neither the resource nor service approaches to scaling are appropriate, they may use what is termed a *valuation* approach. In this proceeding natural resources must explicitly be valued in monetary terms. Both use and non-use values can be considered. For the latter a wide variety of speculative techniques are allowable, including contingent evaluation, hedonic price models, and models of market supply and demand.

Once the trustees have developed a range of restoration alternatives, they must select a restoration plan after public review and comment. The trustees must prepare and circulate both a Draft Restoration Plan and a Final Restoration Plan for public comment before making their selection. The criteria for selecting a Final Restoration Plan are very broad. They include:

(1) The cost of carrying out the alternative;
(2) The extent to which each alternative is expected to meet the trustees' goals and objectives in returning the injured natural resources and services to baseline and/or compensating for interim losses;
(3) The likelihood of success of each alternative;
(4) The extent to which each alternative will prevent future injury as a result of the incident, and avoid collateral injury as a result of implementing the alternative;
(5) The extent to which each alternative benefits more than one natural resource and/or service; and
(6) The effect of each alternative on public health and safety.

3.4. Restoration Implementation Phase

Upon completion of the restoration planning phase, the trustees must implement the decisions concerning restoration. These tasks include (1) closing the administrative record; (2) presenting a demand for implementation and/or the payment of damages by the responsible parties; (3) monitoring and supervising restoration actions; and (4) determining that final restoration has been achieved.

The trustees can enforce their determinations by bringing a civil suit or by seeking an appropriation from the Oil Spill Liability Trust Fund.

4. CONCLUSION

The Final Rule for Natural Resource Damage Assessments issued by the Department of Commerce is a good-faith effort to simplify the process and to focus on environmental restoration of damaged resources. Nevertheless, there are reasons to doubt whether the rule will be effective.

First, although the process is streamlined, it is open-ended and vague, with virtually unlimited discretion in the hands of the trustees. Because of the enormous number of discretionary decisions, the process will move very slowly, and there will be ample opportunity to challenge the trustees' decisions.

Secondly, although the regulation attempts to focus on restoration, there is ample authority allowing the trustees to levy virtually unlimited monetary damages to compensate for 'non-use' values using questionable methodologies. Again, the extent these methods are used is a case-by-case judgement by the trustees.

Thirdly, the Department of Commerce's Final Rule concerns only spills of oil;

hazardous substance spills are subject to a different regime under the Comprehensive Environmental Response, Compensation, and Liability Act (CERCLA). The natural resource damage assessment regulations promulgated under CERCLA,[54] which are quite different in many ways, are under the authority of the United States Department of the Interior. There is an obvious need to co-ordinate and harmonize the two sets of regulations.

Another concern is the fact that the emerging American regime for liability and recovery of damages for an oil spill incident is quite different from international standards. Despite the fact that the United States rejected ratification of the 1969 Convention on Civil Liability for Oil Pollution Damage (CLC) and the complementary 1971 Convention on the Establishment of an International Fund for Compensation for Oil Pollution Damage (Fund Convention), every effort should be made to harmonize American and international practice when possible. It would be particularly unfortunate if the divergence between international and American practice extended to the recovery and measurement of natural resource damages.

It would be useful if both the American and international liability systems would agree on common standards for the restoration of natural resources that are damaged by oil spills. Spurred on by an emerging consensus under national laws in France, Italy, and Germany in favour of restoration damages for injury to natural resources, the international liability regime is moving rapidly towards accepting restoration as a central concept in oil spill liability. Protocols to the CLC and Fund Convention adopted in 1992 expand the definition of pollution damage to include compensation 'for the impairment of the environment limited to the costs of reasonable measures of reinstatement actually undertaken or to be undertaken'. These protocols entered into force on 30 May 1996. The Comité Maritime International (CMI) has adopted 'draft guidelines' for assessing claims for 'reinstatement' of natural resources.

Although the gap between American practice and the international regime remains great, now is the time for both US officials and those responsible for the IOPC Fund to make every effort to harmonize both procedures and the substantive provision dealing with restoration of the environment. Both are now in the process of formulating natural resource damage policies; after final rules are promulgated, it will be largely too late.

Restoration is the key concept upon which agreement should be sought. Common criteria that reject extreme views on both sides—that only exact replication is acceptable, on the one hand, and pure natural forces restoration on the other.

Restoration should be based upon ecological principles that emphasize the continuing biological functioning of the resource. NOAA has set out five standards for evaluating restoration:[55]

---

[54] Codified at 43 CFR Part 11.

[55] Hearing on Oil Spill Response Technology before the Subcommittee on Oceanography, Great Lakes and the Outer Continental Shelf of the House Comm. on Merchant Marine and Fisheries, 102d Cong., 1st Sess. 126 (18 June 1991) (Statement of David Kennedy).

There are five generic criteria that restoration efforts must demonstrate to be considered complete in providing the holistic services that occurred prior to the impact: (1) sustainability: being capable of perpetuating itself and resilient to natural disturbances; (2) invisibility: demonstrated ability to resist invasion by new species; (3) productivity: demonstrated ability to support plant and animal populations at similar levels of productivity to predisturbance conditions; (4) nutrient retention and transformation: demonstrated nutrient processing and cycling to support microbial, plant and animal communities; and (5) biotic interactions: being capable of providing food chain support and maintaining local gene pools. A long-term monitoring process or assessment program is required to ensure the establishment and continuation of the resorted structure and functional value and, more importantly, to evaluate the need for mid-course corrections in restoration methodologies.

Although restoration is a case-by-case endeavour, these principles go far in establishing criteria that can be accepted both by the United States and the international community.

PART IV

*Problems involved in the Practical Application
of New Approaches—the US Example*

10

The Role of Government Trustees in Recovering Compensation for Injury to Natural Resources

WILLIAM D. BRIGHTON AND DAVID F. ASKMAN*

1. INTRODUCTION

Any nation's natural resources are vital to its wealth, well-being, and identity. While some resources, such as land and minerals, can be purely private property, many important natural resources cross legal boundaries and are not 'owned' by anyone. These include wildlife, birds, and fish, as well as most rivers and costal waters. Such 'common' resources are of enormous value not only to identifiable groups of users—fishermen, hunters, bird-watchers, hikers, swimmers, and shippers—but also to the general public through the consumption of natural products, through economic growth fuelled by outdoor recreation and tourism, and through local, regional, or even national pride in specific resources (like bald eagles or the Maryland blue crab) or natural areas (like Yellowstone, the Grand Canyon, or Glacier Bay).

Protecting common natural resources from pollution has traditionally depended on government regulation or public nuisance actions. These remedies may compel a polluter to stop the harmful activity, but they generally do not require restoration of the quality of injured resources or compensation for direct and indirect losses resulting from the injury. While many jurisdictions allow private claims for lost profits and other personal economic losses when pollution has damaged the claimant's own property or health, for most of this nation's history the fact that an oil spill killed thousands of seabirds or that acid drainage from mining wastes cleansed twenty river miles of fish did not give anyone a right to compensation, because no one owned the birds or the fish.[1]

Over the last twenty years, a series of United States laws has dramatically expanded the authority of both federal and state governments to respond to oil spills and releases of hazardous materials. These laws—most importantly, the Comprehensive Environmental Response, Compensation, and Liability Act of 1980

* The views expressed in this Ch. are those of the authors alone, and do not represent positions of the US Government.

[1] See e.g. *In re Steuart Transportation Co.*, 495 F.Supp. 38, 40 (E.D. Va. 1980) ('no individual citizen could seek recovery' for waterfowl killed by an oil spill).

(CERCLA or Superfund) and the Oil Pollution Act of 1990 (OPA)[2]—provide broad authority to clean up oil or hazardous substance releases and to recover clean-up costs from those responsible for the pollution. In addition, recognizing that oil and hazardous substances can harm natural resources in ways that persist long after clean-up, these laws authorize federal and state government officials, acting as trustees on behalf of the public, to recover damages for injury, destruction, or loss of natural resources resulting from the hazardous substance or oil pollution.

These natural resource damage laws share three crucial features: first, the government is empowered to recover damages not as a proprietor of resources, but as a trustee of the public's interest in the injured natural resources.[3] Secondly, as a corollary to the trusteeship principle, all damages recovered from polluters must be used *only* to restore, replace, rehabilitate, or acquire the equivalent of injured resources.[4] Thirdly, the parties who caused or contributed to the pollution are strictly liable for full compensation to the public: the costs of restoring or replacing the injured resources, *plus* the value of the public's loss between the time the injury began and the time restoration or natural recovery is complete.[5]

The underlying theory is plainly that the nation's natural resources are not the 'property' of the government nor the chattels of those who are permitted to use them at the moment, but are a common heritage of all citizens, both now and for future generations. Thus, the federal and state governments must act on the entire public's behalf to rebuild the natural resources 'trust' when pollution erodes it. As discussed below, the theory that natural resources are impressed with a public trust has roots going back at least as far as the Roman Empire. Its application in practice, however, has been at best sporadic, and it has most often been ignored. Incorporating the public trust theory into CERCLA, OPA, and similar laws is thus a dramatic development, one that makes it impossible to ignore the question of what type of trusteeship this is. In other words, what duties do government trustees owe the public, what rights does the public have against arbitrary or inadequate action by its trustees?

---

[2] CERCLA is codified at 42 USC § 9601 ff.; 33 USC § 2701 ff. Other laws in this series include that Trans-Alaska Pipeline Authorization Act of 1973, 43 USC §§ 1651–1655; the Deepwater Port Act of 1974, 33 USC §§ 1501–1524; the Federal Water Pollution Control Act, 33 USC § 1251 ff.; the Outer Continental Shelf Lands Act, 43 USC § 1813; Title III of the Marine Protection, Research, and Sanctuaries Act, 16 USC § 1402 ff. (as amended 1978); and the National Forest System Protection Act, 16 USC § 19jj. This Ch. focuses primarily on CERCLA and OPA, and to a lesser extent on the Federal Water Pollution Control Act, because they are the laws of broadest application.

[3] See 42 USC § 9607(f)(2)(A)–(B) (the President and the Governor of each state shall designate federal and state officials to 'act on behalf of the public as trustees for natural resources'); 33 USC § 2706(a)(2)–(3) (federal and state trustees act on the public's behalf under OPA).

[4] See 42 USC § 9607(f)(1); 33 USC § 2706(f).

[5] See generally F. Anderson, 'Natural Resources Damages, Superfund, and the Courts' (1989) 16 *Boston College Environmental Affairs Law Review* 405–67, at 408–9 (discussing inadequacy of compensation under early CERCLA regulation, which measured damages by the lesser of restoration costs or lost use values).

This Chapter examines the powers and duties of federal and state governments as natural resource trustees under US law. Section 2 reviews the common law roots of the public trust doctrine. Section 3 describes the major US laws that allow natural resource damage claims by government trustees, focusing primarily on CERCLA and OPA. Section 4 explores a series of issues relating to the scope of the government's trustee authorities, including what natural resources are subject to trustee claims, the measure of damages, permissible uses of recovered funds, and co-trusteeship of the same resource by multiple levels of government. Finally, section 5 addresses the legal avenues that may be available for citizens to influence the government's exercise of its statutory trustee responsibility.

2. ORIGINS OF NATURAL RESOURCE TRUSTEESHIP

The concept that the government holds certain natural resources in trust on behalf of the public is extremely old, but has been honoured much more in theory than in practice. The precept may have originated in the writings of the Emperor Justinian.[6] The public trust doctrine first recognized by the United States Supreme Court, however, was gleaned from the English common law.

The seminal case in the development of the public trust doctrine in the United States is *Illinois Central Railroad* v. *Illinois*,[7] in which the Supreme Court first recognized the principle discussed in English common law decisions that certain resources, namely the navigable waters and underlying land traditionally open to the public for navigation and fishing, are held in trust for the public and cannot be alienated or otherwise utilized in a manner which would violate that trust.[8]

---

[6] Justinian wrote that '[b]y the law of nature these things are common to mankind—the air, running water, the sea and consequently the shores of the sea', *The Institutes of Justinian* 2.1.1. (1841). Professor R. Lazarus notes that this statement was in the context of primer on the laws, and was probably not a concept implemented in any meaningful way in Roman Law. In fact, coastal resources were conveyed by the Roman government to private ownership to 'promote commercial exploitation of the sources'; R. Lazarus, 'Changing Conceptions of Property and Sovereignty in Natural Resources: Questioning the Public Trust Doctrine' (1986) 71 *Iowa Law Review* 631–716, at 634, n. 12 (citing P. Deveny, 'Title, Jus Publicum, and the Public Trust: An Historical Analysis', (1976) 1 *Sea Grant LJ* 13–81, at 33–34. Regardless of whether it was applied in his time, the doctrine survived in Justinian's writings and, in the thirteenth century, was taught at Bologna, the oldest of the Italian universities. Students from throughout the medieval world studied at Bologna, and the concept of commonly held rights in a public trust would eventually find favour in the law of France (and thus eventually to the Louisiana Civil Code of 1870), Spain and the Spanish colonies (see *Lux* v. *Haggen*, 10 P. 674 (Cal. 1886)), and the English common law.

[7] 146 US 387 (1892).

[8] Ironically, the New Jersey court's recitation of the English common law in *Arnold* v. *Mundy*, on which the Illinois Central Court bases its opinion, is widely considered incorrect. See G. J. MacGrady, 'The Navigability Concept in the Civil and Common Law' (1975) 3 *Florida State University Law Review* 511–615, at 513. See also J. L. Sax, 'The Public Trust Doctrine in Natural Resource Law: Effective Judicial intervention' (1970) 68 *Michigan Law Review* 471–506, at 485 ('only the most manipulative of historical readers could extract much binding precedent from what happened a few centuries ago in England. But that the doctrine contains the seeds of ideas whose importance is only beginning to be perceived . . . can hardly be doubted').

The court explained that the state's title in submerged lands is 'different character from that which the State holds in lands intended for sale . . . It is a title held in trust for the people of the State that they may enjoy the navigation of the waters, carry on commerce over them, and have the liberty of fishing therein freed from the obstruction or interference of private parties.'[9] Because the trust 'can only be discharged by the management and control of property in which the public has an interest', the court said, such lands can be conveyed to a private party only to the extent the public's interests in the property would be promoted by the conveyance, and the state's ultimate control over those resources can *never* be alienated.[10]

The Illinois Central Court faced an extreme situation: a state legislature's conveyance of almost the entire Chicago waterfront to a private corporation, which the legislature itself, after elections changed its composition, was seeking to repudiate. The court plainly stretched to find a theory to invalidate such an obvious abuse of the public interest.[11] The principle embraced by the court, however, that government agencies holding resources in trust for the public may not act in violation of their trust responsibility, has broad implications that have become ever more apparent as development and population growth have shrunk the nation's natural resource base.

Under US law, the fifty states have inherent sovereign authority over most natural resources within their borders.[12] The federal government derives its authority over natural resources from specific legislation regarding, for example, the management of public lands, parks and forests, marine fisheries, migratory birds, and endangered species. Historically, the public trust doctrine was applied almost exclusively as a check on *the states'* power to alienate the public's traditional rights of access to the foreshore, submerged lands of the oceans and the Great Lakes, navigable waters, and fishing grounds. However, courts confronted with other alleged government abuses of natural resources for the benefit of narrow private interests have been drawn into expanding the doctrine's uses far beyond these historical boundaries.

State courts have extended the trust doctrine to non-navigable waters, parks, air and other natural resources not historically protected, and to such uses as the protection of wildlife and ecological values and water conservation.[13] Courts have also invoked the public trust doctrine as justification for the broad exercise

---

[9] N. 7 above, at 452.   [10] *Ibid.* 452–3.

[11] The Court acknowledged that it could cite no authority where a grant of this kind was held invalid, but it built upon the 'numerous [decisions] which declare that such property is held by the state . . . in trust for the public': *ibid.* 455.

[12] See, e.g. *Georgia* v. *Tennessee Copper Co.*, 206 US 230, 237 (1906) ('[T]he State has an interest independent of and behind the titles of its citizens in all the earth and air within its domain').

[13] See C. Carlson, 'Making CERCLA Natural Resource Damage Regulations Work: The Use of the Public Trust Doctrine and Other State Remedies' (1988) 18 *Environmental Law Reporter* 10299–307, at 10302 (citing authorities).

of federal authority over public lands[14] and as a source of a duty on federal agencies to take action even outside the boundaries of federal land to protect the resources for which they are responsible.[15] This evolution of the courts' application of the doctrine has apparently been a result of changing congressional and, presumably, public perceptions concerning the importance of preserving public resources.[16]

Of particular interest are the decisions of a few courts finding that the public trust doctrine, combined with the right of sovereigns to sue as *parens patriae* to vindicate rights of their citizens, can be used by government agencies to recover damages for injuries to natural resources. In *In re Steuart Transp. Co.*,[17] the court held that both the United States and the State of Virginia have 'the right, and the duty' pursuant to the public trust doctrine, 'to protect and preserve the public's interest in natural wildlife resources'.[18] The court held that the public trust doctrine was available to seek damages for the destruction of 30,000 migratory birds by an oil spill. Similarly, in *United States* v. *Burlington Northern R. Co.*,[19] the court held that the United States' suit seeking damages for injury to 354 acres of a waterfowl production area (including destruction of forage, ducks, pheasants, other wildlife, and firefighting expenses) stated a colourable claim. The court found that the public trust doctrine applies to the United States as well as the states, and that the United States may 'maintain an action to recover for damages to its public lands and the natural resources on them, which in this action would encompass the destroyed wildlife'.[20]

Although the clear trend of these decisions has been toward broader recognition of the government's trust responsibilities for natural resources, such *ad hoc* judicial activism is a shaky foundation for the long-term protection of public

[14] See, e.g. *Light* v. *United States*, 220 US 523 (1920), in which the Supreme Court upheld the Forest Service's authority to regulate grazing lands, holding that '[a]ll public lands of the nation are held in trust for the people of the whole country': *ibid.* 537.

[15] In *Sierra Club* v. *Department of the Interior*, 376 F.Supp. 90 (N.D. Cal. 1974), the court stated that the Department of the Interior (DOI) had an affirmative duty to protect resources within a national park by conducting activities outside the park boundaries. The court derived this duty from both the federal statutes requiring the Secretary of the Interior to establish and regulate the park to preserve designated redwood forests and the public trust doctrine, under which the court found DOI is 'the guardian of the people of the United States over the public lands'. The court found that 'any discretion vested in the Secretary concerning time, place and specifics of the exercise of such powers is subordinate to his *paramount legal duty imposed, not only under his trust obligation but by the statute itself*, to protect the park': *ibid.* 95–6 (emphasis added). See also *Massachusetts* v. *Andrus*, 594 F.2d 872, 890 (1st Cir. 1979) (finding that the Outer Continental Shelf Lands Act 'implied an underlying duty to exercise due diligence that the resources be in fact protected', and that such a duty is consistent with the Secretary's role as trustee of the public domain).

[16] For a synopsis of the statutory evolution in the federal public lands law, see C. F. Wilkinson, 'The Public Trust Doctrine in Public Land Law' (1980) 14 *UC Davis Law Review* 269–316, at 293–8.

[17] N. 1 above.   [18] *Ibid.* 40.   [19] 710 F.Supp. 1286 (D.Neb. 1989).

[20] *Ibid.* 1287. See also *Maine* v. *M/V Tamano*, 357 F.Supp. 1097 (D. Maine 1973) (Maine suit for damages *parens patriae* for injuries to coastal waters and marine life within the public trust which resulted from the spill of 100,000 gallons of oil in Casco Bay).

rights. Moved by the same changes in public attitudes that fuelled these judicial decision, Congress began to strengthen that foundation by incorporating the public trust principle explicitly in statutory law.

3. US NATURAL RESOURCE DAMAGE STATUTES

The first federal environmental law expressly to use public trust language was the Deepwater Port Act of 1974, which applies to pollution from offshore oil unloading facilities.[21] Although the Act has yet to be used to bring a claim, it set the basic pattern for later natural resource damage legislation by designating a government official (the Secretary of Transportation) to 'act on behalf of the public as trustee of the natural resources of the marine environment' and by directing that '[s]ums recovered shall be applied to the restoration and rehabilitation of such resources'.[22]

Congress greatly expanded the scope of the natural resource damage cause of action in 1977 amendments to the Federal Water Pollution Control Act (the Clean Water Act).[23] Section 311(f) of the Clean Water Act originally made the owners or operators of vessels and facilities from which oil or a hazardous substance was spilled into water liable for clean-up costs. The amended statute broadened these parties' liability to include the costs of 'restoration or replacement of natural resources damaged or destroyed as a result of a discharge of oil or a hazardous substance'.[24] Section 311(f)(5) authorizes state representatives as well as federal officials to 'act on behalf of the public as trustee' to recover such damages and provides that '[s]ums recovered shall be used to restore, rehabilitate, or acquire the equivalent of such natural resources by the appropriate agencies of the Federal Government or the State Government'.[25]

The Clean Water Act's natural resource damage provisions created a potentially powerful cause of action, but they had a serious flaw. The Act did not designate any specific agency to be responsible for recovering damages and restoring the injured resources. Quantifying natural resource injury and determining how to repair a damaged ecosystem are remarkably complex tasks, and often require the co-ordinated efforts of several scientific disciplines as well as economists. The lack of specific delegated responsibility meant that no agency had the motivation or mandate to develop the structured programme needed to perform such assessments on a regular basis. Congress finally set the stage for such a programme with CERCLA's enactment in 1980.[26]

---

[21] 33 USC §§ 1501–1524.   [22] 33 USC § 1517(i)(2).

[23] Pub. L. No. 95–217, 91 Stat. 1566 (1977), codified as amended at 33 USC §§ 1251–1387. Among other things, the Clean Water Act establishes a comprehensive federal permitting scheme for discharges of pollutants from point sources into most United States waters.

[24] 33 USC §§ 1321(f)(4).   [25] 33 USC §§ 1321(f)(5).

[26] The evolution of early US natural resource damage legislation is reviewed in B. Breen, 'Citizen Suits for Natural Resource Damages: Closing a Gap in Federal Environmental Law' (1989) 24 *Wake Forest Law Review* 851–80, at 855–63. Some of the 50 states have comparable legislation. See

3.1. The Comprehensive Environmental Response, Compensation, and Liability Act

The Comprehensive Environmental Response, Compensation, and Liability Act of 1980[27] was passed by Congress in response to severe environmental and health problems posed by the past disposal of hazardous substances.[28] CERCLA created a comprehensive scheme for remedying a release or threatened release of 'hazardous substances'[29] anywhere in the environment—to land, air, or water. The statute established the 'Superfund' with tax dollars to be replenished by costs recovered from liable parties, to pay for clean-ups if necessary. It conferred on the Environmental Protection Agency (EPA) control of the Superfund and broad powers to investigate contamination, select appropriate remedial actions, and either order liable parties to perform the clean-up or do the work itself and recover its costs.

CERCLA also contained the most complete provisions for the recovery of natural resource damages to that time. Section 107(a)(4)(C) provides that any person who is responsible for a release of a hazardous substance is liable, to federal, state and tribal governments for (in addition to clean-up costs): '(C) damages for injury to, destruction of, or loss of natural resources, including the reasonable costs of assessing such injury, destruction, or loss resulting from such a release'.[30] In addition, CERCLA contains two innovations that were crucial to the development of a natural resource damages programme. First, it authorized the designation of federal, state, and tribal officials to act as trustees to recover damages for injured resources within their jurisdictions.[31] The federal and state trustees are directed to act 'on behalf of the public' and are responsible for spending recovered damages 'only to restore, replace, or acquire the equivalent of' the injured natural resources.[32] Secondly, section 301(c) of CERCLA required the federal government to issue regulations identifying the 'best available procedures' for assessing natural resource damages.[33] Damages measured by a

---

generally L. W. Landreth and K. M. Ward, 'Natural Resource Damages: Recovery Under State Law Compared With Federal Laws' (1990) 20 *Environmental Law Reporter* 10134–48, at 10134. In our experience, however, most states rely on federal law to bring natural resource damage claims.

[27] Pub. L. No. 96–510, 94 Stat. 2767 (11 Dec. 1980), codified at 42 USC §§ 9601–9675. CERCLA was significantly amended by the Superfund Amendments and Reauthorization Act of 1980 (SARA), Pub. L. No. 99–499, 100 Stat. 1613 (1986).

[28] Congress intended that those responsible for hazardous substance pollution bear the costs of cleaning it up. See, e.g. *Lone Pine Steering Comm.* v. *EPA*, 777 F.2d 882, 886 (3rd Cir. 1985), cert. denied, 476 US 1115 (1986).

[29] 'Hazardous substance' includes virtually all materials that are toxic, flammable, corrosive, or reactive except for oil or petroleum products: 42 USC § 9601(14); 40 CFR Part 302 (1994).

[30] 42 USC § 9607(a)(4)(C).   [31] 42 USC § 9607(f)(2).

[32] 42 USC § 9607(f)(1). Tribal trustees act on behalf of the tribe and members. Tribal natural resource damage claims raise a host of issues beyond the scope of this Ch.

[33] 42 USC § 9651(c).

federal or state trustee in accordance with these damage assessment regulations are given a 'rebuttable presumption' of correctness.[34]

Although the standard of liability is not explicit in the statute, courts generally have held that CERCLA liability is strict (i.e. does not require a showing of fault) and that all persons who contributed to a contaminated site are jointly and severally liable for clean-up costs and damages.[35] The persons deemed responsible for the contamination include current owners or operators of the site, anyone who owned or operated the site when hazardous substances were disposed of there, persons who arranged to dispose of hazardous substances found at the site; and transporters of the substances to the site.[36] The statute provides only a limited number of exclusive defences and exceptions.[37]

CERCLA provides no specific measure of damages. The statute states, however, that awards are *not* limited by the sums which can be used to restore or replace the injured resources,[38] implying that substantial damages may be awarded even if restoration is not technically possible. The statute also directs that the damage assessment regulations address 'both direct and indirect injury, destruction, or loss and shall take into consideration factors including, but not limited to, replacement value, use value, and the ability of the ecosystem to recover'.[39]

3.2. The Oil Pollution Act

The Oil Pollution Act of 1990[40] is the latest congressional statement regarding the nature and scope of natural resource damages. It was passed in the wake of the *Exxon Valdez* oil spill to consolidate and reform the perceived patchwork of

---

[34] 42 USC § 9607(f)(2)(C). No court has yet addressed the significance of this presumption. It is unclear whether the presumption merely shifts the burden of coming forward with evidence to the defendant, or whether the presumption shifts to defendants the burden of proving by a preponderance of the evidence that the correct measure of damages differs from that found by the trustee.

[35] See, e.g. *United States* v. *Colorado & Eastern R.R. Co.*, 50 F.3d 1530 (10th Cir. 1995); *Idaho* v. *The Hanna Mining Co.*, 882 F.2d 392, 394 (9th Cir. 1989). Joint and several liability is the common law rule where multiple parties contributed to a tort, and most cases interpreting s. 107 have found that intended to allow its application under the statute. See, e.g. *United States* v. *R. W. Meyer*, 889 F.2d 1497, 1506–8 (6th Cir. 1989), cert. denied, 494 US 1057 (1990); *United States* v. *Monsanto Co.*, 858 F.2d 160 (4th Cir. 1988), cert. denied, 490 US 1106 (1989) (CERCLA permits courts to impose joint and several liability in cases where the harm is indivisible).

[36] 42 USC § 9607(a)(1)–(4).

[37] One of the most significant exceptions is for 'federally permitted releases', that is releases of a hazardous substance pursuant to a permit issued under a federal law, including the Clean Water Act and the Clean Air Act. See 42 USC § 9607(j). CERCLA also contains exceptions for: damages resulting from the application of a registered pesticide, 42 USC § 9607(i); natural resource losses that were specifically identified in an environmental impact statement and were then authorized by permit, 42 USC § 9607(f)(1); and economic damages where both the release and the damages occurred 'wholly before' CERCLA's enactment on 11 Dec. 1980, 42 USC § 107(f)(1); see *In re Acushnet River & New Bedford Harbor*, 716 F.Supp. 676, 683–6 (D. Mass. 1989). Both CERCLA and OPA bar the double recovery of damages for the same release and natural resource injury: 42 USC § 9607(f)(1); 33 USC § 2701(d)(3). [38] 42 USC § 9607(f)(1).

[39] 42 USC § 9651(c)(2). [40] Pub.L. No. 101–380, 104 Stat. 486 (18 Aug. 1990).

federal laws pertaining to oil spills,[41] and to provide a comprehensive response to oil spills that affect navigable waters. One of the most important and controversial elements of this response was OPA's treatment of natural resource damages. Section 1002(a) of OPA[42] provides that:

[E]ach responsible party for a vessel or a facility from which oil is discharged, or which poses the substantial threat of a discharge of oil, into or upon the navigable waters or adjoining shorelines or the exclusive economic zone is liable for the removal costs and damages specified in subsection (b)

Section 1002(b) provides for recovery of, among other things, '[d]amages for injury to, destruction of, loss of, or loss of use of, natural resources, including the reasonable costs of assessing the damage, which shall be recoverable by a United States trustee, a State trustee, an Indian tribe trustee, or a foreign trustee.'[43] Liability under OPA is expressly joint and several, and strict.[44] Congress exempted claims under OPA from the Limitation of Liability Act of 1851, a Victorian relic that limited a vessel owner's liability for an accident involving the vessel to the value of the vessel *after* the accident, subject to narrow exceptions.[45] Instead, OPA provides its own, more generous, limits on liability, subject to a number of important exceptions that can lead to unlimited liability.[46]

The measure of natural resource damages under OPA is similarly broad. Where CERCLA provides no specific measure of damages, OPA provides that the measure of damages is:

(A) the cost of restoring, rehabilitating, replacing, or acquiring the equivalent of, the damaged natural resources;
(B) the diminution in value of those natural resources pending restoration; plus
(C) the reasonable cost of assessing those damages.[47]

OPA parallels CERCLA by requiring the designation of federal, state, and tribal natural resource trustees but also allows foreign governments to assert claims for damage to their natural resources.[48] Like CERCLA, OPA requires trustees to use awards of natural resource damages only to reimburse assessment costs and to restore, rehabilitate, replace, or acquire the equivalent of injured resources, and it directs the Under Secretary of Commerce for Oceans and Atmosphere to issue regulations to guide natural resource damage assessments.[49]

---

[41] See S. Rep. No. 94, 101st Cong., 1st Sess. 2 (1989), reprinted in 1990 US Code Cong. & Adm. News 722, 723. [42] 33 USC § 2702(a).
[43] 33 USC § 2702(b)(2)(A).
[44] Conference Report, H. Rep. No. 653, 101st Cong., 2nd Sess., reprinted in 1990 US Code Cong. & Adm. News 722, 780; S. Rep. No. 94, 101st Cong., 1st Sess. 11 (1989), reprinted in 1990 US Code Cong. & Adm. News 722, 733.
[45] See Limitation of Liability Act of 1851, 46 USC § 183; Conference Report, n. 44 above, at 103, 1990 US Code Cong. & Adm. News at 781. [46] See 33 USC § 2704.
[47] See 33 USC § 2706(d)(1).   [48] 33 USC § 2706(b).
[49] 33 USC § 2706(e) (regulations), 2706(f) (use of funds).

3.3. The Natural Resource Trustees

Only the federal and state officials designated as trustees, representatives of Indian tribes, and (under OPA but not CERCLA) trustees designated by the head of a foreign government may recover natural resource damages under CERCLA or OPA.[50] Federal natural resource trustees are designated in the National Oil and Hazardous Substances Contingency Plan (NCP).[51] In general, the federal trustees are:

— The Secretary of Commerce, trustee for all marine resources and associated habitats and for anadromous fish (such as salmon).
— The Secretary of the Interior, trustee for migratory birds, endangered species, some marine mammals, minerals, and most marshes and fresh water resources.
— The heads of federal land managing agencies, principle the Department of Agriculture (for National Forest System lands), the Department of Defense, and the Department of Energy, trustees of natural resources located on the land in its jurisdiction.

The Secretary of Commerce, acting through the National Oceanic and Atmospheric Administration (NOAA), and the Department of the Interior (DOI) have been by far the most active of the federal trustees.

The governors of most states have designated one or more state officials to act as trustees for natural resources within the state. Some Indian tribes have also designated trustees, who are generally entitled to act with respect to natural resources within a tribal reservation, owned by members of the tribe, or subject to off-reservation hunting or fishing rights provided by treaty or federal law.

3.4. Natural Resource Damages Assessment Regulations

Section 301(c) of CERCLA directed the President to promulgate regulations for the assessment of natural resource damages within two years of the passage of the Act—by 11 December 1982.[52] The statute requires two types of regulations: procedures that allow the trustees to estimate damages with minimal field analysis, by means of a computer model or other simplified method ('Type A regulations'), and protocols for conducting assessments in individual cases for which the simpler procedures would not be appropriate ('Type B regulations'). The original Type B regulations were finally promulgated almost four years after the statutory deadline, on 1 August 1986.[53]

---

[50] CERCLA has been interpreted to preclude private parties from bringing statutory natural resource damage actions. See *Artesian Water Co.* v. *New Castle County*, 851 F.2d 643, 649–50 (3rd Cir. 1988); *Lutz* v. *Chromatex, Inc.*, 718 F.Supp. 413, 419 (M.D. Pa. 1989).
[51] 40 CFR § 300.600.   [52] 42 USC § 9651(c).
[53] 51 Fed. Reg. 27674 (1 Aug. 1986) (codified at 43 CFR §§ 11.60–84). This first rule included only the Type B regulations. DOI promulgated an initial applicable only to marine environments,

Numerous states, environmental groups, and industry challenged the damages assessment rules in the US Court of Appeals for the District of Columbia. The court addressed these challenges in two cases, *State of Ohio* v. *Department of the Interior* (hereinafter *Ohio* v. *DOI*)[54] (Type B rule) and *State of Colorado* v. *Department of the Interior*[55] (Type A rule). Although the court upheld most of the regulation, it struck down two important elements concerning the measure of damages: the 'lesser of' rule, which provided that the measure of damages should be the lesser of restoration costs or lost economic values; and the 'hierarchy' of assessment methodologies, under which DOI stated a preference for lost market value as the measure of damages.[56] The court remanded both rules for redrafting.

A revised Type B damages assessment rule was promulgated on 25 March 1994.[57] The Type B regulations set forth a five-stage administrative process, which includes a 'pre-assessment screen' to determine whether there is likely to be enough resource injury to justify a full assessment; a plan for the assessment; a report describing the trustees' findings on the nature and amount of natural resource injury; and a final report that includes the trustees' proposed plan for restoration of the injured resources and the amount of damages the trustee is seeking from responsible parties.[58] The regulations require the trustee to give the public (including responsible parties) opportunities to review and provide comments on the trustee's plans and findings at several stages.

The DOI regulations provide guidance and standards on many issues likely to arise in a damage assessment.[59] For example, the DOI regulations define 'injury' to a natural resource as 'a measurable adverse change, either long- or short-term, in the chemical or physical quality or the viability of a natural resource'.[60] Proof of injury is allowed by either (1) empirical evidence of an adverse change (e.g.

Type A rule, on 20 Mar. 1987: 52 Fed. Reg. 9042 (condified at 43 CFR §§ 11.40–41). Both sets of regulations were amended to conform to the 1986 CERCLA amendments: 53 Fed. Reg. 5166 (22 Feb. 1988).

[54] 880 F.2d 432 (D.C. Cir. 1989).   [55] 880 F.2d 481 (D.C. Cir. 1989).

[56] The Court held that Congress expressed a clear preference for restoration costs as the measure of damages: n. 54 above, at 444. The Court also held that the Department's 'rigid hierarchy of permissible methods for determining "use values"' which emphasized market-based values, was not a reasonable reading of CERCLA: *ibid*. 462.

[57] 59 Fed. Reg. 14262 (25 Mar. 1994). Revised Type A regulations for the Great Lakes and marine waters have been proposed but not issued as final rules. See 59 Fed. Reg. 40319 (8 Aug. 1994). The DOI regulations apply to cases under CERCLA or the Clean Water Act. NOAA was charged with issuing regulations for natural resource damage assessments under OPA and recently published the final rule significantly different from the DOI regulations. See 61 Fed. Reg. 439 (5 Jan. 1996).

[58] See 43 CFR § 11.13, for an overview of regulation's assessment process.

[59] The DOI Type B regulations have often been criticized as overly prescriptive and rigid, and there is yet no case in which a trustee has completed a damages assessment fully conforming to the Type B regulations. Nonetheless, parties routinely cite to portions of the regulations to support their contentions on how an assessment should be conducted and what substantive standards should apply.

[60] 43 CFR § 11.14(v).

lower hatching rates or increased incidence of tumours) or (2) proof that the hazardous substance is present in the resource at a level exceeding a regulatory standard or threshold for protection of the resource or consumers. Such regulatory standards for proof can significantly simplify a damages case.[61]

Importantly, the damages assessment regulations specify that the goal of restoration is to return the injured resources to 'baseline', defined as the 'conditions that would have existed at the assessment area had the discharge of oil or the release of a hazardous substance under investigation not occurred'.[62] Thus, trustees generally do not seek to restore an injured natural resource to its historical or 'pre-injury' condition but, rather, to a condition that takes as given other changes to the environment—such as development activity or damage from causes other than oil or hazardous substances—that have occurred since the release. For example, in the assessment of damages resulting from toxic metals released at the Blackbird Mine in Idaho, the trustees set a goal for restoration of chinook salmon at a level one-tenth of their historical population, because dams in the Columbia River system presently block the passage of approximately 90 per cent of the salmon before they reach the Blackbird Mine. A salmon population at 10 per cent of historical levels is therefor the condition that the salmon would be in today if the hazardous substance releases had not occurred.

Trustees need not conduct their damage assessments in accordance with the regulations to recover damages or the costs of assessment. The rules are optional, and the only legal consequence of a choice not to follow them is the loss of 'rebuttable presumption' that attaches to an assessment that conforms to the DOI regulations.[63]

4. THE SCOPE OF TRUSTEE AUTHORITY

4.1. The Trust Corpus

Both CERCLA and OPA allow trustees to reach all natural resources necessary to restore damage to the ecosystem. 'Natural resources' is defined broadly in both statutes as 'land, fish, wildlife, biota, air, water, ground water, drinking water supplies, and other such resources *belonging to, managed by, held in trust by, appertaining to, or otherwise controlled by* the United States . . . , any State or local government, any foreign government, [or] any Indian tribe.'[64]

---

[61] See, e.g. *In re Acushnet River & New Bedford Harbor: Proceedings re Alleged PCB Pollution*, 716 F.Supp. 676, 685 (D. Mass. 1989) ('injury' to fish and aquatic life established by showing that the organisms were contaminated with PCBs in excess of 'tolerance level' set by the Food and Drug Administration for safe consumption of seafood).   [62] 43 CFR § 11.14(e).

[63] See 40 CFR § 300.615(c)(4) (as revised 8 Mar. 199); *Utah* v. *Kennecott Corp.*, 801 F.Supp. 553, 567 (D. Utah 1992).

[64] 33 USC § 2701(20); 42 USC § 9601(16) (emphasis added). The ellipses in this quotation remove minor wording differences that are immaterial to this discussion.

The leading case interpreting this provision found that 'a substantial degree of government regulation, management or other form of control over property would be sufficient' to bring it within the trustees' jurisdiction.[65] Given the states' sweeping regulatory authority over fish and wildlife and any other resources that affect the health or welfare of their citizens,[66] and comprehensive federal regulation of waters and wetlands, anadromous fish, threatened or endangered species, migratory birds, and federal lands, the statutory trusteeship encompasses virtually all of the nation's natural resources.

This includes many natural resources on private land. Although Congress apparently meant to exclude 'purely private' resources,[67] the exception is narrow. Virtually any privately-owned lake or marsh, and most undeveloped land, is part of an integrated ecosystem that sustains fish, birds, and wildlife subject to state or federal authority. Restoring damaged habitat on private land may be essential to rebuilding injured wildlife populations, and the damages provisions of CERCLA and OPA are clearly broad enough to include restoration of key habitat regardless of whether it is in public ownership.[68]

4.2. Monetary Compensation and Other Relief

No issue related to natural resource damages law has been so controversial as how to measure the monetary compensation due for harm to 'environmental goods' that have no market price.[69] The debate has sometimes become very technical, centring on the reliability of specific economic methods for valuing natural resources.[70] Despite this controversy, a few basic principles are reasonably clear.

---

[65] *Ohio* v. *DOI*, n. 54 above, at 461.

[66] See, e.g. *Artesian Water Co. New Castle County*, 851 F.2d 643, 650 (3rd Cir. 1988) (an aquifer is a natural resource whose injury gives the state a cause of action under CERCLA); *Idaho* v. *Southern Refrigerated Transport Co.*, No. 88–1279, slip op. at 11–12 (D. Idaho, 25 Jan. 1991) (state is trustee under CERCLA and common law *parens patriae* for all of Idaho's wildlife and sport fish). It has long been settled that 'the state has an interest independent of and behind the titles of its citizens, in all the earth and air within its domain': *Georgia* v. *Tennessee Copper Co.*, 206 US 230, 237 (1907). [67] *Ohio* v. *DOI*, n. 54 above, at 460.

[68] The legislative history of OPA clearly indicates that Congress intended to include resources on privately-owned land. See S. Rep. No. 94 101st Cong., 1st Sess. 11, 14 (1989), reprinted in 1990 US Code Cong. & Admin. News 722, 730, 733. See also H. Rep. No. 242, Part 2, 101st Cong., 1st Sess. 53 (1989) (Congress intended that the term 'natural resource' to include 'living and nonliving resources, whether or not possessing commercial value').

[69] An excellent overview of resource valuation methods is provided by F. B. Cross, 'Natural Resources Damage Valuation' (1989) 42 *Vanderbilt Law Review* 269–341, at 269.

[70] The most controversial technique, known as contingent valuation (CV), is the only widely applicable technique for measuring lost 'non-use' or 'passive use' values (also known as existence and bequest values)—the enjoyment that people derive from the existence of certain resources even though they have no expectation of using the resources themselves. See generally Cross, n. 69 above. In oversimplified terms, a CV survey asks a representative sample of people in a target population how much they would be willing to pay to preserve a natural resource described in the survey. CV has been vigorously attacked, mainly because it necessarily relies on responses to hypothetical questions that cannot be directly validated in a market or by other observations of

Under all US natural resource damages laws, the *minimum* measure of damages is normally the cost of restoring or replacing the injured resources or the cost of acquiring equivalent resources (referred to collectively as 'restoration costs').[71] This fundamental rule was initially in doubt under CERCLA. The first damage assessment regulations, published by DOI in 1986, took the position that the proper measure of natural resource damages is the *lesser of* (a) the costs of restoring, replacing, or acquiring the equivalent of the injured resources, and (b) the lost or reduced 'use value' of the resources.[72] In July 1989, the US Court of Appeals for the D.C. Circuit struck down that aspect of the DOI rule, holding that 'CERCLA unambiguously mandates *a distinct preference for using restoration cost as the measure of damages*, and so precludes a "lesser of" rule which totally ignores that preference'.[73] The court found that this presumption, that injured natural resources should always be restored regardless of their estimated economic value, derived from Congress' perception 'that natural resources have value that is not readily measured by traditional means'.[74]

The costs recoverable under this basic measure of damages are described in four different terms: restoration, replacement, rehabilitation, and acquisition of the equivalent of the injured resources.[75] Regardless of which term has which meaning, they include four types of actions:

(1) returning the injured resource to its baseline condition.
(2) creating or improving the condition of the same type of resource in a nearby location. A common example is the creation of a new marsh to replace one that has been so severely contaminated that the best remedial option is simply to fill and cover it to prevent further exposure of people and wildlife to the hazardous substances.
(3) replacing an injured resource with a substitute resource at the injured site. For example, it might be necessary to substitute one sport fish for another that, due to changes in environmental conditions, cannot be re-established.

---

behaviour. See, e.g. J. C. Dobbins, 'The Pain and Suffering of Environmental Loss: Using Contingent Valuation to Estimate Non-Use Damages' (1994) 43 *Duke Law Journal* 879–946; Note: ' "Ask a Silly Question . . .": Contingent Valuation of Natural Resource Damages' (1992) 105 *Harvard Law Review* 1981–2000. Indeed, Mobil Corporation recently published advertisements in the *New York Times, Wall Street Journal, Washington Post*, and other major newspaper attacking the validity of CV. Nonetheless, DOI included CV as an acceptable method for resource valuation in its damages assessment regulations, and the Court of Appeals upheld that part of the regulations: see *Ohio* v. *DOI*, n. 54 above, at 476–8.

[71] See *Ohio* v. *DOI*, n. 54 above, at 444. OPA, the Marine Protection, Research, and Sanctuaries Act and the Clean Water Act expressly state that restoration or replacement costs are recoverable. 33 USC § 2706(d)(1)(A); 16 USC § 1432(6); and 33 USC § 1321(f)(4).

[72] See 43 CFR § 11.35(b)(2) (1988) (now superseded).

[73] *Ohio* v. *DOI*, n. 54 above, at 444 (emphasis added).   [74] *Ibid.* 457.

[75] OPA uses all four terms, 33 USC § 2706(d)(1). CERCLA contains only 'restore, replace, or acquire the equivalent': See 42 USC § 9607(a)(4)(C). The damages assessment regulations attempt to define these terms individually: 43 CFR § 11.82(b)(1)(i)–(ii). See also the definitions in NOAA's proposed damages assessment regulations under OPA, 59 Fed. Reg. 1062, 1166–7 (7 Jan. 1985).

(4) acquiring similar resources or land for such purposes as parks, wildlife refuges, buffer zones to prevent the disturbance of vulnerable habitat areas, or to provide public access that would not otherwise be assured.

Although many have argued that trustees should give priority to on-site restoration of the same resources whenever practicable, the DOI regulations allow trustees to select among these alternative approaches without priority, based on case-specific factors.[76]

In addition to restoration costs, the damages provisions enacted after CERCLA, and judicial decisions under CERCLA, empower the trustees to recover damages for the reduction in the injured natural resources' value to the public from the time injury occurred until restoration or natural recovery of the resources is complete.[77] There will almost always be some period of time, often many years, between the injury to natural resources and the time they are restored or recover by natural processes, and the public may suffer significant losses— fishery closures, loss of recreational opportunities, or reduced tourism and economic growth—in the interim. While trustees may choose not to assess such interim losses, because they may be more difficult to measure than they are worth,[78] interim losses can be significant, especially in cases where heavily-used resources were severely injured and will not fully recover for a substantial time.

Measuring interim lost values, or the lost value of natural resources for which there is no feasible method of restoration or replacement, is a job for economists. Economic damages to the public for the interim loss of enjoyment or for continuing injury to resources may include, in addition to the costs of restoration or replacement, (1) lost *use values* (benefits derived from the availability of a resource for current and expected future uses by identifiable persons), and (2) lost *'non-use' or 'passive use' values* (benefits that people derive from the knowledge that certain resources exist and are available for the future).[79] Many natural resources have no ascertainable market value, and the market generally does not capture the full value of those resources that have market prices.[80]

---

[76] See 43 CFR § 11.82(a). The State of Montana has filed an action challenging DOI's decision not to accord priority for actions to restore injured resources on site. The case is currently pending in the US Court of Appeals for the District of Columbia Circuit.

[77] See *Ohio* v. *DOI*, n. 54 above, at 454, n. 34 ('Congress intended that trustees in some cases be permitted to recover damages greater than the sum required to restore the resource. The excess would represent interim use value, the value of the lost uses from the time of the spill until the completion of the restoration project').

[78] The DOI damage assessment regulations expressly state that the recovery of interim lost value is 'at the discretion of the [trustee]': 43 CFR § 11.80(b) (1994). See 59 Fed. Reg. 14262, 14272 (25 Mar. 1994).

[79] See generally Cross, n. 69 above; E. J. Yang *et al.*, 'The Use of Economic Analysis in Valuing Natural Recource Damages' (1984). See also C. M. Augustyniak, 'Economic Valuation of Services Provided by Natural Resources: Putting a Price on the Priceless' (1993) 45 *Baylor Law Review* 389–421.

[80] While it is not irrational to look at market price as *one* factor in determining the use value of a resource, it is unreasonable to view market price as the *exclusive* factor, or even the predominant one. From the bald eagle to the blue whale and snail darter, natural resources have values that are not fully captured by the market system: *Ohio* v. *DOI*, n. 54 above, at 462–3 (emphasis in original).

Thus, the methods of measuring these values in most cases are necessarily indirect. As noted above, the accuracy of many of these techniques, including the only one capable of estimating passive use values, is disputed.

A possible alternative to these economic valuation methods is suggested by the statutory scheme. Federal and state natural resource trustees are required to use all damages exclusively for restoration actions. CERCLA and OPA, however, only authorize the collection of monetary damages, apparently assuming that the trustees, not the liable parties, will perform the restoration work. Under this scheme, trustees first recover damages, based on preliminary restoration cost estimates and economic studies, and then prepare a final plan of restoration actions that they will then implement.

The alternative methodology, known as 'habitat equivalency', skips the economic damages calculation and goes straight to determining what restoration actions will provide compensation to the public 'equivalent' to the interim lost resource values. The trustee could either negotiate with the responsible parties to perform the chosen actions themselves or seek the costs.

The federal government is increasingly taking this approach in settlements and has begun to test it in litigation.[81] A relatively simple example of how the technique can be used is an oil spill that kills one acre of coastal mangrove trees. If it will take twenty years for the mangroves to regenerate and grow enough to provide the same quality of 'services'—habitat for birds, juvenile fish, and wildlife and stabilization of the coast, for example—the public has been deprived of twenty 'acre-years' of those services. Instead of calculating the economic value of the lost services for that time, fair compensation to the public can be measured in the same currency that was lost, by the work or costs needed to create twenty acre-years of mangrove swamp of the same quality. The area required may be determined by a formula that considers, among other factors, the amount of time it will take the newly created mangrove area to reach maturity.[82]

There may be some cases where restoration or replacement of an injured resource is technically feasible but it seems intuitively obvious, even with a healthy scepticism of man's ability to accurately value natural resources, that the costs of restoration or replacement are excessive. The *Ohio* v. *DOI* court noted 'that CERCLA permits [the Department of the Interior] to establish a rule exempting

---

[81] The United States used this approach in assessing interim lost use damages for the destruction of salmon habitat in the headwaters of the Columbia River system, in *United States* v. *Blackbird Mining Co. et al.; State of Idaho* v. *M. A. Hanna Mining Co.*, Consolidated Case No. 83–4179 (D. Idaho), discussed at 4.4 below. Even though the parties had widely divergent views of the cost of implementing certain actions that were clearly necessary to restore the damaged ecosystem, the impasse was broken by the defendants' agreement to do the work themselves, instead of continuing to argue about how much they should pay in damages so that the trustees could do it.

[82] Habitat equivalence has begun to be discussed in the economic literature. See R. Bishop and R. Unsworth, 'Assessing Natural Resource Damages Using Environmental Amenities' (1994) 11 *Ecological Economics* 35–41. NOAA has included habitat equivalence analysis as an acceptable method for calculating interim lost values in its proposed damages assessment regulations under OPA. See 60 Fed. Reg. 39803, 39825 (3 Aug. 1995).

responsible parties *in some cases* from having to pay the full cost of restoration of natural resources'.[83] The court suggested that some other measure might be used where the cost of restoration is '*grossly disproportionate* to the use value of the resource'.[84]

This type of common sense, rough proportionality test seems perfectly appropriate in theory. In practice, however, it requires resort to the controversial economic valuation techniques mentioned above—techniques that are generally anathema to the same liable parties who may be inclined to argue that the cost of restoration is disproportionate to the value of the injured resource. Moreover, if a grossly disproportionate test is employed, it should be done consistently with the statutory presumption that injured natural resources will be restored or replaced. In particular, the burdens of raising the issue and of persuasion should both be on the party who claims that restoration costs are disproportionate to value.[85]

Finally, the measure of damages under CERCLA and OPA includes the trustees' 'reasonable' assessment costs.[86] Assessment costs may be substantial.[87] Allowing trustees to recover such costs, and to use the recovered funds to perform other damages assessments, is extremely valuable to the development of an effective natural resource damages program.

4.3. Use of Recoveries

Assessing and recovering damages is at best half of the trustees' job. When that has been accomplished, and the litigators have gone on to the next case, the trustee agencies must still focus on their original objective, actual restoration, replacement, rehabilitation, or acquisition of the equivalent of the injured resources.

Trustees are not necessarily required to implement the restoration plan used to determine the amount of damages. This flexibility is essential, both because a trustee may be unable to recover the full amount of restoration costs it initially claimed and because new information, including scientific advances while the case was in litigation or even the opposing parties' evidence, might point the

---

[83] N. 54 above, at 443 (emphasis in original).

[84] *Ibid.* 443, n. 7 (emphasis added). See also *ibid.* 456, 459; *Puerto Rico* v. *SS Zoe Colocotroni*, 628 F.2d 652, 675–6 (1st. Cir. 1980). In its recent revision of the damages assessment regulations, however, DOI declined to limit the recovery of restoration costs by a 'grossly disproportionate' rule: see 59 Fed. Reg. 14262, 14271 (25 Mar. 1994). DOI reasoned that the procedures and standards imposed by the regulations, including consideration of the cost-effectiveness of a range of alternatives, would eliminate unduly expensive restoration actions.

[85] See generally Anderson, n. 5 above, at 436–40.

[86] See 42 USC § 9607(a)(4)(C); 33 USC § 2706(d)(1)(C).

[87] The settlement for natural resource damages resulting from the *Exxon Valdez* oil spill included a provision for reimbursement of up to $67 million to the United States for damages assessment costs, and an additional $72 million to the State of Alaska for damages assessment and litigation costs. While the magnitude of those costs is as unique as the size of that oil spill—the largest by far in US history—the costs of investigating injury, developing restoration alternatives, and preparing estimates of interim lost values can be expected to cost over $1 million in many cases.

way to more efficient restoration actions.[88] Recognizing the need for this flexibility, the DOI regulations require the trustee to prepare a final, post-litigation restoration plan, allowing the public to submit written comments and, if requested, to make oral presentations at a public hearing.[89]

As discussed above, trustees have discretion to choose among a range of approaches to restoration.[90] Selecting wisely among these approaches and the many possible variants within each approach can be an extraordinarily complex task. Of course, it is technically feasible to return resources at the site of impact to a good condition at a reasonable cost, the problem is manageable. In cases where a major oil spill or many years of hazardous substance releases caused large-scale harm to the ecosystem, repairing the ecosystem directly is often beyond current scientific ability. Trustees then must consider indirect actions—replacement or acquisition—to mitigate the environmental harm.[91]

In making those choices after the litigation has ended, trustees may be exposed to pressure from citizens or groups that have a particular, arguably self-interested, perspective on how the restoration fund should be spent. Individuals and businesses interested in recreation or tourism argue that, to make up for recreation opportunities lost because of the environmental damage, the trustees should improve facilities useful for access to recreation—cabins, trails, boat docks, fishing piers, visitor information centres, even roads and car parks. Some fishermen and the operators of fish hatcheries assert that the fastest way to replace depleted fish populations is by stocking streams with hatchery fish. Rural communities, which often depend on hunting and fishing for a significant part of their diet, seek subsidies of 'replacement' actions such as fish farming. Landowners in the vicinity argue that their land is important to the ecosystem and should be acquired by the trustees for preservation.

Trustees face a real dilemma in addressing such demands. On the one hand,

[88] The DOI regulations state that this final plan 'shall be based upon' the restoration plan used to determine the restoration costs component of damages: see 43 CFR § 11.93(a). The preamble to the regulations clarify that this is not a rigid requirement: see 59 Fed. Reg. 14262, 14278–9 (25 Mar. 1994).

[89] As noted above, both CERCLA and OPA require the development of a restoration plan, and must provide opportunities for public review and comment on the plan and for one or more public hearings, before federal or state trustees may expend finds recovered for natural resource damages: see 42 USC 9611(i); 33 USC § 2706(c)(5).

[90] See pp. 190–1 above. There have been very few judicial decisions that discuss restoration alternatives. One federal district court noted that improvements to river habitat to promote increased steelhead trout populations, including fencing to restrict cattle access and the removal of barriers to fish passage, serve as replacement or acquisition of the equivalent of injured resources: *Idaho* v. *Southern Refrigerated Transport*, n. 66 above, at 26. See also *Puerto Rico* v. *SS Zoe Colocotroni*, n. 84 above ('[a]lternatives might include acquisition of comparable lands for public parks or, as suggested by the defendants below, reforestation of a similar proximate site').

[91] Congress allowed the replacement or acquisition of equivalent resources in recognition that the trustees could not always restore the exact same resources that were injured: see 58 Feb. Reg. 39328, 39339 (22 July 1993). The DOI regulations provide that, to determine what resources are 'equivalent', trustees should consider the 'services' provided by the resources—including both human uses, such as recreation, and benefits to other resources due to their ecological functions: *ibid.* 39340.

they are charged with acting on behalf of the public, and political acceptance of their decisions is one measure of how well they have succeeded. Moreover, those making demands may in fact have had their lives altered by the environmental damage, and ensuring that the restoration programme addresses their loss is a legitimate objective for the trustees. On the other hand, consistently with the principles behind the original public trust doctrine, trustees represent the interests of the whole public in preserving the availability of natural resources held in trust for the future. That suggests that trustees should give priority to actions that accelerate recovery of the ecosystem, even at the cost of failing to redress short-term effects on some interested members of the public while the recovery occurs.[92]

4.4. Co-Trusteeship

The scope of trusteeship under CERCLA and OPA creates the potential for overlapping jurisdiction by federal, state, and tribal governments over the same resources. Both statutes prohibit double recovery by two trustees for the same loss.[93] But that prohibition does not prevent more than one trustee from bringing natural resource damage claims with respect to the same resource, as long as the responsible party does not pay twice for the same damage.[94] For example, if migratory birds or fish subject to Indian harvest rights are killed by an oil spill within state waters, federal, state, and tribal trustees could each assert claims for the loss. In fact, several federal and state agencies may claim trusteeship, potentially under both federal and state law.[95] The statutes provide no clear method for drawing a line between the trustees' competing claims to natural resources.

This overlap of trustee jurisdictions creates issues of fairness to defendants as well as legal risks to the trustees if they fail to co-ordinate their claims. When

[92] An example from the aftermath of the *Exxon Valdez* oil spill illustrates the balancing act required of trustees. The oil spill forced the closure of rich salmon fishing grounds in Prince William Sound for a full season, and caused increased mortality of salmon eggs and fry which might have contributed (along with other factors unrelated to the spill) to a decline in certain salmon runs the next two seasons. Though the trustees performed several projects to enhance the existing wild salmon runs, their short-term effects were small compared to the decline in available fish for the commercial fleet. There is strong pressure from commercial fishing groups to fund the expansion of salmon hatchery operations to introduce large numbers of fish into the Sound for commercial catch. Although there is no question that hatchery releases can be effective, at least in the short term, at increasing the number of fish for harvest, studies have suggested that hatchery releases can harm wild fish populations. Therefore, the trustees have decided to evaluate the risk of such further damage to wild stocks carefully before agreeing to fund any large-scale hatchery projects.

[93] 33 USC § 2706(d)(3).

[94] Furthermore, because neither CERCLA nor OPA preempts state law, state trustees are free to pursue natural resource damage claims under state law. See 42 USC § 9614(a); 33 USC § 2718(a).

[95] A discussion of state natural resource damage law is beyond the scope of this Ch. It should be noted, however, that state law may differ considerably from federal law both procedurally and substantively. For example, some states provide civil penalties or compensation tables for injury to natural resources either in lieu of, or in addition to, a damage remedy. See, e.g. Alaska Stat. §§ 46.03.758, 46.03.759, 46.03.760, 46.03.822; Alaska Adm. Code §§ 75.500 ff.; Wash. Rev. Code §§ 90.48.366, 90.48.368, 90.56.370; Wash. Adm. Code §§ 173–183–010 ff.; Wash. St. Reg. 92–13–083 (1 July 1992); Wash. St. Reg. 92–10–005 (20 May 1992).

multiple trustees assess damages for injury to the same resources, any difference in methodology or results provides ammunition for defendants to attack both assessments. More importantly, if one trustee settles or obtains a judgment independently of the others, it creates difficult issues of what claims the remaining trustees may still pursue without exposing the defendants to impermissible double recovery. Therefore, in practice, the prohibition on double recovery creates a strong incentive for trustees whose claims may overlap to bring their claims jointly whenever possible.[96]

Despite the potential for conflicts when federal, state, and tribal trustees are all allowed to seek damages for the same harm, the scheme has important advantages. Federal, state, and tribal trustees each bring different sensitivities and different types of expertise to the task of assessing natural resource damages and developing a restoration plan. For example, two federal agencies, NOAA and the US Forest Service, joined forces with the State of Idaho to assess damages resulting from acid mine and toxic metals releases at the Blackbird Mine in central Idaho. Seepage from mine audits and two million tons of mill tailings had killed all life in several creeks in the headwaters of the Columbia River system. These creeks were historically a rich trout fishery and spawning grounds for chinook salmon, now listed as a threatened species under the Endangered Species Act. The combination of NOAA's expertise as overseer of salmon recovery for the entire Columbia River system, the Forest Service's expertise in mining and hydrogeology, and the state's detailed knowledge of the watershed produced an unprecedented plan to restore water quality and reintroduce salmon that the mining company defendants have agreed to implement as part of a settlement of their damages liability.[97]

Furthermore, co-trusteeship by federal, state, and tribal governments provides a check on the potential for any one trustee to abuse, or fail to exercise, its authority. This is particularly significant where a trustee agency is also liable for the natural resource injury, and therefore has an arguable incentive to be less than aggressive in assessing damages.[98]

---

[96] Congress anticipated this very situation: '[t]here may be instances where two or more trustees share jurisdiction or control over natural resources. In such cases, trustees should exercise joint management or control of the shared resources. Thus, one class of trustee cannot preempt the right of other classes of trustees to exercise their trusteeship responsibilities.' Conference Report, n. 44 above, at 109, 1990 US Code Cong. & Adm. News at 787; See also H. Rep. No. 242, Part 2, 101st Cong., 1st Sess. 33 (1989). Both the National Contingency Plan and DOI's damages assessment regulations encourage trustees to coordinate their activities with respect to natural resources. See 40 CFR § 300.615(a) (1994); 43 CFR § 11.32(a)(1)(ii) (1994) ('[a] lead authorized official shall be designated to administer the assessment'). See also 60 Fed. Reg. 39803, at 39827 (3 Aug. 1995), s. 990.14(a) of proposed NOAA rule, addressing co-ordination among co-trustees.

[97] *United States* v. *Blackbird Mining Co. et al.*; *State of Idaho* v. *M. A. Hanna Mining Co.*, Consolidated Case No. 83–4179 (D. Idaho), n. 81 above. Notice of the settlement has been published at 60 Fed. Reg. 25250 (11 May 1995).

[98] The federal trustees who manage large areas of public land—DOI, the Department of Agriculture (through the Forest Service), and the Departments of Defense and Energy—are especially likely to find themselves in this situation.

If, for example, the federal landowner/trustee is liable for a hazardous waste dump that is leaching toxins into a river and killing fish, the state in which the facility is located, and any Indian tribe with trusteeship over affected resources, would have the authority to sue the United States for natural resource damages under CERCLA.[99] Even if the state or tribe refrains from filing a lawsuit as a matter of comity, the authority to bring suit can serve as a goad to ensure that the federal trustee gives full consideration to measures needed to return injured resources to full productivity.

5. PUBLIC OVERSIGHT OF TRUSTEE ACTIONS

As discussed above (section 2), the common law public trust doctrine was used primarily by citizens seeking to enforce the government's duties to the public. The codification of natural resource damage claims, however, has made this an exclusively governmental cause of action.[100] The obvious question, then, is what opportunities remain for citizens to influence the government's exercise of trusteeship over natural resources on the public's behalf or to hold the government accountable for its actions as natural resource trustee.

Writing about the public trust doctrine, Professor J. L. Sax asserted that for the doctrine to be a satisfactory tool for resolving resource management problems, it 'must contain some concept of a legal right in the general public [and] it must be enforceable against the government'.[101] The need for the general public to provide an effective check on government discretion is no less in the natural resource damage assessment and restoration process. The need arises primarily from the fact that governments are inherently required to balance competing aspects of the public interest. Thus, the federal and state agencies that act as natural resource trustees typically have a range of other statutory obligations, also owed to the public, which may be in competition with their responsibilities as natural resource trustees.

One of the key types of potential conflict is between the statutory responsibility of a land management agency to encourage 'multiple use' of public lands by both public and commercial interests and its obligations to act as trustee for resources located on those lands. For example, the Department of Agriculture, through the US Forest Service, is a trustee under both CERCLA and OPA of National Forest System lands and the plants and wildlife that inhabit

---

[99] S. 120(a)(1) of CERCLA expressly waives the United States' sovereign immunity to such suits. Only one state has filed a natural resource damages claim against the federal government to date. That case, *State of Coloado* v. *US Department of the Army*, Civ. No. 86–19549 (D. Colo.), concerns extensive contamination from weapons manufacturing and other operations at the Army's Rocky Mountain Arsenal in Colorado. The litigation has been stayed while the Army, in co-ordination with EPA and the state, prepares a plan to clean up the site. [100] See n. 50 above.

[101] Sax, n. 8 above, at 474.

them.[102] The Forest Service is also charged, by the National Forest Management Act of 1976,[103] with managing those lands for multiple uses, including timber-harvesting, grazing, recreation, and wildlife habitat. Forest management plans, adopted by the Forest Service after a formal process that includes public notice and comment, are used to determine how these multiple uses are allocated in a particular forest. Under this scheme, it is entirely possible for the Forest Service to be allowing timber companies to log breeding habitat for marbled murrelets, small birds that nest in undisturbed forest near the marine waters in which they feed, while at the same time seeking damages under OPA for the deaths of the same type of bird resulting from an oil spill in the vicinity. The permitted logging activity may worsen the harm to the very species injured by the oil spill, and directly impact its population. But nothing in OPA suggests that the Forest Service's status as a natural resource trustee empowers it to stop the logging authorized by the Forest Management Plan, even if that is clearly the most effective way to promote recovery of the injured bird population.

Furthermore, it is not unusual for the same government agency designated to act as natural resource trustee to have caused part, or even all, of the environmental damage at issue. That is especially likely to occur at facilities owned by the Departments of Defense or Energy,[104] many of which have severe hazardous substance contamination. However, any federal or state trustee may find itself in the same situation. The agency experiences a very real conflict between its responsibility to make the public whole for any loss of natural resources and its obligation, also imposed by law, to spend no more than Congress or the state legislature has appropriated for natural resource restoration. Nothing in CERCLA or OPA indicates that the natural resource trustee duties should or could prevail.

This understanding that governmental agencies often represent competing interests underlines the need for mechanisms by which the public can assure itself that the trustees are acting reasonably in the public's interest and, to the extent possible, in accordance with the various laws. Alternatives that have been suggested or already used include using the citizen suit provisions of CERCLA or OPA to enforce trustee obligations or to recover damages from a trustee,[105] and intervention in a government natural resource damages action to assert more

---

[102] 40 CFR § 300.600(b)(2) (1994). Likewise, the Bureau of Land Management (BLM), through the Department of the Interior, is also a trustee under CERCLA and OPA of BLM lands, and the resources thereon. The BLM is charged by the Federal Land Policy and Management Act of 1976 with managing lands in their control for multiple uses: Pub. L. No. 94–579, 90 Stat. 2743; codified at 43 USC §§ 1701–1782 (1976). Each of the federal trustee agencies has similar statutory obligations to permit, subject to regulatory controls, economic uses of public resources. See, e.g. Mining Act of 1872, 30 USC §§ 22–54 (allowing private parties to stake out and work mining claims on most federal land, including vast areas managed by DOI and the Forest Service).

[103] Pub. L. No. 94–588, 90 Stat. 2949; codified at 16 USC §§ 1600–1614 (1976).

[104] As noted above, the Secretaries of Defense and Energy were both designated trustees of natural resources on the land they manage: see 40 CFR § 300.600(b)(3) (1994).

[105] Anderson, n. 5 above, at 414; Comment: 'Natural Resource Damages: Trusting the Trustees' (1990) 27 *San Diego Law Review* 407–66, at 453–4.

aggressive positions against the defendants.[106] In addition, the damages assessment regulations provide important procedural opportunities for citizen input into damage assessments and, importantly, into the development and implementation of restoration plans.

5.1. Citizen Suits

CERCLA authorizes citizens to bring actions to enforce the government's non-discretionary statutory duties. In section 310 the statute provides that 'any person' may bring an action in either of two circumstances:

(1) against any person . . . who is alleged to be in violation of any standard, regulation, condition, requirement, or order which has become effective pursuant to this chapter . . . ; or (2) against the President or any other officer of the United States . . . where there is alleged a failure of the President or of such other officer to perform any act or duty under this chapter, . . . which is not discretionary with the President or such other officer.[107]

Citizen suits are distinctly appropriate to enforce explicit statutory requirements applicable to government agencies—often referred to in case law as 'mandatory duties'.[108] While certain provisions of CERCLA and OPA arguably impose mandatory duties on agencies that are performing clean-up actions, in general, the natural resource damage provisions appear to be a broad grant of discretionary authority to trustee agencies and contain little in the way of explicit commands that could be enforceable by citizen suits against a trustee.

Perhaps the strongest candidate for creating a mandatory duty is the language in both CERCLA and OPA which states that the trustees 'shall' assess damages for injury to natural resources resulting from a release of hazardous substances or oil.[109] The use of seemingly compulsory language in this context, however, does not always mean that an agency has a 'mandatory duty' to take enforcement

---

[106] See, e.g. *In re Acushnet River & New Bedford Harbor: Proceedings re Alleged PCB Pollution*, n. 61 above (D. Mass. 1989) (intervention by citizens' group in natural resource damages lawsuit that had been pending for nearly six years). One commentator has suggested that the next logical legislative step would be to authorize citizen suits for the recovery of natural resource damages: see Breen, n. 26 above, at 852–4. While in theory the recovery of damages by citizens' groups could fill any real or perceived gaps in recoveries attributable to limited appropriations of trustee agencies or competing intra-agency pressures, the practical effect would be substantially less. The assessment of damages can be an extremely costly and time-consuming endeavour, especially if that assessment is done in accordance with the regulations. As discussed above, recovery of damages is not, and in a citizen suit presumably would not, require compliance with the regulations. A citizens' group that did not comply with the regulations, however, would then be required to put forth an affirmative case—certainly a more daunting prospect.   [107] 42 USC § 9659(a)(1)–(2).

[108] Because the citizen suit provision prescribes specific forms of relief that a court may impose, including the authority that an action be taken consistent with statutory mandates, but does not include a provision for assessing or awarding damages, both citizen suits and private causes of action for damages are precluded. See *Middlesex Cty. Sewerage Auth.* v. *National Assoc. of Sea Clammers*, 453 US 1, 14–15 (1981); *Conservation Law Found. of New England* v. *Browner*, 840 F.Supp. 171, 177–8 n. 11 (D. Mass. 1993).

[109] See 42 USC § 9607(f)(2)(A)–(B); 33 USC § 2706(c)(1)–(2).

action. In *DuBois* v. *Thomas*, a citizen suit under the Clean Water Act, the plaintiff had sought to require EPA to investigate an allegedly contaminated creek and, if it determined it was contaminated, exercise its authority under the Act to abate the conditions. The Court of Appeals reasoned that finding a mandatory duty to enforce the Clean Water Act would undermine EPA's efforts to achieve the objectives of restoring and maintaining water quality.[110] The reasoning is convincing. If EPA were not allowed to use its expertise to determine which enforcement activities to conduct, the agency could be compelled to employ its limited resources investigating multitudinous complaints, irrespective of the magnitude of their environmental significance. Any agency exercising its enforcement authorities may be unable to efficiently investigate the myriad of complaints it receives and, regardless of seemingly mandatory duties, should be allowed to use its expertise to determine what violations are the most suitable for enforcement.

The reasoning of *DuBois* provides a compelling response to the claim that a trustee that chooses not to assess damages at a particular site has violated a mandatory duty.[111] Trustee agencies rely on very limited appropriated budgets to conduct damage assessments. If a trustee agency were required to assess damages at every site where hazardous substance or oil may have injured natural resources under its jurisdiction, without the opportunity to set priorities, the agency's assessment capacity would be overwhelmed almost immediately. Even allowing citizens to bring suits challenging the trustees' priority decisions could lead to a very inefficient use of those resources. Conducting the assessment, choosing an appropriate restoration alternative for injured natural resources, or, perhaps, accepting a particular amount of damages in settlement, each involves the trustee making informed decisions that require a balancing of priorities and allocation of limited agency resources necessarily within its discretion.

There are, however, other arguably mandatory duties incumbent on trustees which could effectively be enforced through citizen suits. Most importantly, CERCLA and OPA expressly limit the permissible uses of natural resource damages recovered to the restoration, replacement, or acquisition of equivalent resources.[112] In effect, the law impresses a constructive trust on damages recoveries. If a trustee

---

[110] 820 F.2d 943, 947–8 (8th Cir. 1987). *DuBois* has also been relied on in the context of CERCLA. See *McCormick* v. *Anschutz Mining Corp.*, 29 ERC (BNA) 1707 (E.D. Mo. 1989) (relying on *DuBois* where a plaintiff had contended that EPA was required to act whenever a violation of CERCLA is brought to its attention, and that it is liable under s. 310 for a failure to do so).

[111] Thus far there has been one case in which citizens sued the Administrator of EPA for a 'failure to assess and evaluate the hazardous waste problems in each of approximately 840 federal waste sites, located throughout the United States': *Conservation Law Found. of New England* v. *Browner*, n. 108 above, at 172. The lawsuit was dismissed on appeal on the ground that the groups had failed to demonstrated a 'personal stake' in the case and therefore lacked standing to sue: *Conservation Law Found.* v. *Reilly*, 950 F.2d 38 (1st Cir. 1991).

[112] See 42 USC § 9607(f)(1) and 33 USC § 2706(f). OPA also provides for the 'rehabilitation' of injured resources: 33 USC § 2706(c), and both statutes provide for the reimbursement of assessment costs.

decides to expend funds recovered for natural resource damages in a manner inconsistent with this statutory command, that would appear to be the violation of a mandatory duty, which could be actionable under the citizen suit provisions.

5.2. Intervention to Challenge the Adequacy of Compensation

Section 113(i) of CERCLA creates a right of intervention in any judicial action brought under CERCLA, where the person seeking to intervene 'claims an interest relating to the subject of the action and is so situated that the disposition of the action may, as a practical matter, impair or impede the person's ability to protect that interest'.[113] The requirements for intervention under this section are virtually identical to those that already exist for intervention of right in Federal Rule 24(a)(2).[114] The CERCLA provision recognizes that private interests may be affected by actions taken or not taken in the context of CERCLA and that participation in CERCLA litigation should be allowed when the public's rights were not being adequately represented by the agency action.

When the government has resolved a natural resource damages claim brought on behalf of the public, the settlement acts as a bar to any separate claim for *public* damages by citizens.[115] Thus, citizen intervention in the government's lawsuit may be essential to protect the citizens' interests in assuring full restoration of the injured resources.

Citizens or organizations seeking to intervene in a natural resource damages action must overcome a number of hurdles, including establishing that they have a sufficiently concrete interest in the subject of the lawsuit to have 'standing' to sue[116] and that their petitions to intervene are timely. Courts have not hesitated to find these requirements satisfied by citizen intervenors in natural resource damage cases, even when the citizens sought to intervene after the litigation was apparently settled. For example, in *In re Acushnet River & New Bedford Harbor*,[117] the National Wildlife Federation sought to intervene over three years after the suit had been filed to allege that its interests were not represented by the amount recovered in a proposed settlement. The court found that the application was timely, reasoning that until the proposed settlement was filed, the intervenor believed that its interests were being adequately represented. 'To do otherwise would promote a sort of prophylactic intervention whereby parties would be compelled to intervene in matters simply to protect their rights to participate in

---

[113] 42 USC § 9613(i).   [114] Fed.R.Civ.P. 24(a)(2).

[115] See *Alaska Sport Fishing Ass'n* v. *Exxon Corp.*, 34 F.3d 769 (9th Cir. 1994); *California* v. *Southern Pacific Transp. Co.*, No. CIV. S–92–1117 LKK (E.D. Cal. 19 Dec. 1994).

[116] In general, this means that a would-be intervenor must demonstrate that it risks suffering some actual injury to a protectible interest as a result of the outcome of the litigation, beyond a mere concern for the public good. See, e.g. *Conservation Law Foundation* v. *Reilly*, n. 111 above, 41–2 (1st Cir. 1991).   [117] N. 37 above.

those matters downstream on the more or less remote chance that a party apparently protecting the intervenors' interest might someday betray them.'[118]

Relying on similar reasoning, the federal district court in *United States* v. *Exxon Corp.*[119] found that a citizens' group's motion to intervene to allege that the trustees had failed to fulfil their trust obligations was timely, even though it was field over three years after the entry of a consent decree. The intervenors argued that it was not clear whether their interests were at risk until the trustees drafted a post-litigation restoration plan indicating how they intended to use the damages recovered from Exxon. The court reasoned that it was 'not untimely to seek intervention at the time when the trustees have allegedly digressed from their duties'.[120]

Persons who satisfy both the prudential standing requirements and the various factors governing intervention have the potential to affect the outcome of some natural resource damages cases. First, intervenors may find that the amount of damages assessed in a particular assessment do not capture all of the values which have been lost due to an injured resource. Obviously, a challenge to the amount of damages assessed could have a direct impact on the amounts which are recoverable in an action. Secondly, private parties could challenge the amount of damages agreed upon by the trustees and defendants in settlement of a natural resource damages claim. Finally, intervenors may choose to assert that trustee agencies have failed to fulfil their responsibilities in implementing the provisions of the ultimate restoration plan at a site.

One issue on which intervention by private parties has abundant potential is in determining whether the amount of damages agreed upon by the trustees and the defendants in a settlement is adequate. CERCLA provides that the federal trustee may agree to a damages covenant in a remedial action consent decree 'if the potentially responsible party agrees to undertake *appropriate actions necessary to protect and restore* the natural resources damaged by [the release at issue]'.[121]

The meaning of this provision was discussed in the *In re Acushnet River & New Bedford Harbor* case,[122] where the National Wildlife Federation argued that only a commitment to pay for or perform full restoration would satisfy the requirement of 'appropriate actions necessary to protect and restore the [injured] natural resources'. The court rejected that argument and found a $2 million settlement with one of the five defendants (out of an estimated total claim of $50 million) was consistent with the statutory standard. In so finding, the court stated that 'an

---

[118] N. 37 above, at 1023–4.   [119] No. A91–0082 (D. Alaska, 17 May 1995).

[120] *Ibid.* 6. The court denied the motion because the interveners failed to allege independent grounds for jurisdiction, as required for permissive intervention under Rule 24(b), Fed.R.Civ.P. Presumably, an allegation that CERCLA s. 310 provides jurisdiction (if the action had been brought under CERCLA) would be sufficient to satisfy this requirement. The court also found that the intervenors had failed to claim any injury to themselves or to one of their members, and had thus failed to meet Art. III standing requirements: *ibid.* 8, n. 13.

[121] 42 USC § 9622(j)(2) (emphasis added).   [122] N. 37 above, at 1032–8.

interpretation more in keeping with the intent of, as well as the language employed by Congress is one that requires the United States to assess the strengths and weaknesses of its case and drive the hardest bargain it can'.[123] Obviously, if the reviewing court emphasizes CERCLA's intention to promote settlement of disputes, and defers to the government's assessment of its case in achieving the best resolution it can, the prospects for intervenor's challenges to settlements appears bleak.

Two recent cases, however, suggest that the courts will not only be receptive to citizen challenges to the adequacy of settlements, but may at times raise independent judicial concerns when natural resources in the public trust are at issue. In *State of Utah* v. *Kennecott Corp.*,[124] the district court undertook a far more searching inquiry into the adequacy of the State of Utah's proposed $12 million settlement for injury to groundwater than had the district court in *Acushnet*. After an evidentiary hearing regarding the rationale for the settlement, the court rejected it. According to the court, the state's determination that restoration of the injured resources was infeasible lacked foundation, the state failed to require adequate source control measures to prevent further groundwater contamination, and applied the wrong measure of damages because it considered only the market value of the resource and failed to consider its 'passive use' value.[125]

The Ninth Circuit Court of Appeals decision in *United States* v. *Montrose Chemical Corp.*[126] also considered the fairness of a natural resource damages settlement, in that case between the Untied States and a county sanitation district in Los Angeles. Though the challenge to the consent decree was made by a non-settling defendant and not by the public, and the criteria for determining whether the settlement was adequate were not whether the government agencies had fulfilled their trust responsibilities,[127] the court's discussion of the adequacy of the settlement is instructive. The court vacated the entry of the decree, in which the county had agreed to pay over $45 million for damages, and remanded to the district court for a determination of an 'estimate of total potential damages'.[128]

While these decisions may demonstrate a trend toward requiring a more introspective investigation when a settlement concerns resources with the attributes of the public trust, neither *Montrose* nor *Kennecott* addresses the specific issues which will confront a court when a non-party seeks to intervene to challenge trustees' actions. There is, however, no reason to believe that the inquiry undertaken in

---

[123] *In re Acushnet River & New Bedford Harbor*, n. 37 above, at 1036. The court further ruled, however, that Congress' policy of requiring a 'reopener' for unknown conditions in remedial action settlements, set forth in 42 USC § 9622(f)(6)(A), should also be applied to natural resource damage settlements: *ibid.* 1038. The court declined to approve a settlement without such a reopener.

[124] 801 F.Supp. 553 (D. Utah 1992); appeal dismissed, 14 F.3d 1489 (10th Cir. 1994).

[125] 801 F.Supp., at 566, 568–71.   [126] 50 F.3d 741 (9th Cir. 1995).

[127] In determining whether a consent decree is a fair settlement, the district court reviewing the decree must find that it is fair, reasonable, and consistent with the purpose of the statute. See, e.g. *United States* v. *Montrose Chemical Corp.*, n. 126 above, at 746; *United States* v. *Charles George Trucking*, 34 F.3d 1081, 1084–5 (1st Cir. 1994).   [128] N. 126 above, at 747.

that instance would be any less stringent. In fact, courts may be more willing to entertain the types of challenges addressed in these cases, if put forward by members of the general public to whom the trust duty is owed.

5.3. Public Participation in Damages Assessment and Restoration Planning

Though citizen suits, intervention and challenges to the adequacy of settlements may be avenues for enforcing the public's rights *vis-à-vis* resources held in trust by governmental agencies, potentially the most viable and potent option is active, informed participation by interested citizens and non-governmental organizations in the assessment of damages and the formulation of the plan for restoration of the injured resource.

Both CERCLA and OPA require trustees to develop a plan for restoration or replacement of injured resources, to publish notice of the proposed plan, and to allow opportunities for public comment and a hearing before natural resource damage recoveries are expended.[129] As a result, both the DOI and the NOAA regulations on damage assessment (discussed in section 3 above) set forth an explicit administrative record process, and provide for meaningful opportunities for the public to participate in that process.[130]

There may be several advantages to participating in this manner. Obviously, participation at this level does not demand the financial and scientific resources that may, and in larger cases will, be required if citizens are to intervene in litigation. Secondly, as discussed above, if members of the public have the opportunity to intervene, it will likely be at a very late stage in the litigation, tantamount to, in effect, a *post mortem* on an already negotiated settlement. While *parties* to litigation in both the *Montrose* and *Kennecott* cases were successful in challenging resource damages settlements, intervenors have, to date, no such track record. In fact, it seems likely that in the wake of those decisions, agencies and district courts can simply make the types of findings the *Montrose* and *Kennecott* courts believed were necessary to sustain entry of those decrees.

Legal uncertainty about the standard for judicial review of a natural resource damages assessment has, up to now, been a recurring obstacle to effective public participation in the damages assessment process. Under federal law, agency decisions made by an administrative process open to the public and to potential (or actual) defendants are generally reviewed by courts using a deferential standard that acknowledges the agency's special expertise, and the information on which the court bases its review of such decisions is generally limited to the administrative decision-making record. However, several courts have ruled that

---

[129] See 42 USC § 9611(i), 33 USC § 2706(c)(5) ('Plans shall be developed and implemented under this section only after adequate public notice, opportunity for hearing, and consideration of all public comment').

[130] See 43 CFR § 11.82(e)(2) (1994); 61 Fed. Reg. 439 (5 Jan. 1996) (s. 990.14(d) of the final NOAA regulations).

defendants are constitutionally entitled to a jury trial on a CERCLA natural resource damages claim, with the outcome turning on the jury's evaluation of competing expert testimony and no deference accorded to the trustees' expertise.[131] In the damages assessment following the *Exxon Valdez* oil spill in Alaska, for example, concern about the risks of prematurely exposing the federal and state governments' expert evidence to attack by Exxon led the trustees to keep their studies of injury and damages confidential until very late in the process, giving the public no opportunity to help shape the assessment.

The exclusion of the public from the damages assessment in *Exxon* deprived the trustees of opportunities both to learn from public input and to build trust in their efforts to restore injured resources efficiently. That is an outcome to be avoided if it is possible to do so consistently with the trustees' obligation to prevail in litigation, so that they can obtain the funds needed for restoration. Public participation in the early stages of development of a damage assessment could guide the trustees to consider both alternatives more palatable to the interested public and, of course, activities consistent with the government's trust responsibilities, and could serve to improve the quality of the assessment planning and restoration alternatives.

6. CONCLUSION

The natural resource damage cause of action in CERCLA, OPA, and similar US laws is a significant expansion from common law public trust and *parens patriae* principles. By requiring polluters to compensate the public for restoration costs and the public's economic loss resulting from natural resource injury, it forces the government plaintiffs, defendants, and the public to confront several hard questions that are central to the quest for an enduring balance between economic activity and preservation of natural resources on which our future welfare depends: What is the value of the public's loss when resources are destroyed or put off-limits by contamination? How do we repair frayed or missing strands in the complex web of an ecosystem? What measures to create or enhance substitute resources, or to acquire and preserve parklands or habitat, adequately compensate the public for damaged natural resources that cannot be directly restored?

The concept of government trusteeship on behalf of the public adds an important dimension to these questions, because it suggests a duty to preserve and enhance natural amenities for the long-term benefit of the entire public, including future generations. However, the statutory obligation to act as a trustee of

---

[131] See *United States* v. *Montrose Chemical Corp.*, No. CV 90–3122 AAH (C.D. Cal. 27 Mar. 1991) (bench ruling); *United States* v. *City of Seattle*, No. C90–395WD, slip op. (W.D. Wash. 28 Nov. 1990); *Acushnet River & New Bedford Harbor: Proceedings re Alleged PCB Pollution*, n. 61 above, 1000 (D. Mass. 1989); but see *United States* v. *Wade*, 653 F.Supp. 11, 13 (E.D. Pa. 1984) (costs of rehabilitating or restoring injured resources 'would properly be characterized as equitable for the same reasons that recovery of . . . response costs is considered equitable').

natural resources does not necessarily supersede other statutory duties of the trustee agencies. Government trustees generally have broad responsibilities, also owed to the public, to encourage the productive use of public resources and to minimize the government's own liability for natural resource damages. There is a compelling need to develop both a coherent theory and practical guidance on how government trustees should integrate their often-competing obligations to restore and preserve our natural heritage and to permit economic activities that also contribute to our common welfare.

For this balancing of competing objectives to work consistently, effective checks on the trustees' discretion are essential. The scheme of overlapping federal, state, and tribal trusteeships in US natural resource damages legislation provides one check, but it may not be enough by itself. Codification of natural resource damage claims has effectively precluded independent damages claims by citizens. Nonetheless, intervention in government natural resource damage cases by private citizens who are able to establish standing, to challenge the adequacy of settlements or the appropriateness of restoration plans, may be a valuable supplement to trustee actions.

The opportunities for citizen participation are greatest and least disruptive when the process is conducted on an open record. Although the damages assessment regulations under CERCLA and OPA encourage an open administrative process for assessing damages, the prevailing judicial view that the trustees' assessment should be tested by jury trial tends to undermine the value of public participation in assessments and should be changed by legislative action.

11

Litigating and Settling a Natural Resource Damage Claim in the United States: The Defence Lawyer's Perspective

CHARLES B. ANDERSON

1. INTRODUCTION

Natural resource damage assessment (NRDA) is an adversarial process in the United States. Although virtually all natural resource damages cases settle before trial, they are generally preceded by a multitude of assessment studies and analyses, prolonged debates between experts on both sides, and seemingly endless meetings with trustees representing federal, state, and local governments. This Chapter will discuss the NRDA process from the perspective of lawyers representing responsible parties in actions brought under both the Oil Pollution Act of 1990 (OPA) and the Comprehensive Environmental Response, Compensation, and Liability Act of 1980 (CERCLA), and will evaluate some of the problems likely to be encountered in trying and settling a natural resource damage action in the United States.

2. BACKGROUND

2.1. Natural Resource Damages under OPA

OPA establishes a comprehensive scheme for liability and damages resulting from the discharge of oil into the navigable waters of the United States and the exclusive economic zone. Section 1002(a) provides that:

[N]otwithstanding any other provision or rule of law, and subject to the provisions of this Act, each responsible party for a vessel or a facility from which oil is discharged, or which poses the substantial threat of a discharge of oil, into or upon the navigable waters or adjoining shorelines or the exclusive economic zone is liable for the removal costs and damages specified in subsection (b).[1]

---

[1] 33 USC § 2702(a).

Section 1002(b) provides for recovery of '[d]amages for injury to, destruction of, loss of, or loss of use of, natural resources, including the reasonable costs of assessing the damage, which shall be recoverable by a United States trustee, a State trustee, an Indian tribe trustee, or a foreign trustee.'[2] In addition, private claimants may recover damages for loss of subsistence use of natural resources without regard to the ownership or management of the resources, and loss of profits or impairment of earning capacity due to the injury, destruction, or loss of natural resources.[3] Natural resources are defined to include:

land, fish, wildlife, biota, air, water, ground water, drinking water supplies, and other such resources belonging to, managed by, held in trust by, pertaining to, or otherwise control-led by the United States (including the resources of the exclusive economic zone) any State or local government or Indian tribe, or any foreign government.[4]

The measure of natural resource damages under OPA is set forth in section 1006(d):

(1) the cost of restoring, rehabilitating, replacing, or acquiring the equivalent of, the damaged natural resources;
(2) the diminution in value of those natural resources pending restoration; plus
(3) the reasonable cost of assessing those damages.[5]

2.2. *Ohio* v. *Department of the Interior*

The legislative history indicates that section 1006(d) of OPA is intended to be consistent with *State of Ohio* v. *United States Department of the Interior*.[6]

The most significant issue in the *Ohio* decision concerned the validity of proposed regulations published by the Department of the Interior (DOI) in 1986 providing that damages for injury to natural resources under CERCLA shall be 'the lesser of: restoration or replacement costs; or diminution of use values'.[7] The petitioners' challenge rested on CERCLA's mandate that damages be at least sufficient to pay the cost in every case of restoring, replacing, or requiring the equivalent of the damaged resource. According to the state and environ-mental petitioners, in enacting CERCLA Congress intended restoration costs as a minimum measure of damages. The petitioners relied on several sections of CERCLA to support their position. The petitioners relied first on § 107(f)(1) of CERCLA, which states that natural resource damages recovered by a govern-ment trustee are 'for use only to restore, replace, or acquire the equivalent of such natural resources'.[8] The petitioners relied further on a provision according to which 'the measure of damages in any action under [§ 107(a)(C)] shall not be limited by the sums which can be used to restore or replace such resources'.[9]

Both the DOI and the industry petitioners argued that Congress intended that

[2] 33 USC § 2702(b)(2)(A).   [3] 33 USC § 2702(b)(C) and (E).   [4] 33 USC § 2701(20).
[5] 33 USC § 2706(d)(1).   [6] 880 F.2d 432 (D.C. Cir. 1989).
[7] 43 CFR § 11.35(b)(2) (1987).   [8] 42 USC § 9607(f)(1).   [9] 42 USC § 9607(a)(C).

damages under CERCLA would be calculated according to traditional common law rules, under which damages are measured as the lesser of lost use value or restoration costs. Alternatively, they argued that the 'lesser of' rule should be adopted because of economic efficiency. In other words, as the cost of a restoration project goes up relative to the value of the injured resource, at some point it becomes wasteful to require parties responsible to pay the full costs of restoration. The court of appeals rejected both arguments, finding that a motivating force behind CERCLA's natural resource damage provisions was Congress' dissatisfaction with the common law. As to the economic efficiency argument, the court stated: '[t]he fatal flaw of Interior's approach, however, is that it assumes that natural resources are fungible goods, just like any other, and that the value to society generated by a particular resource can be accurately measured in every case—assumptions that Congress apparently rejected'.[10] After a detailed analysis of CERCLA's legislative history, the court concluded that restoration costs were intended to be the presumptive measure of recovery in natural resource damages cases.[11] Unfortunately, the goal of restoration articulated in the *Ohio* decision is frequently obscured in litigation. In the wake of a substantial oil spill, for example, there may be considerable pressure on trustees to utilize the damage assessment process in a punitive manner. In addition, trustees may be tempted to reject restoration proposals until the completion of injury studies and formal restoration planning, thus delaying the primary objective of the NRDA process—restoration of the environment.

2.3. Natural Resource Damages under CERCLA

Section 107 of CERCLA provides that the owner and operator of a vessel or a facility shall be liable for '[d]amages for injury to, destruction of, or loss of natural resources, including the reasonable cost of assessing such injury, destruction, or loss resulting from such a release'.[12] The term 'natural resources' is nearly identical to the OPA definition.[13]

Recovery of natural resource damages is, of course, predicated on the accrual of a cause of action under OPA or CERCLA and a finding of liability. Under both statutes there is a broad threshold of liability and very narrow defenses. The liability schemes are briefly summarized below.

---

[10] N. 6 above, at 456.

[11] The court stated: 'Congress established a distinct preference for restoration costs as the measure of recovery in natural resource damage cases.' The court nevertheless recognized that there may be some class of cases where other considerations, i.e. infeasibility of restoration or grossly disproportionate cost-to-use value, may warrant a different standard: n. 6 above, at 459.

[12] 42 USC § 9607(a)(4)(C).

[13] Liability is to 'the United States Government and to any State for natural resources within the State or belonging to, managed by, controlled by, or pertaining to such State': 42 USC § 9607(f)(1). CERCLA provides for the designation of federal and state trustees who are authorized to assess natural resource damages and assert claims for the recovery of damages under both CERCLA and under s. 311 of the Federal Water Pollution Control Act (FWPCA).

2.4. Liability Regime under OPA

The cornerstone of liability under OPA is § 1002, which provides:

[N]otwithstanding any other provision or rule of law, and subject to the provisions of this Act, each responsible party for a vessel or a facility from which oil is discharged, or which poses the substantial threat of a discharge of oil, into or upon the navigable waters or adjoining shorelines or the exclusive economic zone is liable for the removal costs and damages specified in subsection (b) that result from such incident.[14]

A 'vessel' is defined to mean every description of watercraft or other artificial contrivance used, or capable of being used, as a means of transportation on water, other than a public vessel (a vessel owned or bareboat chartered and operated by the United States, a state, or foreign nation, except when the vessel is engaged in commerce[15]). In the case of a vessel, 'responsible party' means any person owning, operating, or demise chartering the vessel.[16]

The liability provisions also apply to a 'facility' which is defined to mean 'any structure, group of structures, equipment, or device (other than a vessel) which is used for one or more of the following purposes: exploring for, drilling for, producing, storing, handling, transferring, processing, or transporting oil'.[17]

Liability is strict, joint, and several, and is established by proof of a 'discharge' of 'oil' into the navigable waters of the United States. A 'discharge' is broadly defined to mean 'any emission (other than natural seepage), intentional or unintentional, and includes, but is not limited to, spilling, leaking, pumping, pouring, emitting, emptying, or dumping'.[18] 'Oil' means 'oil of any kind or in any form, including, but not limited to, petroleum, fuel oil, sludge, oil refuse and oil mixed with wastes other than dredged spoil'.[19] The definition specifically exempts any substance which is listed or designated as a hazardous substance under CERCLA. Under the natural resource damage assessment regulations originally proposed by the National Oceanic and Atmospheric Administration (NOAA), 'injury' was defined as 'any adverse change in a natural resource or impairment of a service provided by a resource relative to baseline, reference, or control conditions'.[20] This definition differed from the definition contained in the CERCLA damage assessment regulations. Under CERCLA, injury is defined as 'a measurable adverse change' to the quality of a natural resource resulting either directly or indirectly from exposure to a discharge of oil or a release of a hazardous substance. Thus, the CERCLA definition incorporates concepts of injury and causality. Under the new NOAA rule, discussed in further detail below, the definition has been modified to require a demonstration of an 'observable or measurable adverse change in a natural resource or impairment of a natural resource service'.[21] Thus under the OPA regulations, the concept of 'injury'

[14] 33 USC § 2702(a).   [15] 33 USC § 2701(37).   [16] 33 USC § 2701(32)(A).
[17] 33 USC § 2701(9).   [18] 33 USC § 2701(7).   [19] 33 USC § 2701(23).
[20] 59 Fed. Reg. 1169 (7 Jan. 1994).   [21] 61 Fed. Reg. 504 (5 Jan. 1996).

is substantially identical to that under CERCLA. The trustees may recover for injuries resulting from a discharge only upon a demonstration that:

(1) the definition of injury, as defined above, has been met; and
(2) an injured resource has been exposed to the discharged oil, and a pathway can be established from the discharge to the exposed natural resource; or
(3) an injury to a natural resource or impairment of a natural resource service has occurred as a result of response actions or a substantial threat of a discharge of oil.[22]

OPA specifies limits to liability. For tank vessels larger than 3,000 gross tons, liability is limited to $1,200 per gross ton or $10 million. For tank vessels of 3,000 gross tons or less, liability is limited to the greater of $1,200 per gross ton or $2 million.[23] For all other types of vessels, liability is limited to the greater of $600 per gross ton or $500,000.[24] Offshore facilities other than deepwater ports are subject to unlimited removal costs plus $75 million.[25] Onshore facilities and deepwater ports are subject to a liability limit of $350 million.[26] The limits do not apply if the incident is 'proximately caused by (A) gross negligence or wilful misconduct of, or (B) the violation of an applicable federal safety, construction, or operating regulation by the responsible party', or the agent, employee, or contractor of the party responsible.[27]

Defences to liability under OPA are likewise limited. Liability is avoided only where the discharge was caused solely by (1) an act of God; (2) an act of war; or (3) an act or omission of a third party other than an employee, agent or contractor of the responsible party.[28]

2.5. Liability Standards under CERCLA

Section 107(a) of CERCLA identifies four categories of parties subject to natural resource damage liability: (1) the current owner or operator of a vessel or facility from which there is a release of a hazardous substance; (2) the owner or operator at the time of disposal of a hazardous substance; (3) any person who arranged for disposal or treatment of hazardous substances at the facility; and (4) any person who accepts hazardous substances for transport to a facility selected by that person.

CERCLA defines 'release' broadly to include 'any spilling, leaking, pumping, pouring, emitting, emptying, discharging, injecting, escaping, leaching, dumping, or disposing into the environment (including the abandonment or discarding

---

[22] Potential categories of injury include adverse changes in survival, growth, and reproduction; health, physiology and biological condition; behaviour; community composition; ecological processes and functions; physical and chemical habitat quality and structure; and public services: 61 Fed. Reg. 506.   [23] 33 USC § 2704(a)(1)(A), (B)(ii).
[24] 33 USC § 2704(a)(2).   [25] 33 USC § 2704(a)(3).   [26] 33 USC § 2704(a)(4).
[27] 33 USC § 2704(c)(1).
[28] 33 USC § 2703(a)(1)–(3). Defences to liability are subject to limitations similar to those imposed on liability ceilings.

of barrels, containers, and other closed receptacles containing any hazardous substances or pollutant or contaminant)'.[29] The term 'hazardous substance' is also broadly defined with reference to a wide variety of federal environmental statutes. Under CERCLA, a plaintiff must prove a causal connection between the release and the incurring of response costs and damages resulting from the release. The causation requirement in the case of damages to natural resources differs from the requirement for response costs. With respect to the latter, the alleged costs need only be incurred as part of a clean-up or response to a hazardous substance problem.[30] With respect to natural resource damages, however, the release must be a substantial contributing factor to the injury.[31] Thus, in CERCLA cases, where damages are apportionable, recovery is only for injury resulting from the release. However, since the burden of proof is on the defendant to prove that the injury is divisible, potentially liable parties must devote considerable effort to assessment studies designed to identify or 'fingerprint' hazardous substances and their effect on the environment.[32]

Liability under CERCLA is subject to the same statutory defences as are contained in OPA.[33] Under CERCLA, the liability limit for vessels carrying a hazardous substance as cargo or residue is the greater of $300 per gross ton or $5 million. For facilities, the liability limit per incident is the total of all response costs plus $50 million.[34] As under OPA, these limits do not apply to incidents resulting from wilful misconduct, wilful negligence, or where the primary cause of the release was a violation of applicable safety, construction, or operating standards or regulations.[35]

Under both CERCLA and OPA, in the event of a major maritime casualty involving a substantial release of oil or hazardous substances, it is likely that the plaintiffs will allege gross negligence, wilful misconduct, or a violation of regulatory requirements. Particularly with respect to regulatory violations, it can be anticipated that liability limits may easily be broken. As discussed in more detail below, this is often a powerful incentive for parties responsible to explore settlement rather than proceeding to trial to disprove such allegations.

3. NATURAL RESOURCE DAMAGE ASSESSMENT REGULATIONS

Both OPA and CERCLA require the promulgation of regulations for assessment of damages for injury to natural resources. Trustees are not required to employ these regulations in assessing natural resource damages; however, if the trustees

---

[29] 42 USC § 9601(22).
[30] *Pennsylvania Urban Development Corp.* v. *Golen*, 708 F.Supp. 669, 671–2 (E.D. Pa. 1989).
[31] *Dedham Water Co.* v. *Cumberland Farms Dairy, Inc.*, 889 F.2d 1146, n. 7 (1st Cir. 1989).
[32] See *United States* v. *Monsanto*, 858 F.2d 160, 172 (4th Cir. 1988).
[33] 42 USC § 9607(b)(1)–(3).   [34] 42 USC § 9607(c)(1)(A) and (D).
[35] 42 USC § 9607(c)(2)(A).

opt to utilize these assessment methods, their determination has the effect of a rebuttable presumption of correctness in any subsequent administrative or judicial proceeding.[36] It is thus crucial for potential litigants to understand these regulatory assessment methods.

3.1. Department of the Interior Final Rules

On 25 March 1994 the Department of the Interior issued final rules amending the regulations for assessing natural resource damages resulting from a discharge of oil into navigable waters under the Clean Water Act or a release of a hazardous substance under CERCLA.[37]

Under the DOI rules, the preparation of an NRDA consists of four phases: (1) the pre-assessment phase; (2) the assessment plan phase; (3) the assessment phase; (4) the post-assessment phase. During the pre-assessment phase, the trustees receive notification from the Environmental Protection Agency or US Coast Guard of a release of hazardous substance or discharge of oil, gather relevant information, and determine actual or potential injuries. During the assessment planning phase, the trustees determine the assessment procedure to be used and develop an assessment plan. The rules provide the trustees with two alternative assessment procedures.

3.1.1. Type A Assessment

Type A assessments involve the use of the Natural Resource Damage Assessment Model for Coastal and Marine Environments (NRDAM/CME). This computer model contains extensive chemical, biological, and economic databases that represent average conditions for coastal and marine environments. The model consists of the three submodels: (1) physical fates; (2) biological effects; (3) economic damages.

The physical fates submodel computes rates of surface spreading of oil or hazardous substances and concentrations of these materials over time and space. The biological effects submodel determines injury to fish and wildlife arising from direct mortality due to toxic concentrations, and indirect mortality due to loss of food organisms in the food chain. It also provides data on populations expected seasonally within the area and calculates losses through the period of resource restoration and recovery. The economic damages submodel calculates the dollar amount of compensation based on lost use values. The economic database uses market and non-market prices for the resources and includes direct and indirect mortality or wildlife as well as damages foreclosures of fishing, boating, or beach areas.

---

[36] 33 USC § 2706(e)(2); 42 USC § 9607(f)(2)(c).

[37] 59 Fed. Reg. 19262 (25 Mar. 1994). The DOI regulations were challenged by industry groups in *Chamber of Commerce* v. *Department of the Interior*, No. 94–1462 (D.C. Cir. 1994). Because this case is still pending at the time of writing it remains uncertain whether the court will declare the DOI regulations legally valid.

3.1.2. Type B Assessment

Type B assessments involve the implementation of scientific studies to document and quantify injury. They use a wide variety of methodologies rather than a single, all-inclusive model. Although the Type B assessments are more time-consuming, the breadth of the assessment studies may allow the party responsible to use site-specific criteria rather than a generic model. The trustees may allow the party responsible to perform the assessment itself under official direction, guidance, and monitoring. Consistently with the *Ohio* decision, the DOI rules eliminate the requirement that trustees select the most cost-effective restoration alternative. Instead, cost-effectiveness is only one of ten factors to be used in evaluating alternatives, which include technical feasibility, the relationship of costs to benefits, consistency with federal and state laws, and the potential for additional injury resulting from the proposed actions.[38]

The DOI rules also require that, in addition to restoration costs, damages be based on 'compensable values', defined as 'the amount of money required to compensate the public for the reduction in services provided by the injured resources between the time of the discharge or release and the time the resources and the services those resources provide are fully returned to their baseline conditions'.[39] Compensatable values include passive or non-use values, calculated by use of the highly controversial contingent valuation methodology (CVM).[40]

During the post-assessment phase, a report of assessment is produced which consists of all the documentation supporting the determinations required in the assessment phase. The post-assessment phase also contains a demand for damages which is presented to the party responsible. Upon a determination of the amount of the damages claim, a restoration plan is prepared together with a restoration financial account.

3.2. Final NOAA Rule

On 5 January 1996 NOAA issued its final rule regarding NRDA. The NRDA rule took effect on 5 February 1996.

The rule divides the assessment process into three phases: (1) a pre-assessment phase, in which federal and state trustees determine if restoration of injured resources is appropriate; (2) a restoration planning phase, in which the trustees evaluate and quantify potential injuries; and (3) a restoration implementation phase, in which a written demand is made to the parties responsible to implement the plan. In the planning phase, the trustees may consider a range of alternatives comprised of primary restoration actions—including natural recovery—designed directly to restore natural resources and services to pre-spill conditions, and

---

[38] 59 Fed. Reg. 14285.   [39] 59 Fed. Reg. 14286.
[40] For a detailed discussion of CVM, see K. Ward and J. Duffield, *Natural Resource Damages: Law and Economics* (1992), 281–309.

compensatory restoration actions, which compensate for the loss of resources and services pending recovery. The rule also introduces the concept of 'scaling' as a means of determining how to make the environment and the public whole. If, for example, the trustees cannot design a restoration plan that provides resources of the same type or quality as the injured resources, they may select a plan using different resources that produce the same value as the lost resources, or alternatively estimate the dollar value of the resources and choose a restoration programme equivalent in cost to the lost value.

In essence, any assessment procedure determined to be valid and appropriate by the trustees may be utilized. Trustees may choose from an extensive menu of procedures, including computer models, compensation formulas, contingent valuation, and various economic models, or a combination of these techniques.

There are limitations on the trustees' discretion, but they are so vague as to be almost meaningless. First, the procedure must be capable of providing assessment information of use in determining the type and scale of restoration appropriate for a particular injury. Secondly, the additional cost of a more complex procedure must be reasonably related to the expected increase in the quantity and/or quality of relevant information provided by that procedure. Thirdly, the procedure must be reliable and valid for the particular incident.

If the trustees conduct the assessment in accordance with the rule and meet these broad criteria, their damage determination will receive a rebuttable presumption of correctness in any judicial or administrative proceeding. While a responsible party may propose an alternative assessment procedure, the regulations allow the trustees to reject the proposal if, in their sole judgement, the proposal is not technically feasible or adequate. The trustees are required to document the basis for their assessment decisions in an administrative record, but they largely control the contents of the record. Since courts generally limit their review to the administrative record, challenges to the trustees' assessment decision are likely to fail unless it can be shown that the decision was arbitrary and capricious.

4. LITIGATION OR SETTLEMENT?

The foregoing discussion has highlighted some of the technical complexities of natural resource damage assessments under the NOAA regulations. In addition, the statutes and regulations contain several evidentiary and procedural devices which must be carefully considered by responsible parties in deciding whether to litigate or settle a natural resource damages claim.

4.1. The Rebuttable Presumption

Both OPA and CERCLA provide that any determination or assessment of damages to natural resources made by federal or state trustees in accordance with the regulations promulgated under the Acts shall have the force and effect of a rebuttable presumption on behalf of the trustee in any administrative or judicial proceedings.[41] The effect of the rebuttable presumption is to shift the burden of proof from the trustees to the party responsible. The quantum of proof necessary to rebut the presumption has been the subject of considerable debate. In most civil cases, a preponderance of the evidence is generally sufficient to rebut the presumption. However, some courts have held that where policy considerations require deviation from the preponderance standard, the presumption can be rebutted only by the more stringent clear and convincing evidentiary standard.[42]

The advantages provided to the trustees by the rebuttable presumption may actually impede co-operation in the NRDA process and provide a disincentive for settlement. For example, the force of the rebuttable presumption may cause trustees to deny parties responsible the opportunity to participate in the NRDA process. Moreover, the presumption may create a preference for use of simpler, cost-effective computer models or compensation formulas, which carry the same rebuttable presumption as more expensive, albeit more accurate, scientific studies.

The impact of the rebuttable presumption may promote challenges to proposed damage assessment regulations before they become effective. Both OPA and CERCLA provide for judicial review of any regulations issued under the Acts within ninety days of promulgation of the final regulations. The statutes further provide '[a]ny matter with respect to which review could have been obtained under this subsection shall not be subject to judicial review in any civil or criminal proceeding for enforcement or to obtain damages or recovery of response costs.'[43] The impact of these sections is to preclude judicial challenge to the natural resource damage assessment regulations in any litigation so long as the claim is based on an assessment conducted in accordance with the regulations. Thus, potentially responsible parties may be well advised to make such challenges within the statutory time-frame. In *Ohio* v. *Department of the Interior*, above, DOI natural resource damage regulations promulgated under CERCLA were successfully challenged in court and were remanded to DOI for revisions in accordance with the court's decision, which found the regulations inadequate because they failed to give priority to the 'restoration' measure of damages.

4.2. Judicial Review and the Administrative Record

Section 1006(c)(5) of OPA provides that 'plans shall be developed and implemented under this section only after adequate public notice, opportunity for a hearing and consideration of all public comments'.[44] As noted above, NOAA has implemented this provision by requiring the trustees to document the development

---

[41] OPA § 1006(e)(2), 33 USC § 2706(e)(2); CERCLA § 107(f)(2)(C), 42 USC § 9607(f)(2)(C).

[42] See C. R. O'Connor, 'Natural Resource Damage Actions under the Oil Pollution Act of 1990: A Litigation Perspective' (1993) 45 *Baylor Law Review* 441–57, at 450–3.

[43] OPA § 1017, 33 USC § 2717; CERCLA § 113(a), 42 USC § 9613(a).

[44] 33 USC § 2706(c)(5).

of restoration plans in an administrative record through notice and comment procedures. The basis for limiting judicial review of assessment/restoration plans is that assessments involve highly technical and scientific findings in which the courts have traditionally treated the agency's determination with deference. Limiting judicial review to the administrative record means that an arbitrary and capricious standard will probably be applied to the agency's determination. Several commenters have contended that specifying any judicial standard of review in the regulations would exceed NOAA's statutory authority because a party responsible has the legal right to a jury trial in natural resource damage assessment cases as guaranteed by the US Constitution.[45]

Use of the administrative record has several important implications for the party responsible. First, defendants who wish to challenge the trustees' assessment decision will be precluded from deposing or examining on-scene co-ordinators, government response managers, and consultants or other decision-makers with respect to any assessment decision or engaging in other discovery activity. Secondly, defendants must act quickly to complete their own preliminary assessment studies so that their position is set forth in the administrative record. Once the administrative record is compiled and a decision made, it is very difficult to supplement the record, even if new and important information comes to light. The administrative record may be supplemented with post-decisional documents only at the trustee's discretion, unless the defendant can establish that the record does not disclose the factors considered in making a particular decision; the decision is inadequate; or there is strong evidence that the agency acted improperly or in bad faith.[46] Thirdly, while the record normally should include all documents relied upon by the trustees, pre-decisional, deliberative internal agency memoranda may be excluded, even though they may have a bearing on the validity of the assessment decision. Fourthly, the arbitrary and capricious standard of judicial review severely limits the responsible parties' opportunity to obtain *de novo* review of the agency's decision.

4.3. Use of Experts

The complexity of the NRDA process requires that defence counsel utilize a multitude of technical disciplines. After the discharge of oil or release of hazardous substances into marine ecosystems, use of experts in such varied fields as chemistry, marine biology, oceanography, toxicology, and economics is often required. The use of such experts is vital to show the presence or absence of a causal relationship between the discharge and release and the injuries to natural resources for which recovery is sought. This, in turn, raises questions as to the admissibility of the opinions and scientific evidence proffered by the experts.

---

[45] Many courts have upheld the right to jury trial for natural resource damages claims. See, e.g. *In Re Acushnet River and New Bedford Harbor Proceedings*, 712 F.Supp. 994 (D. Mass. 1989).

[46] See *US* v. *Wastecontrol of Florida, Inc.*, 30 ER Cases 1491 (M.D. Fla. 1989).

In *Frye* v. *United States*,[47] the US Court of Appeals for the District of Columbia Circuit held that testimony regarding novel technical or scientific issues could only be introduced if the principles underlying the testimony had gained general acceptance in their particular field. *Frye*, however, was decided before the adoption of the Federal Rules of Evidence and has been superseded by a more liberal view of expert testimony embodied in rule 702 of the Federal Rules of Evidence. Rule 702 states: 'If scientific, technical, or other specialized knowledge will assist the trier of fact to understand the evidence or to determine a fact in issue, a witness qualified as an expert by knowledge, skill, experience, training, or education may testify thereto in a form of an opinion or otherwise.'

Recently, the US Supreme Court in *Daubert* v. *Merrell Dow Pharmaceuticals*[48] held that 'general acceptance' is not a necessary precondition to the admissibility of scientific evidence; rather, the court held that the task of ensuring that an expert's testimony has a reliable foundation and is relevant to the case rests with the trial judge. The court appeared to devise a balancing test which would promote resolution of legal disputes rather than scientific certainty:

It is true that open debate is an essential part of both legal and scientific analyses. Yet there are important differences between the quest for truth in the courtroom and the quest for truth in the laboratory. Scientific conclusions are subject to perpetual revision. Law, on the other hand, must resolve disputes finally and quickly. . . . Conjectures that are probably wrong are of little use, however, in the project of reaching a quick, final, and binding legal judgment—often of great consequence—about a particular set of events in the past. We recognize that in practice, a gate-keeping role for the judge, no matter how flexible, inevitably on occasion will prevent the jury from learning of authentic insights and innovations. That, nevertheless, is the balance that is struck by the Rules of Evidence not for the exhaustive search for cosmic understanding but for the particularized resolution of legal disputes.[49]

The Supreme Court's holding in *Daubert* has understandably raised concerns in both the legal and scientific community about the standards which courts may now use to measure scientific evidence. The *Daubert* standard places great reliance on the scientific abilities of a particular judge as well as on the ability of experts and attorneys to convince the court of the reliability of their arguments. As a result, demonstrable, objective procedures for the assessment of natural resource damages are likely to suffer, and the results of litigated cases will lack any measure of predictability.

5. CONCLUSION AND OUTLOOK

As the foregoing discussion shows, under the new NRDA regulations, litigation is clearly a last resort in resolving natural damages claims, yet the regulatory and

---

[47] 293 F. 1013 (D.C. Cir. 1923).   [48] 113 S.Ct. 2786 (1993).   [49] *Ibid.* 2798–9.

settlement process is often equally expensive and time-consuming. As a result, the statutory objective of restoring damaged resources as quickly as possible is likely to suffer. Many options to traditional litigation have been proposed for resolution of NRDA disputes both inside and outside the courtroom. These alternatives include the empanelling of a jury composed solely of scientific experts, or appointment of a special master to review data provided by both sides and present to the judge a recommendation based on objective scientific analysis; binding arbitration or mediation consisting of scientific, economic, and legal experts mutually agreed upon by plaintiffs and defendants, and abolition of the rebuttable presumption in order to foster greater co-operation between trustees and parties responsible.[50] Outside the litigation forum, there is growing sentiment that co-operation between parties responsible and trustees is essential if natural damage claims are to be resolved in a cost-effective and impartial manner. Use of objective technical experts mutually agreed upon by trustees and parties responsible, enhanced training in the NRDA process for legal, scientific, and economic participants, and full participation by responsible parties in the damage assessment process, as well as standardization of methods used to assess complex environmental damage issues are key to improving such co-operation. Finally, there appears to be growing understanding that the United States may be out of step with the world maritime community in its methods for compensating injury to natural resources. The adoption of international guidelines, such as those recently formulated both by the Comité Maritime International and the International Oil Pollution Compensation Fund may ultimately provide the best solution for resolution of conflicts of admissibility and assessment of claims for oil pollution damage.[51]

[50] See *The Use and Misuse of Science in Natural Resource Damage Assessment*, Technical Report IOSC–002, 1995 International Oil Spill Conference.
[51] See 'Admissibility and Assessment of Claims for Pollution Damage: Report of the Chairman of the International Sub-committee', in Comité Maritime International, *Yearbook 1993 (Sydney I, Documents for the Conference)*, 88–139; International Oil Pollution Compensation Fund, *Report of Seventh Intersessional Working Group*, FUND/WGR. 7/21 (20 June 1994).

PART V

On Complementary Compensation

COSCA: A Complementary System for Compensation of Accidental Pollution Damage

HENRI SMETS*

1. INTRODUCTION: LATENT CONFLICT BETWEEN POLLUTERS AND THEIR NEIGHBOURS

When there is a case of serious accidental pollution, it is generally agreed that the victims of this pollution should be compensated for the prejudice suffered. Whatever the reason for a Bhopal-type accident, whether it was caused by bad management on the employer's part, sabotage by an employee with a grudge, or even lightning, the victims deserve compensation. Whatever the reason for the accidental pollution of a river, riparians and anglers should be compensated and the river should be rehabilitated. Pollution is an act of social aggression, which should at least be compensated for, whenever it is not possible to avoid it.

The victims' right to compensation, together with the polluter pays principle, shows *who* the payer should be. The fact that governments recognize this principle in domestic law and even go so far as to declare that the polluter pays principle is a 'principle of international environmental law'[1] should have resulted in the efficient organization of full and rapid compensation of victims by the polluter.

The reality is that, while the polluter frequently compensates the victims of the most serious cases of pollution, many other victims remain without compensation. For the polluter to be the payer, it is necessary to be able to identify the culprit, who may have chosen surreptitiously to discharge toxic products into

---

* The author would like to express his sincere thanks to Professor H. Bocken, whose works were at the origin of this study.

[1] *International Convention on Oil Pollution Preparedness, Response and Cooperation* (1990). The Single European Act (1986) and the Treaty of Maastricht (1992) also make reference to the polluter pays principle. On the polluter pays principle and pollution insurance, see OECD Environment Monographs, *The Polluter Pays Principle and Pollution Insurance* (1992). See also H. Smets, 'Le principe pollueur-payeur, un principe économique érigé en principe de droit de l'environnement' (1993) 97 *Revue Générale de Droit International Public* No. 2, 339–64; *idem*, 'The Polluter Pays Principle in the Early 1990s', in L. Campiglio *et al.* (eds.), *The Environment after Rio* (1994), 131–48; and *idem*, 'Les exceptions admises au principe pollueur payeur' (1994) 20 *Droit et Pratique du Commerce International* No. 2, 211–37.

a sewer or a river. To make the polluter pay, he must have no legal loophole to escape his liability, and he has to be solvent, even if the pollution results from an accident that has totally destroyed the enterprise concerned.

There have been many uncompensated victims, sometimes with considerable sums involved. As regards disasters on land, during a fire in a chemical products warehouse in Saint-Basile-le-Grand (Canada), the fear of dioxin contamination meant that about 5,000 people were evacuated for eighteen days. This accident has cost the victims about C$ 38 million, entirely borne by themselves because the insolvent polluter left the country and was not properly insured.[2] In any event, the warehouse was operated illegally and the insurer could have refused to cover the damages even if they had been included in the terms of the policy. A similar situation occurred again in Canada in 1990, when a used tyre dump caught fire, causing almost C$ 10 million of uncompensated pollution damage.[3]

Accidental pollution does not usually cost as much as this, but it can easily cause loss in the order of FF 0.5 to 5 million. Recently a few cases of contaminated soil in France involved clean-up expenditures which could be as high as FF 10 million. A fish farm might be destroyed, for example, causing damage in the order of FF 1 million[4] and the bankruptcy of its owner while the polluter is unknown. A water bottling plant can be driven out of the market by pollution,

---

[2] In Aug. 1988, at Saint-Basile-le-Grand (30 km from Montreal), a fire was started by an arsonist in a warehouse containing 3,800 drums of used transformer oils containing polychlorobiphenyls and inflammable solvents. Because of the risk of contamination by dioxins and furans and the possible similarity between this accident and the notorious Seveso affair in Italy (1976), the entire area beneath the pall of smoke was evacuated (14 km^2, 1,800 dwellings, 5,000 people). Authorization to return home was given 18 days after the accident, once it was proved that the potential contamination was lower than the permitted maximum. Because of this fire, the public authorities had to spend almost C$ 38 million, of which C$ 10 million went in compensation to individuals, businesses, and farmers. There is little hope that these costs will be reimbursed either by the arsonist or the owner of the warehouse. Even if the enterprise had been insured (under comprehensive or third party liability policies covering operation or under fire policies), it still seems likely that most of the damage suffered by the authorities or third parties would not have been covered (quantities in excess of authorized limits, illegal storage of certain substances, incorrect disclosure of risk to the insurer, very limited cover for off-site material damage, indirect prejudice not covered by the insurance policy, etc.).

[3] In Feb. 1990, a fire started by an arsonist consumed 14 million used tyres at Hagersville (Ontario) in Canada. It took 14 days to extinguish the fire. The soil and subsoil were seriously contaminated by the combustion residues and the water used to fight the fire, and 1,700 people were evacuated. The clean-up and compensation costs could reach C$ 10 million, but it appears likely that neither the owner nor the arsonist will be able to pay. There was also another big tyre fire in Canada the same year (Saint Amable) but fewer than 200 people did evacuate. Decontamination costs were very significant. It should be noted that, in France, this type of enterprise would at best be insured for up to FF 5 million for its liability resulting from a fire. In case of a serious contamination resulting from fire it is likely that, the enterprise would be bankrupt.

[4] The destruction of a fish farm by toxic pollutants released into a river can cause the loss of 50 tonnes of fish (FF 500,000 loss to be borne by the enterprise). The cost of cleaning up the river after a toxic release may also reach FF 500,000 (to be borne by the public authorities) (source: Assurpol, 1990). In 1989, French fish farmers lost over 400 tonnes of fish as the result of pollution of unknown origin. In 1990, the loss was over 200 tonnes (source: Ministry for the Environment).

as was the case with Katell Roc in France. An anglers' association may spend the equivalent of over five years of members' fees in restocking a river polluted by an unknown person. An enterprise may suffer a loss of millions of francs because of soot coming from a neighbouring enterprise but receive no compensation because it cannot legally prove who the polluter was.[5] The intervention of the fire brigade to combat oil pollution in a river is often at the expense of the taxpayer because the polluter cannot be identified. In 1988, the whole city of Tours was deprived of drinking water for a few days, but neither the harm suffered by the inhabitants nor the losses suffered by enterprises have as yet been compensated.[6]

Every year in France there are dozens cases of serious accidental pollution for which the victims remain uncompensated. This situation results from the fact that, because of their limited resources, their dispersion, and the nature of the legal system, victims are often in a position of inferiority *vis-à-vis* potential or

[5] A textile enterprise was the victim of soot emissions from another enterprise, which were drawn into the premises by the ventilation system. The machines were covered with dirt, the output was sullied, and a substantial market was lost. The damage suffered was estimated by Assurpol at FF 7 million. The enterprise was not compensated because it was not able to establish the link of causality with the furnace of an incineration plant from which the soot was probably released due to a construction defect (source: Assurpol, 1990).

[6] The Protex accident in 1988 caused the hospitalization of three persons, the intoxication of 15 rescue workers and the evacuation of 200 persons, the death of 15 to 20 tonnes of fish over 45 km of the watercourse and the suspension of the drinking water supply for a few days (serving 155,000 people in Tours). According to the official inquiry, the losses and expenditure caused by the accident amounted to FF 49 million, a figure obtained by adding the claims and evaluating the damage suffered by the victims as a result of the accident. This figure (which exceeds what the victims could obtain if they took the case to court) is made up of: (a) expenditure and costs directly connected with the fire and the pollution: FF 15.6 million (of which 10.4 million for various administrations, 1.4 million for the loss of work by Protex employees and for industrial accidents, and 3.7 million for the private sector and sundry costs); (b) loss of earnings and harm suffered: FF 22 million (of which 1.2 million for the private sector and 4.5 million for damage to fish stocks and ecological damage); and (c) rehabilitation measures: FF 11.5 million (of which 9.3 million to restore the image and 1.4 million for the ecosystems (see Ministère de l'Environnement, *Données économiques de l'environnement*, (Paris, 1988)).

Protex itself suffered a loss of FF 53 million due to the fire, a substantial part of which is to be borne by the fire insurer. On this subject see *Le Monde*, 7 Dec. 1988, *Rapport de la Commission d'évaluation* (M. Leynaud) and *Rapport sur le sinistre Protex* (MM. Langlais and Martin). After the accident in June 1988, urgent work was undertaken (FF 8 million) and the enterprise was punished for earlier pollution (FF 60,000 fine and FF 100,000 damages and interest).

In 1992, the two directors of Protex were given suspended sentences of one year and six months respectively for pollution in 1988 and fined FF 120,000 and FF 60,000. The plaintiffs obtained FF 456,000 damages and interest for the damage to the fish and the Anglers' Federation a provisional payment of FF 300,000 (12 to 15 tonnes of fish taken dead from the Brenne over 23 km and from the Cisse over 5 km). At this stage, the compensation amounts to 56 F/kg or 27,000 F/km. The TOS Association has been compensated on the basis of 0.5 F/m^2 of river destroyed, but other associations and groups have also received compensation. The City of Tours has initiated another case and is claiming FF 10 million from the enterprise. In the end, the damages paid by Protex to third parties may amount to no more than FF 15 million. This case is typical of the gap that exists between the initial estimates (made by the victims) and the decisions taken by the courts. In order to frighten potential insured persons, make anti-pollution propaganda, or cause a hue and cry in the press, it is best to emphasize the highest figures, even if they turn out to be exaggerated or lack any legal basis.

actual polluters, and they also suffer from the fact that there are as yet no mechanisms to ensure the effective implementation of the polluter pays principle.

This observation has the corollary that if the potential victims of accidental pollution were to act rationally, they would insist that potential sources of risk should be made as safe as possible and, in certain cases, should even be relocated or shut down. The NIMBY (not in my back yard) syndrome will become the rule and efforts to make dangerous enterprises ever safer could cause unjustified prevention expenditure. If this happens, industry will no longer find anywhere to locate the more hazardous installations because they are capable of causing uncompensated harm to their neighbours.

A new approach for potential polluters would be collectively to undertake to indemnify all accidental pollution victims in all circumstances and to admit that it is their duty to pay compensation before determining who is actually responsible for the pollution. Through this new approach which separates compensation from liability,[7] potential polluters and their possible victims might be able to find common ground, because those at the origin of the risks would undertake to accept all the consequences. The polluter pays principle would then become a reality and the social tensions around high-risk installations would become less highly charged.

2. COMPENSATION FOR THE VICTIMS OF ACCIDENTAL POLLUTION

How can one ensure that the victims are compensated? How can one ensure that the polluter pays? The answer to the first of these two questions is to require the polluter, where he can be identified, to bear the cost of the damage out of his own resources or through insurance cover. In other words, a regime of strict liability for polluters should be instituted, at least up to the limit of risk insurability. This policy is promoted by member countries of the Council of Europe, which adopted a regime of strict liability for abnormal pollution.[8] Germany adopted a law along these lines[9] and a number of other European countries have

---

[7] The French Council on prevention of technological risks (advising the Prime Minister) gave its views on liability and risk prevention in Mar. 1995. It stated that '[d]amage is such that its compensation should not be dependent on the chance that the party liable is capable of paying it'; '[a]ny damaging risk is becoming compensable'; '[i]t is essential to distinguish compensation mechanisms from liability concepts'. The Council is in favour of a reduced use of strict liability balanced by a greater use of insurance and other collective systems to provide compensation. It proposes to 'separate clearly compensation mechanisms and the legal concept of liability'. See (1995) 21 *Préventique Sécurité* 73–5.

[8] European Convention on Compensation for Damage resulting from Activities Dangerous to the Environment, Council of Europe (1993). The following countries have signed the Convention: Cyprus, Finland, Greece, Iceland, Italy, Liechtenstein, Luxembourg, and the Netherlands. No ratification has been received as at July 1995.

[9] *Umwelthaftungsgesetz*, Dec. 1990. See Code Permanent Environnement et Nuisances, 141 (15 Mar. 1991) 8399, and D. von Breitenstein, 'La loi allemande relative à la responsabilité en matière d'environnement, pierre angulaire du droit de l'environnement' (1993) 93 *Revue Juridique de l'Environnement* No. 2, 231–8.

done the same.[10] Discussions are under way in many other countries with a view to increasing liability of the polluter.[11] In the area of land transport, strict liability is the preferred regime when hazardous goods are involved (see Convention on Civil Liability for Damage Caused during Carriage of Dangerous Goods by Road, Rail and Inland Navigation Vessels, 1989 etc.).

If polluters are subject to a strict liability regime and are obliged to take out insurance, as will be the case in Germany, or to furnish some equivalent financial guarantee,[12] will there still be a problem in guaranteeing compensation for the victims?

The answer is unfortunately in the affirmative for several reasons: (i) it might not be possible to identify the polluter;[13] (ii) he might be able to evade

---

[10] Austria, Switzerland, Denmark, Finland, the Netherlands, Norway, Sweden, Greece, Portugal, and Turkey already have a strict liability regime for accidental pollution. Finland adopted in 1995 an Act on Compensation for Environmental Damage which imposes strict liability for bodily injury, material loss, and environmental damage. In France and Italy, liability is already very close to strict liability. Strict liability was introduced in 1990 in the United Kingdom for waste. Art. 9 of the 'Loi du 9 mai 1990 relative aux établissements dangereux, insalubres ou incommodes' (Law on Dangerous, Insalubrious and Harmful Establishments) in Luxembourg requires that installations 'which create a risk for man and the environment shall underwrite civil liability insurance and constitute a guarantee for reinstatement of the site after closure'. The problem is that such cover is not easily available on the local insurance market. For Germany and Austria, see H. D. Sellschoop, 'Topical Issues Concerning Environmental Liability and Its Insurance' (1993) 18 *Geneva Papers on Risk and Insurance* No. 67, 115–28. Belgium also has a mandatory insurance requirement for hazardous plants.

[11] In the Netherlands and in Austria discussions are under way to adopt new liability provisions for pollution damage. The Flemish Executive is examining a proposal to create a regime of strict liability for the operator of a polluting facility with a mandatory system of financial guarantees. If, in addition, the operator buys excess liability cover with a state fund (e.g. 4 billion Bfr.), he may limit his liability at the level of the mandatory guarantee (e.g. 1 billion Bfr.). Otherwise liability would be unlimited. In addition, a public fund would be created to cope with compensation not otherwise available (insolvent or unknown polluter). See H. Bocken, 'Responsabilité civile et fonds de compensation' (1992) 22 *Environmental Policy and Law* 160–3 and also idem, Draft Decree on Environmental Policy unpublished paper, (1995) (Part. 9: compensation of damage caused by environmental pollution).

[12] France first introduced the obligation to provide financial guarantees in its Law of 22 July 1987. Three recent laws, Law 92–3 of 3 Jan. 1992 (water), Law 92–646 of 13 July 1992 (waste), Law 93–3 of 4 Jan. 1993 (stone quarries), have specified instances where such guarantees are required: hazardous installations, waste dumps, oil storage, stone extraction. The issue consists in organizing the availability of such guarantees whenever insurance companies and banks refuse to provide them. A mutual fund for all similar risks could be set up by the industrial sector concerned, or alternatively this sector could seek a group insurance to cover the excess while sharing the first layer within the sector. According to French Decree 94–484 of 9 June, 1994, hazardous installations which require the setting up of a safety (buffer) zone have to provide a financial guarantee to cover clean-up and other urgent remediation costs undertaken by public authorities after an accident. This guarantee is to be paid if the polluter does not reimburse the authorities for their emergency activities. Technical details for implementation of this decree are not yet available.

[13] An unidentified firm released hexavalent chromium (from a plating shop) into the drainage network. The purification station not having sufficiently purified the waste waters, a watercourse was polluted. The cost of cleaning the river over 2 km amounted to FF 300,000 and had to be borne by the municipality owning the purification station (and not the unknown polluter) (source: Assurpol, 1990). In many countries (France, Norway, Sweden, etc.), clean-up costs are borne by the municipality (or the beneficiary) when the polluter remains unknown.

responsibility in certain specific cases; (iii) he might not benefit from insurance cover;[14] and, finally, (iv) the accident could be so costly as to exceed the polluter's limit of liability or limit of solvency.

In order to guarantee indemnity the solution is to *create a fund to substitute for defaulting or unknown polluters* (hereafter COSCA which stands for COmplementary System for Compensation of Accidental pollution damage).

This type of fund already exists in France to compensate the victims of aggression or acts of terrorism or of damage caused by hunting or road accidents when there is no payer. With respect to pollution, a fund has been created in the Netherlands to compensate victims of air pollution who are not compensated in any other way. Another fund (CRISTAL) has been set up by oil companies to compensate victims of oil spills over and above what shipowners would pay and, more recently, Sweden has established a fund to compensate for abnormal pollution damage.[15] Discussion concerning creating a similar fund is under way in Finland.[16] In the United States, many funds have been created at state level to cover pollution damage caused by oil spills or leakage from underground storage tanks.

The creation of such a fund guarantees compensation for victims, but it also implies an extra cost for potential polluters, i.e. for a number of industry sectors. It would therefore be reasonable to compare this cost with the expenditure that would be avoided by industry if a fund were set up. If this cost is low as compared with the expenditure avoided, it could be 'profitable' for industry to favour the creation of such a compensation fund without waiting for it to be imposed by the state. As early as the 1970s, the oil industry realized that in the case of oil spills it was better to complement the limited compensation costs

[14] The loss caused by the temporary evacuation of an industrial zone was estimated by Assurpol at FF 3 million in 1990. The mere threat of toxicity due to an explosion in an incineration plant caused the evacuation of the industrial zone for 24 hours. This type of loss is rarely covered by civil liability insurers because it is a matter of immaterial non-consecutive damage. More generally, many insurers do not cover pollution damage caused by non-compliance with the regulations, faulty maintenance, poor state of the plant, or, of course, an intentional act on the part of the insured.

[15] C. Oldertz, 'Swedish Environmental Damage Insurance', in H. Bocken and D. Ryckbost (eds.), *L'assurance des dommages causés par la pollution* (1991), 363–73. The Swedish fund received 26 claims between 1990 and 1993 but polluters bore all the costs and the fund did not have to pay anything. The limits of the fund are Skr. 200 million per year, Skr. 5 million per person and Skr. 50 million per event (for material damage) and Skr. 100 million per event (for material damage and injury). The fund is set up by five major insurance companies. See Ordinance (1989:365) on Environmental Damage Insurance. Note that the fund does not reimburse the clean-up costs of public authorities, or damage suffered by large companies. In Sweden, since the creation of the compensation fund in July 1990, no request for compensation has been accepted and the fund's accident expenditure has been nil. This situation is partly due to limitations on what the fund can be used for. An inquiry is under way with a view to extending the scope of intervention of the Swedish fund.

[16] *Complementary Schemes for Compensating Environmental Damage, Environment Economics Committee*, W. G. Report No. 3, 1993, Ministry of the Environment, Helsinki. Finland has operated an Oil Pollution Compensation Fund since 1974. This fund compensates for damage caused to third parties by oil pollution and for the cost of response action by the combat authorities (FIM 40 million/ year). It also covers the cost of acquiring and maintaining readiness to combat oil pollution. The current charge is FIM 2.2/t of oil (or FIM 4.4/t if the oil is carried in a tanker without a double skin).

borne by shipowners and come to the aid of the victims of oil spills, even if the accident was entirely due to the shipowner's negligence.

As will be shown below, COSCA represents only a relatively modest cost, the impact of which is virtually negligible for potential polluters. This result is due to the fact that accidental pollution is a rare phenomenon and usually less costly than is generally believed. Due to the media concentration on industrial disasters occurring around the world, the public tends to believe that a serious pollution accident could well happen soon at any hazardous installation. Since insurers are not willing to cover certain accidental pollution risks,[17] the public is led to believe that these risks are high. Since firms insist that their liability has to be limited in the case of accident,[18] the public assumes that this limit will be exceeded and the cost could be very high.

In reality however, serious accidental pollution is a fairly rare phenomenon and on average not all that costly. On the other hand, non-accidental pollution is at the origin of very costly damage. For instance, pollution damage by abandoned waste dumps or contaminated industrial sites can be very expensive and the cost of chronic pollution (air, water, etc.) which does not call for compensation vastly exceeds accidental pollution damage. Compensating non-accidental damage would call on financial resources which are simply not available at present.

3. THE COST OF ACCIDENTAL POLLUTION IN OECD COUNTRIES

In order to clarify the cost aspect we may consider the 1976 Seveso disaster in Italy, which cost FF 1 billion in 1980 for decontamination of the polluted ground and compensation to the victims. Since 1976, i.e. for a period of eighteen years, there has been no other 'Seveso-type' disaster in Western Europe and there was none since 1960 either. One catastrophe of this scale in thirty-four years means for France (which represents 10 per cent of the total of GDPs of the European

[17] French insurers are at present reluctant to cover pollution risks for over FF 200 million under pollution liability policies provided under Assurpol (current aggregate premium collected: FF 50 million per year for 500 contracts). Reinsurers refuse to cover what is known as 'gradual' pollution under comprehensive general liability policies and have decided not to cover any pollution event whatsoever unless under a special policy. This decision means that pollution damage would now be excluded from fire insurance and comprehensive general liability insurance, and that most French firms are no longer covered for their pollution liability. Large firms are able to find large cover for sudden and accidental pollution outside the French market (e.g. up to FF 600 million). Lloyd's has suffered large losses as a result of asbestos pollution and the *Exxon Valdez* oil spill, two areas not covered by this Ch. (product liability, occupational disease, maritime civil liability). US insurers have suffered losses in respect of contaminated sites, although most losses remain unpaid.

[18] In Germany, for example, the ceiling for strict liability under the new law has been fixed at DM 320 million or about FF 1 billion but insurance policies with such large cover are generally not available (except for large firms). In the case of liability for water pollution (under the strict liability regime since 1957) there is no limit. The ceiling as introduced by way of a compromise when the law was discussed in 1990.

Harm to the Environment

Table 1: *Fatal accidents in France*

	1987	1988	1989	1990	1991	1992	1993
Number of accidents	10 (18 d.)	9 (14 d.)	16 (23 d.)	14 (23 d.)	15 (16 d.)	11 (21 d.)	12 (35 d.)
Industrial installations (oil, explosives chemicals, metallurgical sectors, etc.)	5 (5 d.)	5 (9 d.)	8 (12 d.)	3 (3 d.)	3 (3 d.)	4 (9 d.)	4 (14 d.)
Road transport	2 (4 d.)	2 (3 d.)	3 (3 d.)	3 (3 d.)	6* (6 d.)	3* (4 d.)	5** (14 d.)
Maritime transport	1 (6 d.)	1 (1 d.)	0	1 (2 d.)	0	1 (4 d.)	0
Pipeline (oil, gas)	0	0	1 (3 d.)	0	0	0	0
Gas leaks	1 (1 d.)	0	0	2 (4 d.)	0	0	0
Standing gas (e.g. in wells)	0	1 (2 d.)	0	1 (1 d.)	0	1 (2 d.)	0
Grain silo	1 (1 d.)	0	1 (1 d.)	0	1 (1 d.)	0	0
Fire and explosion in carpentry shop, furniture warehouse, framing shop, hardware shop, pesticide/fertilizer storage, waste dump, etc.	1 (1 d.)	0	1 (1 d.)	3 (8 d.)	5 (6 d.)	2 (2 d.)	3 (7 d.)
Cleaning tanks in gasoline line stations and waterworks	0	0	1 (2 d.)	1 (1 d.)	0	0	0
Motor explosion in carpentry shop	0	0	1 (1 d.)	0	0	0	0

Notes: d. death
(*) Not related to hazardous substances
(**) 3 accidents not related to hazardous substances
Source: Ministry of the Environment, SEI-BARPI, 1987–1993 (ARIA accident data base).

OECD countries), an expenditure of FF 100 million over thirty-four years, or FF 3 million a year. If this is divided among the 300 major polluting enterprises capable of creating another Seveso-type disaster in France, this means that each enterprise would have to pay FF 10,000 a year to cover this type of disaster.

Another method of measuring the size of the risk would be to count the number of people killed off-site by accidents at hazardous industrial plants in Europe. In France, there is about one off-site death in twenty-five years (Feyzin, 1966 and Paris La Défense, 1994). This constitutes a small risk for the areas round industrial plants. Evaluated in monetary terms, this death may represent a compensation payment of perhaps as much as FF 2.5 million, or FF 100,000 a year to be shared between 300 major polluting enterprises, i.e. FF 330 per enterprise per year. Even if other damage to third parties located off-site amounts to ten or even thirty times that of the lives lost, the cost per enterprise still remains very small.

The OECD has calculated what would be the average annual cost of compensating all the victims of accidental pollution in France. On the basis of the different statistics available, an inventory of all the accidents causing water, air, or soil pollution was drawn up, together with the compensation that should have been paid to victims. Fatal accidents are rare and of fairly limited scale (Table 1). The average total annual cost was finally estimated to be in the order of FF 100 million[19] for industrial plants in 1990, i.e. less than the price of *one postage stamp per inhabitant per year*.

While the cost of compensation is very low for the state, industry, and insurers, it is high for the victims and for the firms causing accidental pollution. In particular, the cost of compensation is very low as compared with what industry spends on combating pollution (FF 17.6 billion a year), the cost of industrial accidents (FF 37.4 billion a year for injury to workers), and the cost of major industrial fires (FF 7.8 billion a year). It should therefore be possible to insure accidental pollution damage to third parties at very little extra cost, i.e. by a very small increase in the insurance premiums already paid by industrial enterprises.

To give a more precise idea, the damage caused by accidental pollution arising from the chemicals industry or from chemical products can be estimated as being in the order of FF 56 million a year, while the turnover of this sector is FF 280 billion a year. Such damage could be covered by an average contribution of 0.2 thousandths of turnover. For the high-risk enterprises, the premium might be higher, but it would still remain fairly modest. Thus a big French chemicals group, Rhône-Poulenc, has spent about FF 8 million a year on average over the

---

[19] H. Smets, 'Indemnisation des dommages exceptionnels à l'environnement causés par les activités industrielles', in R. Dupuy (ed.), *L'avenir du droit international de l'environnement* (1985), 275–356; *idem*, 'The Cost of Accidental Pollution' (1988) 11 *Industry and Environment* No. 4, 28–33; *idem*, 'Le coût de l'indemnisation des tiers victimes de la pollution accidentelle en France', in Bocken and Ryckbost, n. 15 above, 95–117; 'Smets, L'assurance pollution et les fonds d'indemnisation des poutions accidentelles' (1991) 627 *L'Assurance française* 383–9.

past ten years in compensation for accidental pollution, while the corresponding turnover was some FF 40 billion a year. Here again we see that accidental pollution costs about 0.2 thousandths of turnover, while the fight against pollution costs 20 thousandths of turnover, or 100 times as much.

More evidence that accidental pollution does not generally involve high cost is furnished by Swedish insurers, who recently decided to return to covering accidental pollution in the normal enterprise comprehensive general liability policies, because they considered that the cost of polluting accidents had not turned out to be as high as they initially thought. This decision does not apply to high-risk plants, however, which remain subject to special requirements. Discussion along the same lines is also taking place in France.

Lastly, indirect evidence that accidental pollution does not cost very much can be inferred from the fact that insurers have not kept full statistics on this type of accident and that in France there are few lawyers specializing in pollution damage compensation.

If compensation for accidental pollution costs relatively little to potential polluters, and if polluters generally compensate their victims, it is obvious that the cost of compensation not paid by polluters must be very low when shared among all potential polluters. Tables 2 and 3 provide a list of uncompensated pollution accidents in France.

4. COSCA

As explained above, COSCA will facilitate the compensation of victims in the case of an industrial disaster (accidental pollution, explosion, fire, etc.) or, in the case where compensation is not paid from any other source, whether the pollution be sudden or gradual, provided it is fortuitous.[20] COSCA has a direct advantage for the polluter involved in catastrophic pollution ('excess' insurance) and an indirect advantage for all potential polluters, among whom are those who have actually caused pollution.

The probable scale of intervention by COSCA is calculated below by evaluating the damage over and above a certain amount and in cases where the origin of the pollution cannot be determined.

[20] H. Bocken, 'Alternative Compensation Systems for Pollution Damage' (OECD/ENV/ECO(89)8) (1989); *idem*, 'Deficiencies of the System of Liability and Liability Insurance as a Mechanism for the Indemnification of Environment Damage Suffered by Individual Victims', in Bocken and Ryckbost, n. 15 above, 133–42; H. Smets, 'Guaranteed Compensation for Accidental Pollution' (1990) 166 *OECD Observer* 28–31; *idem*, 'Pour une indemnisation garantie des victimes de pollution accidentelle', in Bocken and Ryckbost, n. 15 above, 397–420; *idem*, 'Indemnisation des victimes de catastrophes industrielles' (1991) 6 *Cahiers de la Sécurité Intérieure* 165–76, also updated in *Colloque Crise et Droit de la Sécurité Civile* (1994); *idem*, 'L'indemnisation complète des victimes de la pollution accidentelle' (1992) 11 *Risques* 49–71; *idem*, 'Le FIPA, un instrument financier pour l'indemnisation des pollutions accidentelles', in A. Kiss (ed.), *A Law for the Environment* (1994), 131–42; *idem*, 'Mieux indemniser les atteintes à l'environnement' (1994) 10 *Sécurité* 2; *idem*, 'L'assurance obligatoire et la responsabilité civile pour pollution' (1994) 18 *PRINT Industries* 73–5; *idem*, 'Pollution accidentelle, l'indemnisation des tiers' (1994) 32 *Préventique* 54; *idem*, 'Des caisses mutuelles pour les pollueurs' (forthcoming 1995).

Table 2: *Examples of pollution of indeterminate origin (France, 1990)*

19/1/1990 Lizis (56)	Petroleum pollution of the spring supplying a mineral water bottling plant (Katell Roc). Baby hospitalized. Bottles taken out of sale. Production halted.
16/3/1990 Villers St-Paul (60)	Discharge of ammonia into the air. Ten lycée students and one teacher ill. Two children under observation.
26/3/1990 Hasparren (66)	Spillage of 300 kg of ammonia into a river. Pollution over 12 km. Fish killed.
13/4/1990 Bayonne (64)	30 litres of chloromethane escaped from a broken carboy. Four people slightly intoxicated.
20/4/1990 Loison-sous-Lens (62)	Acid products in sewers. Purification station out of service for several days. During this period untreated waste water discharged into the Lens Canal.
7/5/1990 Plouzevède (57)	River polluted over 30 km. 10 tonnes of dead fish.
22/5/1990 La Serre (02)	River polluted by nitrogen fertilizers. 3 tonnes of dead fish.
3/6/1990 Morlaix (29)	Discharge of a toxic product into a river, 100 tonnes of trout destroyed. Fish killed over 5 km.
4/6/1990 Wingersheim (67)	River polluted. Several tonnes of dead fish.
6/6/1990 La Deule (62)	River polluted. Several tonnes of dead fish.
10/6/1990 Premery (58)	Drinking water supply cut off due to pollution of the network.
2/7/1990 Boulogne (92)	Pollution of the Seine. 100 tonnes of dead fish retrieved.
30/8/1990 Plumerel (56)	Pond polluted. 30 tonnes of fish killed.
11/12/1990 Laluque (40)	Fish farm polluted. 60 tonnes of trout killed.

Notes: The number after the name of the city is the number of the French department. In some instances, pollution may be caused by stormwater after a dry spell in the city.
Source: French Ministry of the Environment.

4.1. Covering Damage above the Insured Ceiling

A prime function of COSCA would be to cover damage when this damage exceeds the insurance cover, limited to a certain amount per event, and thus to intervene as an 'excess' insurer with respect to contributors, forming a kind of mutual aid society for losses due to pollution. In this case, substantial contributions will be called for after major accidents. Otherwise, COSCA could reinsure

Table 3: *Cases of pollution of indeterminate origin in France (1990)*

Water pollution

Hydrocarbons (fuel, oil, gasoline)
— Without intervention of specialists services   16
— With intervention of specialist service (booms, etc.)   28
— Spring polluted   2

Agro-food sector
— Pesticides, fertilizers   4
— Manure   3

Unidentified chemicals
— Without fish kill   12
— With fish kill   23
— With pollution of the drinking water supply network   5

Chemical industry
Coke dust/soot

Atmospheric pollution   3

Soil pollution
— Pyralène   3
— Waste   1
                                                              110
                                                            cases

Source: Inventory of accidents (French Ministry of the Environment).

to attenuate the fluctuations in contributions, and this under favourable conditions because it represents a big market.

If all potential polluters were contributors to COSCA, the compensation paid by way of excess would be equal to the cost of the accidents after deducting the amount covered by usual insurance or the liability layer covered by the polluter. It might be assumed, for example, that COSCA would intervene in the case of accidents costing over FF 50 million and up to a maximum sum of FF 450 million (in the French context, the lower limit could be FF 200 million if contributors are insured with Assurpol).

Damage of over FF 50 million in civil liability pollution[21] has not occurred in France in the last twenty years in the case of accidents on land, but the pos-

---

[21] Accidents costing FF 50 million are said to have occurred in Germany, but this figure included the cost of restoring soil soaked by oil from a refinery that had been leaking for a long time. Similar costs (FF 15 to 60 million) were also found in France when a leak in a refinery remained undetected or when an aquifer was seriously polluted. Much larger sums were involved when large toxic waste dumps were involved (e.g. FF 300 million for Montchanin toxic waste dump) but such installations are not considered in this Ch.

sibility cannot be ruled out in the light of accidents in Mexico (gas explosion), Bhopal (release of toxics), or Seveso (contamination of the soil by a toxic cloud). Since 1976, the most costly accidents in Western Europe in terms of civil liability for pollution have been at Seveso (FF 1 billion in 1980) and at Basle (FF 125 million in 1986). If we assume that the industrial disasters in OECD Europe since 1976 have cost FF 2.2 billion for pollution damage to third parties (1988 francs) and that this cost is distributed proportionally to GDP among the European OECD member countries, France would have to pay FF 25 million a year to cover accidents costing over FF 50 million. If the upper limit (ceiling) of COSCA compensation were fixed at FF 500 million, COSCA payments by France for catastrophic accidents in Europe would be in the order of FF 8 million a year (combined effect of the lower limit and the ceiling).

The possibility of an accident occurring that is more costly than Bhopal (US$ 470 million) for example a FF 5 billion accident cannot be ruled out. Assuming that such an accident occurs once every twenty-five years somewhere in the twenty-four OECD countries and that the probability of its happening in France is proportional to GDP (6.3 per cent of the OECD total), the average impact for France would be FF 12.6 million a year, but French payments to COSCA would be in the order of only FF 1.1 million a year because of the compensation ceiling.

On the basis of these calculations, it would seem that COSCA would cost on average only FF 10 million a year for large accidents. This rough evaluation, however, has the disadvantage of being based on a doubtless incomplete inventory of accidents costing over FF 50 million and rather too short a period of time.

Another approach for calculating the cost of major accidents would be to evaluate the cost of accidents between FF 0.5 and 5 million and between FF 5 and 50 million, then extrapolate the available information to evaluate accidents costing between FF 50 and 500 million. An estimate of the excess of accidents costing between FF 0.5 and 5 million is twenty cases a year in France for fixed industrial plants, or a total of some FF 26 million a year. There is little information available for accidents costing between FF 5 and 50 million. It would no doubt be reasonable to work on the basis of a maximum of two accidents a year with a total cost of FF 26 million a year. On this basis, and taking account of the Pareto law of distribution[22] (which we assume here to be of the first order for the cost of industrial accidents), we could expect to see *at most* two accidents every ten years costing between FF 50 and 500 million (average annual cost: FF 26 million). In this case the COSCA would pay 260 − (50 × 2) = 160 million francs (or FF 16 million a year). Finally, it might be envisaged that there would

[22] On Pareto law, see H. Smets, 'Major Industrial Risks and Compensation of Victims' (1988) 27 *Social Science & Medicine* 1085–95; and *idem*, 'Frequency distribution of the consequences of industrial accidents involving hazardous substances in OECD countries' (forthcoming, 1996). As a matter of fact, it seems likely that a second-order Pareto law is applicable for large accidents in OECD countries whether measured in lives lost or in money. i.e. that the expected cost of accidents between 50 MF and 500 MF is smaller than FF 26 million.

be a case of catastrophic pollution (FF 2 billion) every 100 years. This would imply a further COSCA contribution of FF 450 million (or FF 4.5 million a year).

All in all, COSCA would on average pay victims about FF 20 million a year for catastrophic pollution. This figure is probably too high because it is based on the somewhat pessimistic assumption that the monetary cost of accidents varies according to the first-order Pareto law, whereas it is probable that the consequences of major accidents are less frequent than assumed. Be this as it may, we shall retain this figure for calculating the financial impact of COSCA. It will subsequently be possible to increase the COSCA ceiling to FF 1 billion and call upon the state in cases where the damage exceeds the ceiling.

4.2. Covering Damage not Compensated in any other Way

A second function of COSCA would be to intervene in cases where the victims could not otherwise be compensated. This is the case where nobody can be held responsible (unknown or unidentified polluter, etc.)[23] or where the person responsible is insolvent (e.g. if he has insufficient civil liability insurance cover or if the polluting event corresponds to an event excluded by the policy). This type of damage can occur in the case of water pollution caused by hydrocarbons of unknown origin, by chemicals used in agriculture, or by the illicit discharge of dangerous substances into the sewer system. Such pollution affects waste water treatment plants (rendered inoperative), fish farms (destruction of fish), drinking water supply networks, and, more generally, ecosystems. There can also be damage due to air pollution whose origin is difficult to establish legally, or pollution of the soil by transformer oil or toxic waste. Tables 2 and 3 give recent examples of this type of pollution, but they no doubt reflect only part of the true picture.

An economic evaluation of the damage caused by this type of pollution is very difficult to carry out. An extremely rough estimate might be something like FF 10 million a year, that is, 100 cases a year averaging FF 100,000 a case. More precisely, accidents may be evaluated as follows. If we assume that each intervention by the fire brigade to deal with a discharge of hydrocarbons costs FF 15,000, this means an annual expenditure of FF 0.45 million in France. If compensation for *damage* to fish farms costs FF 500,000 per accident and there are six such accidents a year, we need to allow FF 3 million.[24] Damage caused to river fish could be compensated on the basis of the total length of river polluted (100 km) and the total quantity of dead fish removed (100 tonnes), estimating the cost at $100 \times 10,000$ F/km + $100 \times 1,000 \times 10$ F/kg = FF 2 million/year. Damage caused by the pollution of springs and by accidental air pollution[25] could also each amount to FF 2 million a year. In total, damage of

---

[23] See n. 5 above.   [24] See n. 4 above.

[25] Since its creation in 1977, average payments by the Dutch Air Fund have amounted to Fl. 146,000 a year (FF 480,000 per year). Between 1980 and 1990, the following compensation was paid (sums over Fl. 30,000): Fl. 1.1 million (1989), 110 victims (crops lost) due to smog in the west of the country; Fl. 0.55 million (1982), 11 market gardeners in the west of the country, following

Table 4: *Average yearly cost of a COSCA in France*

	Type of damage (FF Millions)		
	'Excess' cover (damage over and above pollution insurance limit)	Damage caused by an unidentified, non-responsible or insolvent polluter	Total damage
Origin of the pollution			
Polluter being identified and solvent	15	0	15
Polluter insolvent or unidentified	5	10	15
Cost of COSCA for all contributors of which	20	10	30
an extra cost of:	5	10	15

Note: Costs of accidental pollution amount to FF 100 million per year of which 70 FF million is borne by polluters and their insurers.

unknown origin could amount to about FF 10 million a year in France. This very rough evaluation depends to a large extent on the more or less generous estimate of the environmental damage as assessed by the courts.[26]

5. ECONOMIC IMPACT OF COSCA ON INDUSTRY

According to the above calculations, the cost of COSCA could amount to about FF 30 million a year on average, i.e. FF 20 million to finance pollution compensation above the insurance ceiling and FF 10 million for damage caused by unidentified or insolvent polluters (see Table 4). As compared with the present situation, the extra cost imposed on industry by COSCA would be considerably

abnormal photochemical atmospheric pollution; Fl. 0.18 million (1984), a stockfarmer in Overijssel who lost an animal killed by a cloud of smoke; Fl. 40,000 (1985), arson in a toy factory caused atmospheric pollution. 4 farmers were compensated for damage to their crops; Fl. 31,000 (1984), 6 farmers were compensated for damage caused by abnormal photochemical atmospheric pollution. In addition, a tree grower received Fl. 18,448 (1978) following dust pollution from a Belgian cement works.

[26] The cost of the compensation calculated could be higher if the courts were more generous in compensating for the loss of fish (for example 50 F/kg dead fish removed, as was awarded by a French court). It is very likely that judges will award greater compensation for ecological damage but this will not have much impact on the total compensation. The greater risk consists in requiring an 'unreasonable' level of clean-up, i.e. a very expensive undertaking. The latter risk does not affect compensation of third parties but rather the liability of the polluter.

less than FF 30 million a year, because in the absence of any 'excess' insurance industrial polluters would have to bear the cost of any compensation above the insurance limit themselves. In concrete terms, it can be estimated that three-quarters of the premiums for the 'excess' insurance cover provided by COSCA correspond to compensation that the polluter would have had to pay himself. Under these conditions, the extra cost to industry due to the creation of COSCA (like the benefit for the victims of accidental pollution) amounts to FF 15 million a year (or 15 per cent of the damage qualifying for compensation). Such a sum may justify the adoption of special legislation, but is modest enough not to cause any undue anxiety among contributors (potential polluters).

For industry in general, the creation of COSCA would mean a maximum increase in expenditure of one thousandth of environmental protection expenditure or of workman's compensation expenditure. For the chemical industry, in particular, the increase would be in the order of 1 per cent of the industrial accident contribution (workman's compensation) or one thousandth of expenditure in the field of environmental protection. In return for this relatively modest expenditure, industry would be able to announce that it will compensate all victims in all cases of accidental pollution, thus demonstrating that it *supported and applied the polluter pays principle* and fully assumed all its responsibilities.

The positive impact of this decision on public opinion must not be underestimated, especially when it comes to applying for authority to operate new dangerous plants. The regulatory zeal of national or European Community authorities would no doubt be abated and the gains in the form of regulatory constraints avoided could greatly outweigh the costs of COSCA. In the final analysis COSCA appears to be a realistic approach to alleviate public perception of pollution risk. Considering that the public demands more safety and pollution prevention, it is likely that its demand will be less onerous if there is little doubt that the damage will be fully compensated.

Experience shows that accidental pollution damage is caused by installations owned by public authorities, industry, farmers, and individuals. It might therefore be envisaged that the different economic agents involved should contribute to the financing of COSCA, for example through a budget allocation (general taxation) and/or a specific tax.

A more realistic approach would be to reduce the number of contributors to COSCA, for example by imputing the damage caused by fuel oil tanks owned by individuals to the oil industry, or damage caused by farmers' pesticides and fertilizers to the chemical industry. It might be considered that in the final analysis only certain industrial sectors should finance COSCA. Whatever the solution adopted, the additional cost involved would be so low that contributors would hardly be aware of it.

In addition, it might be justifiable for the state to intervene financially, for example through bearing a proportion of the cost of COSCA in the name of solidarity to aid non-industrial polluters or in recognition of the damage caused by dangerous installations owned by local authorities (waste water treatment plants, waste dumps, incineration plants, etc.).

In any event, the most hazardous plants should pay a higher contribution because they could be at the origin of exceptional damage. These enterprises are to be found mainly in the chemicals industry and the oil and gas sector (so-called 'Seveso' plants).

In the extreme case, the entire extra cost of FF 15 million could be financed by the 300 major 'Seveso' plants in France. Although this is obviously an exaggerated and unfair scenario, it would still only mean a COSCA contribution of FF 50,000 a year by each enterprise. In reality, the individual contributions by potential polluters would be much lower than this because there would be over 300 of them. The chemical industry in France is made up of:

— 10 enterprises employing 5,000 people or over;
— 109 enterprises employing 500 to 4,999 people;
— 951 enterprises employing 20 to 499 people.

A COSCA contribution of FF 7.6 million for the French chemical industry would result in the following payments:

— 10 enterprises contributing FF 250,000 each;
— 109 enterprises contributing FF 25,000 each;
— 951 enterprises contributing FF 2,500 each.

This contribution would amount to roughly FF 10 per year for each worker in the chemical industry, i.e. a little more than the price of a newspaper per year for each worker. With respect to the industry turnover (FF 280 billion), the extra cost of COSCA would be 3 per cent of one thousandth. It can be seen that COSCA causes no noticeable extra cost for the chemical industry, and the situation would necessarily be similar for all other polluting sectors.

If a COSCA were to be created, industry could run it on a private basis and manage it with the help of insurers as a private or captive fund.[27] In such a case industry could establish the methods of intervention so as to maximize the social role of COSCA and minimize the risk of its being used for purposes unconnected with the original objective. Despite the advantages of a private COSCA created by industry itself, so far only Swedish industry and the world oil industry have recognized the merits of the system.

Therefore numerous proposals, both national and international, are now being made for the creation of COSCA under state control like the Dutch Air Fund, the IOPC Fund (the intergovernmental oil spill compensation fund, managed at

---

[27] COSCA could be organized on the same lines as a mutual P and I club between all industrial contributors (equivalent to shipowners) or in a captive form. The latter method has enjoyed increasing success in the United States (over 30 per cent of the damage insurance market). There are, however, serious reservations among industrialists about these approaches because of the lack of homogeneity of the risks to be covered and because most potential polluters do not have much in common.

Table 5: Compensation funds for underground storage tanks in various states of the United States

State	Fund (million $) Minimum	Maximum	Annual Contribution ($/tank)	Deductible ($)	Ceiling (M$)	Civil Liability	Clean up	Comments
Alabama	7.5	10	100 to 150	5,000	1	x	x	
Delaware	—	—	50	100,000	1	NA	x	
Florida	—	—	?/tank	300,000	1	x	NA	
Georgia	10	20	0.1 c/gal	500	1	x	NA	
Illinois	—	—	100	10,000	1	x	x	
Indiana	—	—	partially through tax	100,000	1	NA	x	
Louisiana	2	6	100 to 150	10,000	1	x	x	
Maine	—	—	25 to 50	—	—	x	x	Recursory action
Michigan	—	—	?	10,000	1	NA	x	
Minnesota	1	—	1 c/gal	10,000	—	NA	x	25% of expenses between $10,000 to 100,000 not covered
Mississippi	4	6	0.2 c/gal	100,000	1	NA	x	
New Hampshire	2.5	5	?c/gal	5,000 to 30,000	1	x	x	

State								Recursory action
New Jersey	—	—	? c/gal	—	—	NA	x	
New Mexico	2	10	0.2 c/gal	100,000	—	NA	x	Cover 50% of expenses liability operator max. $450,000
North Carolina	5	15	30 to 60	100,000	1	NA	x	Trade
				0	1	x	NA	Non-trade
South Carolina	—	—	60	100,000	1	NA	x	
				300,000	1	x	NA	
South Dakota	—	—	1c/gal	10,000	0.1	NA	x	
Tennessee	3	5	100	75,000	1	NA	x	
				150,000	1	x	NA	
Vermont	—	—	partially through tax	100,000	1	NA	x	
				300,000	1	x	NA	
Virginia	—	—	tax	100,000	1	NA	x	
				300,000	1	x	NA	
Wisconsin	—	7.5M$/yr max	—	5,000	97,500	NA	x	Max. 50% clean-up cost

NA = non applicable

x = applicable

IMO in London), or the many American funds for compensating gradual pollution caused by underground storage tanks (Table 5).[28] The OECD has explained
the merits of the system[29] and the Commission of the European Communities has
proposed the creation of a compensation fund.[30] This 'state' solution can be implemented more quickly, but it carries the risk of the authorities giving COSCA the
task of compensating damage caused by past or historical pollution, in addition
to future accidental pollution. Furthermore, it is very likely that a state inspired
or managed COSCA would emphasize clean-up costs rather than third party
damage.[31]

If a fund were supposed to cover the errors of the past in addition to the
accidents of the future,[32] if it had to accept responsibility for the contaminated

---

[28] Compensation funds for accidental pollution are envisaged in the Basel Convention on the
Control of Transboundary Movements of Hazardous Wastes and their Disposal 1989. The current
draft (Mar. 1995) of the Protocol on Liability and Compensation for Damage Resulting from
Transboundary Movements of Hazardous Wastes and Their Disposal contains a draft proposal to set
up an international fund for compensation to the extent that compensation for damage under the civil
liability regime is inadequate or not available.
A draft IMO Convention on Liability and Compensation for Damage in Connection with the Carriage of Hazardous and Noxious Substances by Sea (HNS) contains a scheme or fund which would
provide compensation when the shipowner is not liable, when he is unable to meet its obligations,
or when the damage exceeds the limits of shipowner liability. This convention is scheduled for adoption at a diplomatic conference in early 1996. The IMO Fund for emergency response in the case of
oil pollution of the sea was endowed with over US$ 5 million in voluntary contributions (after the
Gulf War), while the corresponding Convention (International Convention on Oil Pollution Preparedness, Response and Co-operation, OPPRC) of Nov. 1990 had not come into force (now in force). In
Canada, New Zealand, the United States, etc., funds were set up to cover clean-up costs after an oil
spill. The US fund under the 1990 Oil Pollution Act has a ceiling of $1 billion.
[29] See n. 1 above.
[30] The Communication from the European Commission to the Council and Parliament on Environmental Liability (1993) (so-called 'Green Paper') also argues in favour of complementary civil
liability funds. While the European Parliament is in favour of the creation of compensation funds
for accidental pollution, it would seem that the Member States are not yet ready to create this type
of institution in the Community. A trend in favour of such a fund is nevertheless to be observed and
it would only need some catastrophe for the reservations to disappear.
[31] The Ecology and Public Action Committee (Commission Ecologie et Actions Publiques) set
up by the French administration in 1990 proposed that a national environment fund should be created, notably to make it possible to repair damage without having to wait for reimbursement by
the polluter (*Le Monde*, 6 July 1991). Art. 18 of the French Law on Water ([1992] *Journal Officiel*
187) states that 'legal entities having taken action . . . have the right to reimbursement by the
person . . . responsible for the accident, of the expenses incurred by them'. Where the person liable
is unknown or insolvent, this reimbursement cannot take place unless there is a fund, however.
[32] Art. 18 of the proposed Council Directive of 22 May 1991, on the landfill of waste ([1991] OJ
C190/1) provides for the creation of a fund that would bear the costs of damage caused by the waste
dump where the operator does not pay them. The amended proposal for a Council Directive on civil
liability for damage caused by waste ([1991] OJ C192/6) provides that liability for the producer of
wastes will be covered by insurance or some other financial guarantee. This type of provision means
will be covered by insurance or some other financial guarantee. This type of provision means that
if the insurer refuses to cover non-fortuitous damage, the producer has to furnish a guarantee from
a bank, another enterprise, or an industrial guarantee fund. The sum insured or guaranteed necessarily has to be limited in order to be available, so that it is then necessary to find a payer for any
sum above this limit. In this field, the UK dump operators (the National Association of Waste
Disposal Companies) have proposed a fund financed by a tax in order to cover liability after closure.

soils of the industrial wastelands, if it were to be used to rehabilitate old waste dumps and compensate the victims of wastes discharged in the past, then this fund would cost very much more than what was calculated above. In the United States for example, the cost of remedying soil pollution caused by waste amounts to over $10 per inhabitant per year and could double in the near future. In the Netherlands expenses could reach FF 60 per year per inhabitant. Such figures are on a totally different scale from the cost of accidental pollution, which is in the order of FF 2 per inhabitant per year for hazardous plants in France, or with the cost of a COSCA, which is only 30 centimes per inhabitant per year.

For reasons of budgetary equilibrium and to permit proper planning, COSCA should clearly be limited to future accidental pollution and should not serve to finance remedial measures to correct past mistakes. It is for the state to create a special fund to rid the environment of the accumulated rubbish of the past and to finance it through a budget allocation or a tax. The scale of the dismal heritage of the past can be so great that in former East Germany it blocked financial transactions until the state accepted responsibility for the heritage of many years of total disregard for the environment.

6. FINANCING COSCA

COSCA should primarily be financed by fees, charges, or taxes borne by potentially polluting enterprises. These fees would be proportional to one or more of the following parameters:

— number of employees;
— turnover;
— capital investment;
— contribution to worker compensation scheme;
— premium for fire insurance;
— premium for comprehensive general liability insurance;
— registration fee/permit fee;
— pollution charges;
— quantity of hazardous substances bought or produced;
— quantity of hazardous waste generated (or waste charge).

COSCA can also receive a budget allocation from the state (e.g. a 25 per cent subsidy). If there is an accident, the polluter should be asked to pay a higher premium for a few years after the accident (*malus*). Conversely polluters who have a good record should benefit from a reduction in premium (*bonus*).

The new French law on reinforcing environment protection (95–101, Feb. 1995) has created a tax on waste disposal to provide financial resources to clean up contaminated sites contaminated by unknown polluters. Similar systems also exist Canada, Austria, etc. In the United States, activities under Superfund for 1980–92 induced the following expenditures: clean-up by polluters: $7.5 billion (in part paid by insurers); legal costs: $2 billion; clean-up by public authorities: $20.5 billion.

COSCA would have an annual budget to cover pollution cases of indeterminate origin (e.g. FF 10 million per year), administrative costs, and a premium
for reinsurance. In addition, calls or retrospective additional payments would
be made after a large accident. Experience of the international oil compensation
funds (IOPC Fund and CRISTAL) shows that management and administrative
costs represent 7 to 10 per cent of all claims paid.

7. KEEPING COSCA COMMITMENTS WITHIN REASON

While COSCA does not cost very much *on average*, fluctuations in its yearly
payments may be very large because of rare and very costly disasters. In order
to avoid making the management of COSCA too difficult, it will perhaps be
necessary, at least initially, to limit certain commitments, as discussed below.

7.1. Major Disasters: Limitation of Payment per Accident

By its very nature, COSCA could have to pay hundreds of millions of francs,
or even several billion. In order to guard against having to bear the whole of
this risk, COSCA could limit its payment (to FF 500 million, for example) or
resort to reinsurance (for example, for the US$ 100–200 million range, i.e. FF
500–1,000 million). In addition, the state could undertake to intervene in the case
of major disasters, covering for example the US$ 200–400 million range (special
state outlay for man-made disasters). The counterpart of such state intervention
could be that COSCA pays a 'premium' to the state for this coverage or agrees
to intervene in cases of risks of unknown origin but in fact created by public
authorities (e.g. accidental pollution that might be due to a municipal waste
dump). The aim is not to derogate from the polluter pays principle, but to share
the risks among all polluters by efficient economic methods.

7.2. Limitation of Payment per Period or Site

For reasons of financial stability, it might also be useful to introduce a limit of
total COSCA payments in any one year or for any pollution site. This approach
has the disadvantage of reducing the scope of the guarantee given. For reasons
of equity and good public relations, it may be appropriate to make provision for
exceeding any such limits, where appropriate and on a voluntary basis or, better,
to set multi-year limits.

 If the state co-operates in the creation of COSCA, it could provide a financial
guarantee and ensure that COSCA meets its financial commitments even during
a 'bad' year.

7.3. Accumulated Pollution and Previously Authorized Pollution

In the past, several cases of pollution have turned out to be particularly costly because the polluter had allowed large quantities of pollutants to accumulate (for example, toxic waste dumps such as found at Love Canal, chronic pollution discharge into the environment such as found near lead or zinc smelters). Victims may suddenly appear for pollution that started a long time ago, perhaps of ill-defined origin, but very serious and with high clean-up costs.

If the polluter cannot meet his financial responsibilities or if he is exonerated from all liability, COSCA may be called upon to intervene to compensate the victims even though there is no accident[33] but rather the unfortunate consequences of known activity by the polluter, perhaps even condoned by the authorities. For instance, damage may reveal itself twenty years after exposure and concern all the neighbours of a number of similar factories. This may be the case with many zinc or lead smelters which created physical harm in their neighbourhood by pollutants emission whose long-term toxicity was underestimated at the time.

If COSCA has to cover this type of risk, the cost may be limited by restricting the cover to physical and material damage suffered by specified third parties, i.e. by excluding pure economic losses, clean-up costs paid by officials bodies, and environmental damage suffered by many people. Public authorities could pay for damage caused by previously authorized pollution. Another possible solution would be to establish priority compensation for certain types of damage when the ceiling per site is exceeded (e.g. to pay for physical injury only if there are many injured people, as was the case in Bhopal).

---

[33] As regards civil liability pollution insurance, the expression 'accidental pollution' may cover, depending on the case, both sudden pollution and gradual pollution that occurs because of a fortuitous event due to an accidental fault, a sudden and unforeseeable failure, an equipment break-down. It may also include leaks in storage tanks and underground pipework by reason of unforeseen corrosion or other defects provided these leaks have not been detected and were not expected to occur. It generally excludes pollution resulting from spills, leaks, discharges, or emissions of polluting substances which occur as a result of the normal use of these substances or the negative consequences for the environment of industrial operations which are inevitable, necessary, or tolerated, provided that, on the basis of the available knowledge, the operator could not know the consequences at the time of the initiating events. Outside pollution liability policies, accidental pollution often means only sudden and fortuitous pollution, but there is often vagueness about what 'sudden' should refer to (cause, effect, damage, injury). From the standpoint of full compensation for victims (pollution damage insurance for the benefit of victims), accidental pollution should be defined very broadly, for instance, abnormal, excessive, and unacceptable pollution causing prejudice to the victims, whatever the cause of this pollution (fortuitous or deliberate action on the part of the polluter), provided this pollution has not been authorized by the authorities or by the victims. Such pollution is compensated because it causes abnormal prejudice and is unforeseen by the victim. The same applies in the case of road accidents: the driver's insurer or a guarantee fund has to compensate the victim even if the driver is drunk or has no licence or no insurance. The fact that certain cases of pollution cannot be covered by civil liability pollution insurance (e.g. deliberate pollution) in no way removes the obligation to repair the damage, unless the state decides that the victims have to bear the cost (exoneration from liability) or decides to compensate them itself in the name of national solidarity.

7.4. Cases Qualifying and Not Qualifying for Compensation

In the period immediately following the creation of COSCA, where the probable cause of the accident is not established, it may sometimes be difficult to establish whether the accident originated before or after the creation of COSCA, i.e. whether it qualifies for compensation or not. A solution might be to compensate for a limited list of damage only whenever the cause is ill-defined, or to impose a lower ceiling for accidents of unknown origin but probably preceding the creation of COSCA.

7.5. Victims: Individuals and/or Legal Entities

Another way of limiting COSCA intervention would be to disregard claims by public authorities where they are involved in clean-up operations. While this approach is perfectly conceivable in the case of central authorities, it is much less justifiable at local level. Similarly, compensation may not be paid to legal entities constituted under private or public law possessing substantial financial resources (for example, a large private or nationalized enterprise) in order to reserve COSCA resources for SMEs and individuals.

7.6. Exclusion of Certain Types of Pollution

COSCA would not intervene in accidents already subject to special liability regimes, such as radioactive pollution or pollution of maritime origin or connected with aerial or terrestrial transport. Pollution coming from waste dumps or industrial derelict lands would need to be clearly delineated and no doubt excluded unless the origin of the pollution is subsequent to the creation of COSCA (because existing waste dumps may generate expenditure out of proportion with accidental pollution damage).

7.7. Expenses on the Site of the Insured; Decontamination of Polluted Ground

A particularly effective method of limiting COSCA commitments is to exclude any intervention on the site of the insured (first party liability) where there is no damage suffered by third parties. Such an approach makes the polluter or the state pay for certain costly work involved in combating ground water pollution resulting from contamination of the ground beneath an industrial plant.

7.8. Possible Abuses

In so far as COSCA has to intervene to compensate for pollution damage of unknown origin, there is a risk that pollution is caused deliberately by a claimant in order to 'get rid of' waste (which he himself is responsible for producing) or derive benefit from the situation. Thus it might be decided that compensation for certain types of damage will be limited to a fraction of the loss suffered (after deduction of a fixed sum). Experience will show whether it is necessary to maintain such safeguards against abuse (e.g. a fish farm destroyed by pollution when there is overproduction or when fish are selling badly). Similarly, reimbursement of the authorities could be limited to 'reasonable' clean-up costs rather than all the costs incurred by them (in order to exclude useless action carried out for purely 'political' reasons).

7.9. Comments

Any limitations on COSCA intervention as regards the amount of compensation or the type of damage covered greatly reduce the credibility of the scheme in the eyes of the public and should therefore be avoided as far as possible. Since certain limitations are necessary, particular care should be taken to give priority to the victims with the least resources, for reasons of equity and solidarity. Such an approach was adopted by the Swedish Government, which agreed not to be reimbursed by the Swedish fund for the cost of its clean-up operations. If COSCA is created by the private sector, such limitations will be all the easier to implement. On the other hand, experience of oil spill compensation shows that governments by no means give priority to the interests of private victims over their own interests. A COSCA created by the state is therefore likely to be more expensive than one created by the private sector.

COSCA should be perceived by the public as a fund created to protect the victims rather than to protect the interests of polluters. Thus it is essential that COSCA should be able to have recourse to persons responsible for causing accidents and, in certain cases, the polluters. If COSCA pays substantial compensation for damage caused by one of its contributors, it should retain the ability to take legal action if it appears that the accident was not fortuitous or was the result of serious fault or negligence on the part of the insured. Such a provision is intended to encourage accident prevention and to avoid making industry bear the cost of irresponsible behaviour by one of its members.

COSCA intervenes as the collective guarantor of compensation for the victims of accidental pollution, and thus has every interest in ensuring that potential polluters take all necessary preventive measures and do not relax their efforts on the pretext that COSCA will look after them. This may mean, in particular, that contributors (who benefit from coverage of the excess above the limit of their civil liability insurance) should be subject to prior audit and/or inspection by authorized bodies. In addition, contributors who are not insured or who cannot provide a sufficient financial guarantee could be made to pay a higher contribution to COSCA because there is a risk that they may cause COSCA to have to intervene in cases of damage below the normal floor for excess coverage. Lastly, it may be useful to graduate COSCA contributions according to the real risk, i.e. not to take account only of the traditional economic parameters (turnover, etc.).

The financial stability of COSCA will always be a difficult problem. If COSCA has an annual ceiling of FF 600 million and if there are 300 main contributors, the maximum risk per contributor is FF 2 million. While this may be tolerable because the maximum loss would not occur every year, it is unlikely that the same ceiling would be acceptable if there were only 60 main contributors (as would be the case in a small country).[34]

8. CONCLUSIONS

The creation of COSCA by potential polluters to guarantee compensation of pollution victims has the merit of effectively putting the polluter pays principle into practice, and bringing with it great advantages in terms of public relations. This solution is relatively inexpensive for industry and will be even less costly if industry itself creates and manages the compensation system.

The difficulties of creating COSCA are far from negligible, but they can be overcome as shown by the positive experience of the world oil industry and the pollution funds already created in Sweden and the Netherlands.

If COSCA is not created by the private sector, the following consequences have to be envisaged:

(a) compulsory insurance or guarantee could be instituted and industry would have to bear higher insurance or guarantee costs;

(b) the state could create a public COSCA costing more than a private one;

(c) costly regulatory measures could be introduced in response to inadequately compensated accidents occurring in the period preceding the introduction of a public COSCA.

In view of the advantages of creating COSCA and the correspondingly low costs, it would appear that industry should seriously study this option rather than run the risk of one or two highly publicized and poorly compensated accidents having very costly indirect consequences for it. In France, no COSCA has so far been created, although the matter is being examined by both public authorities and groups of large enterprises. In the meantime, the French Government has set up a financial guarantee system under which many hazardous polluting enterprises must provide a guarantee and it has created a waste tax to take care of orphan waste disposal sites.

[34] COSCA could be created at national level or at regional level provided the region was homogenous enough. The concept would be viable for large countries, such as France, or for groups of smaller countries (e.g. Benelux). Smaller countries could also operate COSCA provided that the state would provide financial support in case of need. However, in such a case, the ceilings of COSCA are likely to be small. A European Union-wide COSCA is also conceivable but may be difficult to set up because of alleged differences in safety standards and practices in the 15 member countries.

Bibliography

'Admissibility and Assessment of Claims for Pollution Damage: Report of the Chairman of the International Sub-Committee', in *Comité Maritime International, Yearbook 1993 (Sydney I, Documents for the Conference)* (Antwerp, CMI, 1993), 88–139.

AGELL, A., 'Adekvans eller skyddsändamål: Om rättsvetenskaplig metod och skadeståndsrättslig regelbildning' (1994–5) 13 *Juridisk Tidskrift* No. 4, 799–810.

ANDERSON, F., 'Natural Resources Damages, Superfund, and the Courts' (1989) 16 *Boston College Environmental Affairs Law Review* 405–67.

ANDERSON, F. R., 'Natural Resource Damages, Superfund, and the Courts' (1989) 16 *Environmental Affairs* 405–81.

ANDERSSON, HÅKAN, Skyddsändamål och adekvans: Om skadeståndsansvarets gränser (Uppsala, Justus, 1993).

AUGUSTYNIAK, C. M., 'Economic Valuation of Services Provided by Natural Resources: Putting a Price on the Priceless' (1993) 45 *Baylor Law Review* 389–421.

BATES, J. H., and BENSON, C., *Marine Environmental Law* (London, Lloyd's of London Press Ltd., 1993).

BERLINGIERI, F., 'Il sistema internazionale di risarcimento dei danni causati da inquinamento da idrocraburi' (1992) 94 *Il diritto marittimo* 3–29.

BIANCHI, A., 'The Harmonization of Laws on Liability for Environmental Damage in Europe: An Italian Perspective' (1994) 6 *Journal of Environmental Law* 21–42.

BINGER, B. R., COPPLE, R. F., and HOFFMAN, E., 'The Use of Contingent Valuation Methodology in Natural Resource Damage Assessments: Legal Fact and Economic Fiction' (1995) 89 *Northwestern University Law Review* 1029–115.

BIRNIE, P. W., and BOYLE, A. E., Basic Documents on International Law and the Environment (Oxford, Oxford University Press, 1995).

—— and ——, *International Law and the Environment* (Oxford, Oxford University Press, 1992).

BISHOP, R., and UNSWORTH, R., 'Assessing Natural Resource Damages Using Environmental Amenities' (1994) 11 *Ecological Economics* 35–41.

BLAY, S., and GREEN, J., 'The Development of a Liability Annex to the Madrid Protocol' (1995) 25 *Environmental Policy and Law* 24–37.

BOCKEN, H., 'Alternative Compensation Systems for Pollution Damages' (OECD/ENV/ECO(89)8, 1989).

—— 'Deficiencies of the System of Liability and Liability Insurance as a Mechanism for the Indemnification of Environment Damage Suffered by Individual Victims', in H. Bocken and D. Ryckbost (eds.), *L'assurance des dommages causés par la pollution* (Brussels, Story Scientia, 1991), 133–42.

—— 'Milieuwetgeving en onroerende goederen: Aansprakelijkheid voor de kosten van bodemsanering' [1992] *Tijdschrift voor Privatrecht* 1–88.

—— 'Responsabilité civile et fonds de compensation' (1992) 22 *Environmental Policy and Law* 160–3.

—— 'Developments with Respect to Compensation for Damage Caused by Pollution', in

B. S. Markesinis (ed.), *The Gradual Convergence: Foreign Ideas, Foreign Influences, and English Law on the Eve of the 21st Century* (Oxford, Clarendon Press, 1994), 226–51.

—— 'Achievements and Proposals with Respect to the Unification of the Law on Environmental Liability for Damages Caused by Particular Types of Operation', in Dr. C. von Bar (ed.), *Internationales Umwelthaftungsrecht I: auf dem Wege zu einer Konvention über Fragen des Internationalen Umwelthaftungsrechts* (Cologne, Carl Heymanns Verlag, 1995), 31–67.

—— 'La réparation des dommages causés par la pollution: La situation en 1992' (1992) 4–5 *Revue de droit civil belge* 284–327.

—— RYCKBOST, D., and DELODDERE, S., 'Herstel van milieuschade door milieuverontreiniging', in Interuniversitaire Commissie tot Herziening van het Milieurecht in het Vlaamse Gewest, *Voorontwerp Decreet Milieubeleid* (Bruges, Die Keure, 1995), 833–994.

BODANSKY, DANIEL, 'Managing Climate Change' (1992) 3 *Yearbook of International Environmental Law* 60–74.

—— 'The United Nations Framework Convention on Climate Change: A Commentary' (1993) 18 *Yale Journal of International Law* 451–558.

BOSSI, P., 'Sulla quantificazione del danno all'ambiente ex art. 18 legge n. 349/1986; la prima pronuncia del giudice penale' [1989] *Diritto e pratica nell'assicurazione* 867–76.

BOWETT, D., 'Estoppel before International Tribunals and Its Relations to Acquiescence' (1957) 34 *British Year Book of International Law* 176–202.

BOWMAN, M., 'The Convention on Civil Liability for Damage Resulting from Activities Dangerous to the Environment' (1994) 2 *Environmental Liability* Issue 1, 11–13.

—— 'Nuisance, Strict Liability and Environmental Hazards' (1994) 2 *Environmental Liability* Issue 5, 105–10.

BOYLE, A., 'Nuclear Energy and International Law: An Environmental Perspective' (1989) 60 *British Year Book of International Law* 257–314.

—— 'The Convention on Biological Diversity', in Luigi Campiglio, Laura Pineschi, Domenico Siniscalco, and Tullio Treves (eds.), *The Environment After Rio: International Law and Economics* (London, Graham & Trotman, 1994), 111–27.

BRANS, E. H. P., 'The *Braer* and the Admissibility of Claims for Pollution Damage under the 1992 Protocols to the Civil Liability Convention and the Fund Convention' (1995) 3 *Environmental Liability* Issue 4, 61–9.

BREEDING, C. W., and CRESS, L. R., JR., 'Natural Resource Damages under CERCLA: A New Beginning?' (1992) 20 *Northern Kentucky Law Review* 23–45.

BREEN, B., 'Citizen Suits for Natural Resource Damages: Closing a Gap in Federal Environmental Law' (1989) 24 *Wake Forest Law Review* 851–63.

BREITENSTEIN, D. VON, 'La loi allemande relative à la responsabilité en matière d'environnement, pierre angulaire du droit de l'environnement' (1993) 93 *Revue Juridique de l'Environnement* No. 2, 231–8.

BROWNE, B., 'Compensating Marine Oil Pollution Victims: A Case Study', Paper delivered at the Conference 'Access to Environmental Justice in Europe', organized by the Robert Schumann Centre (Working Group on Environmental Studies) at the European University Institute in Florence, 18–19 March 1994.

BROWNLIE, I., *Principles of Public International Law* (4th edn., Oxford, Clarendon Press, 1990).

CAMERON, J., and O'RIORDAN, T. (eds.), *Interpreting the Precautionary Principle* (London, Cameron May, 1994).

CAMPIGLIO, LUIGI, PINESCHI, LAURA, SINISCALCO, DOMENICO, and TREVES, TULLIO (eds.), *The Environment After Rio: International Law and Economics* (London, Graham & Trotman, 1994).

CARAVITA, B., *Diritto pubblico del'ambiente* (Bologna, Il Mulino, 1990).

CARLSON, C., 'Making CERCLA Natural Resource Damage Regulations Work: The Use of the Public Trust Doctrine and Other State Remedies' (1988) 18 *Environmental Law Reporter* 10299–307.

CARTWRIGHT, C., 'Natural Resources Damage Assessment: The Exxon Valdez Oil Spill and Its Implications' (1991) 17 *Rutgers Computer & Technology Law Journal* 451–92.

CHARNEY, J., 'Third State Remedies for Environmental Damage to the World's Common Spaces', in Francesco Francioni and Tullio Scovazzi (eds.), *International Responsibility for Environmental Harm* (London, Graham & Trotman, 1991), 149–77.

CHURCHILL, R., and FREESTONE, D. (eds.), *International Law and Global Climate Change* (London, Graham & Trotman, 1991).

COMITÉ MARITIME INTERNATIONAL, *Yearbook 1994 Annuaire (Sydney II, Documents of the Conference* (Antwerp, CMI, 1995).

CONDORELLI, L., *Il giudice italiano e i trattati internazionali (gli accordi self-executing e non self-executing nell'ottica della giurisprudenza)* (Padua, Cedam, 1974).

CONFORTI, B., 'Do States Really Accept Responsibility for Environmental Damage', in Francesco Francioni and Tullio Scovazzi (eds.), *International Responsibility for Environmental Harm* (London, Graham & Trotman, 1991), 179–80.

—— *International Law and the Role of Domestic Legal Systems* (Dordrecht, Martinus Nijhoff, 1993).

CROMBRUGGHE, N. VAN, 'Belgium: Class Action for Environmental Issues' (1993) 2 *European Environmental Law Review* No. 10, 275–6.

CROSS, F. B., 'Natural Resource Damage Valuation' (1989) 42 *Vanderbilt Law Review* 269–341.

—— 'Restoring Restoration for Natural Resource Damages' (1993) 24 *University of Toledo Law Review* 319–44.

DOBBINS, J. C., 'The Pain and Suffering of Environmental Loss: Using Contingent Valuation to Estimate Non-Use Damages' (1994) 43 *Duke Law Journal* 879–946.

DUNFORD, R. W., 'Natural Resource Damages from Oil Spills: A Comparison of the Ohio Decision and the Oil Pollution Act' (1992) 22 *Environmental Law Reporter* 10263–67.

DUNNÉ, J. M. VAN, 'Environmental Liability—Continental Style' (1992) 1 *Reciel* No. 4, 394–401.

——, BIERBOOMS, P. F. A., and VAN, A., 'Liability Developments in the Netherlands' (1993) 1 *Environmental Liability* Issue 3, 72–6.

ENDERS, R., and REITER, B., 'Die Umwelthaftung im System des Umweltgesetzbuches' (1991) 42 *Versicherungsrecht* 1329–41.

EUROPEAN ENVIRONMENTAL LAW ASSOCIATION, 'Repairing Damage to the Environment—A Community System of Civil Liability', Report of Working Party: Submission to the Commission of the European Communities (1994) 2 *Environmental Liability* Issue 1, 1–10.

FAYETTE, L. DE LA, 'Nuclear Liability Revisited' (1992) 1 *Reciel* No. 4, 443–53.

—— 'Towards a New Regime of State Responsibility for Nuclear Activities' (1992) 50 *Nudear Law Bulletin* 7–35.

FEOLA, D., 'L'Art. 18 L.349/1986 sulla responsabilità civile per il danno all'ambiente: dalle ricostruzioni della dottrina alle applicazioni giurispurdenziali' (1992) 9 *Quandrimestre* 541–68.

FRANCARIO, L., *Danni ambientali e tutela civile* (Naples, Jovene, 1990).

FRANCIONI, F. (ed.), *International Environmental Law for Antarctica* (Milan, Giuffré, 1992).

FREESTONE, D., 'The Precautionary Principle', in R. Churchill and D. Freestone (eds.), *International Law and Global Climate Change* (London, Graham & Trotman, 1991), 21–39.

GALLAGHER, J., 'In the Wake of the *Exxon Valdez*: Murky Legal Waters of Liability and Compensation' (1990) 25 *New England Law Review* 571–616.

GASKELL, N. J. J., 'Economic Loss in the Maritime Context' [1985] 1 *Lloyd's Maritime and Commercial Law Quarterly* 81–117.

GESAMP, *The State of Marine Environment* (Oxford, Blackwell, 1990).

GIAMPIETRO, F., *La responsabilità per il danno all'ambiente* (Milan, Giuffré, 1988).

—— 'La valutazione del danno all'ambiente. I primi passi dell'Art. 18 della legge n. 349 del 1986' (1989) 65 *Foro amministrativo* 2957–61.

—— 'Damage to the Environment: Meaning and Function of the Assessment of Damage', in F. Giampietro and S. Miccoli, *Assessment of Damage to the Environment* (Strasbourg, Council of Europe Press, 1993), 9–28.

—— 'Access to Environmental Justice in Italy: The Innovative Role of the Judge', Paper delivered at the Conference 'Access to Environmental Justice in Europe', organized by the Robert Schumann Centre (Working Group on Environmental Studies) at the European University Institute in Florence, 18–19 March 1994.

—— 'Responsabilità per danno all'ambiente: la Convenzione di Lugano, il Libro verde della Commissione CEE e la novità italiane' (1994) 9 *Rivista giuridica dell'ambiente* 19–33.

GÖRANSSON, M., 'The 1984 and 1992 Protocols to the Civil Liability Convention, 1969 and the Fund Convention', in C. M. De La Rue (ed.), *Liability for Damage to the Marine Environment* (London, Lloyd's of London Press Ltd., 1993), 71–82.

HAGER, G., 'Das neue Umwelthaftungsgesetz' [1991] *Neue Juristische Wochenschrift* 134–43.

—— 'Umwelthaftungsgesetz: The New German Environmental Liability Law' (1993) 1 *Environmental Liability* Issue 2, 41–5.

HALTER, F., and THOMAS, J. T., 'Recovery of Damages by States for Fish and Wildlife Losses Caused by Pollution' (1982) 10 *Ecology Law Quarterly* 5–47.

HANDL, G., 'National Uses of Transboundary Air Resources: The International Entitlement Issue Reconsidered' (1986) 26 *Natural Resources Journal* 405–67.

—— 'Après Tchernobyl: Quelques Réflexions sur le Programme législatif Multilateral' (1988) 92 *Revue Générale de Droit International Public* 5–62.

—— 'Towards a Global System of Compensation for Transboundary Nuclear Damage', in *Nuclear Accidents, Liabilities and Guarantees: Proceedings of the Helsinki Symposium 31 August–3 September 1992* (Paris, Nuclear Energy Agency, 1993), 497–520.

HARPER, F. V., JAMES, F., and GRAY, O. S., *The Law of Torts* (2nd edn., Boston, Mass., Little, Brown & Co., 1986).

HARRIS, J. W., 'Private and Non-Private Property: What Is the Difference?' (1995) 111 *Law Quarterly Review* 421–44.

HEYDE, J., 'Is Contingent Valuation Worth the Trouble?' (1995) 62 *University of Chicago Law Review* 331–62.

HOHMAN, H. (ed.), *Basic Documents of International Environmental Law* (London, Graham & Trotman, 1992), i.

HONORÉ, A. M., 'Causation and Remoteness of Damage', in A. Tunc (ed.), *International Encyclopedia of Comparative Law, Vol. XI, Torts* (Tübingen, Mohr, 1983), 7–45.

HOUSE OF LORDS SELECT COMMITTEE ON THE EUROPEAN COMMUNITIES, Session 1989–90, 25th Report, *Paying for Pollution: Civil Liability for Damage Caused by Waste* (London, HMSO, 1990).

INTERNATIONAL OIL POLLUTION COMPENSATION FUND: *Annual Reports 1990, 1993, 1994* (London, IOPCF).

IWASAWA, Y., 'The Doctrine of Self-Executing Treaties in the United States' (1986) 26 *Virginia Journal of International Law* 627–92.

JACOBSSON, M., 'The International Convention on Liability and Compensation for Oil Pollution Damage and the Activities of the International Oil Pollution Compensation Fund', in C. M. De La Rue (ed.), *Liability for Damage to the Marine Environment* (London, Lloyd's of London Press Ltd., 1993), 39–55.

—— and TROTZ, N., 'The Definition of Pollution Damage in the 1984 Protocols to the 1969 Civil Liability Convention and the 1971 Fund Convention' (1986) 17 *Journal of Maritime Law and Commerce* No. 4, 467–91.

JAMES, F., JR., 'Limitations on Liability for Economic Loss Caused by Negligence: A Pragmatic Appraisal' (1972) 25 *Vanderbilt Law Review* 43–58.

JONES, B., 'Remedying Environmental Damage: The European Commission's Green Paper' (1994) 8 *TMA—Environmental Liability Law Review* Issue 1, 1–7.

JUSTINIAN, Institutes 2.1.1. (2nd edn., translated by T. Cooper, s.l., Halsted and Voorhies, 1841).

KINKEL, K., 'Möglichkeiten und Grenzen der Bewältigung von umwelttypischen Distanz- und Summationsschäden' (1989) 22 *Zeitschrift für Rechtspolitik* 293–8.

KINNANE, THOMAS W., 'Recovery for Economic Losses by the Commercial Fishing Industry: Rules Exceptions, and Rationales' (1994) 4 *Journal of Environmental Law* 86–112.

KLIK, P., 'Group Actions in Civil Lawsuits: The New Law in the Netherlands' (1995) 4 *European Environmental Law Review* No. 1, 14–16.

KLOEPFER, M., REHBINDER, E., SCHMIDT-AßMANN, E., and KUNIG, P., *Umweltgesetzbuch—Allgemeiner Teil* (Berlin, Schmidt, 1991).

KOCH, W., *Aktualisierte Gehölzwerttabbellen* (2nd edn. Karlsruhe, Verlag Versicherungswirtschaft e.V., 1987).

KOLODKIN, A., KISELEV, V., and KOROLEVA, N., 'Some New Tendencies in Legislation of the Russian Federation and Its Attitude Towards Conventions with Regard to Marine Pollution', in C. M. de la Rue (ed.), *Liability for Damage to the Marine Environment* (London, Lloyd's of London Press Ltd., 1993), 33–8.

KOSKENNIEMI, M., 'Transfrontier Pollution Damage Liability' (1990) 2 *International Environmental Affairs* No. 2, 309–16.

KREUZER, K., 'Environmental Disturbance and Damage in the Context of Private International Law' (1992) 44 *Revista española de derecho internacional* 57–78.

254 *Bibliography*

KRÄMER, L., *EEC Treaty and Environmental Protection* (London, Sweet & Maxwell, 1990).

KUOKKANEN, T., 'Defining Environmental Damage in International and Nordic Environmental Law', in T. Tervashonka (ed.), *The Legal Status of the Individual in Nordic Environmental Law* (Rovaniemi, Northern Institute for Environmental and Minority Law, University of Lapland, 1994), 53–62.

LADEUR, K.-H., 'Schadenersatzansprüche des Bundes für die durch den Sandoz-Unfall entstandenen "ökologischen Schäden"?' (1987) 40 *Neue Juristische Wochenschrift* 1236–41.

—— 'Der "Umwelthaftungsfonds"—ein Irrweg der Flexibilisierung des Umweltrechts?' (1993) 44 *Versicherungsrecht* 257–65.

LANDRETH, L. W., and WARD, K. M., 'Natural Resource Damages: Recovery under State Law Compared with Federal Laws' (1990) 20 *Environmental Law Reporter* 10134–48.

LAYARD, A., 'Contaminated Land: Law and Policy in the United Kingdom, the Environmental Bill, Clause 54' (1995) 3 *Environmental Liability* Issue 1, 52–60.

LAZARUS, R., 'Changing Conceptions of Property and Sovereignty in Natural Resources: Questioning the Public Trust Doctrine' (1986) 71 *Iowa Law Review* 631–716.

LEIGH, K., 'Liability for Damage to the Global Commons' (1993) 14 *Australian Year Book of International Law* 129–56.

Liability and Compensation for Nuclear Damage: An International Overview (Paris, OECD, Nuclear Energy Agency (NEA), 1994).

LINKOLA, P., 'Försäkringsprincipen som miljöekonomiskt styrmedel' (1989) 69 *Nordisk Försäkringstidskrift* No. 2, 90–100.

LOUDENGOUGH, E., 'The Role of Science in Valuing Natural Resources after *State of Ohio* v. *Department of Interior* 880 F.2d 432 (D.C. Cir. 1989)' (1992) 32 *Natural Resources Journal* 137–48.

LUCAS, A., 'Canada—Economic Loss from Natural Resource Damage: The *Norsk Pacific* Case' (1994) 2 *Environmental Liability* Issue 2, 38–41.

LUNDSTROM, R.-M., 'Environmental Liability in Sweden: Context and Main Features' (1993) 1 *Environmental Liability* Issue 5, 117–23.

MACGRADY, G. J., 'The Navigability Concept in the Civil and Common Law' (1975) 3 *Florida State University Law Review* 511–615.

MADDALENA, P., *Il danno pubblico ambientale* (Rimini, Maggioli, 1990).

MAFFEI, M. C., 'The Compensation for Ecological Damage in the "Patmos" Case', in F. Francioni and T. Scovazzi (eds.), *International Responsibility for Environmental Harm* (London, Graham & Trotman, 1991), 381–94.

MALINCONICO, C., *I beni ambientali* (Padua, Cedam, 1991).

MARTICKE, H.-U., 'Liability for Ecological Damage: Report' (1992) 22 *Environmental Policy and Law* No. 1, 28–31.

MAUGERI, M. R., 'Liability for Environmental Damage in Italy', in I. Koppen, M. R. Maugeri, and F. Pestellini, *Environmental Liability in a European Perspective*, European University Institute Working Paper EPU No. 91/12, Badia Fiesolana, San Domenico (FI), 1991.

MCCORMACK, T., and SIMPSON, G., 'The International Commission's Draft Code of Crimes against the Peace and Security of Mankind' (1994) 5 *Criminal Law Forum* 1–55.

MCINTYRE, O., 'European Community Proposals on Civil Liability for Environmental Damage—Issues and Implications' (1995) 3 *Environmental Liability* Issue 2, 29–38.

McKay, David A., 'CERCLA's Natural Resource Damage Provisions: A Comprehensive and Innovative Approach to Protecting the Environment' (1988) 45 *Washington and Lee Law Review* 1417–59.

Medugno, M., 'Il caso della Patmos' (1989) 4 *Rivista giuridica dell'ambiente* 35–52.

Mensah, T., 'The Question of the Unit of Account for the Limitation Amounts under the 1971 Fund Convention and the Method of Conversion into National Currency' [1992] *Il diritto marittimo* 547–61.

Merialdi, A., 'La sentenza sulla quantificazione del danno all'ambiente nel caso *Patmos*' (1995) 10 *Rivista guiridica dell'ambiente* 145–52.

Michelson, S., 'Skadeberäkning vid miljöskada' (1989) 74 *Svensk Juristtidning* 721–4.

Minogue, K. R., 'The Concept of Property and Its Contemporary Significance', in J. R. Pennock and J. W. Chapman (eds.), *Property* (Nomos No. 22, New York, New York University Press, 1980).

Moore, J. B., '*Hisber and Digest of the International Arbitration to which the United States has been a Party*' (Washington, Government Printing Office, 1898), i.

Morehouse, W., 'Unfinished Business: Bhopal Ten Years After' (1994) 24 *Ecologist* No. 5, 164–9.

Nedelsky, J., *Private Property and the Limits of American Constitutionalism: The Madison Framework and Its Legacy* (Chicago, ILL., University of Chicago Press, 1990).

Nicoll, J. L., Jr., 'Marine Pollution and Natural Resources Damages' (1993) 5 *University of San Francisco Maritime Law Journal* 323–58.

Note: ' "Ask a Silly Question . . .": Contingent Valuation of Natural Resource Damages' (1992) 105 *Harvard Law Review* 1981–2000.

O'Connor, C. R., 'Natural Resource Damage Actions under the Oil Pollution Act of 1990: A Litigation Perspective' (1993) 45 *Baylor Law Review* 441–57.

OECD, *OECD and the Environment* (Paris, OECD, 1886).

OECD, *The Polluter Pays Principle* (Paris, OECD, 1992).

—— *The Polluter Pays Principle and Pollution Insurance* (Paris, OECD, 1992).

Oldertz, C., 'Swedish Environmental Damage Insurance', in H. Bocken and D. Ryckbost (eds.), *L'assurance des dommages causés par la pollution* (Brussels Story Scientia, 1991), 363–73.

—— and Tidefelt, E. (eds.), *Compensation for Personal Injury in Sweden and Other Countries* (Stockholm, Juristförlaget, 1988).

D'Oliveira, J., 'The Sandoz Blaze: The Damage and the Public and Private Liabilities', in Francesco Francioni and Tullio Scovazzi (eds.), *International Responsibility for Environmental Harm* (London, Graham & Trotman, 1991), 429–45.

Opschoor, J. B., *Economic Instruments for Environmental Protection* (Paris, OECD, 1989).

Pagh, P., 'The New Danish Act on Strict Liability for Environmental Damage' (1995) 3 *Environmental Liability* Issue 1, 15–19.

Paul, E. F., Miller, F. D., Jr., and Paul, J. (eds.), *Property Rights* (Cambridge, Cambridge University Press, 1994).

Peck, N., and Page, K., 'USA—Natural Resource Damage: A Defence of the Economic Loss Doctrine or Bright-Line Rule Limiting Recovery' (1993) 1 *Environmental Liability* Issue 3, 53–61.

Pfennigstorf, W., 'Environment, Damages, and Compensation' (1979) 2 *American Bar Foundation Research Journal* 347–448.

—— 'Liability and Insurance for Pollution Damage: New Approaches in the Federal Republic of Germany' (1990) 71 *Nordisk Försäkringstidskrift* No. 2, 139–51.

—— (ed.), *Personal Injury Compensation: A Comparative Analysis of the Major European Jurisdiction* (London, Lloyd's London Press Ltd, 1993).

PISSILLO-MAZZESCHI, R., 'Forms of International Responsibility for Environmental Harm', in Francesco Francioni and Tullio Scovazzi (eds.), *International Responsibility for Environmental Harm* (London, Graham & Trotman, 1991), 15–35.

POHL, A., 'Die Altlastenregelungen der Länder' (1995) 48 *Neue Juristische Wochenschrift* 1645–50.

POSTIGLIONE, A., 'Danno ambientale e Corte di Cassazione' (1989) 4 *Rivista giuridica dell'ambiente* 106–9.

RAUCHER, S., 'Raising the Stakes for Environmental Polluters: The Exxon Valdez Criminal Prosecution' (1992) 19 *Ecology Law Quarterly* 147–85.

REICH, C., 'The New Property' (1964) 73 *Yale Law Journal* 733–87.

RODRIGUEZ, A. J., and JAFFE, P. A. C., 'The Oil Pollution Act of 1990' (1990) 15 *Tulane Maritime Law Journal* 1–35.

ROSAS, A., 'Issues of State Liability for Transboundary Environmental Damage' (1991) 60 *Nordic Journal of International Law* 29–48.

—— 'Property Rights', in A. Rosas and J. Helgesen (eds.), *The Strength of Diversity: Human Rights and Pluralist Democracy* (Dordrecht, Martinus Nijhoff Publishers, 1992), 133–57.

—— 'State Responsibility and Liability under Civil Liability Regimes', in O. Bring and S. Mahmoudi (eds.), *Current International Law Issues: Nordic Perpectives. Essays in Honour of Jerzy Sztucki* (Stockholm, Norstedts Juridik, 1994), 161–82.

RUE, C. DE LA 'Environmental Damage Assessment', in R. R. Kroner (ed.), *Transnational Environmental Liability and Insurance* (London, Graham & Trotman, 1993), 67–78.

SALJE, P., *Umwelthaftungsgesetz* (Munich, Verlag C. H. Beck, 1993).

SANDS, P., *Principles of International Environmental Law* (Manchester, Manchester University Press, 1994), i.

SANDVIK, B., 'Broadening the Scope of Compensation for Damage to Natural Resources— What Can We Learn from US Law?' (1995) 218 *Marius*. 1–40.

SAX, J. L., 'The Public Trust Doctrine in Natural Resource Law: Effective Judicial Intervention' (1970) 68 *Michigan Law Review* 471–506.

SAXE, D., 'Canadian Reflections on Environmental Restoration: The Legal Questions' (1994) 2 *Environmental Liability* Issue 2, 51–6.

—— 'Canadian Reflections on Environmental Restoration: The Legal Questions (Continued)' (1994) 2 *Environmental Liability* Issue 3, 57–64.

SAXÉN, H., *Skadeståndsrätt* (Åbo, Åbo Akademi, 1975).

SCHIMIKOWSKI, P., *Umwelthaftungsrecht und Umwelthaftpflichtversicherung* (3rd edn., Karlsruhe, Verlag Versicherungswirtschaft e.V., 1994).

SCHLEGELMILCH, G. (ed.), *Geigel, Der Haftpflicthprozeß* (19th edn., Munich, Verlag C. H. Beck, 1986).

SCHMIDT-SALZER, J., *Kommentar zum Umwelthaftungsrecht* (Heidelberg, Verlag Recht und Wissenschaft, 1992).

SCHOENBAUM, T. J., 'Liability for Spills and Discharge of Oil and Hazardous Substances from Vessels' (1984) 20 *The Forum* 152–63.

SELLSCHOOP, H. D., 'Topical Issues Concerning Environmental Liability and Its Insurance' (1993) 18 *Geneva Papers on Risk and Insurance* No. 67, 115–28.

SHELLER, C. S. C., 'Frank Stewart Dethridge Memorial Address 1994, Pride and Precedent: Economic Loss—The Search for a New Bright Line' (1994) 10 *MLAANZ Journal* Part 2, 7–34.

SMETS, HENRI, 'Indemnisation des dommages exceptionnels à l'environnement causés par les activités industrielles', in R. J. Dupuy (ed.), *L'avenir du droit international de l'environnement* (Dordrecht, Martinus Nijhoff, 1985), 275–356.

—— 'Major Industrial Risks and Compensation of Victims' (1988) 27 *Social Science & Medicine* 1085–95.

—— 'The Cost of Accidental Pollution' (1988) 11 *Industry and Environment* No. 4, 28–33.

—— 'Guaranteed Compensation for Accidental Pollution' (1990) 166 *OECD Observer* 28–31.

—— 'Le coût de l'indemnisation des tiers victimes de la pollution accidentelle en France', in H. Bocken and D. Ryckbost (eds.), *L'assurance des dommages causés par la pollution* (Brussels, Story Scientia, 1991), 95–117.

—— 'Pour une indemnisation garantie des victimes de pollution accidentelle', in H. Bocken and D. Ryckbost (eds.), *L'assurance des dommages causés par la pollution* (Brussels, Story Scientia, 1991), 397–420.

—— 'Indemnisation des victimes de catastrophes industrielles' (1991) 6 *Cahiers de la Sécuritè Intérieure* 165–76.

—— 'L'assurance pollution et les fonds d'indemnisation des pollution accidentelles' (1991) 627 *L'Assurance française* 383–9.

—— 'L'indemnisation complète des victimes de la pollution accidentelle' (1992) 11 *Risques* 49–71.

—— 'Le principe pollueur-payeur, un principe économique érigé en principe de droit de l'environnement' (1993) 97 *Revue Générale de Droit International Public* No. 2, 339–64.

—— 'L'assurance obligatoire et la responsabilité civile pour pollution' (1994) 18 *PRINT Industries* 73–5.

—— 'Les exceptions admises au principe pollueur payeur' (1994) 20 *Droit et Pratique du Commerce International* No. 2, 211–37.

—— 'Le FIPA, un instrument financier pour l'indemnisation des pollutions accidentelles', in A. Kiss (ed.), *A Law for the Environment* (Bonn, IUCN, 1994), 131–42.

—— 'Mieux indemniser les atteintes à l'environnement' (1994) 10 *Sécurité* 2.

—— 'The Polluter Pays Principle in the Early 1990s', in L. Campiglio, L. Pineschi, D. Siniscalco, and T. Treves (eds.), *The Environment after Rio* (London, Graham & Trotman, 1994), 131–48.

—— 'Pollution accidentelle, l'indemnisation des tiers' (1994) 32 *Préventique* 54.

—— 'Des caisses mutuelles pour les pollueurs' (forthcoming 1995).

—— 'Frequence distribution of the consequences of industrial accidents involving hazardous substances in OECD countries' (1996, mimeo).

SMITH, J. T. II, 'Natural Resource Damages under CERCLA and OPA: Some Basics for Maritime Operators' (1993) 18 *Tulane Maritime Law Journal* No. 1, 1–32.

SPRINGER, A., 'Towards a Meaningful Concept of Pollution in International Law' (1977) 26 *International and Comparative Law Quarterly* 531–57.

STEWART, RICHARD, 'Liability for Natural Resources Injury: Beyond Tort', in Richard E. Revesz and Richard Stewart (eds.), *Analysing Superfund, Economics, Science and Law* (Washington, DC, Resources for the Future, 1995), 219–47.

STÅHLBERG, P., 'Causation and the Problem of Evidence in Cases of Nuclear Damage' (1994) 53 *Nuclear Law Bulletin* 22–9.

SULLIVAN, M. P., 'Annotation, Robins Dry Dock Doctrine Limiting Recovery for Economic Losses Due to Unintentional Maritime Torts' (1988) 88 *American Law Reports Federal* 295–334.

SZÖLLÖSY, P., 'Compensation for Personal Injury in Western Europe' (1994) 74 *Nordisk Försäkringstidskrift* No. 3, 221–42.

TECLAFF, L. A., 'Beyond Restoration: The Case of Ecocide' (1994) 34 *Natural Resources Journal* No. 4, 933–56.

THOMAS, PATRICIA (ed.), *Environmental Liability* (London, Graham & Trotman, 1991).

TOMCZAK, M., 'Defining Marine Pollution' (1984) 8 *Marine Policy* 311–22.

TOTTEN, C. H., 'Recovery for Economic Loss under *Robins Dry Dock* and the Oil Pollution Act of 1990: *Sekco Energy* v. *M/V Margaret Chouest*' (1993) 18 *Tulane Maritime Law Journal* 167–78.

TREPTE, P.-A., 'Civil Liability for Environmental Damage: The Green Shoots of a Community Policy' (1992) 1 *Reciel* No. 4, 402–10.

TREVES, T., 'Aspetti internazionali sulla responsabilità civile per danni all'ambiente' (1994) 9 *Rivista giuridica dell'ambiente* 105–16.

TROMANS, S., 'Environmental Liability' (1992) 22 *Environmental Policy and Law* 43–8.

UDA, M. J., 'The Oil Pollution Act of 1990: Is There a Bright Future Beyond Valdez?' (1991) 10 *Virginia Environmental Law Journal* 403–33.

WAGNER, T. J., 'The Oil Pollution Act of 1990: An Analysis' (1990) 21 *Journal of Maritime Law and Commerce* No. 4, 569–95.

WARD, K., and DUFFIELD, J., *Natural Resource Damages: Law and Economics* (New York, Wiley Law Publications, John Wiley & Sons, Inc., 1992).

WETTERSTEIN, P., *Damage from International Disasters in the Light of Tort and Insurance Law*, General Report submitted to the Association Internationale du Droit des Assurances 8th World Congress on Insurance Law, in Copenhagen, 18–22 June, 1990.

—— *Environmental Impairment Liability in Admiralty: A Note on Compensable Damage under US Law* (Åbo, Åbo Akademis Förlag, 1992).

—— 'Trends in Maritime Environment Impairment Liability' [1994] 2 *Lloyd's Maritime and Commercial Law Quarterly* Part 2, 230–47.

—— 'The Finnish Environmental Compensation Act—and Some Comparisons with Norwegian and Swedish Law' (1995) 3 *Environmental Liability* Issue 3, 41–8.

WILKINSON, C. F., 'The Public Trust Doctrine in Public Land Law' (1980) 14 *UC Davis Law Review* 269–316.

WILKINSON, D., 'EC Green Paper on Remedying Damage to the Environment COM (93)47' (1993) 2 *European Environmental Law Review* 159–61.

—— 'Moving the Boundaries of Compensable Environmental Damage Caused by Marine Oil Spills: The Effect of Two New International Protocols' (1993) 5 *Journal of Environmental Law* No. 1, 71–90.

WILLIAMS, D., 'Valuing Natural Environments: Compensation, Market Norms, and the Idea of Public Goods' (1995) 27 *Connecticut Law Review* 365–491.

WILMOWSKY, P., and ROLLER, G., *Civil Liability for Waste* (Frankfurt am Main, P. Lang, 1992).

WOODARD, D., and HOPE, M. R., 'Natural Resource Damage Litigation under the Comprehensive Environmental Response, Compensation, and Liability Act' (1990) 14 *Harvard Environmental Law Review* 189–215.

WOODER, J. B., and SOUTHCOTT, R. F., 'Canadian Maritime Law Update: 1992–1993' (1994) 25 *Journal of Maritime Law and Commerce* 421–50.

YANG, E. J., DOVER, R. C., and MENEFEE, M., 'The Use of Economic Analysis in Valuing Natural Resource Damages', unpublished report, US Department of Commerce, June 1984.

Index

act of God 160, 211
act of war 160, 211
act or omission of a third party 160–162,
   211
actio popularis 93–94, 99

bankruptcy 224
Basle 235
biological diversity 47, 84–87, 94
Bophal 29, 62, 223, 235, 245

causality 17, 20, 22–23, 29–30, 32, 42–43,
   46, 62–63, 132, 137, 146–147, 171, 210,
   211–212, 217, 223–224, 246
celestical bodies 84
cessation 79, 107, 112
Chernobyl 29, 62, 88–89, 156
citizen intervenors 106, 201–204, 206
citizen suits 32, 52–55, 106–107, 199–201
claim rights 31, 63
clean-up 14, 25, 30, 57, 61, 70, 88, 93,
   96–100, 105, 112, 114, 119, 143,
   146–149, 154–156, 160–161, 178,
   182–183, 199, 212, 224, 227–229, 231,
   242–243, 245–247
climate change 85, 87, 89, 94
common heritage 83–85, 178
common interest or concern 84–86
common property 83–84
compensation formulas. *See* damage
   assessment methods
computer models. *See* damage assessment
   methods
contingent valuation. *See* damage assessment
   methods
contributory negligence 120, 161
criminal law 12, 15, 26, 93, 98–100,
   106–108, 158, 168

damage assessment costs 164, 167, 183, 185,
   193, 207–208
damage assessment methods
   compensation formulas 139–140, 151,
      215–216
   computer models. *See* Type A regulations
   contingent valuation 137, 167, 171,
      189–190, 214–215
   costs of restoration. *See* restoration
   equitable appraisal of damages 49, 105,
      108, 115–116, 118–121, 129

eguitable assessment of damages 67–68,
   80–81
habitat equivalency 192
hedonic pricing 80, 167, 171
hierarchy of 187
   'lesser of' 187, 190, 208–209
   market price 33, 79, 119–121, 123, 136,
      149–151, 164–166, 177, 191, 213
   'methodica' 67–68, 123
   rebuttable presumption of 165, 168, 184,
      188, 213, 215–216
   travel costs 80, 166–167
deep seabed 84–86
defective installations 145, 147
defective objects 144–145, 147
diminution in value 48–50, 66, 68–69, 151,
   164, 190–192, 208–209. *Cf. also* damage
   assessment methods
double recovery of damages 50, 165–166,
   184, 196
dumping 98

economical loss
   consequential 29, 31, 57, 61, 64, 70, 156,
      177
   pure 13–15, 18, 30–32, 33–46, 54, 57, 61,
      64, 70, 73, 76, 78, 122, 132, 135,
      156–157, 163, 167–168, 208
environmental impact statement 184
environmental values
   aesthetic values 30, 67, 75–77, 150–151,
      158
   archaeological values 49
   bequest values 49, 189
   cultural values 30, 33, 67, 74–75, 84
   ecological values 53, 67, 150–151, 153, 158
   emotional value 136
   existence values 49, 166, 189
   historical values 33
   intrinsic values 67, 77, 153
   landscape values 60, 75–76
   non-use values 49, 75–77, 116, 189, 191,
      214
   use values 48–49, 75–77, 165–166, 172,
      184, 187, 190–191, 208–209, 213
   option values 166
   passive use values 189, 191–192, 203, 214
estoppel 91, 127–128
exclusive economic zone 97–98, 159, 185,
   207–208, 210

Exxon Valdez 30, 159, 164, 184, 193, 195,
    202, 205

fault liability 18, 24–27, 34, 91, 105–106,
    112, 132, 143–144, 147
financial guarantees 147–148, 157, 227, 244
force majeure 145
fungible goods 209

gross negligence 161, 211–212

habitat equivalency. *See* damage assessment
    methods
hedonic pricing. *See* damage assessment
    methods
the high seas 84–86, 88, 93

inflation 122
injunction 112, 153
insolvency 224, 236–237
insurance 26, 39, 41, 46, 62, 127, 148, 224,
    226–229, 231–239, 243–244, 248
interest 122, 139–140
intervention in judicial actions. *See* citizen
    interventors

jurisdiction 170, 189, 195–197
jury trial 205, 217

the 'lesser of' rule. *See* damage assessment
    methods
liability for risk 70
limitation of liability
    in Belgium 148
    in the Netherlands 227
    in the United States 161–163, 185, 211
    under the 1969 CLC 113, 123
loss of enjoyment 73, 116, 120, 135,
    149–150. *Cf. also* moral damages
loss of profit. *See* economical loss

'methodica'. *See* damage assessment methods
moral damages 78, 149–150, 157–158

navigable waters 179, 185, 207, 210, 213
non-navigable waters 180
nuisance 13, 33, 132, 145–146, 149, 151

offshore facilities 161, 170, 182
onshore facilities 161
outer space 85–86
the ozone layer 85, 87, 152

pain and suffering 32–33, 133, 135, 149–150.
    Cf. also moral damages
parens patriae 181, 189, 205
period of limitation 62, 147

personal injury 13, 16, 23–24, 29–30, 32–33,
    37, 53, 57, 61–63, 70–71, 73, 76, 88–89,
    106, 135, 149, 151, 231
polluter pays principle 17, 19–20, 39, 45, 65,
    95–100, 116, 146, 155, 170, 223, 226,
    238, 248
precautionary measures 69–70, 89
precautionary principle 97
pre-spill planning 169–170
preventive measures 12, 14, 32, 37, 57, 61,
    69–70, 73, 81, 96–97, 115, 154–156
preventive principle 70, 92
product liability 25–26. *Cf. also* defective
    objects
property damage 13, 16, 29, 31–33, 37, 47,
    53–54, 57, 61, 63, 70, 73, 76, 78, 106,
    135–137, 149–151, 157, 163
public health 172. *Cf. also* public safety
public nuisance 44, 177
public oversight 197–199
public participation 204–205, 206, 216–217
public safety 133
public vessel 161, 170, 210
punitive damages 98, 108, 123

rebuttable presumption. *See* damage
    assessment methods
reinstatement. *See* restoration
remedial actions 12, 47, 133–134, 183
remoteness of damage 34, 39–40, 91–92
removal costs 47, 163, 185, 207
res communis omnium 32, 46–47, 53, 113,
    152–153
response costs 154–156, 170, 212, 216
responsible parties 147, 155, 160, 207, 209–211
restoration
    acquisition of equivalent resources 33, 47,
        49, 51, 61–62, 65–71, 73, 79, 111, 134,
        141, 153–154, 164, 166, 185, 190–191,
        194–195, 208
    baseline conditions 48, 169, 171–172, 188,
        190, 210, 214
    compensatory restoration 170–172, 214
    cost-effectiveness 214
    costs of restoration undertaken 12, 33,
        47–54, 57, 61, 65–71, 73, 78–79, 81, 93,
        96–100, 105–108, 111–112, 117, 122,
        131–141, 149–151, 153–154, 157–158,
        164–166, 168–174, 182, 185, 190–191,
        208
    costs of restoration to be undertaken 48,
        52, 65, 67, 73, 81, 117
    disproportionate expenditures 107–108, 141,
        164, 165–166, 192–193
    natural recovery 47, 80, 122, 142, 164,
        166, 171, 184
    primary restoration 170–171

restoration assessment 168, 170, 187, 213–214
restoration planning 168, 170–172, 213–214, 217
restoration implementation 168, 172, 214
technical feasibility 47, 165, 184, 194, 214–215
revenues 163

sabotage 223
salvage 97
self-help 114
Seveso 229–231, 235, 239
space objects 58–59, 88, 91
special drawing right 123–124
strict liability 16–17, 19, 24–27, 91, 109–110, 112, 132, 133–135, 144–146, 148, 155, 157, 160, 185, 210, 226–227
subsistence use 44–45, 163, 208

taxes 148, 156, 183, 225, 238, 242–244, 248
territorial waters 97, 113–115, 119–120
travel costs. *See* damage assessment methods
trustees 50, 77, 84, 86, 88, 104–105, 152–153, 159, 164, 169–172, 177–208, 212–217, 219
Type A regulations 186–187, 213, 215–216
Type B regulations 186–187, 214

unknown polluters 224–225, 227, 232–234, 236–237
use of recovered damages 80, 167, 178, 182, 185, 192–195, 208

wilful misconduct 161, 211–212
wilful negligence 212
wreck removal 122